John Murray

Lessons in English literature

With a short dictionary of British, Irish, and American authors

John Murray

Lessons in English literature

With a short dictionary of British, Irish, and American authors

ISBN/EAN: 9783337124991

Printed in Europe, USA, Canada, Australia, Japan

Cover: Foto ©Paul-Georg Meister /pixelio.de

More available books at **www.hansebooks.com**

LESSONS

IN

ENGLISH LITERATURE.

WITH A

SHORT DICTIONARY

OF

BRITISH, IRISH, AND AMERICAN AUTHORS.

BY

JOHN O'KANE MURRAY, M.A., M.D.,

Author of "The Prose and Poetry of Ireland," "The Catholic Pioneers of America,"
"Little Lives of the Great Saints," and "Popular History of the Catholic
Church in the United States."

The foundation of knowledge must be laid by reading.—DR. JOHNSON.

It is only great names and great works that make a literature.
—DR. CRAIK.

BALTIMORE:
JOHN MURPHY & CO.
1892.

Entered according to Act of Congress, in the year 1877, by
JOHN O'KANE MURRAY,
in the Office of the Librarian of Congress.

This Book

IS MOST AFFECTIONATELY DEDICATED TO MY SISTER

Miss Murray.

"To thee no star be dark!
Both heaven and earth
Befriend thee ever."

PREFACE.

The title of this little volume scarcely conveys an adequate idea of the wide range of subjects discussed between its covers. The work is divided into four Books. Book I. gives a brief history of the English Language, a bird's-eye view of its composition, and a history of English Literature from Cædmon to Chaucer. Book II. covers the English Literature of Great Britain from Chaucer to the present time. Book III. treats of the Literature of Ireland—Celtic and English. Book IV. embraces in brief the English Literature of America, and ends with a Short Dictionary of Authors.

The Historical Introductions—each of which should be carefully read before proceeding to the lessons that follow—give a rapid view of British, Irish, and American history, with special reference to the progress of letters, learning, and civilization. Literature takes a color from the times in which it is produced. It is best studied in connection with history.

I have omitted long extracts. In a work of this nature they serve no good purpose. A literary masterpiece should be read from the first word to the last —or not at all. The whole should never be judged by a part. How silly and illogical it is to represent *Julius Cæsar* or *Evangeline* by two or three pages! The quotations I have scattered here and there are so many gems to be fixed in the mind as an exercise of taste and memory.

My book has grown by degrees during the last ten years. It has been prepared with a high, well-defined purpose, and has cost me much earnest, patient labor. The final chapters, I may be permitted to say, were written during periods of painfully poor health. It now goes forth on its mission, and may that be *ad majorem Dei gloriam!* I hope it will be found a pleasant guide over the wide world of English Literature—a guide equally safe and suitable for the class-room and the home-circle.

JOHN O'KANE MURRAY.

1734 OXFORD STREET,
PHILADELPHIA, July 22, 1884.

INDEX TO THE PRINCIPAL WRITERS.

☞ This index is confined to the authors noticed in the lessons. For others the reader is referred to the *Short Dictionary* at the end of the volume.

	PAGE		PAGE
Adamnan, Saint	311	Curran, John P	336
Addison, Joseph	211	Cusack, Miss Mary	375
Alcuin	40	Davis, Thomas O	366
Aldhelm, Saint	35	De Foe, Daniel	213
Alfred the Great	42	De Vere, Aubrey	376
Arbuthnot, John	211	Dickens, Charles	265
Ascham, Roger	153	Douatus, Saint	304
Bacon, Lord	189	Douglas, Bishop	132
Bacon, Roger	69	Doyle, Bishop James	357
Bancroft, George	407	Dryden, John	185
Banim, John	361	Duffy, Sir Charles G	379
Barbour, John	92	Dunbar, William	134
Bede, Saint	37	Eliot, George	238
Boswell, James	226	Emerson, Ralph W	412
Browning, Mrs. E. B	250	England, Bishop	410
Brownson, Orestes A	413	Evin, Saint	310
Bryant, William C	404	Everett, Edward	403
Burke, Edmund	333	Exter, Joseph of	69
Burke, Thomas N	373	Faber, F. W	262
Burns, Robert	207	Fiacc, Saint	310
Butler, Alban	216	Fielding, Henry	214
Butler, Samuel	182	Fisher, Bishop	153
Byron, Lord	242	Fitzpatrick, W. J	378
Cædmon	32	Franklin, Benjamin	387
Campbell, Thomas	246	Freeman, Edward A	241
Carleton, William	372	Freneau, Philip	390
Carlyle, Thomas	267	Geoffrey of Monmouth	68
Caxton, William	113	Gibbon, Edward	221
Challoner, Bishop	216	Gildas, Saint	31
Chaucer, Geoffrey	80	Goldsmith, Oliver	330
Clarendon, the Earl of	192	Gower, John	88
Cobbett, William	241	Grattan, Henry	336
Coleridge, Samuel T	242	Green, John R	241
Colgan John	311	Griffin, Gerald	361
Columbkille, Saint	26, 304	Grote, George	241
Cooper, James F	399	Hallam, Henry	253
Cowper, William	207	Hamilton, Alexander	389

	PAGE		PAGE
Harper, Thomas	241	Moore, Thomas	359
Hawthorne, Nathaniel	399	More, Sir Thomas	149
Henry, Patrick	390	Napier, Sir W. F. P.	379
Hildreth, Richard	407	Newman, Cardinal	270
Holmes, Oliver W.	405	O'Callaghan, John C.	379
Hooker, Richard	153	O'Clery, Michael	309
Howard, Henry	137	O'Connell, Daniel	363
Hughes, Archbishop	410	O'Curry, Eugene	369
Hume, David	218	O'Donovan, John	369
Irving, Washington	397	O'Duggan, John	306
James I. of Scotland	106	O'Hanlon, John	378
Jameson, Mrs. Anna	375	O'Kane, Rory Dall	306
Jefferson, Thomas	389	Ossian	303
Jeffrey, Lord	260	Parkman, Francis	409
John of Salisbury	69	Phillips, Wendell	404
Johnson, Samuel	223	Plegmund	45
Jonson, Ben	172	Pope, Alexander	203
Joseph of Exter	69	Prendergast, J. P.	379
Keating, Geoffrey	308	Prescott, William H.	408
Langland, William	94	Procter, Miss Adelaide A.	250
Langton, Cardinal	66	Richardson, Samuel	214
Lanigan, John	357	Robert of Gloucester	64
Layamon	61	Robertson, William	218
Leckey, W. E. H.	379	Ruskin, John	267
Lever, Charles J.	371	Sackville, Thomas	147
Lingard, John	251	Scott, Sir Walter	258
Longfellow, H. W.	401	Shakspeare, William	166
Lover, Samuel	371	Sheil, Richard L.	363
Lowell, James R.	412	Sheridan, Richard B	334
Lydgate, John	108	Sidney, Sir Philip	153
Lynch, Bishop John	308	Smith, Sydney	260
Macaulay, Lord	254	Smollett, Tobias	214
MacCarthy, Justin	379	Southwell, Robert	140
MacCarthy, Denis F.	376	Spalding, Archbishop	411
MacHale, Archbishop	373	Spenser, Edmund	143
MacLaig	305	Steele, Sir Richard	327
MacNamee	305	Sullivan, A. M.	379
MacWard	305, 306	Swift, Jonathan	327
Madden, R. R.	378	Tennyson, Alfred	252
Madison, James	389	Thackeray, W. M.	265
Mallory, Sir Thomas	110	Tighernach	307
Malmesbury, William of	68	Trumbull, John	390
Mandeville, Sir John	90	Wace, Richard	66
Mangan, James C.	366	Walton, Isaac	193
Manning, Cardinal	270	Washington, George	389
Manning, Robert	64	Webster, Daniel	403
Marlow, Christopher	139	Whipple, Edwin P.	413
Massinger, Philip	174	Whittier, John G.	405
Meehan, C. P.	379	Wickliff, John	94
Milton, John	176	Williams, Richard Dalton	366
Minot, Lawrence	94	Wiseman, Cardinal	262
Mitchel, John	378	Wordsworth, William	246
Monmouth, Geoffrey of	68	William of Malmesbury	68

LESSONS IN ENGLISH LITERATURE.

DEFINITIONS.

1. LANGUAGE is the instrument by which we communicate our thoughts to each other.

2. LITERATURE is thought, feeling, or imagination expressed in written language.*

3. LITERATURE is divided into *Poetry* and *Prose*.

4. POETRY is the product of an excited creative imagination expressed in the form of *verse*.

Examples: Longfellow's *Evangeline*, Moore's *Irish Melodies*.†

5. PROSE is the term applied to all compositions that are not in verse.

Ex.: Edmund Burke's *Speeches*, Lingard's *History of England*.

6. RHYME is the chiming of one syllable with

---

* Everything written or printed is not literature. Books intended only for certain trades, professions, or classes of people belong not to literature; such are works on navigation, engineering, law, medicine, theology, grammar, arithmetic, book-keeping, etc. These, and all similar productions, are published for the uses of particular classes of men. But the distinctive feature of literature is that *it addresses all mankind*. It speaks to every head and every heart. It embraces all forms of composition from the simple rhyme or charming story to the dignified history and the sublime poem. The choice, artistic productions in English poetry, history, biography, fiction, travels, oratory, criticism, and popular scientific and religious works—whether written by English, Scotch, Irish, or American authors—constitute what we term *English Literature*.

† The student will do well to read the examples carefully.

another at regular intervals in poetry—generally at the end of a line.

> Ex.: "There is not in the wide world a valley so *sweet*
> As that vale in whose bosom the bright waters *meet*."
> *Moore.*

7. BLANK VERSE is poetry that does not rhyme.

> Ex.: "There is a tide in the affairs of men,
> Which, taken at the flood, leads on to fortune."
> *Shakspeare.*

8. A COUPLET is *two* successive lines rhyming together.

> Ex.: "Who has not felt, with rapture-smitten frame,
> The power of grace, the magic of a name?"
> *Campbell.*

9. A TRIPLET is *three* successive lines rhyming together.

> Ex.: "Round thy path white lilies twine,
> True emblems of that soul of thine,
> Yearning to grow e'er more divine."
> *Murray.*

10. A STANZA is a number of lines taken together, and properly adjusted to each other, the whole forming a distinct portion of a poem.

> *A stanza may consist of almost any number of lines from two upwards.*

11. A POEM is a composition in verse.

> Ex.: Longfellow's *Evangeline*, Griffin's *Sister of Charity.*

12. LYRIC POETRY is so called because among the ancients it was sung to the accompaniment of the lyre. It includes *songs, odes,* and *sonnets.*

13. A SONG is a short poem intended to be sung.

> Ex.: *The Angel's Whisper, The Last Rose of Summer, The Star-spangled Banner.*

14. A BALLAD is a popular song.

15. AN ODE is a short dignified song or poem.

> Ex.: Dryden's *Ode on St. Cecilia's Day.*

16. A SONNET is a poem of *fourteen lines*, with the

rhymes arranged in a particular manner, and ending in some pointed thought or sentiment.

Ex.: The Sonnets of Shakspeare, Milton, or Wordsworth.

17. A HYMN is a sacred song.

Ex.: Mother Seton's *Jerusalem, My Happy Home.*

18. AN ELEGY is a short pathetic poem in commemoration of the death of some person.

Ex.: Milton's *Lycidas,* Gray's *Elegy written in a Country Churchyard.*

19. PASTORAL POETRY is poetry in which country scenes, life, and manners are celebrated.

Ex.: Pope's *Pastorals,* Shenstone's *Pastoral Ballad.*

20. NARRATIVE POETRY recounts the particulars of some interesting event, enterprise, or transaction. It embraces metrical tales, romances, and historical poems.

Ex.: Chaucer's *Canterbury Tales,* Moore's *Lalla Rookh,* Scott's *Lady of the Lake.*

21. DIDACTIC POETRY is poetry employed for the purpose of instruction in some branch of knowledge.

Ex.: Pope's *Essay on Criticism,* Dryden's *Hind and Panther.*

22. DRAMATIC POETRY is poetry founded upon a regular plot or story, and fitted for representation on the stage.

Ex.: Shakspeare's *Plays,* Sheridan's *Plays.*

23. DRAMATIC POETRY is of two kinds—*tragedy* and *comedy.*

24. A TRAGEDY is a dramatic poem representing some remarkable deeds performed by illustrious persons, and generally having a fatal termination.

Ex.: Shakspeare's *Macbeth, Hamlet,* and *Romeo and Juliet.*

25. A Comedy is a dramatic poem of a light and amusing character.

Ex.: S eridan's *Rivals*, S akspeare's *Measure for Measure*.

26. An Epic Poem is the poetical recital of some great and heroic enterprise.*

Ex.: M ilton's *Paradise Lost*.

The epic poem is the highest kind of poetry. Among the most celebrated epics of all time are Homer's Iliad *in Greek, Virgil's* Æneid *in Latin, Tasso's* Jerusalem Delivered *in Italian, and Milton's* Paradise Lost *in English. No literature has reached perfection till it can boast of a great epic poem and a great history.*

27. A Letter is a written communication from one person to another.

Ex.: Goldsmith's *Letters*, Lord Macaulay's *Letters*, the *Letters of Junius*.

28. A Review is generally a critical examination of some new book.

Ex.: Macaulay's *Review of Boswell's Life of Johnson*.

29. A Lecture is an instructive discourse on *any* subject.

Ex.: Father Burke's *Lectures and Sermons*, Reed's *Lectures on English Literature*.

30. A Speech is a discourse in a court of justice, legislative assembly, or other popular convention.

Ex.: Grattan's *Speeches*, Webster's *Speeches*, O'Connell's *Speeches*.

31. An Oration is a discourse of the most formal and elaborate kind.

Ex.: Everett's *Orations*.

---

* The *subject* of the epic poem must be some *one great complex action.* The *principal personages* must belong to the high places of society, and must be grand and elevated in their ideas. The *measure* must be of a sonorous dignity, befitting the subject. The *action* is developed by a mixture of dialogue, soliloquy, and narrative. — *Thomas Arnold.*

DEFINITIONS.

32. An ESSAY is a composition on any particular subject.

Ex : Bacon's *Essays*, Macaulay's *Essays*, Brownson's *Essays and Reviews*.

33. TRAVELS give an account of a long journey.

Ex.: Vetromile's *Tour in Both Hemispheres*.

34. A FICTION is a story invented for some purpose.

Fictions are commonly divided into NOVELS *and* ROMANCES.

35. A novel is a work of fiction, either founded on events of real life, or at least bearing some resemblance to them.

Ex.: Goldsmith's *Vicar of Wakefield*, Dickens' *David Copperfield*.

36. AN HISTORICAL NOVEL is one in which the events and personages of history are introduced under the guise of fiction.

Ex.: Scott's *Waverley Novels*.

37. A ROMANCE is an extravagant fiction, whose wild and unnatural incidents place them beyond the bounds of probability.

38. HISTORY is a written account of past events.

Ex.: Parkman's *Jesuits in North America*, Prescott's *History of the Conquest of Mexico*, Justin MacCarthy's *History of Our Own Times*.

Like the epic in poetry, history holds the highest place in prose composition.

39. A BIOGRAPHY is the history of one person.

Ex.: Boswell's *Life of Dr. Johnson*, Fitzpatrick's *Life and Times of Bishop Doyle*.

40. AN AUTOBIOGRAPHY is the life of a person written by himself.

Ex.: Franklin's *Autobiography*, Trollope's *Autobiography*.

1*

BOOK I.

CHAPTER I.

OUR MOTHER-TONGUE.

INTRODUCTION.

"Words are mighty, words are living—
Serpents with their venomous stings,
Or bright angels crowding round us
With heaven's light upon their wings.

Every word has its own spirit,
True or false, that never dies:
Every word man's lips have uttered
Echoes in God's holy skies."
A. A. Procter.

"There is no impiety in saying that it was scarcely in the power of the Almighty to confer on man a more glorious gift than Language, by the medium of which He Himself has been revealed to us, and which affords at once the strongest bond of union and the best instrument of communication."
F. Schlegel.

Languages are divided into classes or families. The English language is a member of the great INDO-EUROPEAN family* of languages. The chief branches of the Indo-European family, which includes all the leading languages from the Himalaya mountains in

---

* This family has been called the *Japhet'ic*, because the nations included in it are supposed to have been descended from *Japhet*, one of the sons of Noe. It is also termed the *Ar'yan*, which signifies *high*, *noble*, *illustrious*.

Asia, westward to the Atlantic shores of Europe, are as follows:

(1) THE SANS'KRIT,* and all the Asiatic tongues derived from it.
(2) THE ZEND,† and its derivatives.
(3) THE CELTIC.‡
(4) THE GREEK.§
(5) THE LATIN, and its modern derivatives—the Italian, French, Spanish, and Portuguese.
(6) THE TEUTONIC, and its modern derivatives— the languages of Germany, Denmark, Sweden and Norway. Our English, through its parent, the *Anglo-Saxon*, is an offshoot of the Teutonic.
(7) THE SCLAVONIC, under which name may be included the languages of Russia, Poland, Bohemia, and Bulgaria.‖

There is a close connection between language and literature. Some knowledge of the eventful history of our tongue is needed to arrive at a clear understanding of English literature. The study of English is a precious study. The labor spent in its mastery

---

* Sanskrit is the ancient language of India. It ceased to be spoken about 300 B C. Its modern derivatives are the present languages of India.
† The Zend is the ancient language of Persia. The chief living tongues derived from it are the Persian and the Armenian.
‡ Now chiefly represented by the *Irish*, the *Welsh*, and the *Gaelic* of the Scottish Highlands.
§ Now represented by the modern Greek, commonly called Romaic.
‖ The word *mother*, as written in the languages of the Indo-European family, gives us a glimpse at the relationship and curious resemblance that still exist among the many members of that vast family:

SANSKRIT: *matri*.
ZEND: *mader*.
CELTIC: *mathair*.
GREEK: *meter*.
LATIN: *mater*.
ITALIAN: *madre*.
FRENCH: *mère*.

SPANISH: *madre*.
GERMAN: *mutter*.
SWEDISH: *moder*.
DANISH: *moder*.
SAXON: *moder*.
ENGLISH: *mother*.
RUSSIAN: *mat*.

will be amply rewarded. And every young person should resolve to acquire simple and beautiful language, as after early life it can never be attained.

Our mother-tongue is one of the noblest languages with which the earth has ever sounded. It is spoken to-day in every quarter of the globe. It is surely destined to wield a preponderating influence in the future of the world's history and literature.* It is the key to a great literature enriched with the productions of immortal genius. It is worthy of study, and love, and veneration, for through it we have learned to know God and the truths of our holy religion.

"I consider the care of the national language," says Frederick Schlegel, "as at all times a sacred trust. Every man of education should make it the object of his unceasing concern to preserve his language pure and entire, to speak it, so far as is in his power, in all its beauty and perfection."

LESSON I.

THE STORY OF THE ENGLISH LANGUAGE BRIEFLY TOLD.

1. What nations speak the English language?

English is spoken by the people of the *United States, Great Britain, Ireland, Canada, Australia,* and other English colonies.

---

* English is, doubtless, the great language of the future. It has now a firm foothold in Europe, Asia, Africa, America, and Australia; and every year its outposts are extending, and the number of lips that speak it is increasing. Fifty years hence there will, very probably, be *one hundred and fifty millions* of people in the United States alone using English as their mother-tongue!

2. English is the mother-tongue, then, of a great number of people?

Yes; about ninety millions of people speak English.*

3. Was English at all times the language of England?

No; in its *present form* it has been the language of England for about *six hundred years*.†

4. Then, it is not the *first* language that was spoken in England?

Certainly not; other languages have been current in England at different periods in history.

5. What language was used by the earliest known inhabitants of England?

The *Celtic language*.

6. Who were the *Celts*? ‡

The *Celts* were an ancient and powerful people who first inhabited Western and Southern Europe, Great Britain, and Ireland.

7. Who gives us the earliest historical account of the British Celts?

Julius Cæsar, the celebrated Roman general and writer, who invaded England in the year 55 B.C.

8. When the Romans took possession of England, did they attempt to force the Latin tongue § on the inhabitants?

No; the Romans simply held England as a province of the Roman Empire, but without driving out

---

* The number of people speaking the four chief languages of Europe and America has been thus set down by a recent writer:

English.................... spoken by 90 millions.
Spanish...................   "   " 63   "
German....................   "   " 53   "
French....................   "   " 41   "

† After the *middle of the thirteenth century* the language assumed the general shape and physiognomy of the English which we now write and speak. It may be called *English rough-hewn.*—Craik.

‡ Sometimes written *Kelts*.

§ Latin was the Roman language.

OUR MOTHER-TONGUE. 11

the native Celts, or forcing them to change their speech.

9. Is the Celtic language now spoken in any country?

Yes; that ancient and venerable language is yet spoken in various parts of *Ireland*, in *Wales*, the *Scottish Highlands*, and *Brittany* in France.

10. How long did the Romans retain possession of England?

Nearly four hundred years.

11. At what date did the Roman power cease in England?

A.D. 410, after which the British Celts were left to govern themselves until conquered by the *Angles*, *Saxons*, and *Jutes*.

LESSON II.

THE STORY OF THE ENGLISH LANGUAGE, CONTINUED.

12. At what time did the Celtic language cease to be the national speech of England?

About the *middle of the fifth century*.

13. What language then took the place of the Celtic?

The *Anglo-Saxon*, or tongue of the Saxon invaders. It was the parent of our present English.*

14. What caused this change of language in England?

The conquest of England by the Angles, Saxons, and other German tribes.

15. Give the date of that event.

A.D. 450.

---

* The term *Anglo-Saxon*, whether as applied to the *language* or to the *people* by whom it was spoken, must be understood to mean properly *Saxon of England* as distinguished from Saxon of the Continent; just as *Anglo-Norman* means Norman of England, as distinguished from Norman of the Continent. It is a compound formed on the principle of assuming *Saxon* as the name of the people and of the language, and *England* as that of the country.— *Craik*.

16. How did the Angles and Saxons so rapidly introduce their own language?

Unlike the Romans, they drove out the British Celts with fire and sword, settled down, and took possession of the country for themselves.

17. Did the Angles and Saxons become mast rs of all England?

No, not the whole of it. They occupied all Eastern, Central, and Southern England, leaving Wales, Cornwall, and the western coast in the hands of the ancient Britons.

18. Whence came those tribes known as Angles and Saxons?

Chiefly from the present districts of *Sleswick* and *Holstein*, south of what we now call Denmark.*

19. During what time did Anglo-Saxon continue to be the language of the English people and their rulers?

Down to the time of the *Norman Conquest*—a period of over six hundred years.

20. During what famous king's reign did the Anglo-Saxon attain its pre-eminence as a literary language?

During the reign of *Alfred the Great*, which came to a close at the beginning of the tenth century.

21. What effect had the invasion of the D nes on the language of England?

It produced little or no change in the national language.

---

* The *Angles, who seem to have been the most numerous portion,* established themselves in the east and north of Britain, but left the Scottish Highlands to their Gaelic population. The *Saxons* occupied the south and west, but left Wales and Cornwall to their Cymric population. A third fraction, of far inferior numbers, the *Jutes*, had possession of Kent in the southeast of England. There is reason to believe that there was a difference of dialect among these settlers; and, particularly, that the idiom of the Angles varied in some degree from that of the Saxons; but it cannot well be doubted that *they all spoke substantially the same language.—Hadley.*

22. How can that be explained?

(1) England was ruled but a short time by the Danes. (2) In both race and speech the Danes and Anglo-Saxons were kindred nations.

LESSON III.

THE STORY OF THE ENGLISH LANGUAGE, CONTINUED.

23. What language did William the Conqueror introduce into England?

Norman-French, the dialect spoken in the north of France.

24 Give the date of the Norman Conque t.

A.D. 1066.

25. Whence came William and his followers?

From *Normandy*,* in France.

26. What did William do on taking possession of the English throne?

He placed his *Norman followers* in all offices of trust and power. The court, the nobility, the higher clergy, and the army were composed of Normans.

27. In regard to language, what singular spectacle was exhibited in England at that period?

With no line of separation but that of rank, two languages were spoken in the same country at the same time—*Norman-French* by the *ruling classes*, *Anglo-Saxon* by the *common people*.

---

* The Normans (or Northmen) were a body of Scandinavian adventurers who, while their countrymen, the Danes, were making conquests in England, succeeded in establishing themselves on the opposite coast of France. In 912 King Charles the Simple ceded to Duke Rollo and his Norman followers the province which took from them its name of *Normandy*. Here they soon ceased to speak their own language, adopting that which was spoken by the native population.—*Hadley.*

28. From two races and two languages thus living side by side what finally resulted?

The final result was the *blending of the two races and the two languages.*

29. What did the blending of the Anglo-Saxon and the Norman-French produce?

The blending of these two languages *formed a compound* which constitutes the *foundation* and *framework* of our *present English.*

30. Was this blending process rapid?

It was far from rapid. The *growth* and *development* of our present English speech was the *slow* and *gradual result of over five hundred years of almost continual change.*

31. During what space of time did the Norman-French and the Anglo-Saxon continue without intermixing?

From the Norman Conquest till about the year 1150, or nearly a century.

32. What is commonly called the *Semi-Saxon* period of English speech?

From A.D. 1150 to 1250—a period during which the process of blending was very rapid.

LESSON IV.

THE STORY OF THE ENGLISH LANGUAGE, CONTINUED.

33. What period begins with the middle of the thirteenth century?

The earliest dawn of our English speech in its present form. From A.D. 1250 to 1350 is known as *the period of Early English.*

34. What may be termed *the period of Middle English?*

From A.D 1350 to 1500.

35. What especially marked the growth of our language during the period of Middle English?

During this period the English vocabulary was swelled by an *immense accession of new words from the French.*

36. What name is usually given to such English as has been written since the year 1500?

It is called *Modern English.**

37. Can you point out the principal changes by which Anglo-Saxon was transformed into modern English?

The principal changes were: (1) The loss of the Anglo-Saxon inflexions;† (2) Shortening the mode of spelling; and (3) The introduction of thousands of new words from the French, Latin, Greek, Celtic, and other languages.

38. What great genius by his works first stamped, so to speak, the seal of fixity on our language?

Shakspeare.

39. Is the English language no longer subject to change?

It is still subject to changes. As with all things human, no living language ceases to change.

40. Explain one form of this ever-changing condition of our language.

New words are invented, and gradually come into use; while some *old ones* are dropped and forgotten.

---

* Confining ourselves to the history of the English language since the Norman Conquest, we may call the *first century* after that date its *Infancy;* the *second* its *Childhood;* the *third* its *Boyhood;* the *fourth* and *fifth* its *Youth;* and the time that has since elapsed its *Manhood.* Its Infancy and Childhood will thus correspond with what is usually designated the period of *Semi-Saxon;* its Boyhood with that of *Early English;* its Youth with that of *Middle English;* and its Manhood with that of *Modern English.—Craik.*

† For example, nouns in Anglo-Saxon had *four* cases, commonly distinguished by different case-endings. There were about *twenty* varieties of declension. Modern English has only *one* case-ending, the possessive—*'s;* and the declensions are few, and are easily mastered.

41. Mention one of the greatest difficulties the student encounters in perusing works written in Early and Middle English.

A *barbarous orthography* which is often *so different from the present mode of spelling* as almost entirely to disguise a word.*

42. Who had the honor of first giving our language a good dictionary?

Dr. Samuel Johnson, in 1755.

43. What good did Johnson's Dictionary effect?

It introduced greater *uniformity in spelling*, and was of inestimable value *in fixing the exact meaning of words.*

LESSON V.

THE COMPOSITION OF THE ENGLISH LANGUAGE.

44. How many words are there in the English language?

About 118,000, according to the last edition † of Webster's *Unabridged Dictionary.*

45. What is the distinctive character of English?

The distinctive character of English is that it is a COMPOSITE LANGUAGE.

46. Explain what you mean by saying that English is a *composite* language.

I mean that it is COMPOSED or COMPOUNDED of words from *many other languages.* English was formed by the gradual blending of a greater number

---

* Here are a few examples of spelling in Early and Middle English: *Englenelande* (England), *Ennglissh* (English), *Goddespelles* (Gospel), *sette* (set), *lippes* (lips), *thatte* (that). Clothed in their old dress, these well-known words look like strangers to a reader of the present day.

† Edition of 1880.

of languages, perhaps, than has ever entered into the formation of any other speech.

47. Which are the chief languages of which our present English is composed?

The FOUNDATION and FRAMEWORK of the language are ANGLO-SAXON; but it has borrowed largely from the LATIN, FRENCH, GREEK, CELTIC, DANISH, HEBREW, and many other tongues.*

48. How may we generally distinguish the *Anglo-Saxon* words from the other words in our language?

The ANGLO-SAXON words are generally *short, simple, homely*, and *well fitted* to express *common feelings, common wants*, and *every-day events*.

49. Which of the *articles* are Anglo-Saxon?

All the articles—*a, an*, and *the*—are *Anglo-Saxon*.

50. Which of the *pronouns* are Anglo-Saxon?

All the pronouns are derived from the Anglo-Saxon.

51. What *verbs* are derived from the Anglo-Saxon?

All the AUXILIARY and DEFECTIVE VERBS.

52. What other two parts of speech derive nearly all their words from the Anglo-Saxon?

The PREPOSITIONS and CONJUNCTIONS.

53. What *nouns* are Anglo-Saxon?

Nearly all the NAMES OF COMMON THINGS, as *heat, cold, night, day, sun, moon; the names of the days of the week;* the names of the various PARTS OF THE BODY; and of all that CLUSTERS AROUND HOME, making

---

* There is perhaps no language so full of words evidently derived from the most distant sources as English. Every country of the globe seems to have brought some of its verbal manufactures to the intellectual market of England. Latin, Greek, Hebrew, Celtic, Saxon, Danish, French, Spanish, Italian, German—even Hindustani, Malay, and Chinese words—lie mixed together in the English dictionary.—*Max Müller.*

it dear to the heart, as *father*, *mother*, *sister*, *brother*, *friend*, *child*, etc.

54. Whence come nearly all the *irregularities* of our grammar?

From the ANGLO-SAXON. ALL NOUNS forming their plural by a change of vowel, as *man*, *men*, and ADJECTIVES which compare irregularly, as *bad*, *good*, can be traced back to the language once spoken by the Venerable Bede and Alfred the Great.

55. What may be said of the simple and direct language of childhood?

IT IS ALMOST WHOLLY SAXON.

LESSON VI.

THE COMPOSITION OF THE ENGLISH LANGUAGE, CONTINUED.

56. Next to Anglo-Saxon, what element enters most largely into the composition of the English language?

The *Latin*, which has thoroughly penetrated the whole structure of our language.

57. How came so many Latin words to find their way into our speech?

(1) Through the medium of Norman-French, which was mainly an offshoot from the Latin. (2) Directly from the Latin itself by the study of theology, philosophy, and the ancient classics. It must be remembered that Latin is the official language of the Catholic Church, which for nearly a thousand years was the religion of England.

58. How may words derived from the Latin generally be distinguished from the Anglo-Saxon ones?

By their *greater length*, the Latin words being on

an average more than *twice as long* as the Saxon ones.*

59. Which departments of our vocabulary have been especially enriched by Latin terms?

The greater portion of our words relating to *mind, morals,* and *philosophy* are from the Latin.

60. Mention certain divisions of time the names of which are derived from the Latin.

All the months of the year.

61. Does the Latin element enter into our active business-life?

It does.

62. Mention some commercial terms which we have drawn from the Latin.

Account, balance, bank, capital, currency, discount, finance, and many others.

63. Mention some expressive terms which Latin has added to the language of practical life.

Ink, oil, pen, sir, wine, yoke, and many others.

64. From what source has our language derived much of its dignity and stateliness?

From the Latin, which was once *the imperial tongue of the world.*

LESSON VII.

THE COMPOSITION OF THE ENGLISH LANGUAGE, CONTINUED.

65. Is our language much indebted to the French?

It is; nearly all our terms of *war, law,* and *religion* are borrowed from the *French.*

---

* Among the thousands of English words derived from the Latin and the French—which is a daughter of the Latin—are *all nouns* ending in *tion, sion, ity,* and most of those in *ment;* and *all adjectives* ending in *able, ible, ary,* and *ory.*

66. Mention some terms of *war* that come from the French.

Arms, banner, march, soldier, captain, chivalry.

67. Mention some *legal* terms derived from the same source.

Fee, court, judge, jury, damages, attorney.

68. Give an instance of some *religious terms* derived from the French.

Altar, Bible, ceremony, devotion, penance, prayer.

69. In what general way has the French language influenced ours?

Much of the *refined grace and delicacy of English is owing to its French element.*

70. What proportion of our borrowed words comes from the Latin and the French languages?

About *four-fifths.**

71. Are there many words of Celtic origin in our language?

There are perhaps 4000 words. Nearly all the names of places in Ireland, Scotland, Wales, and many of those in England, are derived from the Celtic. *London, Liverpool, Dee, Kent, Thames,* and *Yarmouth* are Celtic words.

72. Mention some common words derived from the Celtic.

Bard, clan, cradle, druid, glen, shamrock.

73. What can you say of the Greek as an element of English?

About *nine-tenths* of all our terms in *science, art,* and *literature* are borrowed from the Greek; as *astronomy, geology, rhetoric, barometer, telescope, telegraph, telephone.*

74. Mention some proper names derived from the *Danish.*

Whitby, Rugby, and other names of places ending

---

* In many instances it is difficult to determine whether a word of Latin origin has come to us *through the French,* or has been taken *directly from the Latin.—Hadley.*

in *by*.* The termination *son* in the names of English people, as Nelson, Hobson, etc., is said to be Danish.

75. Can you name some common words derived from the Danish?

Blunt, booty, cross, mumble, odd, ugly.

LESSON VIII.

THE COMPOSITION OF THE ENGLISH LANGUAGE, CONTINUED.

76. Mention some words for which our language is indebted to the Hebrew.

Amen, abbot, seraph, jubilee.

77. Give examples of words derived from the *Arabic.*

Alcohol, almanac, assassin, bazaar, lemon, sofa, zero.

78. Mention some words derived from the *Persian.*

Chess, orange, shawl, turban.

79. Mention some words derived from the *Hindoo.*

Calico, muslin, punch, rice, sugar.

80. Mention some words derived from the *Chinese.*

Tea, satin, mandarin.

81. From what source do we derive our terms in *music* and *painting?*

From the *Italian.*

82. Mention some words derived from the *Italian.*

Bust, studio, solo, tenor, soprano.

83. Mention some words derived from the *Spanish.*

Alligator, cargo, cigar, mosquito, negro, tornado.

84. From the Portuguese?

Commodore, porcelain, and a few others.

---

* *By* signifies a *village* or *town :* hence *by-law*, a town-law, to distinguish it from the general law of the nation.

85. From the Dutch?
Block, boom, schooner, sloop, yacht.
86. From the German?
Loafer, nickel, waltz, zinc.
87. From the American Indian?
Canoe, potato, tomahawk, tobacco, wigwam, and most of the beautiful names of our States, lakes, and rivers; as, *Ohio, Ontario, Mississippi.**

SUMMARY OF CHAPTER I.

1. Language is the gift of God to man.
2. The English language is a member of the great Indo-European family of languages. It is spoken by about ninety millions of people.
3. In its present form it has been the language of England for over six centuries.
4. English is not the first language that was spoken in England.
5. Language, like individuals and nations, has its periods of childhood, youth, and maturity.
6. The growth and development of the English language were the slow and gradual result of over 500 years of almost continual change.
7. From A.D. 1250 to 1350 is termed the period of *Early English.*
8. From 1350 to 1500 is termed the period of *Middle English.*
9. From 1500 to the present time is termed the period of *Modern English.*

---

* Some further remarks on our language will be found scattered, here and there, in the various Historical Introductions.

10. Shakspeare moulded all the elements of the English language for the first time into one consistent whole.

11. Dr. Johnson gave the English language its first great dictionary.

12. At present, our language contains about 115,000 words.

13. A greater number of languages enters into the formation of English than into that of any other speech.

14. Anglo-Saxon constitutes the foundation and framework of the English language; but our speech has borrowed largely from the Latin, French, Greek, Celtic, Danish, and many other tongues.

15. Anglo-Saxon words are generally short, simple, and homely.

16. All the articles, pronouns, auxiliary and defective verbs, prepositions, and conjunctions are Anglo-Saxon.

17. Nearly all the names of common things are Anglo-Saxon.

18. About four fifths of all the borrowed words in the English language are from the Latin and French. From these sources our speech has received much of its polish, grace, and dignity.

19. About nine-tenths of all our terms in art, science, and literature are from the Greek.*

---

* Here it may be proper to note that the *Scottish dialect* (or Lowland Scotch) is an Anglo-Danish speech. It contains very few Celtic words. "The Scottish dialect," says a recent writer, "is rapidly hastening to decay; before the end of the present century it will probably be confined to the humble and uneducated classes."

For a fuller account of the history of the English language, see Craik's *Outlines of the History of the English Language* and Shepherd's *History of the English Language*.

CHAPTER II.

LITERATURE OF THE ANGLO-SAXON PERIOD.

A.D. 450 to 1066.

HISTORICAL INTRODUCTION.

1. BIRD'S-EYE VIEW OF EARLY BRITISH HISTORY. —Great Britain comprises England, Scotland, and Wales. The *Celts* were the sole masters of all that fine island from the earliest times to the invasion of *Julius Cæsar* in the year 55 B.C. The Roman power in England may be said to extend over a period of nearly four hundred years, during which the native Celts or Britons made considerable advancement in letters and civilization, and were even converted to Christianity.

The arrival of the *Angles, Saxons,* and *Jutes,* in A.D. 450, is the beginning of an important era in the history of England. Those bold invaders were roving, pagan barbarians,* without arts, literature, or civilization. They drove out or exterminated the native Celts, many of whom found a refuge in the mountains of Wales, or on the shores of France.† But all

---

* That the Angles and Saxons were pagans, we still have a remarkable proof in the names which they gave to *the days of the week,* before their conversion, and retained ever since. *Sunday* and *Monday* were named after the sun and the moon; *Tuesday,* after Tieu, the god of the Teutons; *Wednesday,* after Woden, the god of war; *Thursday,* after Thor, the god of thunder; *Friday,* after Freya, the northern Venus; and *Saturday,* after Saetes, a water god.

† Where the exiled Britons founded a province, named after them

this did not occur in a summer. For more than a hundred and fifty years the Britons maintained a heroic resistance against the foreign foe.

During that period of wild conflict nearly every trace of Christianity and civilization was swept from the soil of England by the ruthless Saxon. What remained of religion and refinement sought a home in Wales, Cornwall, or along the western coast. Finally, however, after long years of bloodshed and fire-and-sword rule, the foundation of the *Saxon Heptarchy* was laid in the year 586.

The Heptarchy, during its continuance of nearly two centuries and a half, presents to the eye, in a political aspect, little else than one unvaried scene of war. Egbert by uniting the seven kingdoms into one, in 827, laid the foundation of the English monarchy; but before his death he saw his dominions ravaged by hordes of warlike freebooters, called *Danes.*

For over two hundred years they were the scourge of England. The bold genius of Alfred the Great checked them for a time; but his successors lacking his watchful energy, the Danes at length became masters of England, the throne of which they held for about a quarter of a century, when the Saxon line was restored in the person of Edward the Confessor, at

---

Brittany, or *Bretagne ;* and there to this day can be seen the hardy, faithful descendants of the ancient Britons, still speaking the Celtic language of their forefathers. " About the year 458," writes Lobineau, " the inhabitants of the island of Britain, flying from the swords of the Saxons, gave to a portion of the territory of Armoric Gaul the name of *Bretagne.*"—*Hist. de la Bretagne.*

* In those early ages the term *Danes* was a common name for bands of roving pirates from the countries around the Baltic Sea. The name was not then limited to the inhabitants of the little peninsula *now* called Denmark. Time makes many changes. The first notice of the appearance of the Danes in England occurs in the *Saxon Chronicle* under the year 787.

whose death, in 1066, William the Conqueror invaded England.

2. SCOTLAND FROM 500 TO 1066.—Before the end of the fifth century Scotland was divided between two races—the *Picts* * and the *Scots*. The Picts occupied the northeastern provinces of Scotland, while the Scots—a colony from Ireland, then called *Scotia*—ruled all the western portions, including the islands. The country was named *Caledonia*,† and the language spoken was the Celtic. In 843 the Scots became the ruling race under Kenneth, who was the first king of all Scotland. The Picts and Scots gradually coalesced into one people. Nothing more of political importance occurred in Scotland during the period under consideration.‡

3. THE CHRISTIAN RELIGION AS THE EARLY CIVILIZER OF GREAT BRITAIN.—The Catholic Church was the great civilizer of Europe. With religion came law, refinement, and literature. Learning has ever found a home under the protection of the Cross; and in tracing the progress of letters in Great Britain, it becomes necessary to say a word about the introduction of the Christian Religion.

The apostle and monastic hero of Caledonia was the renowned *St. Columbkille*. A prince of one of the ancient royal houses of Ireland, he began his missionary career in Scotland by founding a monastery on the little isle of Iona § in the year 563. For over a third of a century he traversed those wild northern

---

* The Picts, like the Scots or Irish, were a Celtic race.
† Which is still the poetic name of Scotland.
‡ The name *Scotland* seems first to have been given to the united kingdom of the Picts and Scots in the tenth century. Ireland, it must be remembered, was the *ancient Scotia*, and the Irish the *ancient Scots*.
§ It is only three miles long by about two in width.

regions—regions inaccessible to the Roman eagle—and at the sight of his miracles and preaching the fierce and stubborn Pict bowed beneath the cross and became a Catholic. This royal monk laid the foundation of Christianity, civilization, and literature in Scotland. The remains of fifty-three of his monasteries are yet to be seen. The noble figure of Columbkille, poet, prince, monk, and missionary, towers aloft in that dim and distant age. His is the brightest name in the early annals of Great Britain. From his famous monastery of Iona religion and learning flashed their genial rays over the neighboring kingdoms. It was "the luminary of the Caledonian regions." Columbkille* ended his illustrious career in 597—the very year that St. Augustine converted the king of Kent. The remains of the Saint were interred at Iona, which, for over two hundred years, was regarded as the most celebrated spot in Europe. At his feet seventy kings were buried. The ninth century, however, had scarcely dawned, when this world-renowned shrine was burned and plundered by the Danes; and from that time "the radiant centre from which Christian civilization shone upon the British Isles grew dim."†

To *St. Augustine* and his forty companions—sent from Rome by *Pope St. Gregory the Great*‡ in 596—belong the honor of having converted the kingdom of

---

* Columbkille is the Irish form of the name, which is often written *Columba*.
† The sacking of Iona is thus recorded in the *Annals of the Four Masters:* "The age of Christ 801. Hi-Columb-kille (Iona) was plundered by foreigners, and great numbers of the laity and clergy were killed by them—namely, sixty-eight." (Vol. I. p. 411.) For safety, towards the close of the same century, the sacred remains of St. Columbkille were transferred to Ireland.
‡ One day the great and holy Gregory chanced to walk through the market-place in Rome. He saw several young slaves for sale,

Kent to Christianity. The former landmarks of religion in England had been swept away. "Here and there," says Montalembert, "might be a ruined church, but not one living Christian among the natives." St. Augustine, at the invitation of the good king Ethelbert whom he had converted, fixed his see at Canterbury, the capital of Kent; and there were founded the *first* Catholic church, the *first* monastery, the *first* school, and the *first* library in the Saxon Heptarchy. In 601 Pope Gregory the Great sent over the books to form the first English library. Some of these manuscript volumes still existed in the reign of Henry VIII.; and there is even yet preserved in one of the libraries of Cambridge University a Latin manuscript of the Gospels, which is believed to have been brought from Rome by St. Augustine.

Northumbria and the three other northern kingdoms of the Heptarchy are indebted to Irish monks, from the famed monastery of Iona, for religion and literature. *St. Aidan* and his Irish fellow-laborers established a monastery, which afterwards became celebrated, in the little island of Lindisfarne, now called

---

and was struck with the beauty of their countenances. He made inquiries as to their country and religion. The slave-dealer informed him that they came from the island of Britain, and that they were heathen. "What evil luck," cried Gregory, heaving a deep sigh, "that the Prince of Darkness should possess beings with an aspect so radiant, and that the grace of these countenances should reflect a soul void of the inward grace! Of what nation are they?" "They are Angles," was the reply. "They are well named," continued Gregory, "for these Angles have the faces of angels; and they must become the brethren of the angels in heaven. From what province have they been brought?" "From Deïra" (in Northumbria). "Still good," answered he. "*De ira eruti*—they shall be snatched from the ire of God, and called to the mercy of Christ. And how name they the king of their country?" "Alle." "So be it; he is right well named, for they shall soon sing the *alleluia* in his kingdom." Gregory purchased the captive Saxons, and the purchase of these three or four slaves was the origin of the redemption of all England.—*Montalembert*.

LITERATURE OF THE ANGLO-SAXON PERIOD. 29

Holy Island. From this retreat they sallied forth, carrying religion and learning among the pagan inhabitants of Northern England. The two remaining kingdoms of the Heptarchy were converted by the combined efforts of the Irish and Italian monks.

4. THE MONASTERIES AND LITERATURE.—Religion having established its benign sway over the land, science and literature soon followed in its wake. In those days every monastery was a school, and the monks were the guardians of knowledge.* The principal religious houses had each its *Scriptorium*, in which the Sacred Scriptures, the classics, and all the great works of the ancients which have passed down to modern times were faithfully copied.† To the monastery prince and peasant alike went in quest of learning. Many of these institutions were founded and presided over by Irishmen, for at that time Ireland sent forth the most renowned scholars in Europe.

In the latter part of the seventh century the English monasteries made great literary progress, under two illustrious foreigners — *St. Theodore*, who became archbishop of Canterbury in 669, and his companion the *Abbot St. Adrian*. The former was a native of Asia Minor, the latter by birth an African; and both were deeply versed in all the learning of their age. They expounded Holy Scripture, and taught Latin, Greek,‡ mathematics, astronomy, music, and other

---

* According to Edmund Burke, it was St. Theodore who *first* introduced the study of Greek—his native language—into England.

† Among the Anglo-Saxons, as well as among the Celts of Ireland, Caledonia, and Cambria, monasteries were the sole centres of a religious and liberal education, and knowledge was there at once much sought, very varied, and very literary.—*Montalembert*.

‡ Without the indefatigable industry of the monks we would not now be able to feast on the eloquence of Cicero and Demosthenes, nor be charmed with the beautiful strains of Homer and Virgil.—*Spalding*.

3*

sciences in the schools of Canterbury. Under these two monks England—for the first time—became an important literary centre.

Among the monasteries which at that period ranked high as seats of learning were *Iona*, in Scotland; *Lindisfarne*, *Yarrow*, *Wearmouth*, *York*, and *Whitby* in Northern, and *Canterbury*, *Malmesbury*, and *Glastonbury* in Southern England. Wales had its great houses of *Llancarvan* and *Bangor*, the latter of which contained over 2000 monks. As schools, *Oxford University* may be traced back to the seventh, and *Cambridge University* to the ninth century.

Such a blossoming of human thought, of study and knowledge, of poetry and eloquence, in the bosom of a fighting and barbarous race, still seemingly absorbed by wars, invasions, dynastic and domestic revolutions, and all the storms and blunders which characterize the childhood of society, is truly a touching and wonderful sight.*

Anglo-Saxon scholarship culminated in the *Venerable Bede*, and then began a decline which, unhappily, was hastened by the ravages of the Danes, who destroyed the churches and monasteries—the only colleges of that age.

It has been well said that the monks made Christian Britain. "The English before their arrival," writes Alban Butler, "were a barbarous nation—utter strangers to the very names of the sciences and the liberal arts. When the monks first came to Britain the inhabitants seem not so much as to have known

---

* Even the Anglo-Saxon ladies were well educated, for it was to them that St. Aldhelm addressed his work. *De Laude Virginitatis* (The Praise of Virginity), and St. Boniface corresponded with ladies in Latin.

the use of letters, but to have borrowed their first alphabet from the Irish."

5. PRINCIPAL WRITERS OF THIS PERIOD.—About *eighty* British writers, many of them men of note, adorned the period which lies between the introduction of Christianity and the date of the Norman Conquest. But the names of CÆDMON (kad'-mon), ALDHELM, BEDE (beed), ALCUIN (ăl'-kwin), and ALFRED THE GREAT are the most brilliant of the literary lights that shone in those past ages of English story. Scotland, however, produced the earliest known British writer—ST. GILDAS THE WISE, a prince and monk, who was b rn at Dunbarton on the Clyde in 516. He was educated in Ireland, and died about the year 570. His best-known work is a *History of the Britons*, written in Latin, and recently translated into English. Gildas was a true Celt, and detested all invaders, Saxon or Roman. " The nefarious Saxon of detestable name," he writes, " hated alike by God and man—a band of devils breaking forth from the den of the barbarian lioness." Montalembert styles Gildas "the most trustworthy of the British annalists."

6. HOW PROSE COMES AFTER POETRY.—The early literature of every nation commonly bursts forth in the form of songs and rude poetry. It is often unwritten. It is always the language of passion and imagination. The oldest monuments of Anglo-Saxon literature are the poems of the venerable monk Cædmon, and the singular epic, named after its hero, *Beowulf*. The Beowulf is a poem of over 6000 lines, and is one of the greatest literary curiosities in existence.* Prose is of later growth than poetry. It

---

* The *Beowulf* seems to be a poem of the eighth century, but the author is unknown. The wild scenes pictured are laid chiefly in

is the form in which cultivated reason and calm judgment best find expression; and it attains perfection only in the more mature stages of language and civilization.

LESSON I.

CÆDMON. DIED 680.

Works: *Anglo-Saxon Poems on Religious Subjects.*

1. Who was Cædmon?

He was a venerable monk of Whitby, who is justly honored in our literature with the title of "Father of Anglo-Saxon Song."

2. Is there anything remarkable about his life?

His life is one of the most remarkable in all literature. From a simple cowherd he was immediately transformed into a gifted poet and monk.

Denmark. *Hrothgar*, the Danish king, builds a great banqueting-hall. Daily it echoes the sounds of song and dance and feasting. But a grim and greedy giant soon puts in an appearance. He is called Grendel. He enters the hall when all are at rest, and seizing thirty of the king's guests, he makes them his prey, and hurries homewards. He repeats such visits. Monarch, warrior, and peasant tremble at the monster's name. The havoc made by Grendel, however, reached the ears of the brave Beowulf. He came with his hardy companions to conquer the man-eating fiend. Hrothgar receives him with great joy. Night comes, and the men seek their beds. When all is still Grendel arrives. The hungry giant hopes to have a dainty feast. He seizes a sleeping warrior, drinks his blood, and devours him body and bones. He then takes hold of Beowulf; but soon the monster feels that he is seized in return by an iron grip. He grows afraid. He tries to run, but he cannot. The hero holds him, and the warriors grasp their swords. After a fearful encounter the worsted giant, with bruised and broken limbs, seeks his wild sea-home. But Beowulf follows, and after a fierce struggle with the mother of the monster, who attacks him in the guise of a sea-wolf, he kills her, and then destroys Grendel. Upon the death of Hrothgar, Beowulf receives his reward. He is made king of Denmark.

LITERATURE OF THE ANGLO-SAXON PERIOD. 33

3. Tell how it occurred.

Up to an advanced age Cædmon was a cowherd, devout but simple and very ignorant. His natural dulness even prevented him from taking an active part in the evening songs and music of his rustic companions. One night, while asleep, a voice commanded him to sing about the creation. After some hesitation he obeyed; and when he awoke in the morning the words of his song still lingered in his memory.*

4. What is related of his life after this event?

Through the influence of the holy princess St. Hilda he was received into the celebrated monastery of Whitby, where, as monk and poet, he spent the remainder of his days in praising God.

5. Was his gift of poetry permanent?

It was; his talents and poetic faculty grew day by day, and he was ever grateful for the gifts he had received.

6. How did he die?

Having lived as a saint, "he died as poets seldom die." After receiving the *Holy Viaticum*, he made the sign of the cross, and gently expired at a good old age.

---

* During his slumber he heard a voice, which called him by name and said to him, "Sing me something." Cædmon replied, "I cannot sing, and that is why I have left the supper and come here." "No matter," said the voice, "sing." "But, then, what shall I sing?" he replied. "Sing the beginning of the world," continued the voice—"sing the creation." On receiving this command, he at once began to sing verses of which before he had no knowledge, but which celebrated the glory and power of the Creator, the eternal God, Worker of all marvels, Father of the human race, who had given to the sons of men the heavens for their roof, and the earth for their dwelling-place. On awaking, Cædmon recollected all that he had sung in his dream, and hastened to tell all that had happened to him to the farmer in whose service he was.—*Montalembert.*

7. Of what did his literary works consist?

Of poems on Scriptural and other religious subjects.

8. Explain more clearly what he versified.

A great portion of the Bible: he put into verse the whole of Genesis, with other parts of the old Testament; and afterwards the life and passion of our Lord, and the Acts of the Apostles.

9. What modern English poet, in his celebrated epic, seems to be much indebted to Cædmon?

Milton, whose *Paradise Lost*, in more than one passage, reveals the fact that he borrowed much from Cædmon. The old monk of Whitby sang of the revolt of Satan and Paradise lost a thousand years before Milton.*

10. What does the Venerable Bede say of Cædmon's sacred songs?

"No Englishman has ever written religious poems to equal those that were written by a man who had only God for his master."

11. What does Montalembert remark of Cædmon and his poems?

"No unworthy subject ever inspired his verse, and

---

* The following is the soliloquy that Cædmon puts into the mouth of Satan after that dark personage was hurled into hell:

"Is this the narrow spot in which my Master shuts me up? How different from the dwellings that we know on high in the kingdom of heaven! Oh, if I had the free power of my hands, and if I could issue forth for once—for one winter only—I and my army! But bands of iron surround me; chains bind me down helpless. I am without a kingdom. The fetters of hell shackle me so firmly—clasp me so tightly! Here are huge flames; above and below I have never seen so horrible a place. The fire never languishes; its heat ascends above hell. The rings that encircle me, the manacles that gnaw my flesh, keep me from advancing, and close the way before me; my feet are tied, my hands imprisoned. Thus has God shut me in."

What a sublime passage! As a recent critic remarks, "it is more than probable that Milton borrowed the ideas of his sublime soliloquy of Satan in Pandemonium from this Saxon monk."

nothing in the whole history of European literature is more original or more religious than this first utterance of the English muse."

LESSON II.

ST. ALDHELM. DIED 709.

Works: (1) *The Praise of Virginity.*
(2) *Anglo-Saxon Poems.* (Lost.)

12. For what is St. Aldhelm remarkable?

He was the *first* of the Anglo-Saxons who became celebrated as a Latin author, and whose works yet remain.

13. What was his social rank?

He was a prince of the royal house of Wessex.

14. By whom and where was he educated?

By the learned abbot St. Adrian, who presided over the celebrated school of Canterbury.* Aldhelm was devoted from youth to religious and literary studies.

15. What monastery did he afterwards enter?

The great monastery of Malmesbury, founded by an Irish monk† whom Aldhelm succeeded as abbot. He retained this dignity for thirty years, but was afterwards consecrated bishop.

16. What may be said of his learning?

The most learned Englishman of his time, he was a thorough master of Latin, Greek, Hebrew, Sacred

---

* "It is you, my beloved," wrote Aldhelm to Adrian many years after, "who have been the venerable teacher of my rude infancy; it is you whom I embrace with the effusion of a pure tenderness, longing much to return to you."
† *Maidulf.*

Scripture, Roman law, arithmetic, astronomy, and music.

17. What is related of his character?

He was a man of kind and gentle heart, a diligent student, and led a singularly pure and austere life.

18. What was his principal work?

A Latin treatise entitled the "Praise of Virginity," the first part of which is in prose, the remainder consisting of a long poem.

19. Give an idea of how the subject is treated?

Besides his own remarks, he inserts at length the high commendations which St. Augustine, St. Jerome, and other Fathers bestow on the state of virginity, and gives abridged examples of many holy virgins.

20. What is said of his style?

While his matter is always good, the same cannot be said of his style, which is stiff and labored. He has neither the fiery originality of Cædmon nor the free and elegant simplicity of Bede.*

21. Did he compose anything in his native Anglo-Saxon?

He was the author of many popular Anglo-Saxon poems which have since been lost.†

---

* The following serious but beautiful passage is from one of Aldhelm's letters to his dear friend *Acircius*, a Northumbrian chief: "Let not the sound of the last trumpet depart from your ears; let it recall to you day and night the Book of the Law, which ought to be meditated day and night. You will never sin if you think always of your last end. What is our prosperity here below?—a dream, a vapor, the foam on the sea. God grant that the possession of present good may not hold to us the place of future recompense; and that the abundance of that which perishes may not be followed by the death of that which endures. I ask this for you and for myself, from Him who for us has hung upon the cross."

† Alfred the Great styled St. Aldhelm "the prince of Anglo-Saxon poetry."

Eight centuries after St. Aldhelm's death his feast was still celebrated at Malmesbury by such a crowd of worshippers that, according to Camden, the presence of a troop of soldiers was necessary to prevent disorder. Then came the Reformation of Henry

LESSON III.

ST. BEDE, COMMONLY CALLED "THE VENERABLE."
DIED 735.

Works: (1) *The Ecclesiastical History of the English Nation.*
(2) *Forty-four* other works.

22. What may be said of the Venerable Bede's rank in literature?

The Venerable Bede is the greatest name in the literature of the whole Anglo-Saxon period. He is often called the "Father of British History" and the "Father of English Learning."

23. What does the word Bede signify?

Bede, in Anglo Saxon, means *prayer*.

24. Where was he born?

In the north of England, near the mouth of the Tyne.

25. Where did he receive his education?

In the monastery of Yarrow, in which he lived from his seventh year up to the date of his death.

26. To what Religious Order did he belong?

He was a Benedictine monk, and was ordained deacon in his nineteenth year, and priest at thirty.

27. How did he spend his life?

In the quiet of his monastery, where he tells us the delight of his life was "to learn, to teach, and to write." He modestly shunned all honors, cared only

---

VIII with its usual train of devastations. The magnificent church of Malmesbury would have been razed to the ground had not a weaver bought it from the king to establish his looms there. The monastery was sacked. *The precious manuscripts of the library were long employed to fill up broken windows in the neighboring houses, or to light the bakers' fires.—Montalembert.*

for virtue and knowledge, and was one of the best examples of the perfect student in all history.

28. For what was he especially renowned during his lifetime?

As one of the greatest educators in Europe. He daily gave instruction to over 600 monks; and some of the most illustrious men of his age considered it an honor to say that they had been Bede's pupils.

29. What honorable rank does he hold in the Church?

The Venerable Bede is one of the Fathers of the Church.

30. Is there anything singular about the manner of his death?

It is one of the most touching and beautiful in the history of mankind. Having lived as a saint and scholar, he died as he had lived—at his work.*

LESSON IV.

VENERABLE BEDE, CONTINUED.

31. Which is the principal work of the Venerable Bede?

The Ecclesiastical History of the English Nation.

---

* Bede's last days were devoted to the translation of the *Gospel of St. John* into Anglo-Saxon. Even severe illness could not prevent his pushing on the work with the help of a young secretary. The evening before the Feast of the Ascension, 735, it was all completed except a few lines. "Most dear master," whispered the young monk, "there is still one sentence unwritten." "Write quickly," answered Bede. A few minutes passed, and the other remarked, "It is now done." "You have well said," replied the dying Bede. "It is now done; indeed, all is finished! Dear child, hold my head that I may have the pleasure of looking towards the little oratory where I was wont to pray; and that while I am sitting I may call upon my Heavenly Father and sing. 'Glory be to the Father, and to the Son, and to the Holy Ghost.'" And as the last word passed from his lips, the Venerable Bede breathed his soul to God. He was 63 years of age.

LITERATURE OF THE ANGLO-SAXON PERIOD. 39

32. Of what does this excellent work treat, and how is it divided?

Its name indicates its subject. It is a complete history of the Catholic Church in England from the arrival of St. Augustine till the year 731—or four years before the death of Bede. The work is divided into twenty-four chapters.*

33. In what language did Bede write nearly all his books?

In Latin. His Church History has often been translated into English.

34. Of what do the majority of his other works treat?

The majority of them were commentaries on Holy Scripture and various other theological topics.

35. On which of the sciences did he write treatises?

All the sciences of his age and every branch of literature were handled by the Venerable Bede. He wrote works on astronomy, philosophy, chronology, music, geography, arithmetic, medicine, grammar, and rhetoric.†

36. What are the merits of his Church History?

It is a book unrivalled among the early historical works of Christianity.

37. What may be further said of Bede's scholarship?

He was an almost universal genius. As a critic he was just, able, and penetrating. As a writer, both prose and poetry were equally within his grasp. And

---

* In the preface Bede touchingly writes: " I entreat all those of our nation who read this *History*, or hear it read, to recommend often to the Divine mercy the infirmities of my body and of my soul. Let each man in his province, seeing the care which I have taken to note down everything that is memorable or agreeable to the inhabitants of each district, pay me back by praying for me."

† Here is the touching prayer with which that venerable scholar ends the list of his literary labors: "O good Jesus, who hast deigned to refresh my soul with the sweet streams of knowledge, grant that I may one day mount to Thee who art the source of all wisdom, and remain forever in Thy divine presence."

taking him all in all, he is "the brightest ornament of the English nation."

38. What does the Protestant writer Bayle say of Bede?

Bayle remarks that in eloquence and copiousness of style he was unsurpassed, and that there is scarce anything in all antiquity worthy to be read which is not found in Bede.

39. Mention the only interesting relic of this famous man which has passed down to our own times?

An old oaken chair which the venerable monk is supposed to have used.

40. How did the infamous Henry VII. show his respect for the "Father of English Learning"?

He plundered and destroyed the beautiful shrine in which the Venerable Bede's remains were deposited.*

LESSON V.

ALCUIN. DIED 804.

Works: (1) *Epistles and Poems.* (Latin.)
(2) *Numerous Theological Works.* (Latin.)

41. Who was Alcuin?

After the Venerable Bede, he was perhaps the most renowned scholar of the Anglo-Saxon period.

42. Where was he born and educated?

He was a native of York, of a noble family, and

---

* The monastic sanctuary towards which the dying look of Bede was turned still remains in part, if we may believe the best archæologists, and his memory has survived the changes of time. An old oaken chair is still shown which he is supposed to have used. It is the only existing relic of this great saint. . . . His relics at Durham were an object of veneration to the faithful up to the general profanation under Henry VIII., who pulled down the shrine and threw the bones on a dunghill along with those of all the other holy apostles and martyrs of Northumberland.—*Montalembert.*

received his education in the great monastic school of that city.

43. What state of life did he embrace?

He became a Benedictine monk.

44. Where did he first obtain renown as a great teacher and scholar?

In the celebrated monastic school of his native city.

45. At the court of what famous emperor did he afterwards spend the greater portion of his life?

That of the Emperor Charlemagne, at whose repeated entreaties he went to Paris, where he established the greatest school in Europe.

46. How did Charlemagne honor Alcuin?

He honored him as his special friend, counsellor, and teacher, "and usually called him his master."

47. How long did he live in France?

From about 780 up to the date of his death, which occurred at Tours in 804. Alcuin's great learning adorned a foreign country, but the glory is not lost to his native land.

48. Which are his principal works that belong to literature?

His letters and poems—all in Latin. The former—about two hundred in number—are generally addressed to kings, queens, prelates, and other high personages.*

---

* In a letter to the monks of Yarrow, Alcuin writes: "Remember the nobility of your fathers, and be not the unworthy sons of such great ancestors; look at your many books, at the beauty of your churches and monastic buildings. Let your young men learn to persevere in the praises of God, and not in driving foxes out of their holes, or wearing out their strength running after hares. What folly to leave the footsteps of Christ, and run after the trail of a fox! Look at the noblest doctor of our country, Bede: see what zeal he showed for knowledge from his youth, and the glory which he has received among men—though that is much less important and less dazzling than his reward before God. Stir up, then, the minds of your sleepers by his example. Study his works,

49. What may be said of his poems?

For a rude, unpoetical age, his poems are very beautiful both in thought and diction.

50. How may we sum up his character as a man, a scholar, and a writer?

As a man he was remarkable for his singular modesty, piety, and good sense; as a scholar his learning was extensive and profound; but as a writer his style is often commonplace and redundant.

LESSON VI.

ALFRED THE GREAT. DIED 901.

Works: (1) *Ten original works.*
(2) *Ten translations.*

51. What is this celebrated prince's rank in Anglo-Saxon literature?

Alfred, the greatest of the kings of England, stands pre-eminent as a writer of Anglo-Saxon prose, and is the last of the great literary names of this period.

52. For what was he remarkable in boyhood?

In boyhood he was distinguished for beauty of person, graceful manners, and early display of talent.

53. What is related of his education?

Owing to the disturbed state of the times he was twelve years of age before he was taught to read. He was a most diligent student, but did not find time during his busy career to study Latin until he was forty. He afterwards became one of the best Latin scholars of his day.

54. At what age did he ascend the throne?

He became king at the age of twenty-two, and

---

and you will be able to draw from them, both for yourselves and others, the secret of eternal beauty."

reigned for thirty years, the first half of which were spent in battling with the fierce and warlike Danes.

55. What characteristic did he admirably unite in one person?

In this wonderful man were united the qualities of the saint, the soldier, the scholar, and the statesman in a most eminent degree.

56. What celebrated university did he found?

The University of Oxford.

57. What great literary work did he perform for the good of his people?

Having restored peace to his kingdom, his next object was to bestow upon his people the benefits of knowledge. For this purpose he translated a number of excellent Latin works into his native Anglo-Saxon.

58. Mention the four principal works which he translated from the Latin.

(1) Bede's *Ecclesiastical History of the English Nation*, (2) *The Pastoral of St. Gregory*,* (3) Orosius's *Roman History*, and (4) *The Consolations of Philosophy*, by Boëthius.

59. What is related of Alfred in connection with two of these works?

To each of his bishops he sent a copy of the *Pastoral of St. Gregory*, and in his bosom he always carried a copy of the *Consolations of Philosophy*, by Boëthius.

60. Was Alfred a good translator?

He was a translator of rare excellence. His literary fame rests almost entirely on his translations.

---

* Referring to the manner in which he translated this work, the great king says, with edifying simplicity: "Sometimes by word of mouth, and sometimes according to the sense, as I had learned it from Plegmund my Archbishop, and Asser my Bishop, and Grimbald my Mass-priest, and John my Mass-priest."

61. What can you say of his original productions?

Many of them are now lost. They were nearly all treatises on law and theology, and hence do not come within the scope of general literature.

62. What praise do critics award to his style?

His style is marked by ease, simplicity, and elegance.

63. What is said of Alfred's general scholarship?

Though he began his serious studies somewhat late in life, he was before his death, which occurred in his fifty-second year, the best poet, the ablest writer, and perhaps the most learned man in his kingdom.*

LESSON VII.

THE ANGLO-SAXON CHRONICLE.

64. What is the last literary monument of the Anglo-Saxon language?

The Anglo-Saxon or National Chronicle.

65. What is the Saxon Chronicle, and what period of English history does it cover?

As its name indicates,† it is a chronological arrange-

---

* Speaking of the Catholic Alfred the Great, Edmund Burke truly says: "One cannot help being amazed that a prince who lived in such turbulent times, who commanded personally in *fifty four* pitched battles, who had so disordered a province to regulate, who was not only a legislator but a judge, and who was continually superintending his armies, his navies, the traffic of his kingdom, his revenues, and the conduct of all his officers, could have bestowed so much of his time on religious exercises and speculative knowledge; but the exertion of all his faculties and virtues seemed to have given a mutual strength to all of them. Thus all historians speak of this prince, whose whole history was one panegyric; and whatever dark spots of human frailty may have adhered to such a character, they are all entirely hid in the splendor of his many shining qualities and grand virtues, that throw a glory over the obscure period in which he lived, and which is for no other reason worthy of our knowledge."--*Abridgment of English History*.

† By some writers it is called the *Old English Chronicle*.

ment of the most notable events in English history from the birth of our Lord to the beginning of the reign of Henry II., A.D 1154.

66. In what language is it written?

In Anglo-Saxon prose, with an occasional attempt at alliterative verse in the same language.

67. Who originated the Anglo-Saxon Chronicle?

PLEGMUND, Archbishop of Canterbury, who continued the annals down to his own day, A.D. 891.

68. From what sources were the early portions of the Anglo-Saxon Chronicle taken?

From various trustworthy sources; but the early portion is, in the main, a compilation from Bede's Ecclesiastical History.

69. During what time may the Saxon Chronicl be regarded as a register of contemporary events?

From about A.D. 950 to 1154.

70. By whom was the Chronicle continued after the death of Plegmund?

It was continued by the monks in several of the great monasteries of England.

71. How many genuine copies of this ancient and valuable historical work yet exist in manuscript?

Seven.

72. What may be said of the style in which the Chronicle is written?

The style is somewhat dry and inelegant, the pious writers aiming rather at brevity, truth, and accuracy of statement than mere beauty of diction.*

---

* Here are a few entries translated into English:

"A.D. 457. At this time Hengest and Aesc his son fought against the Britons at the place which is called Crayford, and there slew four thousand men. And then the Britons forsook Kent-land, and with much dismay fled to London-town."

"A.D. 690. This year Archbishop Theodore died. He was bishop

73. What is the historical value of the Anglo-Saxon Chronicle?

Its historical value can scarcely be overestimated. It is the most ancient history of England, giving us, in a series of unadorned pen-pictures, nearly all the knowledge we possess of the early social life and institutions of that nation.

SUMMARY OF CHAPTER II.

1. The Angles, Saxons, and other German tribes took forcible possession of the greater part of England in A.D. 450; hence the name *England*, which signifies *land of the Angles*.

2. For over a century after this event the history of England is written in blood.

3. The foundation of the Saxon Heptarchy, or *seven kingdoms*, dates from A.D. 586.

4. Egbert founded the English monarchy by uniting those small kingdoms into one, A.D. 827.

5. The Catholic Church converted and civilized *all* the nations in which Christianity is professed to-day. Religion came *first*, and was followed by law, refinement, and literature.

6. St. Columbkille founded the first monastery in

---

for twenty-two years, and he was buried at Canterbury. Berthwald succeeded to the b shopric. Before this the bishops had been Romans, but from this time they were English."

"A.D. 793. In this year dire forewarnings came over the land of the Northumbrians, and miserably terrified the people. Mighty whirlwinds and lightnings there were, and in the air were seen fiery dragons. A great famine soon followed these signs; and a little after that, in the same year, on the VI of the Ides of January, the havoc of heathen men wickedly destroyed God's church at Lindesfarne, through rapine and slaughter."

The "heathen men" were the Danes.

LITERATURE OF THE ANGLO-SAXON PERIOD. 47

Scotland, and established religion, literature, and civilization in that country.

7. St. Augustine, a Benedictine monk, began the conversion of the English nation in A.D. 596. He laid the foundation of learning, literature, and civilization in England.

8. Pope Gregory the Great gave the English people their *first* library in A.D. 601.

9. In those early ages the monasteries were the *only* schools and colleges, and the monks were the *only* guardians of learning and literature.

10. The most renowned institutions of learning in Great Britain, during the Anglo-Saxon period, were the monastery of Iona in Scotland, the monasteries of Lindisfarne, Wearmouth, Yarrow, York, Whitby, Malmesbury, and Glastonbury in England, and Llancarvan and Bangor in Wales.

11. About *eighty* British writers of note appeared between the introduction of Christianity and the Norman Conquest.

12. The chief of these were *Bede, Alcuin, Alfred the Great, Cædmon, Aldhelm,* and *Gildas.*

13. Bede is the most illustrious name in the literature of the Anglo-Saxon period.

14. The greatest historical production of this period is Bede's *Ecclesiastical History.*

15. The *Saxon Chronicle* is the most ancient history of England, and the *last* production written in Anglo-Saxon.*

---

* For a fuller account of the literature of the Anglo-Saxon Period, see *The Development of English Literature* by Brother Azarias, Vol. 1.

CHAPTER III.

LITERATURE OF THE NORMAN PERIOD.

A.D. 1066 TO 1350.

FROM THE NORMAN CONQUEST TO THE AGE OF CHAUCER.

HISTORICAL INTRODUCTION.

1. GLANCES AT THE HISTORY OF ENGLAND, A.D. 1066 TO 1350.—The period we are about to consider covers nearly three centuries. The death of *Edward the Confessor*, the last of the Saxon kings, was soon followed by the hard-fought and decisive battle of Hastings. The flower of England's nobility fell on that blood-stained field. Norman skill and valor had triumphed, and William, henceforth known as the *Conqueror*, was crowned king of England in Westminster Abbey. The Confessor, just before his death, had completed that world-famous structure. He was the first of England's rulers interred within its sacred walls; and the first crowned within it was the Norman Duke.*

Eleven kings reigned during this period, the most

---

* As early as 610 a church and monastery had been founded at Westminster. "This modest monastic colony," says Montalembert, "established itself on a frightful and almost inaccessible site, in the middle of a deep marsh, on an islet formed by an arm of the Thames, and so covered with briers and thorns that it was called *Thorny Island*. From its position to the *west* of London it took a new name, destined to rank among the most famous in the world—that of *Westminster*, or monastery of the West."—*The Monks of the West*.

remarkable of whom were *William the Conqueror, Henry II., Richard the Lion-hearted,* and *Edward III.* The chief events were the eight *Crusades,* in which two English kings took a part; the murder of *St. Thomas à Becket;* the invasion of *Ireland;* the signing of the *Magna Charta;* the first *representative Parliament;* the *conquest* of *Wales* and *Scotland;* and the *battles* of *Bannockburn* and *Crécy.*

2. EFFECTS OF THE NORMAN CONQUEST.—With the Norman Conquest came a new order of things—political, social, and literary. It is true that the nation at large, the great body of the people—about two millions in number—remained unchanged. Saxons, Englishmen, they still were. But William suffered no Englishman to hold any place of trust or honor. The court, the nobility, the superior clergy, and the army were composed of Normans. The uncouth Saxons were left to till the soil, to raise cattle; in short, to be the humble "hewers of wood and drawers of water" to their strange rulers. The Conqueror was a hard master. At eight o'clock each evening the sound of the *curfew* which "tolled the knell of parting day" warned the people to extinguish their lights and retire to rest. They were to beware of killing a stag, boar, or fawn; for an offence against the forest-laws they would lose their eyes. They had nothing of all their property assured them, except as an alms, or on condition of tribute, or by taking the oath of homage. Here a free Saxon proprietor was made a body-slave on his own estate. The Normans sold them, hired them, worked them on joint account like an ox or an ass. The Normans would not and could not borrow any ideas or customs from such boors; they despised them as coarse and stupid. They stood among them

superior in force and culture, more versed in letters, more expert in the arts of luxury. They preserved their own manners and their own speech.*

The Norman baron erected his strong castle on some elevation, and lorded it over his district. Feudalism was introduced, and a new legislature, known as a *parliament*, or talking-ground, took the place of the Saxon *witenagemot*, or assembly of the wise. Indeed, the Norman conquest was one of the most complete in all history.

But while William and his successors governed the country with despotic sway, they failed not to elevate it in the rank of nations. If they stripped it of its liberty and many temporal advantages, it must be owned that by their valor they raised the reputation of its arms, and deprived their native Normandy of its greatest men, both in Church and State, with whom they adorned England. Being at once dukes of Normandy and kings of England, they introduced the latter within the circle of continental nations; and by their efforts the land of Bede and Alfred, for the first time in history, obtained an important voice in the councils of Europe. In truth, the Norman Conquest was to England a blessing in disguise—an event to which much of the future greatness of that nation may be traced.

3. RELIGION AND LIBERTY.—The despotism established by William the Conqueror, and continued by his immediate successors, reached its climax in the reckless reign of King John. His idiotic tyranny became unendurable. The Barons, under the direction of Cardinal Langton, formed a powerful league for

---

* Taine.

the purpose of obtaining a lasting guarantee as security for the rights and privileges of the Church and the people. Cardinal Langton "administered to them an oath, by which they bound themselves to each other to conquer or die in the defence of their liberties."

The Barons and the Cardinal* met John on the famous plain of *Run'nymede*.† There, in 1215, they compelled the king to sign the celebrated document called *Mag'na Char'ta*,‡ which established *the supremacy of the law over the will of the monarch*, and which, to this day, is regarded as the basis of English liberties.

The signing of the Great Charter, in which the nation at large had an interest, served to bring closer together, if not entirely to unite, the hitherto divided Norman and Saxon. It is the starting-point from which we can fairly date the beginning of that commingling and consolidation of races and languages which in time become known to us as the *English People* and the *English Language*.

4. OTHER EVENTS.—Henry III., the son of John, struggled hard to abolish the privileges forced from his father, and to crush the power of the nobles. It was in his reign that the wants and dissensions of the time led to a meeting or conference of representative

---

* Stephen Langton was born in England in the early part of the twelfth century, and was educated at the University of Paris, of which he rose to be Chancellor. He was elevated to the dignity of Cardinal and appointed to the See of Canterbury in 1207, by his former friend and fellow-student, Pope Innocent III. It is well to remember that the name of the patriotic Cardinal Langton is the *first* in the list of subscribing witnesses on Magna Charta. He died in 1228.

† Runnymede is a long stretch of green meadow, lying along the right bank of the river Thames, near Windsor, about twenty miles from London.

‡ Great Charter. A copy of it was sent to every cathedral, and ordered to be read publicly twice a year.

men, which may be regarded as the origin of the *English Parliament.* Edward I., the last of England's kings who performed deeds of valor on the plains of Palestine, on being called to the throne, turned his arms against the Welsh and the Scots under Wallace, subduing both countries. But, after his death, the heroism of *Robert Bruce* and the celebrated victory of Bannockburn, in 1314, annihilated the power of England in North Britain. Years had been employed in forging the fetters of Scotland. One battle made her free and independent. The year 1350 brings us to the age of Chaucer and the long and brilliant reign of Edward III.—a period at which we shall glance in our next Historical Introduction.

5. THE CRUSADES AND THEIR INFLUENCE ON MANNERS, COMMERCE, LEARNING, AND LITERATURE.—The Crusades were the great events of the Middle Ages.* It would not be easy to understand the spirit or literature of these remote times, or the history of the world since, without some knowledge of the bearing which those mighty achievements had on the progress of Europe. It was in those distant days—well named "the heroic ages of Christianity"—that over each castle chimney, carved in oak, might be seen the simple but sublime motto: "*There is only this*—FEAR GOD AND KEEP HIS COMMANDMENTS."

It was then that *chivalry* reigned, the distinctive

---

* The Crusades were military expeditions set on foot under the banner of the cross for the purpose of delivering the Holy Land from the oppressive yoke of the Mahometans. The soldiers wore, as a mark of their engagement, a *cross* made of red stuff, and commonly fastened on the right shoulder; hence the names *Crusade* and *Crusader.* The Crusades were *eight* in number, and extended from 1095 to 1272. It was in the third Crusade that the English king, Richard Cœur de Lion, or the Lion-hearted, performed the prodigies of valor which have immortalized his name. For an account of the Crusades see Fredet's *Modern History*, Part V.

qualities of which were bravery, piety, and modesty. The Catholic knight was the hero of the "Ages of Faith." But it has been well said that with the virtues of chivalry were associated a new and purer spirit of love, an inspired homage for genuine female worth, which was now revered as the acme of human excellence, and, maintained by religion itself under the image of a Virgin Mother, infused into all hearts a mysterious sense of the purity of love.*

The commerce of modern Europe dates from the Crusades, which recovered, reopened, and multiplied the ancient trading routes of the Mediterranean and the East.

The revival of letters, which had occurred some time previously, received a mighty impulse from those historic enterprises which aroused the heart and the intellect of Christian Europe. Greek learning and literature were transported to the West, and studied with avidity. The arts were likewise revived. That lofty style of Christian architecture known as the *Gothic* originated about the time of the Crusades. The Gothic cathedral with its graceful spires pointing heavenward symbolizes the grand religious spirit of the Middle Ages. Its first and greatest object is to express the elevation of holy thoughts, the loftiness of meditation set free from earth and proceeding unfettered to the skies. Such is the sublime impression which is at once stamped on the soul of the beholder —however little he may himself be capable of analyzing his feelings—as he gazes on those far-stretching columns and airy domes. The whole inspires a feeling of awe and a vague sense of the Divinity.†

5*   * F. Schlegel.   † Chateaubriand.

The Middle Ages, in short, were times of great faith, great men, great books,* and great achievements. The Crusades secured the independence of Europe, and gave it a most powerful impulse in the career of civilization. No other events recorded in history are so colossal as the Crusades, in which, as Balmes eloquently remarks, "we see numberless nations arise, march across deserts, bury themselves in countries with which they are unacquainted, and expose themselves to all the rigors of climate and seasons: and for what purpose? To deliver a tomb! Grand and immortal movement, where hundreds of nations advance to certain death, not in pursuit of a miserable self-interest, not to find an abode in milder and more fertile countries, not from an ardent desire to obtain for themselves earthly advantages, but inspired only by a religious idea, by a jealous desire to possess the tomb of Him who expired on the cross for the salvation of the human race! When compared with this what becomes of the lofty deeds of the Greeks chanted by Homer? Greece arises to avenge an injured husband; Europe to redeem the sepulchre of a God!"

6. PROGRESS OF LEARNING IN ENGLAND, A.D. 1066 –1350.—We have already learned of the revival of letters on the continent of Europe—a revival which owed its first impulse to the influence of the Catholic Church, seconded by the efforts of the celebrated Charlemagne, who completed his splendid reign in the early part of the ninth century. But the first

---

* The most famous of these is the *Summa Theologica* of St. Thomas Aquinas, the Angelic Doctor and prince of Christian philosophers. This incomparable man was born at Belcastro, Italy, in 1226, and died in 1274, at the age of forty-eight years. See *Little Lives of the Great Saints*, page 385.

waves of this literary revival only reached England with the Norman Conquest. At that date the country was in a very backward state in regard to everything intellectual. William the Conqueror found the Saxons a rustic and almost illiterate people.

The great leaders of thought and fathers of learning in England, immediately after the Conquest, were two renowned monks who became Archbishops of Canterbury—*Lanfranc* and *Anselm*. Though both natives of the north of Italy, they were superiors of the two chief monasteries in Normandy when William invaded England.

Lanfranc was chosen Archbishop of Canterbury and Primate of England in 1070. He founded many new schools, restored the study of art and science, and inspired the nation with a love for learning. He was an able logician and one of the most eloquent Latin writers of his age. Nor was he less famous for his knowledge of Holy Scripture, the Fathers of the Church, and Canon Law.*

Lanfranc's pupil and immediate successor, St. Anselm, was a man still more illustrious. He was the greatest educator, philosopher, and theologian of his time, and to-day he is honored as one of the Doctors of the Church.† By the lofty zeal of those renowned

---

* Lanfranc was born at Pavia, Italy, in 1005, and educated at Pavia and Bologna. He died in 1089, at the age of eighty-four. His chief writings are *Commentaries on the Epistles of St. Paul*, *Treatise on the Blessed Eucharist* against Berengarius, *Sermons*, and *Letters*—all in Latin. On one occasion after the elevation of Lanfranc to the Primacy of England, he was obliged to visit Rome and have an audience with Pope Alexander II., who paid him such marked respect that some of the Roman clergy asked the reason, "It is not because he is Primate of England," replied the Pope, "that I rose to meet him, but because I was his pupil at Bec, where I sat at his feet and listened to his words of instruction."

† St. Anselm was born in 1033, at Aosta, Italy. He was appointed Archbishop of Canterbury in 1093, and his great sanctity, vigor-

prelates, learning was revived in England, and the light of knowledge shone with renewed brightness.

Nor can we forget the Conqueror and his successors in connection with the progress of knowledge. Kings and nobles vied with each other in the erection of monasteries and the endowment of seats of learning. From the Conquest to the signing of the Magna Charta—about a century and a half—we learn that *five hundred and fifty-seven monasteries* were founded in England. These were the schools and colleges of that age, and the monks were the teachers and professors.

"Such great institutions of persons," says the Protestant Warton, "dedicated to religious and literary leisure, while they diffused an air of civility and softened the manners of the people, must have afforded powerful incentives to studious pursuits, and have consequently added no small degree of stability to the interests of learning."

"The monks," writes Balmes, "were not content with sanctifying themselves. From the first they influenced society. The light and life which their holy abodes contained labored to enlighten and fertilize the chaos of the world."

7. THE CATHOLIC CHURCH AND THE PROGRESS OF LEARNING.—At all times, but more especially in those rude ages of war and conquest, the Church was the guardian of learning and the soul of progress. The clarion tones of her sacred voice were ever heard urg-

---

ous character, and vast intellectual power made him the foremost man of his age. Among the works of this famous saint are, *On Truth, On Original Sin, The Fall of Satan, The Liberty of the Will, The Reason Why God Created Man, Why God was Made Man,* and *The Consistency of Freedom with the Divine Foreknowledge*—all in Latin. These great questions were then uppermost in men's minds, and they were handled by St. Anselm in a new and more attractive mode of appeal to pure reason. He died in 1109.

ing forward the spread of sound knowledge. To her we owe the revival of the arts, sciences, and literature. She taught her children to love learning and to found and endow schools; and she educated eminent men to govern those centres of knowledge.*

Before the rise of the universities, the educational institutions of the Middle Ages were of two classes—the *cathedral schools* and the *monastic schools*. The studies were divided into two courses known as the *Trivium* * and the *Quadrivium*.† The Trivium, or lower course, comprised grammar, logic, and rhetoric. The Quadrivium, or higher course, embraced arithmetic, music, geometry, and astronomy. The doors of these schools were open to all—rich and poor alike. It was the Catholic Church that first taught the world to respect man and merit rather than rank or fortune.

An able writer referring to this period says: "Schools for the poor were especially attended to. The Councils of the Church—those landmarks of civilization—from the beginning decree that every church that has the means provide a master for the *gratuitous instruction of the poor* 'according to the ancient canons.' That of Lateran in 1180 says that, the Church of God 'like a dutiful mother' being bound to provide for the indigent in soul as well as in body, to every church shall be attached a master to instruct the poor gratuitously." ‡

---

* Religion and literature were always cultivated together. The library grew up with the school under the shadow of the Church.—*Spalding*.
† Trivium, or Three Roads, because grammar, logic, and rhetoric constitute a triple way to eloquence.
‡ Quadrivium, or Four Roads. The Trivium and Quadrivium together constituted the *seven liberal arts*, or circle of study in the Middle Ages.
§ Brother Azarias, *Philosophy of Literature*.

8. Rise of the Universities.—Nearly all the great institutions of learning in Europe carry the mind back to the ages of faith. As a spring-time, a time of seed-sowing, have those ages been to modern Europe. "The long and silent process of vegetation," says Schlegel, "must precede the spring, and the spring must precede the maturity of the fruit. The youth of individuals has often been called the spring-time of life. I imagine we may so speak of whole nations with the same propriety as of individuals. They also have their seasons of unfolding intellect and mental blossoming. The age of the Crusades, chivalry, romance, and minstrelsy was an *intellectual spring* among all the nations of the west."

The enthusiasm of the Crusades was followed by an enthusiasm of study. From the *thirteenth century* we may properly date the rise of the great universities — *Paris, Oxford, Cambridge, Bologna, Pavia, Padua, Salamanca,* and others. Before that time those seats of learning had existed as schools; but it remained for the thirteenth century to develop and enlarge them into higher and more permanent centres of thought, art, science, and literature.

In the advancement of learning and civilization the value of the universities cannot be overestimated. "One of the causes," observes Balmes, "that contributed most to the development of the human mind was the creation of great centres of instruction, which collected the most illustrious talents and learning, and diffused rays of light in all directions." These grand institutions were created and sustained by the Catholic Church. "All the universities were founded either by religious princes or by bishops and priests; and all were under the direction of different religious orders."

LITERATURE OF THE NORMAN PERIOD. 59

As time went on the thirst for learning increased. At the beginning of the fourteenth century over 20,000 students attended the University of Oxford,* and the number at Paris was still greater. Albertus Magnus † and Abelard ‡ were professors in the University of Paris. Albertus was compelled to lecture in the public square that still bears his name, and Abelard counted his audience by thousands. We are told that of Abelard's pupils twenty became cardinals and fifty bishops and archbishops. Though Bologna § was the oldest of the universities, Paris stood at the head of them all as a place of general instruction.‖

One of Abelard's English pupils, the famous John of Salisbury, writing from Paris in 1176, gives the following glowing account: "When I saw," he says, "the abundance of provisions, the gayety of the people, the good condition of the clergy, the majesty and glory of all the Church, the varied occupations of men admitted to the study of philosophy, I seemed to see that Jacob's ladder whose summit reached heaven, and on which the angels ascended and descended. I must confess that indeed the Lord was in this place."

---

* At the present time the number of students at Oxford is about 2,000.
† A celebrated Dominican, who was St. Thomas Aquinas' preceptor. He died in 1280.
‡ A famous scholastic philosopher and monk, who died in 1142.
§ Ten thousand students are said to have attended Bologna in 1262.
‖ It seems to have been in the early portion of the thirteenth century that *degrees*, or titles of learning, began to be conferred on such students as passed through the university courses of study with approval. According to the historian Robertson, in his *History of Charles V*, the "first obscure mention of these academical degrees in the University of Paris—from which other universities in Europe have borrowed most of their customs—occurs A.D. 1215. They were completely established A.D 1231. It is unnecessary to enumerate the several privileges to which Bachelors, Masters, and Doctors were entitled."

The great zeal for learning in England was proved by splendid endowments. Between 1250 and 1400 seven new colleges were founded at Oxford, and nine at Cambridge. The Church viewed the growth of the universities with a mother's pride, and encouraged them in their upward career. Pope Clement V., at the General Council of Vienne, ordered that professorships of Greek, Hebrew, Arabic, and Chaldaic be established in the universities of Paris, Oxford, Bologna, and Salamanca.*

9. REMARKS ON BRITISH LITERATURE FROM 1066 TO 1350.—We can look for nothing remarkable in the Anglo-Saxon or English literature of this period. All that was learned, valuable, or witty was given to the world in Latin, or occasionally in French. For two hundred years after the Norman Conquest the chief literary productions of England were written in Latin or in French. In fact, the principal English poets for *three hundred years after the Conquest wrote wholly in French.* Out of more than *two hundred and twenty English authors* who wrote between the Conquest and the middle of the fourteenth century, hardly as many names as could be counted on the fingers of one hand left anything worth remembering in their native language.

The key to this state of Saxon literary degradation is furnished by the history of the times. An old British writer bluntly tells us that "French being the language of the polite, and Latin of the learned, nobody could use the common tongue in composition." All the works on philosophy, theology, and history were written in Latin; while all that was intended to

---

* At the date of the discovery of America, about 8000 students attended the University of Salamanca.

amuse the upper classes and the idlers of the court appeared in French.

But what became of the Anglo-Saxon as a literary language? Obscure and despised, we hear it no more except in the mouths of farmers, peasants, swineherds, and outlaws of the forest. It is no longer, or scarcely, written. In the *Saxon Chronicle* we find that gradually the idiom alters, and is extinguished. The Chronicle itself ceases within a century after the Conquest.*

What we call the *Norman Period* extends from the Norman Conquest to the days of Chaucer. It may be separated into two divisions—the *Semi-Saxon Age* and the *Age of Early English*. Under these heads we shall review the principal English writers and the literary monuments which they left behind. But to make this chapter more complete, a bird's-eye view of several of the most distinguished Latin and French authors of the same period is also added.

LESSON I.

THE SEMI-SAXON AGE, A.D. 1150 TO 1250.

1. The *Brut of Layamon*.
2. The *Ormulum*.
3. The *Ancren Riwle* (ăn-krĕn' ri-ūlə).

☞ *These are the three principal works written in the English of the Semi-Saxon Age.*

1. Who was Layamon?

He was a patriotic priest of Worcestershire, and the author of the famous poem known as the *Brut*

---

* Taine.

of Layamon, which he translated chiefly from the French.*

2. State its length, merits, and date of composition.

It consists of over 32,000 lines, and is very valuable as a specimen of English in its early form. The date of its composition, though not exactly known, may be fixed about the year 1200.†

3. What is the subject of the Brut of Layamon, or, more properly, the Brutus of Britain?

It is a chronicle of British history from the arrival of Brutus—a supposed son of Æneas ‡ of Troy—to the death of the last Celtic prince of England, about the middle of the seventh century.

4. What were Layamon's sources for the material of his poem?

(1) The original Celtic poem on the same subject, since lost; (2) a Latin translation of the original by Geoffrey of Monmouth; (3) and a French translation of Geoffrey's Latin one by Wace, a Norman-French poet.

5. What is the Ormulum?

The Ormulum is a series of metrical homilies having for their subject the Gospels of the various Sundays and holidays in the year.

6. Who was the author?

Orm, a pious and learned English canon of the Order of St. Augustine.

7. Does the Ormulum exist entire?

No; out of the whole number of homilies, which

---
* It is mainly a translation of the *Brut d'Angleterre* (Brutus of England) by Wace, a Norman-French poet.
† The Brut of Layamon was first printed in 1847.
‡ Æneas, the hero of Virgil's *Æneid*, was, according to Homer, ranked next to Hector among the heroes of Troy.

must have amounted to nearly *three hundred*, but *thirty-two* remain—a fine fragment of a grand whole.

8. In its present form, of how many lines does the Ormulum consist, and what are its merits?

It consists of nearly 20,000 lines; is a real landmark in the history of our language; and, in the literature of this period, is second in importance only to the Brut of Layamon.*

9. What do the words "*Ancren Riwle*" signify?

This is the old uncouth way of spelling *Anchoress*† *Rule*.

10. What can you say of this work?

It is a prose work, the author of which is unknown, but he was evidently an ecclesiastic high in authority.

11. Of what does it treat?

It is a somewhat extensive treatise on the rules and duties of the monastic life, written for a number of religious ladies who formed a community in Dorsetshire.

12. What may be said of its vocabulary and the date of its composition?

It contains a larger infusion of Latin words than either the Brut of Layamon or the Ormulum, and was probably written about the year 1225.

---

* The Ormulum was first printed in 1852. Only one manuscript copy exists.
† An anchoress is a female hermit or recluse.

LESSON II.

THE AGE OF EARLY ENGLISH, A.D. 1250 TO 1350.

1. Robert of Gloucester's *Chronicle*.
2. Robert Manning's *Chronicle*.
3. THE ROMANCES OF CHIVALRY.
☞ *These are the chief literary productions in the English of this age.*

13. Who was Robert of Gloucester?

He was a writer about whom we know very little, except that he was a monk of Gloucester Abbey, and the author of a rhyming *Chronicle*.

14. What is the subject of this Chronicle?

It is a versified history of England from the time of the imaginary Brutus of Troy till the death of Henry III., A.D. 1272. The Chronicle was written about the year 1300.

15. Who was Robert Manning, or Robert of Brunne as he is sometimes called?

He was a learned priest and canon of Brunne, who wrote in the first half of the fourteenth century.

16. Which is his principal work?

A *Chronicle*, which is the most voluminous work written in Early English.

17. Is Manning's Chronicle written in prose or in verse, and what period of history does it cover?

It is a metrical history of England from the time of the imaginary Brutus of Troy down to the death of Edward I., A.D. 1307.

18. From what source did Robert of Gloucester and Robert Manning draw largely for the early portions of their *Chronicles?*

From Geoffrey of Monmouth's *History of the Britons*—a famous Latin work of the twelfth century.

19. What may be said of the language and versification of these *Chronicles?*

Robert of Gloucester's *Chronicle* is written in *twelve-*syllable and Manning's in *eight*-syllable rhyming couplets. Both works—but Manning's especially—show considerable improvement in English over the productions of the Semi-Saxon Age.

20. During what period did *metrical romance*, or the *romances of chivalry*, flourish?

English metrical romance began about the year 1200; but its most flourishing period was during the *fourteenth century*, after which it entirely disappeared as an element of early English literature.

21. To what kind of compositions was the name metrical romance, or romances of chivalry, given?

To tales of love and adventure *written in verse*.

22. When and by whom were metrical romances introduced into England?

In the *eleventh* century, by the Normans.

23. Were these romances popular during early times?

Strictly speaking, the romances of chivalry were the only popular literature of the Middle Ages, and were patronized by the court and the castle, by the Norman baron and the Saxon gentleman, by the knight and his lady-love.

24. Which were the usual heroes and events in such tales?

Alexander the Great, Charlemagne, or oftener *King Arthur and his Knights of the Round Table;* but whatever might be the name, date, or place of the events described, the real subjects were always a tale of love and adventure for the true faith, a tournament,* a troubadour,† a Christian knight, and a pagan foe.

---
* A mock battle of armed knights.
† One of a school of French poets.

25. What detracts from the merit of English metrical romance?

The want of *originality;* nearly all the English tales are mere imitations or simple translations from the French. We are even left in ignorance of the translators, who thought so little of their own labors as to affix no name to their works.

26. Name a few of the most celebrated of the metrical romances.

King Horn, King Alexander, Sir Tristram, Havelock the Dane, the *Death of Arthur,* and the *Owl and the Nightingale;* the last, especially, being very interesting as *the earliest English poem not copied from some foreign model.*

27. Who revived the metrical romance in modern times?

Sir Walter Scott, though he did it in a form somewhat original.

LESSON III.

PRINCIPAL NORMAN-FRENCH WRITERS OF ENGLAND.
A.D 1066 TO 1350.

1. *Richard Wace.* Died 1184
2. *Richard Cœur de Lion.* Died 1199.
3. *Cardinal Langton.* Died 1228.

28. Who stands first among the Norman-French poets?

Richard Wace, a priest, who lived in the reign of Henry II.

29. Which are his chief works?

Two exceedingly long poems—*The Brutus of England* * and *The Romance of Rollo.*†

---

* *Le Brut d' Angleterre.* † *Le Roman de Ron.*—According to Chambers, "neither of these works has the slightest poetical merit. They are both interesting only as showing the state of the French language in the twelfth century, as supplying occasional facts and social traits to the historian."

LITERATURE OF THE NORMAN PERIOD. 67

30. What are the subject, ve.sification, and length of the first of these poems?

The *Brutus of England* is chiefly a metrical translation of Geoffrey of Monmouth's Latin *History of the Britons*. It is written in eight-syllable verse, and is over 15,000 lines in length.

31. Describe the *Romance of Rollo*.

The *Romance of Rollo* is an epic poem on the first Duke of Normandy—the famous Rollo the Marcher.* It contains the history of the Norman dukes down to Henry II.

32. What two personages celebrated in English history may be mentioned in connection with Norman-French poetry?

King Richard the Lion-hearted and Cardinal Langton.

33. What did King Richard write?

He composed several military songs known as *Sirventes*. A portion of one of these was printed by Horace Walpole in his *Royal and Noble Authors*.

34. By what is Cardinal Langton known to literature?

We possess but one of Cardinal Langton's literary productions—a beautiful little poem, in a manuscript sermon of his, discovered in the British Museum.

LESSON IV.

PRINCIPAL LATIN WRITERS OF ENGLAND. A.D. 1066 TO 1350.

1. *William of Malmesbury.* Died 1144.
2. *Geoffrey of Monmouth.* Died 1154.
3. *John of Salisbury.* Died 1182.
4. *Joseph of Exeter.* Died 1200.
5. *Roger Bacon.* Died 1292.

---

* So called "because he was of so mighty stature that no horse could bear his weight."

35. Who was William of Malmesbury?

He was a monk of the Abbey of Malmesbury, who, next to Bede, was the greatest historian that England produced in early times.

36. Which are his chief works?

The History of the Kings of England and *The New History*, both written in Latin.

37. Describe these two productions.

The *History of the English Kings* is a long work in five books, extending from the landing of the Saxons in England till the year 1120; the *New History*, in three books, carries the account down till 1142.

38. What a e William of Malmesbury's merits as an historian?

His works are written with care, accuracy, and research; and, for the age in which they were composed, are both learned and philosophical.

39. Who was Geoffrey of Monmouth?

He was a Welsh bishop whose *History of the Britons* is one of the most famous productions of the Middle Ages.

40. What may be said of the *History of the Britons?*

While its historical value seems to be slight, it is forever endeared to the literary mind as a grand storehouse of beautiful Celtic legends which have furnished materials for the masterpieces of some of our greatest poets and prose writers.

41. From what source did Geoffrey of Monmouth obtain the materials for this singular work?

The History of the Britons, it seems, is chiefly a translation of an old Celtic Chronicle, which has since been lost.

42. Name a few of the legends borrowed from this History.

The story of King Lear and his daughters,* Arthur and his Knights of the Round Table, and many others.

43. Who was John of Salisbury?

He was a learned English bishop and well-known Latin writer of the Middle Ages.

44. What is his chief work?

His chief work is *Polycration*, a pleasant and learned treatise on the " frivolities of courtiers and the footsteps of philosophers."

45. What Englishman is esteemed the best Latin poet of this period?

A gifted monk of Exeter Abbey, commonly known as *Joseph of Exeter*.

46. What is his principal work?

An epic poem entitled *The Trojan War*. It is written in elegant Latin.

47. Who was Roger Bacon?

He was a native of England, a learned Franciscan Father, and the most famous philosopher of his age.

48. Which is his chief work?

The *Opus Majus* (or "Greater Work"), a celebrated production which has been styled the encyclopædia of the thirteenth century.

-Summary of Chapter III.

1. With the Norman Conquest there was introduced into England a new order of things, social, political, and literary.

2. The 2,000,000 inhabitants of England were still

---

* This story is the foundation of Shakspeare's great tragedy of *King Lear*.

Saxons, but their rulers were Normans, and Norman-French became the language of the Court and the Castle.

3. Cardinal Langton and the Catholic barons forced King John to sign the Magna Charta on the famous field of Runnymede, A.D. 1215.

4. The first English parliament met A.D. 1265.

5. The commerce of Europe dates from the Crusades, which gave a great impulse to art, science, and literature.

6. Gothic or Christian architecture dates from the Middle Ages, often styled "the Ages of Faith." *

7. Lanfranc and St. Anselm began the revival of learning in England in the Middle Ages.

8. The Norman rulers of England were great patrons of learning. From the date of the Conquest to the signing of the Magna Charta—about 150 years—557 monasteries were founded in England. These were all houses of education.

9. To the Catholic Church we owe the revival of the arts, sciences, and literature. History admits of no doubt on this point.

---

* Nowadays shallow or blindly prejudiced authors write of them as the "Dark Ages"; but the *darkness* is in *themselves*, not in the "Ages of Faith." The "Dark Ages" never had any existence save in unenlightened skulls and diseased imaginations. It is to those much calumniated ages that we must trace the origin of the following inventions and improvements: (1) organs and bells in churches; (2) the mariner's compass, which prepared the way for the discovery of America; (3) banks and double-entry book keeping; (4) post-offices; (5) spectacles for the use of the eyes; (6) clocks; (7) gunpowder; (8) computation from the birth of Christ; (9) the Gothic style of architecture; (10) the *gamut* in music; (11) oil-painting; (12) the making of *paper* from linen rags; (13) modern commerce; (14) all our modern languages; (15) rhyme and the beginning of modern poetry; (16) water-mills; (17) glass windows for churches; (18) the manufacture of silk; (19) the great universities; (20) the art of printing.

10. The doors of the monastic schools were open to all—rich and poor alike.

11. The great universities of Europe, under the fostering care of the Church, began to take shape in the thirteenth century.

12. The most renowned of the ancient universities were those of Paris, Bologna, Oxford, Cambridge, and Salamanca.

13. Between A.D. 1250 and 1400 *seven* new colleges were founded at Oxford and *nine* at Cambridge.

14. The degraded condition and unformed state of the English language during the Norman Period warn us that we need look for nothing great in the native literature of that time.

15. With few exceptions, the famous writers of that period gave their ideas to the world in a Latin or a French dress.

16. The chief productions written in the crude and unformed English of the time, for 200 years after the Norman Conquest, were (1) *The Anglo-Saxon Chronicle*, (2) *The Brut of Layamon*, (3) *The Ormulum*, and (4) *The Ancren Riwle.*

17. The chief literary productions written in Early English (1250-1350) were Robert of Gloucester's *Chronicle*, Robert Manning's *Chronicle*, and the metrical tales known as the *Romances of Chivalry.*

18. The principal English historian of the Norman Period was William of Malmesbury, who wrote in Latin.

19. Joseph of Exeter is esteemed the best Latin poet of that age.

20. Roger Bacon is regarded as one of the most profound philosophers of the Middle Ages. His works are all in Latin.

BOOK II.

CHAPTER I.
THE AGE OF CHAUCER, GOWER, AND MANDEVILLE.

A.D. 1350 to 1400.

HISTORICAL INTRODUCTION.

1. GLANCES AT THE BRITISH HISTORY OF THIS PERIOD.—The latter half of the fourteenth century we call the *Age of Chaucer, Gower, and Mandeville*, because these were its representative literary names. That brief age was the real beginning of English letters. It was the springtime of English literature.

The civil history of this period covers the greater part of the reign of Edward III. and the entire reign of Richard II. That of Edward III. was long and brilliant. The victories of Crécy and Poitiers filled Europe with the fame of English arms and the military skill of the Black Prince.* In him English chivalry reached the pinnacle of glory and greatness.

There are certain periods of history in which, by a mysterious combination of circumstances, the genius, energy, and greatness of a nation are suddenly developed and exhibited to the world. Such was the reign of Edward III. In the Black Prince it pro-

---

* So named on account of the color of his armor.

duced the flower of English chivalry; to all time it
gave Chaucer, "the Father of English Poetry." Then
it was that an English nationality, an English language,
and an English literature fairly began. The victories
gained over a French foe by combined Norman and
Saxon valor welded the two races more firmly than
ever together. Three hundred years of commingling,
of intermarriages, and the possession of common interests nearly completed the work of race-consolida-
tion in this reign. The victories of Crécy and Poitiers led to the gradual disuse of the French language
and the downfall of French influence. The tongue
of the vanquished foe could no longer maintain its
former power and prestige in England.

The last years, however, of the reign of Edward
III. were rendered gloomy by the sickness and death
of the Black Prince, and the consequent loss of nearly
all territory in France. But there was one gain.
With the loss of French possessions foreign ties were
broken. Every man from the English sovereign down
found his common country bounded by the coasts of
England. We hear no more of Norman and Saxon.
The two races and the two languages—as by a chemi-
cal process—became one.

Edward III. was the most accomplished English
sovereign since the Conquest. He was the first king
of England who, for three hundred years, could speak
the language of the people he ruled. English was
made the speech of the courts of law and the schools.
An act passed in 1362 decrees that all cases "shall
be pleaded, showed, defended, answered, debated, and
judged in the English tongue."

The reign of Richard II. witnessed the beginning
of that agitation among the lower classes for their just

rights and privileges which ceases not even to-day. The people were little better than serfs and bondsmen. But soon they began to feel their own power, and, headed by bold and lawless leaders like *Wat Tyler*, the restless multitude were treated to discourses on such curious questions as,

"When Adam delved and Eve span,
Who was then the gentleman?"

In treating the English history of this period, many Protestant writers appear to take pleasure in misrepresenting the Catholic Church and her institutions. They would have us believe that much of the miseries of the people could be traced to the Church. The charge is false and malicious. The Catholic Church was then—as she has ever been—the faithful friend and comforter of the people, the loving mother of the orphan, the poor, the afflicted; but, unhappily, she has not always been able to prevent the tyranny of kings and nobles, to destroy corruption in high places, or to cure all the ills of humanity. This is the testimony of true history.

The story of Scotland during this period (1350–1400) is filled with accounts of disastrous wars with England and struggles between the Scottish monarch and his turbulent nobles. *David II.* was taken prisoner by the English, and remained in captivity for eleven years; but he was finally ransomed by his subjects, and died in 1370. He was succeeded by his nephew, *Robert Stuart*, the *first* of that name that swayed the sceptre of Scotland. The Stuart family is, perhaps, the most unfortunate in the annals of history.

2. INFLUENCING AGENCIES ON THE LITERATURE OF THIS PERIOD.—The age of Chaucer, Gower, and Man-

deville, as we have said, may be regarded as the May-time of English letters. And as the months of the year and their products are influenced by various physical agencies, so the literary productions of different ages bear upon them the impressions not alone of the genius which conceived them, but also of the times in which they were given to the world. Various were the causes which had a bearing, a directing influence, on the English letters of this period. In the history of the reigns of Edward III. and Richard II. must be sought the *home* influences. The chivalry of that period and the brilliant military achievements of the Black Prince have their literary counterpart in the masterpieces of Chaucer, the poems of Gower, and the travels of old Sir John Mandeville.

But other influences were also at work. Chief amongst these may be named (1) the *Italian*, (2) the *French*, (3) the *Latin*.

3. ITALIAN INFLUENCE.—" As was to be expected," writes Bascom, " Italy was the first division of Europe after the barbaric overflow to regain the arts of civilization. In commerce, in freedom, in the industrial and fine arts, in literature and science, she took the lead." In truth, the intellectual brightness of Italy illumined Europe in the fourteenth century. The world is indebted to that age for three illustrious poets, *Dante*,* *Petrarch*,† and *Chaucer*—two Italians, and one Englishman. Of all the Christian poets, Dante is the grandest, the most sublime. He was 'the great Catholic bard of these remote times. His

---

* Dante, born at Florence, 1265; died 1321. He was the father of Italian literature.
† Petrarch, born at Arezzo, 1304; died 1374. He is a poet of great purity.

Divina Commedia is the poetic and religious expression of the Ages of Faith. Dante died a few years before the birth of Chaucer. Petrarch taught modern Europe how to write lyric poetry. *Boccaccio* * was another Italian writer of the same age. The genius of Chaucer was doubtless quickened by his renowned foreign contemporaries. It is generally admitted that the infamous *Decameron* † of Boccaccio suggested the plot of the *Canterbury Tales*, and furnished the most beautiful of them all—the *Knight's Tale*. "Indeed, it is here worthy of remark," says Coppée, writing of the age of Chaucer, "that from that early time to a later period many of the greatest products of English poetry have been watered by silver rills of imaginative genius from a remote Italian source. Chaucer's indebtedness has just been noticed. *Spenser* borrowed his versification and not a little of his poetic handling in the *Fairy Queen* from *Ariosto*. Milton owes to Dante some of his conceptions of heaven and hell in his *Paradise Lost*, while his *Lycidas*, *Arcades*, *Allegro*, and *Penseroso* may be called Italian poems done into English."

4. FRENCH INFLUENCE.—The influence of French taste, although much lessened, still continued to make some impression on English letters. Translations

---

* Boccaccio, born 1313; died 1375.
† The *Decameron* is a collection of one hundred tales written during the period when the plague desolated the south of Europe. The plot is simple. It is assumed that a party of ten retired to one of the villas near Naples to escape the danger of contagion. Each person was to tell a new story on each of the ten days; hence one hundred stories, and the title Decameron. Many of these tales, however, are not only immoral but grossly obscene. No beauty of language can hide or make amends for such a heap of moral rottenness and literary filth. This miserable but much-lauded book was freely circulated in Italy until it was condemned by the Council of Trent. Had Chaucer a better model before him, it is very probable the *Canterbury Tales* would have been more moral.

from the French were numerous. The English poets drew freely from the *Fabliaux*, or tales in verse. Chaucer's most masterly translation—*The Romance of the Rose*—is but an elegant English rendering of one of the poetic gems of early French literature.

5. LATIN INFLUENCE.—We have already glanced at some of the literary storehouses which were built up in the Latin of the Middle Ages. For hundreds of years those ancient collections have furnished an almost inexhaustible source of material for the poets and story-tellers of all lands. Chaucer drew liberally from the *Gesta Romanorum** and other Latin collections. Two, if not more, of his *Canterbury Tales* can be traced to the *Gesta*. From the same abundant source Gower borrowed even more largely.†

6. REMARKS ON SOME OF THE WRITERS OF THIS PERIOD.—The principal British writers of this age were CHAUCER, GOWER, MANDEVILLE, BARBOUR, WICKLIFF, LANGLAND, and MINOT. The little we really know of Chaucer's personal history leaves wide scope for speculation; and, as a consequence, few men have been more misrepresented. It is said " a lie has no legs," but that does not prevent lies from travelling. A disgraceful anecdote about Chaucer's having been "fined two shillings for beating a Franciscan friar in Fleet Street" has made the rounds of nearly every text-book on English literature. The care with which this silly item has been hawked about is painfully suggestive. It has no foundation. Sir

---

* A celebrated collection of fictions written in the Latin of the Middle Ages.

† Shakspeare, Scott, Tennyson, and others owe not a little to the vast literary storehouses of the Middle Ages. For instance, the story of the *Merchant of Venice*, on which Shakspeare founded his famous play, is borrowed from the *Gesta Romanorum*.

Harris Nicholas has proved its utter falsehood. Other bigoted writers assert that Chaucer was a disciple of the heretical Wickliff. This is also untrue. In his life or works there is nothing to prove that the "Father of English Poetry" was anything but a Catholic. His last days were spent within the precincts of a religious house. A record is still extant in the office of the Dean and Chapter of Westminster from which we see that on the 24th of November, 1399—the year before his death—Chaucer took a lease for fifty years, from the abbot, prior, and convent of Westminster, of a house situated in the garden of their chapel. Here the venerable poet's dying moments were, doubtless, soothed by having conferred upon him those mysterious blessings which the Catholic religion alone can bestow. He was devoted to the Most Blessed Virgin. This his works prove. An exquisite little poem, *The Prayer to Our Lady*, was composed by him for Lady Blanche, wife of John of Gaunt. In the opening lines of his *Canterbury Tales*, after referring to the "sweet showers of April," he continues:

"So nature stirs all energies and ages
That folks are bent to go on pilgrimages,
And palmers* for to wander through strange strands
To sing the Holy Mass in sundry lands.
And more especially from each shire's end
Of England they to Canterbury wend,
The holy blissful martyr† for to seek,
That hath upheld them when that they were weak."‡

7. WICKLIFF—HIS RELIGIOUS AND LITERARY POSITION.—So many things have been written about Wickliff that it is quite proper, just here, to glance at the man's religious and literary position. He was a secular priest, doctor of divinity, and for some time

---

* Pilgrims to the Holy Land.
† St. Thomas of Canterbury.
‡ *Chaucer modernized.*

a professor in Oxford University. We first hear of him about 1360, in the reign of Edward III. He was a violent enemy of the Franciscan and Dominican Fathers. Their poverty, above all, aroused his wrath. Those apostolic men had been established in England for more than a century; "and," says Lingard, "by their zeal, learning, and piety had deservedly earned the esteem of the public." But Wickliff did not stop at the monks. Soon his coarse invectives were levelled at the whole body of the clergy, the bishops, and even the Pope. His followers were known as *Lollards*— a fanatical sect of revolutionists. Wickliff was several times commanded to appear before his ecclesiastical superiors. When summoned for the last time by order of Gregory XI. to explain his opinions, he "professed his readiness to submit to the correction of the Church, and revoked whatever he might have taught contrary to the doctrine of Christ." Some years after, he suddenly died while celebrating mass. His English translation of the Bible is from the Catholic *Vulgate*, and, from a literary point of view, merits little praise. Wickliff's writings are in every respect a counterpart of the man—coarse, unpolished productions.*

---

* The pronunciation of English in the days of Chaucer differed in many respects from our present system. The letter A was called *ah*, as in *hat* or *father*. E had the sound of *a* in *dare*, or *ai* in *hair*. It was not until the beginning of the eighteenth century that the present sounds of A and E were established. I had almost the sound of *ee*, or the lengthened sound of *i* in *still*. Long *i*, as in *pine*, is a modern invention. See Ellis's *Early English Pronunciation*.

LESSON I.

GEOFFREY CHAUCER. DIED 1400.

Chief works: (1) *The Canterbury Tales.*
(2) *The House of Fame.*
(3) *The Flower and the Leaf.*
(4) *The Romance of the Rose.*

1. Who was Geoffrey Chaucer?

Geoffrey Chaucer was the "Father of English Poetry" and the "Founder of English Literature." He takes rank with Shakspeare and Milton.

2. Is his personal history well known?

No; it is shrouded in much obscurity. He was born at London of a good family, in the early part of the fourteenth century, and received an excellent education. Both Oxford and Cambridge claim him as a student. It is thought that he finished his studies at the University of Paris.

3. Relate his ea ly career.

In early life Chaucer was a courtier and soldier. The favor of John of Gaunt introduced him to the brilliant court of Edward III. Having gone to France with the English forces, we learn that he was made prisoner at the siege of Retters in 1359, but was enabled to return to England the year following.

4. How did Edward III. treat the "Father of English Poetry"?

The king showered favors on the bold genius who could wield both sword and pen. Chaucer received an annual pension of twenty marks.* He was employed on various foreign missions. During one of

---

* About $1000.

these to Italy it is supposed that he met the celebrated Petrarch. He also held the office of Comptroller of the Port of London.

5. Whom did Chaucer marry?

A lady named *Philippa Picard*, sister-in-law of John of Gaunt, Duke of Lancaster. A marked feature in his life was his devoted attachment to his wife and family.

6. How did Chaucer fall into disfavor with Richard III.?

For some years after the old king's death prosperity continued to cheer and brighten the poet's path. Richard was his friend. But the Duke of Lancaster, Chaucer's patron and brother-in-law, was not a favorite with the king. During a riot in London the poet sided with the friends of Lancaster. This cost him the king's friendship, and he was obliged to fly to France.

7. What befell Chaucer on his return to England?

He was seized and cast into the Tower; but, by the efforts of his friends, he was once more restored to royal favor, and received the lucrative position of Clerk of Works at Westminster.

8. What did the Father of English Poetry do in 1391?

Wearied of public life, he retired to his country-house at Woodstock, and at the advanced age of over threescore years began to write the famous *Canterbury Tales.**

9. Where did he take up his residence in 1399?

In 1399 Chaucer rented from the Abbot of Westminster a house in the garden of the convent chapel. Here, in the quiet of religious seclusion, the great

---

* At the advanced age of sixty-three he commenced his masterpiece, the *Canterbury Tales*, which will be an everlasting source of enjoyment to mankind.—*Horne*.

poet breathed his soul to God in the year 1400. He was buried in what is known as the "Poets' Corner" of the renowned Abbey—the *first* in that long line of English geniuses whose remains are there interred.

10. What may be said of Chaucer's checkered career as a preparation for his literary labors?

His career was such that he had every means to study the great volume of life in men, things, and books. He was a scholar, courtier, traveller, soldier, ambassador, and, above all, a diligent, good-tempered student of human nature.*

LESSON II.

GEOFFREY CHAUCER, CONTINUED.

11. Name Chaucer's principal works.

See page 80.

12. Which is his masterpiece?

The Canterbury Tales.

13. Describe the *Canterbury Tales.*

The *Canterbury Tales* consist of *twenty-four* tales or stories preceded by a prologue or introduction; and, except two of the stories, they are all *in verse*.

14. How long are these *Tales?*

The metrical part extends to over 17,000 lines, being longer than Homer's *Iliad* and nearly twice as long as Milton's *Paradise Lost.*†

---

* "He seems," says Lowell, "incapable of indignation. He muses good-naturedly over the vices and follies of men, and, never forgetting that he was fashioned of the same clay, is rather apt to pity than condemn. There is no touch of cynicism in all he wrote."—*My Study Windows.*

† Some idea of the size of each story may be formed by stating that the *Prologue* contains 860 lines, and the *Knight's Tale*, which is the first, contains 2250 lines.

AGE OF CHAUCER, GOWER, AND MANDEVILLE. 83

15. State the plot of the *Canterbury Tales.*

The plot is very simple. Thirty persons arrive at the Tabard Inn, on the outskirts of London. They are all on a pilgrimage to the celebrated shrine of St. Thomas à Becket at Canterbury, some fifty miles distant. Chaucer, likewise at the inn, is on the same journey, and determines to accompany the band of pilgrims. Harry Bailey, the host, is to act as guide. Before starting, in order to relieve the tedium of the road, each one agrees to relate two stories going and two returning. When the pilgrimage is over, the teller of the best story is to get a grand supper at the expense of the others.

16. What is the nature of the *Prologue* to the *Canterbury Tales?*

It is a minute and somewhat lengthy description of the person, dress, manners, and accomplishments of each of the pilgrims. The first described is a *Knight,* " a worthy man," who had fought for the true faith in fifteen " mortal battles."*

17. Mention some other persons in Chaucer's portrait-gallery.

There are the *Knight's son* with his *yeoman attendant;* a *Franklin,* or country gentleman;† a good parish *Priest,*‡ and his *brother,* an honest Ploughman;

---

* " And of his port as meek as is a maid,
  He never yet a word uncourteous said,
  In all his life, to any mortal wight—
  He was a very perfect gentle knight."
† " With sanguine hues did his complexion shine:
  Well loved he in the morn a sop of wine."
‡ " Wide was his parish—houses far asundr r.
  Yet he neglected naught for rain or thunder;
  But Jesus' lore, which owns no pride or pelf,
  He taught—but first he followed it himself."

a *Miller;* a *Reeve,* or *Bailiff;* * a *Prioress;* several *monks;* the *Wife of Bath;*† a *Merchant;* a *Doctor;* a *Sea-captain;* and many others.

18. Which are perhaps the best-drawn characters?

The *Knight* and the *Parish Priest.*

19. Into how many classes may the stories composing the *Canterbury Tales* be divided?

Into two classes, according to their nature—the *pathetic* or tragic, and the *comic* or humorous.

20. Which is the most beautiful of the pathetic Tales?

The *Knight's Tale,* or the story of Aracite and Palamon, which Chaucer borrowed from the Italian of Boccaccio.‡

21. Mention another of the pathetic Tales which is very striking.

The *Tale of the Prioress,* or the touching legend of how "little Hugh of Lincoln" was murdered for perseveringly singing his hymn to the Most Blessed Virgin.

22. By whom are the two prose Tales related?

By Chaucer himself and the Parish Priest.

23. What is the nature of the Tale related by the Parish Priest?

It is a somewhat elaborate sermon on the seven deadly sins, and their causes and remedies. There breathes throughout it a spirit of sincere piety.§

---

* "Full long were both his spindle legs, and lean,
Just like a walking-stick—no calf was seen."

† "She was a worthy woman to the core;
Five husbands had she brought from the church door."

‡ It tells how two brave young knights, Aracite and Palamon, both fell in love with the beautiful Emily. Aracite, victorious in tournament, falls, and dying bequeaths Emily to his rival.

§ It is the opinion of some eminent critics that this sermon was added by Chaucer to his *Canterbury Tales* at the advice of his con-

24. Do the *Canterbury Tales* contain any account of the visit of the pilgrims to the shrine of St. Thomas, and of their return?

No; as the *Canterbury Tales* now exist they are incomplete—a fragment of what Chaucer designed them to be. His death prevented their completion.*

25. For what is the *Prologue* to the *Canterbury Tales* especially admired?

For its pen-pictures. It is an unrivalled collection of humorous and masterly descriptions of men and manners. In descriptive power, in humor and pathos, Chaucer is unsurpassed by any writer in English literature.

26. In what other way does Chaucer exhibit the most exquisite taste?

With the nicest art, each story is suited to the character of the person who relates it. The rude miller's tales is very different from that of the polished, courteous knight.

27. What may be said of Chaucer's power over language?

His verse forces a music out of our language which few poets have equalled. After the plays of Shakspeare there are few productions in our literature that display more masterly genius than the *Canterbury Tales*.

---

fessor, as a sort of reparation for the light and immoral tone of portions of his *Tales* and other writings.

* Had each of the 31 pilgrims told two stories going and two returning—as was agreed upon—there would be 124 stories in all, with an account of their devotions at Canterbury, adventures by the way, and the grand supper to the victorious story-teller. As they now stand, the *Canterbury Tales* are only 24 in number.

LESSON III.

GEOFFREY CHAUCER, CONTINUED.

28. While the *Canterbury Tales* are the fruit of Chaucer's old age, it may be interesting to inquire if he began to write early in life, and what were his first works?

The "Father of English Poetry" began his literary career early in life. His first productions, however, were all translations or imitations of the French poetry of the time.

29. Which is the most remarkable of his poetical translations?

The *Romance of the Rose*, a beautiful allegory, the original of which is one of the masterpieces of early French literature. Chaucer's translation even surpasses the original, and bears upon it the seal of his genius.

30. In point of time, which is regarded as the first of Chaucer's *original* productions?

The *House of Fame*, a long allegorical poem. Pope's *Temple of Fame* is a somewhat elaborate rendering of the same into modern English.

31. Give, in brief, the plan of the *House of Fame?*

The poem is a curious description of the Temple of Glory and its famous inhabitants, the great authors and heroes of ancient times. Chaucer tells us that in a dream he was carried by an eagle to an immense building, the materials of which were bright as polished brass. It stood upon a rock of ice. The illustrious inmates were standing upon columns of various kinds of metal—iron, copper, and so on—according to their rank. There, seated on a rich throne, Fame ruled. The sight of a venerable personage awakes the poet, which brings his poem to a somewhat abrupt termination.

32. What are the chief merits of this poem?

It excites our admiration by its wealth of imagination, its beautiful imagery, and the richness and splendor of its ornaments. Pope's imitation falls short of its model.

33. Of Chaucer's shorter poems which is considered the most exquisite?

The *Flower and the Leaf*, an inimitable little tale with a happy moral.

34. Repeat Chaucer's description of the knights in the *Flower and the Leaf*, as they rode forth?

After picturing their countenances and "lofty brows which glittered with noble thoughts," he adds:

> "And they rode forth so glorious in array,
> So mannerly and full of gentle grace,
> That every tongue would be compelled to say,
> They were the noblest of a noble race." *

> "Greet well Chaucer when you meet
> As my disciple and my poet."
> *Gower.*

> "Since he of English in rhyming was the best,
> Pray unto God to give his soul good rest."
> *Lydgate.*

> "Great Chaucer—well of English undefied,
> On Fame's eternal bead-roll worthy to be filed."
> *Spenser.*

"I take unceasing delight in Chaucer. His manly cheerfulness is especially delicious to me in my old age."—*Coleridge.*

---

* Chaucer's *Astrolabie*, a prose treatise on astronomy, composed in 1391 for his son Louis, is the *oldest* work in our language now known to exist on any scientific subject. It opens thus: "Lytel Lowys my sonne, I perceive well by certain evidences thine abylytè to lerne sciences touching nombres and proporcions." "Lityl Lowys" (little Louis) was at that time ten years old.

LESSON IV.

SIR JOHN GOWER. DIED 1408.

Chief works: (1) *Confessio Amantis* (The Confessions of a Lover),
(2) *Speculum Meditantis* (The Mirror of Meditation).
(3) *Vox Clamantis** (The Voice of one Crying in the Wilderness).

35. What author ranks next to Chaucer in the literature of the fourteenth century?

Sir John Gower, styled by Chaucer the "moral Gower" on account of the pure moral tone of his writings.

36. What may be said of his personal history?

It is not well known. Gower was the friend and contemporary of Chaucer, whom, in one of his poems, he calls his "disciple." He was a man of rank, wealth, virtue, and literary tastes, and spent his life chiefly in the pursuit of knowledge and in the performance of good works.

37. What may be said of his learning?

He was a man of extensive learning, and wrote in Latin, French, and English.

38. How was Gower afflicted a few years before his death?

He lost his eyesight.

39. What monument of his charity and love of art yet remains?

A beautiful convent-church in London, for the

---

* Though all have Latin titles, the first of these works was written in English, the second in French verse, and the third in Latin. "The *Speculum Meditantis*," says Mr. Hart, "has not been seen in modern times, and has probably perished. The *Vox Clamantis* remained in manuscript until 1850, when it was printed for the Roxburghe Club. The *Confessio Amantis* has been frequently printed." Dr. Hart is mistaken in regard to the *Speculum Meditantis*. Taylor, in his *Annals of St. Mary Overy*, states that there are *two* copies in the Bodleian Library at Oxford.

erection of which, at his death, he left the bulk of his property. His monument can still be seen there.

40. What are Gower's chief writings?

Three large works, one in Latin, one in French, and a third—the *Confessio Amantis*—in English.

41. What is the *Confessio Amantis?*

It is a long poem of over 30,000 lines, divided into a prologue and eight books. One book is devoted to each of the seven deadly sins, and the remaining one to philosophy.*

42. What are the characters in this production?

The characters are but two—a *Lover*, and *Genius*, his confessor. The former confesses his sins to the latter, who before absolving his penitent relates an immense number of tales, each having some reference to *Lover's* moral shortcomings.

43. Are the stories told by *Genius* original with Gower?

Not by any means; in the composition of his poem Gower laid under contribution all the learning of his age. For the tales he ransacked the *Bible*, *Ovid*, the *Gesta Romanorum*, French literature, and other sources.

44. What are the weak points and good qualities of the *Confessio Amantis?*

Its weak points are its length and general tediousness. Gower seems to have aimed less at pleasing the imagination of his readers than at astonishing them by his vast array of learning. On the other hand, the language is easy and smooth, and many of the descriptions are exceedingly agreeable.

---

* The *Confessio* was written at the request of **King Richard II.**, who, one day meeting Gower, told him to "book some new thing."

45. How does Gowe compare with Chaucer?

His genius was less brilliant. He lacked the exquisite humor and rich imagination of "the Father of English Poetry"; but he divides with him the glory of polishing the English language, and of being one of the founders of English literature.

"Gower first garnished our English rude."
Skelton.

"Those of the first age were *Gower* and *Chaucer*."
Sir Philip Sidney.

"He is always sensible and polished."
Hallam.

"Gower mainly helped to polish and refine the language of his country."—*Shaw*.

LESSON V.

SIR JOHN MANDEVILLE. DIED 1372.

Chief work: *Travels*.

46. Who was Sir John Mandeville?

He is sometimes styled "the Father of English Prose," and is considered the most renowned English traveller of the Middle Ages.

47. Where was he born, and for what profession was he educated?

Mandeville was born in the south of England, and was educated for the medical profession. He was a good linguist, and was well read in philosophy and theology.

48. Where did he travel, and why?

He travelled over the then known world. In his twenty-second year the young physician, from some unknown motive, started on his singular career. He spent thirty-four years in roving through every country from England to China, and his friends gave him up for lost. When he came home he found that but few of his old acquaintances were alive to greet him.

49. How did Sir John Mandeville end his singular life?

Having completed the work on which his fame rests, he once more set out to travel. His age, however, did not permit him to go far, for he died at Liége, and was buried in the abbey near that city.*

50. What is his chief work?

Travels, which he wrote in Latin, then translated into French, and finally into English.†

51. Of what does his volume tr at?

As may easily be supposed, it is a detailed account of his third-of-a-century ramble. He relates everything of interest that he saw or heard; and, without doubt, his book is one of the curiosities of English literature.

52. Is Mandeville, as some assert, a mendacious writer?

The charge of mendacity, sometimes brought against good old Sir John Mandeville, is without foundation. When relating what he saw himself he is entirely worthy of credit, as many modern travellers have proved. But the same cannot be said of his hearsay stories, many of which are laughable in the extreme—stories of men with tails, " of people twenty-eight feet long," and of immense birds which could carry elephants through the air.

---

* It is said that the inscription on his monument states that he was very *pious*, very *learned*, and very *charitable* to the poor.

† Speaking of his work, Mandeville writes that he has " put this boke out of Latyn into Frensche, and translated it again into Englyssche, that every man of my nacion may undirstonde it." This is a fair specimen of his spelling.

53. In what point of view is Mandeville's *Travels* especially valuable?

It is a remarkable monument of early English prose; but as a work of art or a polished literary production it does not rank very high.

54. Is it difficult for English-speaking people of the present day to read the book?

It may still be perused with but little difficulty.

55. What can you say of Mandeville's style?

It is a manly, unadorned, and straightforward style of composition.*

LESSON VI.
JOHN BARBOUR. DIED 1396.

Chief work: *The Bruce*—an epic poem.

56. Who is considered the greatest Scottish poet of the fourteenth century?

John Barbour, a gifted and learned priest, and a contemporary of Chaucer.

57. Give a brief outline of his life.

John Barbour was born in Aberdeen, and finished his studies at Oxford. He became archdeacon of his native city, and died a few years before Chaucer.

58. What is his chief literary production?

The Bruce, an epic poem of over 12,000 lines, written in eight-syllable verse.†

---

* " Next to Marco Polo," writes Washington Irving. " the *Travels* of Sir John Mandeville and his account of the territories of the Great Khan along the coast of Asia seem to have been treasured up in the mind of Columbus."—*Life and Voyages of Christopher Columbus.*

† The following lines are from the often-quoted passage on freedom:
 " Fredome all solace to man givis—
  He lives at ease that freely livys!"

Fredome, that is freedom; *givis*, gives; *livys*, lives.

59. What is the subject or action of the poem?

It recounts the life, battles, and adventures of Robert Bruce, the heroic victor of Bannockburn.* This is done with a warmth and enthusiastic patriotism, a clearness of narrative, and dramatic vigor in the depiction of scenes, which must forever give the poem an honorable place among the early monuments of English literature.

60. Has *The Bruce* any real historic value?

As an historical document concerning the great Scottish hero it holds a high rank. It was composed soon after Bruce's death, and while the facts of his life were still fresh in the minds of all.

61. What may be said of the style of the poem?

It is clear and vigorous, the verse is smooth and musical, and the descriptions are bold, animated, and picturesque. The battle-scenes are grandly painted, and we hurry through them charmed with the lofty music of martial verse. More than 2000 lines are devoted to the battle of Bannockburn.

62. What is Barbour's rank among the British poets of the age in which he lived?

He is generally considered as superior to Gower, though he is far from being equal to Chaucer.

63. What do you remark of the Scottish poetry of this period?

It belonged to a school different from that of the English. It is believed that the works of Chaucer were unknown to Barbour.

---

* Robert Bruce, the most heroic of the Scottish kings, was born in 1274. At the battle of Bannockburn, which was fought June 24, 1314, Bruce with only 30,000 men defeated about 100,000 English under Edward II. The English left 30,000 dead upon the field. Bruce died in 1329, and his body was interred in the Abbey Church of Dunfermline.

64. Is there much difference between the English of Barbour and that of Chaucer and Gower?

No; the language of the three is essentially the same, except that Barbour's English is more Saxon, and, of course, more easily read at the present time than that of either Chaucer or Gower. *The Bruce* is the *oldest* monument of the English language in Scotland.*

65. How were Barbour and his poem for a long period honored by the Scottish nation?

Barbour was honored as the Homer of Bruce and Bannockburn; and his poem was treasured as the grand national epic of Scotland until that nation deserted the Catholic faith—the faith of Bruce and Barbour.†

" Fortunate in the choice of a noble theme, Barbour has depicted, in rough but faithful outline, the life, manners, and deeds of a truly heroic time, and given to Scotland not only the first poem in her literature, but the earliest history of her best and greatest king."—*Chambers.*

LESSON VII.

WICKLIFF, LANGLAND, AND MINOT.

66. Who was John Wickliff?

He was a learned but coarse and turbulent priest, who occupies a place in English literature because of his translation of the Bible into English.

67. Give a bird's-eye view of his career.

Wickliff was born in the north of England, studied at Oxford, and was afterwards a professor at that uni-

---

* It was completed about the year 1375.
† The best edition of *The Bruce* was that edited by Dr. Jamieson in 1820. In his *Lord of the Isles*, Sir Walter Scott borrows largely from Barbour's poem.

versity. His insane hatred of the monks soon extended to the whole body of the clergy. He wrote much, and was several times summoned before councils of bishops on the charge of heresy. He died while celebrating Mass. The General Council of Constance condemned *forty-five propositions* in his works.

68. On what is Wickliff's English translation of the Bible founded, and what is its literary value?

His translation is an English rendering of the Latin Vulgate. As a literary production it is a counterpart of the man—rude, unpolished prose.*

69. Who is the author of the somewhat famous poem called *Piers Plowman?*

Tradition—the only authority we have in this case—assigns it to *William Langland,* who was, evidently, a discontented ecclesiastic.

70. State briefly the size and object of the poem.

Piers Plowman is a satirical and allegorical poem of about 15,000 lines in length, composed on the principle of the old Saxon alliteration. It is intended as a scathing denunciation of the real or fancied political and religious abuses of the times, and from beginning to end is little else than versified grumbling.

71. Give the plot and divisions of *Piers Plowman.*

On a morning in May, Peter, a ploughman, goes asleep on the Malvern Hills. He dreams a series of twenty dreams. In these twenty visions the world and its inhabitants, with all their faults and foibles, pass before his eyes. The poem is divided into twenty sections corresponding to his twenty visions;

---

* In the work of translation Wickliff is known to have had several assistants. It is generally believed, however, that he translated the *New Testament* himself.

but there is little connection between the parts, and this want of unity weakens it as a whole.

72. What is generally given as the date of its composition?

A.D. 1370.

73. Who was Lawrence Minot?

Several eminent critics point him out as the *earliest* writer of English verse who deserves the name of poet.

74. When did he write?

In the early part of the reign of Edward III., or in the first half of the fourteenth century.

75. On what subject did he spend most of his poetic abilities?

War. The best of his productions were stirring war-poems which recounted the victorious achievements of Edward III. and the Black Prince.

76. Mention his two best poems.

That on the battle of *Nevill's Cross*, and another on the battle of *Halidon Hill*. These pieces have a polish and warlike ring that entitles them to much praise.

SUMMARY OF CHAPTER I., BOOK II.

1. The works of Chaucer, Gower, and Mandeville mark the real beginning of English letters.

2. Edward III. was the first king of England since the Conquest who could speak English.

3. English was made the language of the law-courts in 1362, and of the schools in 1385.

4. The literature of any age or nation is always an expression of the times in which it is produced.

5. The age of Chaucer, Gower, and Mandeville is

one of the most brilliant in the military annals of England; and this brilliancy is faithfully reflected by the literature of the period.

6. The British authors of this age were much influenced by the works contained in Italian, French, and Latin literatures.

7. The chief British writers of the last half of the fourteenth century were *Chaucer*, *Gower*, *Mandeville*, *Barbour*, *Wickliff*, *Langland*, and *Minot*.

8. Chaucer is styled "the Father of English Poetry," and Mandeville is often called "the Father of English Prose."

9. The *Canterbury Tales* is Chaucer's greatest production.

10. Chaucer died A.D. 1400, and was the *first* great literary genius buried in Westminster Abbey.

11. The *Confessio Amantis* is the best known work written in English by Gower.

12. Mandeville's *Travels* is generally considered the first specimen of real English prose; besides, it is the oldest book of travels in the language.

13. *The Bruce*, by Barbour, is the most ancient monument of the English language in Scotland.

14. Wickliff was the first who translated the entire Bible into English; but as a writer he can claim little merit.

CHAPTER II.

THE ENGLISH LITERATURE OF THE FIFTEENTH CENTURY.

A.D. 1400 to 1500.

THE AGE OF JAMES I. OF SCOTLAND, LYDGATE, AND CAXTON.

HISTORICAL INTRODUCTION.

1. ENGLAND IN THE FIFTEENTH CENTURY.—In many respects the story of England in the fifteenth century is a sad one. The throne was occupied at the dawning of that age by *Henry IV.*, the *first* sovereign of the house of Lancaster. Seven kings ruled during the hundred stormy years that "slowly rolled away." First, we have the three monarchs of the house of Lancaster, *Henry IV.*, *Henry V.*, and *Henry VI.*, with their unwise and unjust wars against France; Henry the Fifth's victory at Agincourt; and, finally, the expulsion of the English from that country through the instrumentality of *Joan of Arc*, known as the "Maid of Orleans."

Joan is one of the most wonderful characters in all history. A country girl but seventeen years of age, pure, pious, patriotic, and beautiful, she headed the armies of her native country, and gave with her own gentle hand the death-blow to English power and English misrule in France.

With some slight intermissions, this unhappy contest lasted over forty years. It taxed the energies and drained the resources of England; and its unfavorable termination hastened a still more terrible struggle at home—the *Wars of the Roses.*

Scarcely had peace with France been concluded, when the crown began to sit lightly on the head of Henry VI., the last of the Lancasterians. The rival house of York kept an envious eye on the royal bauble. Soon the struggle began. The land resounded with the trumpets of war and the shock of arms. The fierce contest lasted over thirty years. It carries us through the reigns of three kings, *Edward IV., Edward V.,* and *Richard III.,* all of the house of York. It was a bloody and unnatural struggle that made Great Britain one extensive theatre of atrocities, was signalized by twelve pitched battles, cost the lives of more than 100,000 men with eighty princes, and almost annihilated the ancient nobility of England.

The Wars of the Roses, which terminated in 1485, led to two important political results: (1) They partially annihilated the Norman nobility. "Many of these perished on the field of battle or on the scaffold. They mutually broke each other in pieces. . . . The law of Henry VII. forbidding the nobles the maintenance of retainers other than domestic servants shows at once how thoroughly the power of the aristocracy was broken."* (2) The rival claims of the two houses were united in the family of *Tudor.* The marriage of Henry VII. to his cousin, Elizabeth of York, brought about this union. Thus the power of the sovereign was vastly increased, and as we glide into the sixteenth century the strong hand of Henry VII. sways the destinies of the nation.

---

* Bascom.

2. SCOTLAND.—At the beginning of the fifteenth century, the second of the Stuart line sat on the throne of Bruce—a shaky and dangerous seat. The nobility, haughty and powerful, were the greatest enemy with which the Scottish king had to contend. Robert III., fearing for the safety of his young and promising son, *James*, prepared to send him to France in 1405. While on the way the royal boy was intercepted by the English, and remained in captivity for eighteen years. For the prince this reverse of fortune was a blessing in disguise. The trials he had to endure developed and moulded his manly character. James I. was perhaps the greatest English poet of his century, and by far the wisest and most accomplished of the Stuart kings. His assassination by a number of his nobles proves—were proof needed—that learning, worth, and wisdom do not always secure the respect of ruffianism.

The fate of his two immediate successors was even more tragic. James II. was killed by the bursting of a cannon. Between James III. and his nobles a fierce contest arose in which both eagerly took the field. The royal army was defeated and James fled. Historians tell that as he rode hastily along he passed through a small hamlet; and at the sight of a woman, who came out for water, his horse took flight, suddenly turned, throwing the king to the ground. Being heavily armed, he was stunned by the fall. Soon people collected and removed him into a mill near by. On recovering, James called for a priest.

Questioned by the miller's wife as to what he was, he replied: "I was your king this morning." The woman, struck with surprise, hastened out and called loudly for a priest to attend the king. Upon this a

LITERATURE OF THE FIFTEENTH CENTURY. 101

stranger rode up and said: "I am a priest; lead me to the king." He was immediately introduced, and kneeling down asked James if he thought he was dangerously injured. The king replied that he did not consider his hurt serious, but in the mean time desired that his confession might be heard, and that he might receive absolution. "This shall absolve you," exclaimed the assassin—for such he was—and drawing a poniard, plunged it into the breast of the unhappy monarch.

James IV. succeeded, and as a ruler was more successful than any of his three namesakes and predecessors. He was a good Christian and an able sovereign. By marrying Margaret, the eldest daughter of Henry VII., he drew the thrones of Scotland and England more closely together. With this event was concluded a perpetual treaty of peace between the two kingdoms, after one hundred and seventy years of war, or of truces little better than war. The reign of James IV. carries us into the sixteenth century.

3. INFLUENCING AGENTS ON THE LITERATURE OF THE FIFTEENTH CENTURY.—The forty years' conflict with France began little more than a decade after the death of Chaucer. This was scarcely over, when a thirty years' fratricidal struggle commenced at home. Those long periods of war blighted literary labor and dwarfed intellectual growth. The camp was not favorable to letters, and in this century the sword took the place of the pen. "The bells in the church-steeples," wrote Fuller, "were not heard for the sound of drums and trumpets."

Hence we must be content if we find no great literary masterpiece in the English prose and poetry of the fifteenth century. True, the names of *seventy*

British poets who wrote in this age have come down to us, but we have room only for the principal of these—JAMES I. of *Scotland*, and JOHN LYDGATE, a *Benedictine monk*. Both acknowledge Chaucer as their master and model in the art poetic. Still more limited, of course, was the number of prose writers, chief among whom were SIR THOMAS MALLORY and WILLIAM CAXTON, the *first* English printer. Thus the English literature of the fifteenth century is principally represented by a king, a monk, a knight, and a printer.*

4. THE AGE OF BALLADS AND PROSE ROMANCE.— The chivalrous tales called metrical romances, which were popular in England from the twelfth century, cease about the middle of the fifteenth. The wants of the time and the tastes of the people demanded something else. A change came. *Ballads* and *prose romances* became the favorites. But the riches of the English literature of this age consist mainly in its ballads, many of which have perished. These ballads, in most instances, are simply *abridged romances*— short tales in verse. The hero of many a ringing rhyme was *Robin Hood*,† the bold outlaw. It is the opinion of Hallam that the Scottish ballads of this period are much superior to the English.

---

* There were, of course, many *Latin* works composed in the various monasteries, but these do not come within the scope of a little text-book on English literature. Over *forty* monks lived from the twelfth to the fifteenth century who wrote the history of England from the earliest times down to the dawn of the sixteenth century. Those of the fifteenth century were *Thomas Walsingham, Thomas Otterbourne, John Whethamstede, Thomas Elmham, William of Worcester*, and *John Rouse*.

† Robin Hood flourished in the reign of Edward II , or the early portion of the fourteenth century. The earliest notice of him is in the *Vision of Piers Ploughman*, a poem composed about 1370. A collection of ballads recounting the deeds and adventures of Robin Hood were printed by Ritson, in 2 vols., in 1795.

Two of the most ancient and beautiful British ballads are *Chevy Chase* and *Sir Patrick Spens*. *Chevy Chase*, which was written in the early part of the fifteenth century, consists of sixty-eight four-lined rhyming stanzas.* It is the soul-stirring, fiery old war-song of which Sir Philip Sidney wrote that he never heard it without feeling himself aroused as by the blast of a trumpet. *Sir Patrick Spens*, which is a true Scottish ballad, consists of twenty-six four-lined rhyming stanzas.† It has been greatly praised. Coleridge calls it a " grand old ballad," and Reed does not hesitate to style it the finest specimen of all the old songs. Though more easily read than *Chevy Chase*, on account of the simplicity of its diction, *Sir Patrick Spens* is commonly considered a more ancient ballad. The authors of both poems are unknown.

---

* " To drive the deer with hound and horn,
  Earl Percy took his way;
The child may rue that is unborn,
  The hunting of that day."

As Earl Percy and his English followers went to hunt in the Scottish woods of Earl Douglas without the latter's permission, a bloody conflict was the result. Percy and Douglas were among the hundreds slain on both sides.

" Of fifteen hundred Englishmen,
  Went home but fifty-three;
The rest were slain in Chevy Chase,
  Under the greenwood tree."

There are two versions of the ballad of *Chevy Chase*, an ancient and a modern. The former is in antiquated English which ordinary readers will find as difficult to peruse as Chaucer's *Canterbury Tales*; the latter is clothed in the language of the age of Elizabeth. Both versions are the same in substance. The two foregoing stanzas belong to the modern version, and are made to conform to our present system of spelling.

† The following is the fourteenth stanza, as in the original:
  " They hadna sailed a league, a league,
    A league but barely three,
  When the lift grew dark, and the wind blew loud,
    And gurly grew the sea."
" Lift," that is *sky*.

5. PROGRESS OF LEARNING, EDUCATION, AND DISCOVERY.—If long years of war and disaster stunted the growth and dimmed the brilliancy of English literature in the fifteenth century, it is but right to add that on the whole it was a very progressive age. The founders of colleges in England were especially active. *Eton*, the most famous of the English public schools, was founded in this century. Scotland added to her seats of learning the universities of *St. Andrews* (1411), *Glasgow* (1450), and *Aberdeen* (1494) —" all," says Thomas Arnold, " under the authority of different Popes."

Then most of the great European nations of to-day were rapidly reaching maturity—making really marvellous progress in art, science, and discovery. For glorious achievements the fifteenth century stands the most brilliant in all history. Protestantism was unknown. The nations were all one in faith—Catholic. Their power for good which sprung from this solidity, this massive religious unity, was not weakened and broken by the unhappy dissensions caused at a later period] by the so-called Reformation. Printing began its mission, and books were rapidly multiplied. The fall of Constantinople into the hands of the barbarous Turks forced the remains of Greek learning and literature to seek a home in western Europe; and since that time the language of Homer and Demosthenes has been honored with a place in every college programme of studies. The compass was invented, and navigation grew into an art. The immortal Columbus doubled the size of the world's map by the discovery of America. The spirit of faith erected the grand Gothic cathedral with its airy domes and graceful spires pointing heavenward. Sixty-four universities shed rays of intellectual light over Europe. In short, the foundations of modern European greatness were laid. Our Catholic forefathers were men of labor and vast enterprise. The monuments they left behind bear witness to their lofty achievements.

6. NOTES ON THE PROGRESS OF THE LANGUAGE.— For the English language the fifteenth century was a period of rapid transition from its obsolete state to its more modern form. These changes were especially hastened by two events: (1) The Wars of the Roses; (2) The introduction of printing by Caxton in 1474. The Wars of the Roses, however singular it may seem, had a considerable influence in bringing about a certain uniformity of speech throughout the kingdom by more or less harmonizing its various dialects. The art of printing did much to polish speech and to make reading popular. It gave a new impulse to literature. The number of books and readers was multiplied. Authors were enabled to address a larger reading public than before. For the first time the language of books began gradually to extend its sway and to supplant local forms and provincial usages, except among the wholly uneducated classes, to whom books were not accessible. With printing also came a certain uniformity of spelling, and the division of sentences by points or stops, now called punctuation.

By examining a few words it can easily be seen that great changes have taken place in English spelling since the fifteenth century.

Some words as spelled in the fifteenth century.	As spelled to-day.
syng	sing
sterre	star
certyn	certain
bookes	books
haiff	have
giffs	gives
kaute	caught

The unaccented final *e* was generally neglected, and at length wholly lost in pronunciation. The attempt to distinguish *gender* by terminations was abandoned, and the rule was adopted of treating the names of all *things without life as neuter.*

The English of the fifteenth century had nearly reached its stature as a full-grown language, but it wanted polish and maturity as an instrument of thought. No Shakspeare had as yet seized the discordant elements of our speech to stamp upon them the seal of fixity and genius. Latin was still—as it had been for hundreds of years—the only great and polished medium of learning. Men who wished to give their thoughts to the world spoke and wrote in the imperial language of Rome.

LESSON I.

JAMES I. OF SCOTLAND. DIED 1437.

Chief work: *The King's Quire* (or Book).

1. Who was James 1. of Scotland?

He was the third and ablest sovereign of the Stuart line, an accomplished scholar, and the most *original* English poet of the fifteenth century.

2. What happened to him in his tenth year?

While on his way to France he was captured by order of Henry IV. of England. This captivity lasted for nineteen years.

3. What benefits did he reap from this seeming misfortune?

For the royal boy it proved to be a blessing in disguise. Adversity strengthened and developed the sterling qualities of his character; and the solitude of those early years inclined him to long and serious study. He excelled in all the learning of his time, and was especially fond of poetry and music.

LITERATURE OF THE FIFTEENTH CENTURY. 107

4. How long did James I. rule over Sco land?

He reigned thirteen years, during which he reformed many abuses; but finally fell a victim to the treachery of a number of his haughty and barbarous nobles by whom he was assassinated.

5. What work has established his literary reputation?

The *King's Quire*, a poem of nearly 1400 lines, divided into one hundred and ninety-seven seven-lined stanzas.

6. What does this poem de cribe?

It gives many particulars of the prince's youthful career—the sad thoughts and hopes and fears of his prison life. It also portrays in glowing terms a May-scene in Windsor garden, the power of love, and the grace, beauty, and virtue of the young lady who finally rewarded his devotion with her hand.*

7. What influence can be traced in the writin s of James I.?

The influence of Chaucer and Gower, of whose works he was an admirer and diligent student.

8. What may be said of the style of the *King's Quire*, and of its rank in early English literature?

In grace and polish of style many of its stanzas are exquisite. The poem is distinguished by delicacy of feeling and tenderness of expression. It is regarded as one of the most original and meritorious productions of the English muse between the days of Chaucer and those of Spenser.

"James I. of Scotland was a true poet and a true man."—*Hart*.

---

* James relates that on a pleasant morning in the month of May he was taking a view from the windows of his prison—the round tower of Windsor Castle. In the garden below, accompanied by her attendants, walked a modest and beautiful girl: This was Lady Jane Beaufort, who afterwards became his wife and queen of Scotland. The *Quire* was written towards the close of his captivity, and evidently while the sunshine of love lit up the poet's breast.

LESSON II.

JOHN LYDGATE.   DIED 1462.

Chief works: (1) *The Fall of Princes.*
(2) *The Story of Thebes.*
(3) *The Destruction of Troy.*

9. Who was Father John Lydgate?

He was the most prolific writer of the fifteenth century, and in every respect the most remarkable native-born English poet of his age.

10. Of what religious order was he a member?

He was a Benedictine monk of Bury St. Edmunds, and spent a pious, useful, and laborious life in study, teaching, and writing.

11. Where was he educated?

At Oxford University; but he greatly increased his knowledge by travelling in France and Italy.

12. n his own day how was the good monk of Bury regarded?

As the greatest poet and scholar of the age. He was a ready pen, which, for over half a century, supplied the various literary wants of his time.

13. When were his talents especially in reque t?

On such occasions as religious festivals and court entertainments. For these his versatile quill dashed off with equal ease hymns, songs, and dramas. He left over 250 pieces behind him.

14. Which are his three chief poems?

The Fall of Princes, *The Story of Thebes*, and *The Destruction of Troy.*

15. What is the *Fall of Princes?*

It is a versified translation from the Latin of Boccaccio, and contains Lydgate's famous reference to his " master Chaucer, the lode-star of our language."

16. What is the *Story of Thebes?*

It is chiefly a translation from *Statius*, a Latin poet of the first century. Lydgate adapts the work of the old Roman to his own times by making it a romance of chivalry, in which adventures, love-scenes, and tournaments take up a large space.

17. Where does Lydgate represent himself as telling the story of Thebes?

He relates that having met Chaucer's pilgrims at an inn in Canterbury, he accompanies them back to London; and on being invited to tell a tale gives the *Story of Thebes*, which is thus represented as an additional Canterbury tale.

18. What is *The Destruction of Troy?*

It is likewise a translation from the Latin, and is very interesting, as it gives occasional pen-pictures of life in the fifteenth century.

19. What may be said of Lydgate's style?

He is very diffuse. This is his chief failing. But the enthusiasm of the good Benedictine often makes the reader forget the length of his poems. His hymns and devotional pieces, however, are generally admired for graceful diction and beautiful sentiment.

"No writer was ever more popular in his own day; but it was a popularity which could not last."—*Thomas Arnold.*

" He is the *first* of our writers whose style is clothed with that perspicuity in which the English phraseology appears at this day to an English reader."—*Warton.*

LESSON III.

SIR THOMAS MALLORY. DIED 1476.

Chief work: *History of King Arthur.**

20. Who was Sir Thomas Mallory?

He was a priest and knight of whose personal history we know nothing except that he lived in the fifteenth century, and wrote his famous work about the year 1470.

21. By whom was the *History of King Arthur* first printed?

By *William Caxton*, in 1485.

22. From what sources does Mallory tell us he collected the materials of his book?

He states that he compiled his *History* "out of certyn bookes of Frensshe, and reduced it into English."

23. At what period did the romances which relate the wonderful career of Prince Arthur originate?

The origin of the romances of Arthur and his Knights of the Round Table is involved in obscurity; but it is generally believed they commenced about the sixth century.†

---

* This work is commonly called the *Morte d'Arthur*, or Death of Arthur.

† King Arthur and his Knights of the Round Table are familiar to all lovers of romance. Arthur was the son of *Pendragon*, King of Britain. After he was crowned king his entire career was one of conquest, either upon a huge scale or in single combat. Nothing earthly, it is told, could withstand the prowess of his stalwart arm; and against the powers of darkness he was fully armed and accoutred by his friend and counsellor, Merlin. He proceeded from

LITERATURE OF THE FIFTEENTH CENTURY. 111

24. Who was King Arthur?

He lives in history and romance as the most celebrated of the British Celtic princes, who made a gallant stand against the Saxon invaders. Arthur, according to tradition, was crowned in 516; and at his death—the date of which is unknown—was buried in the old abbey of Glastonbury.

25. What does Mallory's *History of King Arthur* contain?

It embraces the six distinct romances or narratives of Arthur and his famous Knights of the Round Table.

26. Which is the first of these narratives?

The first is the legend of the *Saint Grail*,* which gives the history of the Chalice used by our Blessed Lord at the Last Supper. Joseph of Arimathéa, it is

---

victory to victory, conquering kingdom after kingdom, slaying innumerable giants, rescuing distressed ladies, destroying "wicked witches," cutting off whole armies of Saracens, and making no more of dragons than greyhounds do of hares—sometimes killing wholesale when alone and unsupported, but more commonly in company with the famous Knights of the Round Table. Arthur's epitaph in the church of the old monastery of Glastonbury runs thus: *Hic jacet Arthurus, rex quondam atque futurus.* His tomb was discovered in the twelfth century. The exhumation took place in 1189. King Arthur's Knights of the Round Table were twenty-four in number—the chosen few among his forces. Around the celebrated table every knight had his appointed seat upon which his name was inscribed in letters of gold. One of these was styled the "seat perilous." It was reserved for the most famous champion of that invincible band. Paulus Jovius relates that when the Emperor Charles V. visited England, Henry VIII. exhibited this table to him as the veritable one of King Arthur. To-day in the chapel of Worcester there is preserved what is affirmed to be Arthur's Round Table. It consists of a stout oak board perforated by many bullets, supposed to have been fired at it by Cromwell's soldiers, who used it for a target. Upon it is painted a royal figure seated beneath a canopy, intended to represent King Arthur. In the centre is painted a large rose, and around it are the words: "Thys is the rounde table of King Arthur and his valiant knights." From the centre radiate twenty-four spaces, each one appropriated to a knight who seated himself in front of the one that had his name painted on it.—*Hall's Book of British Ballads.*

* That is, *Holy Cup*, or *Chalice.*

told, carried the sacred vessel with him to Britain; but, too holy to be looked upon by sinful eyes, it after a time vanished from the gaze of men.

27. Which is the second of the narratives?

The second is the story of *Merlin*, which celebrates the birth and exploits of Arthur, and relates how he gathered around him the peerless knights and heroes of the Round Table.

28. Which is the third of the narratives?

The adventures of *Sir Lancelot du Lac* (of the Lake). This is a wild, weird story of a bold and sinful hero; and of the Lady of the Lake, and her fairy realm beneath the waters.

29. Which is the fourth of the narratives?

The fourth is the legend styled the *Quest of the Saint Grail*. This is the touching and beautiful story of the search for the sacred chalice, which could only be seen by *one who was perfectly pure in thought, word, and action*. Many knights engaged in this search. The object was finally achieved by the young and noble knight, *Sir Galahad*, who, while the vision passed before him, prayed that he might no longer live, and was immediately taken to the happy regions of bliss.

30. Which is the fifth of the narratives?

The fifth is the *Death of Arthur*, which relates the tragic end of the incomparable Celtic hero, who for years had bravely battled against the Saxon foe.

31. Which is the sixth and last of these romantic narratives?

The sixth and last traces the adventures of *Sir Tristram*, a hero somewhat similar in character to Sir Lancelot du Lac.

32. What poet of our day has clothed those ancient tales in the poetic diction of the nineteenth century?

ALFRED TENNYSON in his *Idylls of the King*.*

"Mallory shows considerable mastery of expression; his English is always animated and flowing, and in its earnestness and tenderness occasionally rises to no common beauty."—*Craik*.

LESSON IV.

WILLIAM CAXTON. DIED 1492.

Chief work: *The History of Troy*.

33. Who is commonly styled the "Father of the English Press"?

William Caxton, a name venerable in the history of English letters.

34. Briefly relate Caxton's early history.

He was born in England in the early part of the fifteenth century, was for a time a merchant in London, travelled much in Europe, and on one occasion was employed by Edward IV. to negotiate a treaty with the Duke of Burgundy.

35. Whose service did he enter in 1468?

That of the English princess Margaret, who, about that time, was married to the Duke of Burgundy.

36. Which was his first literary effort?

The History of Troy, which he translated from the French during his leisure hours at the Court of Bur-

---

* Few readers of poetry are unacquainted with Tennyson's beautiful poem of *Morte d'Arthur*, a modern rendering of the concluding part of the romance bearing that title. The *Idylls of the King* are renderings of so many particular passages or episodes in the same great romance.—*Arnold*.

gundy. It was at this period that he began to learn the *new* art of printing.*

37. Where did he first begin his labors as a printer?

At Cologne, where, in 1471, he issued the *first* English book ever printed—his own *History of Troy*

38. In what year did he remove to England?

In 1474, carrying with him his press and types. He settled down to his business in one of the apartments of Westminster Abbey, whither he was most probably invited by the abbot.

39. What work did he print in 1474?

The *Game and Play of Chess*—the *first* book ever printed in Great Britain.

40. How many different works is he known to have printed between th s and his death?

During the remaining eighteen years of Caxton's life *sixty-five* different works, translated and original, came from his press. Many of these were the products of his own industrious pen.

41. How did Caxton die?

Like the Venerable Bede, he piously breathed his last almost at his work.

42. What was his character as a man and a writer?

Caxton was a man of learning, tireless industry, and spotless character. At fifty years of age he learned the art of printing; and with his head silvered

---

* The honor of discovering this simple but marvellous art is contested by the Dutch in favor of *Lawrence Coster*, between 1420 and 1426, and by the Germans on behalf of *John Gutenberg*, about the year 1438. It is very probable that the discovery was made by both about the same time. Between 1450 and 1455 Gutenberg succeeded in printing a Bible, copies of which are now exceedingly rare and valuable. *Mayence, Strasburg*, and *Haarlem* were the places where printing was *first* executed. Coster, Gutenburg, and Caxton were good Catholics. It is well to remember that *the Bible was printed seventy years before the so-called Reformation, and that the art of printing is a Catholic invention.*

over with the white hairs of venerable age he might still be seen in his office to the day of his death.*

"Caxton was a man of learning, and wrote many of the works he printed."—*Hart.*
"Few English names of this century will live as long as William Caxton."—*Shaw.*

SUMMARY OF CHAPTER II., BOOK II.

1. The stormy political history of England and Scotland, and the almost incessant wars of the time, account for the literary barrenness of the fifteenth century.

2. Ballads and romances make up the great bulk of the English literature of the fifteenth century.

3. Two of the most famous of the ancient ballads are *Chevy Chase* and *Sir Patrick Spens.*

4. The English language and higher education made great progress during this age.

5. The chief poets were *James I. of Scotland* and *Father John Lydgate*; the chief prose-writers, *Sir Thomas Mallory* and *William Caxton.*

6. James I. of Scotland is considered the most *original* writer of the fifteenth century; Lydgate, the most *prolific.*

---

* His life, writes Henry Reed, is to be thought of like that of the Venerable Bede, as monitory of "perpetual industry;" for as the aged Saxon expired dictating the last words of a translation of St. John's Gospel—
"In the hour of death,
The last dear service of his parting breath,"
so did the old printer carry forward his last labor, on a volume of sacred lore, to the last day of a life that bore the burden of fourscore years.—*Lectures on English Literature.*

7. Mallory's *History of King Arthur and his Knights of the Round Table* is the most remarkable historical romance of the fifteenth century.

8. William Caxton, the "Father of the English Press," was a pious Catholic. He printed the *first* English book in 1471.

CHAPTER III.

THE ENGLISH LITERATURE OF THE SIXTEENTH CENTURY.

A.D. 1500 to 1600.

The Age of More, Dunbar, and Spenser.

HISTORICAL INTRODUCTION.

1. A Glance at England and Scotland in the Sixteenth Century.—The sixteenth century is the most eventful in English history. It carries us through the reigns of *Henry VIII., Edward VI., Mary,* and *Elizabeth.* Henry VII. died in 1509,* and was succeeded by his son Henry VIII. In the bloom of youth, his mind well stored with knowledge, and bright hopes lighting up his future pathway, Henry mounted the throne of the rich, prosperous, and powerful Catholic kingdom of England. For about twenty years he enjoyed an excellent reputation. Owing mainly to the abilities of his Prime Minister,

---

* Henry VII. was the *first* of the Tudor family that sat on the English throne; Elizabeth was the *last.*

the famous *Cardinal Wolsey*, his home administration was marked by wisdom; and the success of his arms against the Scots and French added to the glory of the nation.

Even in letters Henry made a name. It was in his reign that *Martin Luther*,* a bold, able, and unprincipled monk of Germany, threw off the mask, raised his hand against the Catholic Church in which he had been educated, and stirred up the baser passions of

---

* Luther was born in 1483, and died in 1546. He was the father of the Protestant Reformation. "Let us clearly understand," says WILLIAM COBBETT, a Protestant author, "the meaning of these words—*Catholic, Protestant,* and *Reformation. Catholic* means *universal* and the religion which takes this epithet was called u-niversal because all Christian people of every nation acknowledged it to be the *only true religion*, and because they all acknowledged *one and the same head* of the Church. and this was the *Pope*, who, though he generally resided at Rome, was head of the Church in England, in France, in Spain. and, in short, in every part of the world where the Christian religion was professed. But there came a time when some nations—or rather parts of some nations—cast off the authority of the *Pope*. and, of course, no longer acknowledged him as the *head* of the Christian Church. These nations, or parts of nations, declared, or *protested*, against the authority of their former head, and also against the doctrines of that Church which. until now, had been the *only* Christian Church. They, therefore, called themselves *Protesters*, or *Protestants;* and this is now the name given to all who are not Catholics. As to the word *Reformation*, it means an alteration *for the better;* and it would have been hard indeed if the makers of this great alteration could not have contrived to give it a *good name*.

"Now a fair and honest inquiry will teach us that this was an alteration greatly *for the worse;* that this ' *Reformation*.' as it is called, was engendered in beastly lust, brought forth in hypocrisy and perfidy, and cherished and fed by plunder, devastation, and by rivers of innocent English and Irish blood; and that as to its more remote consequences. they are, some of them, now before us in that misery, that beggary, that nakedness, that hunger, that everlasting wrangling and spite which now stare us in the face and stun our ears at every turn. and which the ·Reformation' has given us in exchange for the ease, and happiness, and harmony, and Christian charity enjoyed so abundantly, and for so many ages. by our Catholic forefathers."—*History of the Reformation.*

"If mere dissent from the Church of Rome be a merit," writes the great Edmund Burke. "he that dissents the most perfectly is the most meritorious. A man is certainly the most perfect Protestant who protests against the whole Christian religion."

rich and poor. The English king was among the first to enter the lists against Luther. He became the champion of the true faith. He wrote a book in Latin entitled *Defence of the Seven Sacraments*, and sent a copy to *Pope Leo X*. Leo, who was a most illustrious patron of arts and literature, conferred upon the royal author the beautiful title of *Defender of the Faith*.*

A change, however, came over King Henry. He allowed himself to become the slave of a vile passion, which finally transformed him into a despicable tyrant, drove him headlong into every cruelty, led to the downfall of the ancient faith in England, covered the country with mourning and venerable ruins, and introduced heresy, pauperism,† and grinding despotism into the once happy land of Alfred the Great. Because the Pope would not—and, in truth, could not—allow him to put away his Queen, the virtuous *Catherine of Arragon*,‡ and to marry her maid of honor, the pretty *Anne Boleyn*, Henry broke the sacred tie which bound himself and his kingdom to the Vicar of Christ.

He sacrilegiously placed himself at the head of the English Church, and butchered without mercy all who dared to oppose his mad career. This English Nero had six wives, several of whom he murdered.

---

* A title to this day retained by the English sovereigns, though they have long since ceased to profess that Cathol c faith for the defence of which the title was conferred.

† " Englishmen in general," says William Cobbett, "suppose that there were always *poor-laws* and *paupers* in England. They ought to remember that for 900 years u der the Catholic religion there were neither."—*History of the Reformation*.

‡ Catherine was the daughter of the celebrated Isabella the Catholic, Queen of Castile, and her husband Ferdinand King of Arragon. Isabella shares with Columbus the glory of discovering America.

The powerful Wolsey died in disgrace, exclaiming, "Had I served my God as I did my king, *He* would not have given me over in my gray hairs!" The venerable *Bishop Fisher* and the great *Sir Thomas More* finished their bright careers at the block, because they chose to obey God and conscience rather than a brutal monarch. Hundreds of monasteries were robbed and crumbled away at the tyrant's destructive touch. Rich and worldly ecclesiastics cowered at his frown and basely became apostates; and the whole fabric of the Catholic Church in England was shaken to its very foundations.

Nothing was sacred in the eyes of this royal savage. The rich shrines which contained the precious remains of the *Venerable Bede* and the "holy, blissful martyr," *St. Thomas of Canterbury*, were rifled of their treasures and the ashes cast to the winds. Even the tomb of *Alfred the Great* was not spared from desecration. Thus, in brief, began the modern religious change in England. The sudden falling away of that nation from the unity of faith in which it had dwelt for nearly a thousand years is a strange and terrible event. Henry VIII., a cruel monster, who was the sport of all the vile and brutal passions, was its originator; and he died as he had lived—scowling on the ruins and desolation which marked his unfortunate and dreadful reign of thirty-seven years.[*]

Henry VIII. was succeeded by his little son *Edward VI.*, who, after a brief rule of six years, died at the age of sixteen. The work of planting the new creed, and breaking the Seventh Commandment by

---

[*] During this reign Wales became a part of the kingdom of England.

robbing and plundering Catholic churches and monasteries, went on briskly during this reign.

Mary, the daughter of the unhappy Catherine of Arragon, became queen in 1553. She was a most zealous Catholic, reigned for five years, and did her best to repair the mischief done by her father and her brother. It was a thankless task. Because she exercised a certain severity towards the leaders, vow-breakers, and sacrilegious fanatics of the English Reformation, some historians, blinded by bigotry, have denounced her in unmeasured terms, styling her " bloody Mary." This is unjust. " Mary," says Lingard, " only practised what *all* taught. It was her misfortune, rather than her fault, that she was not more enlightened than the wisest of her contemporaries."

The long, cruel, and eventful reign of *Elizabeth* opens in 1558, and carries us through the remainder of the sixteenth century. The religious—or rather irreligious—changes set on foot by her father, Henry VIII., were now brought to a close. The work of iniquity and sacrilege was completed. The English Protestant Church was founded on the ruins of the ancient faith, and barbarous laws were enacted against the creed of Bede, Chaucer, and More. The Catholics were treated with savage ferocity and the most revolting cruelty.* The churches and religious houses were finally robbed of everything that could minister to private luxury and godless rascality.

---

* The minority in England who adhered to the ancient faith became the victims of an organized system of persecution and plunder. Open a book by *Cardinal Allen*, and a score of martyred priests, of harried and plundered laymen, of tortured consciences and bleeding hearts, will blot out from your view the smiling images of peace and plenty.—*Thomas Arnold.*

LITERATURE OF THE SIXTEENTH CENTURY. 121

Elizabeth, on one occasion before she became queen, said that she " wished the earth would open if she was not a true Roman Catholic." But she was an artful hypocrite. However brilliant in some respects, hers was, in the highest degree, a blood-stained reign. The execution of the beautiful and unhappy *Mary Queen of Scots*, by order of the English queen, is one of the blackest crimes recorded in history.

The cruelties of her rule in Ireland would fill a volume. *Hugh O'Neill*, Prince of Tyrone, *Hugh O'Donnell*, Prince of Tyrconnell, and other Irish chiefs * bravely battled for faith and country against the female tyrant. For fifteen years they defied the power of England and skilfully routed her best generals. This was at a time when, in the words of a famous historian, " it was enough to be an Irishman to be persecuted, and a Catholic to be crucified." " Has Tyrone submitted?" gasped the dying Elizabeth. " No," answered the statesmen who gathered around her bed; and the last of the Tudors passed from earth appalled by the terrors of coming judgment, and vexed at the thought that an Irish prince still defied her power.

Elizabeth was a vile, vain, able, and imperious woman. At her death 3000 dresses were found in her wardrobe. During her last years the Protestant bishop of London, on one occasion, ventured in his sermon to raise her thoughts from the ornaments of dress to the riches of Heaven; but she told her ladies that if he touched on that subject again she would fit him for Heaven.

2. SCOTLAND, 1500–1600.—In 1502 the Scottish

---

* Principally O'Kane, O'Doherty, MacMahon, MacGuire, Magennis, MacSweeney, and O'Hanlon.

11

monarch, *James IV.*, married the princess Margaret, daughter of Henry VII. of England. The harmony which this alliance produced between the two kingdoms did not last long. James declared war against Henry VIII. The battle of Flodden Field was fought, and on it fell the Scottish king and the flower of his nobility. He was succeeded by his infant son, *James V.*, who, on reaching manhood, found himself involved in war with his uncle, Henry VIII. The military disasters of his reign hastened his death, a few days before which was born to him a daughter destined to be famous in history as *Mary Queen of Scots.*

The beauty, virtue, and accomplishments of this royal lady, her misfortunes and her heroic death, are events well known. The introduction of Protestantism into Scotland, and the preaching of such fanatical apostates as *John Knox*, upset all law and order. The passions ran wild. Mobs ruled. Mary was powerless.

The unhappy queen fled to England and threw herself on the generosity of her cousin Elizabeth, who promised her every protection. But the English queen was as cruel as she was treacherous. She beheld in Mary Stuart a Catholic and a rival to the throne. Her course was worthy of royal ruffianism. Elizabeth had the Queen of Scots thrown into prison, where for eighteen years she languished in captivity, only to end her career at the block.

How impressive was the scene that marked the last moments of that noble woman! Historians tell us that, with an ivory crucifix in her hand, Mary Stuart advanced into the hall of execution with the grace and majesty so often displayed in her happier days and in the palace of her fathers. Her last words were: "Into thy hands, O Lord, I commend my spirit!" And at the third stroke of an axe, the most queenly head in Europe was severed from the body, and the pure and lofty spirit of the last Catholic queen of Scotland passed into eternity.

3. CHIEF AGENTS INFLUENCING THE PROGRESS OF ENGLISH LITERATURE IN THE SIXTEENTH CENTURY.— The chief agents that influenced the progress of English literature in this century were: (1) The printing-press; (2) the mature condition of the English language, which had just reached that advanced stage of growth and development that made it a grand and polished instrument for all the higher purposes of prose and poetry; (3) the study of the Latin and Greek classics and the poetry of Italy; (4) the increased number of colleges and public schools, and the consequent diffusion of education; (5) the rise of the middle classes of the people; (6) the discovery of America, and the circumnavigation of the earth. These last events fired the intellect and enthusiasm of Europe. Human curiosity marched over the globe.

4. ENGLISH LITERATURE AND THE EVENT MISNAMED THE REFORMATION.*—It is the fashion with a large class of non-Catholic writers to view the so-called Reformation as the great agent that gave such a vast and widespread impulse to thought, literature, and social progress in the sixteenth and succeeding centuries. Let us briefly examine this subject by the light of true history. Let facts speak.

(1) PRINTING *owes nothing to the "Reformation,"* which it preceded by nearly a century; and from this

---
* Cardinal Wiseman truly styled it "that terrible event in English history, the horrors of which have been gilded by the name of Reformation."

invention alone literature received its greatest impulse.*

(2) THE ENGLISH LANGUAGE *owes nothing to the "Reformation."* Our speech began, developed, and reached its full growth, if not its present perfection, long before Henry VIII. prepared the way for a new creed by tyranny, wife-murder, and sacrilegious robbery.

(3) THE ANCIENT CLASSICS *owe nothing to the "Reformation."* The careful hand and wise, beautiful taste of the Catholic Church saved the masterpieces of Greek and Roman literature from perishing in the wreck of ages. From Catholic Italy England learned to write poetry and to polish her speech.

(4) THE COLLEGES, PUBLIC SCHOOLS, and EDUCATION *owe nothing to the "Reformation."* The University of Oxford consists of nineteen colleges. *Fourteen* of these were founded *before* the "Reformation," and but five since. The University of Cambridge consists of seventeen colleges. *Thirteen* of these were founded *before* the "Reformation," and but four since. It is the same with the great public schools, such as *Eton*,† nearly all of which existed before the

---

* How did the English "Reformation" treat the art of printing? "By the regulations of the Star Chamber, in 1585," says Thomas Arnold, "no press was allowed to be used out of London, except one at Oxford and another at Cambridge. Thus every check was imposed on literature, and it seems unreasonable to dispute that they had some efficacy in restraining its progress."—*Hist. of English Literature.*

† Eton College is one of the most famous educational establishments in England. It was founded in 1440 by Henry VI. under the title of "*The College of the Blessed Mary of Eton beside Windsor.*" It barely escaped destruction during the period of robbery and plunder that marked the early course of the "Reformation." For instance, in the reign of Henry VIII. alone, *ninety* colleges were destroyed. Indeed, in 1550 Ascham predicted the speedy extinction of the universities of Oxford and Cambridge from the growing calamities which attended the new religious movement.

"Reformation." But no sooner did the new religion assume sway than the high standard of instruction at Oxford and Cambridge was lowered. The Catholic professors were driven out of the country, and their offices were bestowed upon obsequious apostates and bold ignoramuses. "At Oxford," says Warton, "the public schools were neglected by the professors and pupils and allotted to the lowest purposes. Academical degrees were abrogated as anti-Christian. Reformation was turned into fanaticism." Latimer declared, in 1550, that there were 10,000 fewer students in England than twenty years before; and we have it on the authority of Anthony Wood that in 1563— the fifth year of the reign of Elizabeth—there were only *three* men at Oxford qualified to preach in public. Williams, Speaker of the House of Commons in the same reign, complained that more than *one hundred* flourishing schools had perished in the destruction of the monasteries, and that ignorance had prevailed ever since. The good old Catholic times had passed, and with them passed the noble race of generous princes and pious churchmen who founded schools and colleges. It was a sad change. "The rapacious courtiers of Edward VI.," says Craik, "robbed the institutions of learning in the base race to fill their pockets." The same accurate writer doubts if popular education was farther advanced at the close of the reign of Elizabeth than it was at the commencement of that of her father, or even her grandfather. The lower and many of the middle classes were wholly uneducated and illiterate. It is a question whether the father of Shakspeare, an alderman of Stratford, could write his name.

(5) THE ENGLISH PEOPLE *owe nothing to the* "*Re-*

formation," for it did nothing to make them free—to elevate them. It gave them no new rights. Magna Charta is the bulwark of English liberty, but it is the work of Catholics. The " Reformation," on the contrary, strengthened the fetters of despotism by centring all power, spiritual and temporal, in the person of grasping and godless monarchs. " A political and spiritual despotism, such as that of Henry VIII. and Cromwell," says Frederick Schlegel, " would have been impossible but for the Reformation." From the reign of Elizabeth until the act of Catholic emancipation was passed in the present century, religious liberty was trampled to the ground in England, Scotland, and Ireland. This was one of the fruits of the " Reformation," and the tree is known by its fruit. For nearly three hundred years blood flowed in torrents, and to be a Catholic was to be persecuted like a wild beast. The same price was offered for the head of a wolf and that of a priest. The fierce Mohawk was not more eager and skilful on an enemy's trail than was the fanatical and barbarous government of England in its hunt after Catholic clergymen; and the humanity of the American Indian compares very favorably with that of the Protestant Briton.

The Holy Book declares that *truth* alone gives freedom—real mental and moral freedom. But the Catholic Church is the grand depository of truth upon earth—that truth which makes men free. She is the mother of true liberty. Now, to unsettle a man's belief in the religion founded by Christ is not to make him free. It is to make him doubt, and doubt is not freedom. Telling a man to master the mysteries of a badly translated *Bible*, and to think as he pleases in dealing with the truths of religion, is not the wise way to make him free. The lunatic enjoys such freedom. But this is the reprehensible manner in which the so-called Reformation labored to cheat the human mind. It produced doubt, irreverence, infidelity, mental giddiness, moral inconstancy, and a countless number of new "churches," by falsely stigmatizing fixed belief in the sacred dogmas of religion as a state of intellectual bondage.

(6) THE "REFORMATION" HAD NO SHARE *in those gigantic achievements which doubled the size of the world's map and revealed the mysteries of the earth to mankind—the discovery of America, and the circumnavigation of the globe.* Luther was but nine years of age when the Catholic *Columbus* planted the cross on the shores of the New World; and it is uncertain if ever the Catholic *Magellan* heard of the Wurtemberg reformer and mighty "bellower in bad Latin."

The Reformation, in truth, was a sad hindrance to the progress of sound thought and pure, healthy literature. It brought no new truth into the world. It originated no new form of composition. It did not polish speech. It was, at best, a fatal whirlwind that swept over the British mind, leaving behind the scars, changes, hatred, and confusion which marked its pestilential and destroying course. In short, neither English civilization nor English letters owe anything to the "Reformation." For them it was a retrograde movement. Had it never occurred, the career of English literature would, doubtless, have been brighter and grander.

7. THE REFORMATION AND ART, SCIENCE, AND THE WORLD AT LARGE.—The "Reformation" began by showing itself an enemy to the fine arts. To it music, painting, and architecture are certainly under no

obligations. "The Reformation favorable to the fine arts!" writes Archbishop Spalding—"as well might you assert that a conflagration is beneficial to a city which it consumes. Wherever the Reformation appeared it pillaged, defaced, often burned churches and monasteries; it broke up and destroyed statues and paintings, and it often burned whole libraries." Look at the venerable ruins of churches and abbeys in England, Scotland, and Ireland. In mute accents they tell a mournful tale. Over them passed the rude, destroying hand of the Reformation. "With the art of poetry," says Frederick Schlegel, "Protestantism at first disclaimed any connection." It also began by an insane effort to abolish the sciences. Luther pronounced "all science, whether practical or speculative, to be damnable, and all the speculative sciences to be sinful and erroneous; and he even loudly declared that all human learning was "an invention of the devil." The truth of all this is confirmed by history.

Nor does the world at large owe anything to this boasted "Reformation." It was an unhappy rupture between men and their ancestors. It pulled down. It destroyed.* But it neither built up, originated anything really new and useful, nor added to the sum of human happiness. To thought it added no idea of value.

"Protestantism," says the profound Balmes, "has

---

* Challoner states that during the reign of Henry VIII. 645 monasteries, 90 colleges, and 110 hospitals were suppressed or destroyed, and the money was pocketed by the royal robber. The destruction of precious libraries in the same reign was truly deplorable. "Those who purchased the religious houses," writes I. D'Israeli, "took the libraries as part of the booty, with which they scoured their furniture, or sold the books as waste paper, or sent them abroad in ship-loads to foreign book-binders."

not a single idea of which it can say, *This is my own.*" It lives on borrowed ideas, as, in many places, it still worships in stolen churches.* It simply led to wars, bloodshed, rancor, robbery, fanaticism, infidelity, persecution, and endless changes in religion. There is nothing *fixed* in Protestantism, for it is the work of man. To the human intellect tossed about on the ocean of life it offers no place of safe anchorage. It shifts with the times. " You change," said Bossuet to Protestants; " and that which changes is not the truth "

The consequences of the so-called Reformation were wide and deplorable. It introduced discord into the bosom of the Christian people of Europe and America. It broke the unity of European civilization. It weakened the moral influence which Europe exercised over the rest of the globe. It carried fanaticism and religious persecution to the shores of the New World. It dwarfed the growth of Christian missions. It checked the progress of Christian civilization or gave it a wrong direction. The invention of printing, the invention of the compass, the progress of art, science, and literature, and the discovery of America led to the formation of bright hopes, alas! never to be fulfilled. Over three centuries ago the wild tocsin of religious strife sounded; all the baser passions were aroused; and the noise, animosity, and confusion have not yet died away.

8. RISE OF THE ENGLISH DRAMA.—THE DRAMA IS not a modern invention. Regular dramatic entertainments were given in Greece as early as 450 B.C., and at Rome about a century later, according to Livy.

---

* This, of course, does not refer to America.

The ancient drama perished with the downfall of pagan Rome.

In later times Catholic taste and piety revived dramatic exhibitions. First came the MIRACLE PLAYS. For their origin we must go back to the Middle Ages. The earliest miracle-play on record is the *Play of St. Catherine.* It was written in French, and was represented at Dunstable, England, in 1119. The oldest manuscript of a miracle-play in English is one entitled the *Harrowing of Hell*, that is, the conquering of hell by our Blessed Redeemer. It was written about the year 1350.

A miracle-play was some mystery of religion, or story from Holy Scripture, or from the lives of the saints, dramatized for the purpose of instructing the people in a pleasing manner, and initiating them into the spirit of the festivals which the Church celebrated. Few among them could read and study the explanations of the festivals, but all could take in and appreciate what was placed before their eyes. In England the miracle-play did not altogether die out before the early part of the seventeenth century.

The MORAL PLAYS soon partly displaced the miracle-plays, and came into great favor in England about the middle of the fifteenth century. Their object was also to promote religious ideas; but in many respects they differed widely from the miracle-plays. *Virtues* and *abstract qualities* took the place of the historical personages of Scripture. Instead of the *Adam*, *Moses*, *Herod*, and *Pontius Pilate* of the miracle-play, we find *Justice*, *Mercy*, *Temperance*, and *Vice* as characters in the moral play. Virtues and vices talk, jest, and act.

But with the universal popularity of the miracle

LITERATURE OF THE SIXTEENTH CENTURY. 131

and moral plays came their abuse, and they were finally discouraged by the Church. They prepared the way, however, for the modern drama.

We may date the rise of the *English drama* from about the middle of the sixteenth century. The *two earliest English comedies* were *Ralph Roister Doister* and *Gammer Gurton's Needle*. The first dates from about 1540; the second was written about twenty years later. *Gorboduc*,* the first English tragedy, was from the pen of *Thomas Sackville*, and was acted in 1562.

During the next thirty years a number of wild, gifted, and scholarly young men tried their hands at play-writing. At the head of these stood *Christopher Marlowe*. But a greater far was to come. The culminating point in English dramatic literature was reached in the prince of dramatists—the myriad-minded *Shakspeare*.

9. CONDITION OF THE ENGLISH LANGUAGE IN THE SIXTEENTH CENTURY.—With the beginning of the sixteenth century we enter on the period of *Modern English*. The language had, by slow degrees, become a polished and mighty instrument of expression. It was now adequate to all the wants of poetry. And in the hands of the great *Sir Thomas More* it exhibited, for the first time, its real powers as a vehicle for dignified prose. More's *Life of Edward V.*, written about the year 1513, is, according to Hallam, the first good specimen of classical English prose, "pure and conspicuous, well chosen, without vulgarisms or pedantry."

"The English language," says Henry Reed, writing of the sixteenth century, "was now better fitted for

---

* Sometimes called *Ferrex and Porrex*.

all the uses of literature, more adequate to the needs of philosophic thought, and of deep and varied feeling—at once stronger, more flexible, and more copious. It was now *one* mighty flood no longer showing the separate colors of the two streams which filled its channel—colors caught from different soils, the Saxon and Norman, in which they had their springs. The hidden harmonies of the language were disclosed, and its power of more varied music shown. The people's speech had grown to its full stature."

LESSON I.

GAVIN DOUGLAS. DIED 1522.

Chief works: (1) *Translation of Virgil's Æneid.*
(2) *King Hart.*
(3) *The Palace of Honor.*

1. Who has the special honor of having been the *first* to translate any of the ancient classics, Latin or Greek, into English?

Gavin Douglas, a learned Catholic bishop of Dunkeld.

2. Where was he born, and to what historic family did he belong?

Gavin Douglas was born in Scotland, and was a younger son of the fifth Earl of Angus, Archibald Douglas, known in Scottish history as "Archibald Bell-the-Cat."

3. Give some of the chief points in his life.

He studied at the University of Paris, entered the religious state, became abbot, and finally bishop of Dunkeld.

4. Which is the most remarkable production of the poet-bishop's pen?

His elegant and scholarly translation of Virgil's *Æneid* into English. This was the *first* translation of a Latin classic into our language.*

5. Which are his other chief works?

King Hart and *The Palace of Honor*,† two long allegorical poems.

6. Where did Bishop Douglas die?

After the disastrous battle of Flodden Field, misfortune frowned on the warlike house of Douglas, and the gentle and gifted bishop was compelled to fly to London, where he died of the plague in 1522.

7. What was his character?

The member of a warlike family, in a rude age and country, Bishop Douglas was noted for his refinement, scholarly tastes, peacefulness, and gentle virtues.

8. In which of his poems do s Sir Walter Scott draw a touching picture of Gavin Douglas?

In his *Marmion*, where, in a striking scene, he says:

> "A bishop by the altar stood,
> A noble lord of Douglas blood,
> . . . . .
> More pleased that, in a barbarous age,
> He gave rude Scotland Virgil's page."

---

* Bishop Douglas made this translation in 1512 and 1513.
† *The Palace of Honor* was written in 1501. The leading idea of the poem and some of the details seem to be reproduced in Bunyan's *Pilgrim's Progress*, a work composed about 180 years later. It is very probable that the fanatical Baptist preacher drew from the work of the Catholic bishop much unacknowledged material.

LESSON II.

WILLIAM DUNBAR. DIED 1530.

Chief works: (1) *The Dance of the Seven Deadly Sins.* (2) *The Thistle and the Rose.* (3) *The Merle and the Nightingale.*

9. What poet has received the title of ' the Chaucer of Scotland"?

William Dunbar, the greatest of the Scottish poets.

10. Give a short account of his early life.

He was born in Scotland, belonged to a family of distinction, and was educated at the University of St. Andrews, where he took the degree of M.A. He then entered the Order of St. Francis,* was ordained priest, and spent many years as a missionary, travelling on foot through Scotland, England, and France, and living on the alms of the faithful.

11. In what capacity was Dunbar subsequently employed by his sovereign, James IV. of Scotland?

As ambassador in conducting negotiations with various foreign courts. It was thus he gained that wide experience and deep knowledge of men and things which afterwards greatly aided him in his literary labors.

12. Where did he die, and when?

His last days were spent at the Scottish court, a dependent on royal bounty. Here he died, at the age of sixty-five, in 1530.†

---

* In early life Dunbar entered the novitiate of the Franciscan Order, but does not appear to have taken the vows.—*Thomas Arnold.*

† "Dunbar's works, with a small exception," writes Dr. Hart, "remained in manuscript unknown to the world for more than two centuries, and it is only within the memory of persons still living that full justice has been done his merits. His poems began to attract attention about the middle of the last century, and since that

13. Into how many classes are Dunbar's poems divided?
Into three classes—the *allegorical*, the *moral*, and the *comical*.

14. Which are his best and most original allegorical poems?
The Dance of the Seven Deadly Sins and *The Thistle and the Rose*.

15. What is *The Dance of the Seven Deadly Sins?*

It is a long allegorical poem, the scene of which is in the infernal regions. Mahomet furnishes the music. In the fearful dance *Pride* leads the other Deadly Sins. Each of the seven is a terrible personage, painted in horror's darkest hues, and lighted in the dance by the lurid flames in which he leaps.

> And first of all in dance was *Pride*,
> With hair combed back, bonnet on side.
> . . . . . .
> Then *Ire* came in with strut and strife,
> His hand was e'en upon his knife." *

The Dance of the Seven Deadly Sins is a masterpiece.

16. What is the *Thistle and the Rose?*

It is a fine allegorical poem, commemorating the marriage of the English Princess Margaret to James IV. of Scotland in 1503. The *Rose*, the type of beauty, is wedded to the *Thistle*, the type of strength, who is commanded to cherish well and guard his Rose.† Many critics consider this Dunbar's *most perfect poem*.

---

time his fame has been steadily rising; and it became at length so great that in 1834 a complete edition of his works was printed."—*Manual of English Literature.*

* In these lines the spelling is modernized. Dunbar spells pride, *pryd;* back, *bak;* came, *cam;* and knife, *knyfe.*

† The *Thistle* symbolizes Scotland; the *Rose*, England. Dunbar spells the words *Thrissill* and *Rois.*

17. Which is considered the best of Dunbar's *moral* poems?

The Merle* and the Nightingale, a beautiful poem in which the two rival songsters debate in alternate stanzas the merits of earthly and heavenly love. The Merle argues that human love is the best. The Nightingale replies in behalf of the love of God. The last verse comes to the conclusion that "all love is lost but upon God alone."

18. What may be said of his *comic* poems?

Though full of the most genuine fun and the broadest humor, there is in most of Dunbar's comic pieces an element of coarseness and indecency, which unhappily detracts not a little from their merits.

19. What is Dunbar's rank in English literature?

He is one of the great writers of our language, and is certainly *the greatest poet between Chaucer and Spenser*.

"A poet unrivalled by any that Scotland has ever produced."—*Sir Walter Scott.*

"In the poetry of Dunbar we recognize the emanations of a mind adequate to splendid and varied execution. As a descriptive poet he has received superlative praise. In his allegorical poems we discover originality and even sublimity of invention."—*Irving.*

"Burns is the only name among the Scottish poets that can be placed in the same line with that of Dunbar; and even the inspired ploughman, though the equal of Dunbar in comic power and his superior in depth of passion, is not to be compared with the elder poet either in strength or in general fertility of imagination."—*Craik.*

---

* *Merle*, the blackbird.

LITERATURE OF THE SIXTEENTH CENTURY. 137

LESSON III.

HENRY HOWARD, EARL OF SURREY. DIED 1547.

Chief works: (1) *Translation of the Second and Fourth Books of Virgil's Æneid.*
(2) *Songs and Sonnets.*

20. Who was Henry Howard, Earl of Surrey?

Henry Howard, styled "the English Petrarch," was a member of the ancient and noble Catholic family of the Howards, and eldest son of the third Duke of Norfolk. His is one of the youngest, brightest, and most romantic names in the history of English literature.

21. Where did he receive his education?

At Oxford University; but he afterwards travelled much, and during his stay in Italy made himself familiar with the rich literature of that country, especially the writings of Petrarch.

22. What are we told of Surrey's romantic career?

It was very eventful. He was a gay, gifted, brave young man who early learned the secret of joining brain to action. A knight, a great lord, a relative of the king, he had made war, commanded fortresses, mounted to assaults, fought tournaments, and wrote sonnets before his years had filled up a quarter of a century.

23. What was his unhappy fate?

Having fallen under the displeasure of the brutal Henry VIII., the brilliant but unhappy Howard, on a frivolous charge, was cast into the Tower of London; and, while still in the bloom of youth, was bar-
12*

barously executed, his bright hair, all dabbled in blood, sweeping the dust of the scaffold.*

24. Which are Surrey's chief literary productions?

His *Translation of the Second and Fourth Books of Virgil's Æneid into English* and his *Songs and Sonnets.*

25. What is remarkable about his translation of the *Æneid?*

It is the *first* specimen of *blank-verse* in our literature. Surrey deserves the title of Father of English Blank-verse.†

26. What other new form of poetical composition did he introduce into our literature?

The *Sonnet.*‡

" Surrey has the merit of having restored to our poetry a correctness, polish, and general spirit of refinement such as it had not known since Chaucer's time."—*Craik.*

" Surrey, for justness of thought, correctness of style, and purity of expression, may justly be pronounced the *first* English classical poet."—*Warton.*

" In his purification of English verse, he did good service by casting out those clumsy Latin words with which the lines of even Dunbar are heavily clogged."—*Collier.*

---

* Political and religious animosity was the chief but secret cause of Lord Surrey's death. Henry VIII. had him convicted on a flimsy charge of treason, and we all know what treason meant in the reign of that merciless tyrant. The defence of the gifted poet and gallant young soldier was nobly eloquent—unanswerable. But he was condemned to die, and " his early and unmerited death deepens the romantic interest that surrounds his name."

† Surrey borrowed his blank-verse from Italy, where it began to be used in the early part of the sixteenth century. His translation of the two books of the *Æneid* is thought to be simply an imitation of the Italian version of Cardinal de' Medici. Of Surrey, Hallam says: " No one before his time had known how to translate or imitate with appropriate expression."

It is its form in blank-verse that so strikingly distinguishes the language of Shakspeare from that of Chaucer.

‡ The sonnet is also borrowed from Italian literature. There is a remarkable sweetness and polish about Surrey's " Songs and Sonnets." Like the productions of Petrarch, most of them treat of love, the star of inspiration being the beautiful Geraldine, a daughter of the Earl of Kildare, in Ireland. " It was a pure love," says Taine, " to which Surrey gave expression; for his lady, the beauti-

LESSON IV.

CHRISTOPHER MARLOWE. DIED 1593.

Chief works: (1) *The Life and Death of Dr. Faustus.*
(2) *The Rich Jew of Malta.*
(3) *The Life of Edward II.*
} All tragedies.

27. Who was Christopher Marlowe?

The ablest of the English dramatists before Shakspeare, he may be considered the forerunner of that great literary master.

28. Give a few of the chief events in his life.

The son of a shoemaker, Marlowe was born at Canterbury, England, and received a learned education at Cambridge, where he took the degree of M.A. He drifted into atheism, led a wild, disgraceful life, and finally died of a wound which he had received in a miserable tavern brawl.*

29. Give the title of Marlowe's first drama, and mention some remarkable feature of the work.

His first drama was *Tamburlaine the Great.* It was composed before his graduation, and was among the *first English plays* written in *blank-verse.*

30. Which is his second play, and what does it exhibit?

His second play is *The Life and Death of Dr.*

---

ful Geraldine, like Beatrice and Laura, was an ideal personage—a child of thirteen years."
Surrey also translated the *Book of Ecclesiastes* into verse, which shows the serious religious cast of his mind.
* There was, indeed, hardly a Christian element in Marlowe's untamable nature; and, although he was called a skeptic, infidelity in him took the form of blasphemy rather than of denial. He was made up of vehement passions, vivid imagination, and lawless self-will; and what Hazlitt calls "a hunger and thirst after unrighteousness" assumed the place of conscience in his haughty and fiery spirit.—*Whipple.*

Faustus. It exhibits a much higher and wider range of dramatic power than his first tragedy.*

31. What have y u to remark of *The Rich Jew of Malta?*

It is considered a play of much power and originality. It is said that its principal character furnished Shakspeare with the first ideal of his *Shylock.*†

32. What is the play entitled *The Life of Edward II.?*

It is a tragedy, and the *first* truly *historical play* written in English. Eminent critics consider it Marlowe's ablest production, and the best historical play before the time of Shakspeare.

33. Did Marlowe write anything except dramas?

He left some pretty lyrics behind him, a few of which still find a place in collections of poetry.

34. What may be said of Marlowe's style?

It is marked by force and vigor, with which there mingles an element of bombast and exaggeration. Ben Jonson speaks of "Marlowe's mighty line."

LESSON V.

ROBERT SOUTHWELL, S.J. DIED 1595.

Chief works: *Fifty-five Poems.*

35. Who was Robert Southwell?

He was a Jesuit Father, a hero, a charming poet, and one of the real refiners of the English language.

---

* His *Faustus* perhaps best reflects his whole genius and experience. The subject must have taken strong hold of his nature, for, like Faustus, he had himself doubtless held intimate business relations with the great enemy of mankind, and was personally conscious of the struggle in the soul between the diabolical and the divine.—*Whipple.*

† In *The Merchant of Venice.*

LITERATURE OF THE SIXTEENTH CENTURY. 141

36. State some of the chief events in his life.

Southwell belonged to an ancient Catholic family, and was born in Norfolk, England. He made his studies in the English college at Douay.* The poet went to Rome, and in his sixteenth year entered the Society of Jesus. Being raised to the priesthood, he returned to his native country as a missionary, and, for eight years, secretly labored for the salvation of souls in the face of penal laws that threatened him with a death certain and terrible.

37. When was Father Southwell arrested?

In 1592.

38. What followed his arrest?

He was at once thrown into one of the most filthy dungeons in the Tower. For three years the holy and heroic Jesuit bore this imprisonment, was brutally tortured on the rack *ten* different times, and finally executed at Tyburn with the most revolting cruelties.

39. What new element did this venerable man introduce into English poetry?

Southwell, so to speak, Christianized English poetry. He was the *founder* of the modern English style of religious poetry, being the first modern Englishman who showed " how well verse and virtue suit together."

---

* By the zeal of the learned Catholic professors who were banished from Oxford—and especially of the famous Cardinal Allen—an English college was established at Douay, in France, 1568. For nearly two centuries and a half the Catholic students of Great Britain directed their steps to this renowned institution. Here the flame of faith was nourished and the light of knowledge kept burning when all was bigotry and religious darkness in the once Catholic land of England—the home of the holy Bede and the great Alfred. Here were trained those bands of devoted priests who laid down their lives in laboring to restore the true faith among their unhappy countrymen. Here our Catholic Bible was translated into English. Here the pious and learned Alban Butler, author of the *Lives of the Saints*, received his education.

40. When were his poems first issued, and were they popular?

The first edition of his poems was issued the very year he was executed; and so popular were those beautiful productions that during the next hundred years eleven editions were reprinted.

41. Are Southwell's poems numerous?

They are *fifty-five* in number. The longest is *St. Peter's Complaint*.

42. What may be said of their merits?

They are marked by quaint figures, much beauty of language, and purity of sentiment; and as they were chiefly composed in prison, they breathe a tone of quiet, lofty resignation.

43. Did Southwell leave any productions in prose?

He did. *Mary Magdalen's Tears* is his best-known production in prose, which is not less charming than his poetry. A deep, strong, loving heart sanctified all he wrote.

"Southwell shows in his poetry great simplicity and elegance of thought and still greater purity of language. He has been compared in some of his pieces to Goldsmith, and the comparison seems not unjust."—*Angus.*

"Southwell, it seems, was the founder of the modern English style of religious poetry; his influence and example are evident in the work of Crashaw, or of Donne, or of Herbert, or Walker, or any of those whose devout lyrics were admired in later times."—*Thomas Arnold.*

LESSON VI.

EDMUND SPENSER. DIED 1599.

Chief works: (1) *The Fairy Queen.*
(2) *The Shepherd's Calendar.*
(3) *View of the State of Ireland.*

44. Who was Edmund Spenser?

With *Chaucer, Shakspeare,* and *Milton,* he was one of the great old masters of English poetry.

45. What do we know of his early life?

Very little; he was born in London, and educated at Cambridge, where he took the degree of M.A.

46. On leaving college, where did Spenser live for some years?

In the north of England.

47. While residing in the north of England what work came from his pen?

His first production—a poem entitled *The Shepherd's Calendar.*

48. What position did Spenser obtain in 1580 through the influence of Sir Philip Sidney, who was his warm personal friend?

The position of Secretary to Lord Grey, who was at that time appointed Lord-Lieutenant of Ireland.

49. How were his services in Ireland rewarded by Elizabeth in 1586?

By the grant of Kilcolman Castle and 3000 acres of confiscated land in the county of Cork.* This tract of country was one of the most beautiful in beautiful Ireland.†

---

* It was a gift plucked from the bleeding heart of unhappy Ireland.
† The castle of Kilcolman, from which the Desmonds had lately been driven, stood by a beautiful lake in the midst of an extensive

50. What celebrated poem did he write at his Irish residence?

The Fairy Queen.

51. What happened to Spenser the year before his death?

With his family he was obliged to fly from Kilcolman Castle, which was committed to the flames. Hugh O'Neill, the great Earl of Tyrone, was making a gallant struggle to regain the lost liberties of Ireland. The spirit of insurrection spread over the island, and among the English adventurers who sought safety in flight was Edmund Spenser.*

52. Where and when did he die?

At London, in 1599. According to Ben Jonson, he "died for want of bread." He was buried in Westminster Abbey.

53. What is the *Shepherd's Calendar?*

It is a pastoral poem in twelve eclogues, modelled to some extent after the Latin eclogues of Virgil.

54. What is an eclogue?

A pastoral poem in which shepherds are introduced conversing with each other.

---

plain girdled with mountain-ranges. Soft woodland and savage hill, shadowy river-glade and rolling ploughland, were all there to gladden the poet's heart with their changeful beauty and tinge his verse with their glowing colors.—*Collier.*

It was in this retired Irish paradise that Spenser composed the greater part of his works, especially *The Fairy Queen;* and from the banks of the "gentle Mulla" we may still see how his famous poem is pictured with that delightful Munster scenery.

* Spenser was justly regarded with odium by the Irish, who looked upon him as a polished robber and needy adventurer.

LESSON VII.

SPENSER, CONTINUED.

55. Which is Spenser's famous masterpiece?

The Fairy Queen.

56. What is *The Fairy Queen?*

It is a great narrative poem in the form of an allegory.

57. What does Spenser declare its object to be?

He states that the object of the poem "was to fashion a gentleman in virtuous and gentle description."

58. How is this poem divided?

It is divided into six books, each book being subdivided into twelve cantos.

59. What does each book picture to the mind?

Each book has a story and a hero of its own, with a series of connected adventures, all intended to illustrate some *one great moral virtue.*

60. Of what does the first book treat?

It treats of the adventures of *St. George, the Red-Cross Knight*, who represents the virtue of Holiness. The first book is the grandest of all.

61. What does the second book recount?

It recounts the adventures of *Sir Guyon*, or *Temperance.*

62. What does the third book give?

It gives the adventures of *Britomartis*, or *Purity.*

63. What does the fourth book recount?

It recounts the legend of *Cambel and Triamond*, or *Friendship.*

13

64. What does the fifth book give?

It gives the adventures of *Sir Artegal,* or *Justice.*

65. What does the sixth and last book give?

The adventures of *Sir Calydore,* or *Courtesy.**

66. Who is the chief hero of the whole poem?

Prince Arthur, the chivalrous Celtic warrior of the old British legends. The poem opens by his paying a visit to the court of the *Fairy Queen* † in Fairyland, where the hero finds her holding a solemn festival during twelve days.

67. Which are the chief qualities presented for our admiration in this poem?

Heroic daring and ideal purity.

68. As a literary artist, in what way does Spenser especially excel?

As a scene-painter. He drew pen-pictures with unrivalled power. He describes to the eye. He gives the distinctness of real objects to the airy conceptions of allegory.

69. What name is given to the stanza used in the *Fairy Queen?*

The Spenserian stanza, because invented by Spenser. It consists of *nine lines* of a peculiar construction.

70. Mention some of the more serious defects of this fine composition.

The obsolete diction and cold, tedious allegory of the *Fairy Queen* repel most modern readers. It contains dozens of indecent passages, and is pervaded with an anti-Catholic spirit.

---

* The *Fairy Queen* is an unfinished poem. Spenser's plan embraced *twelve books;* only six were completed. Still, it is more than twice as long as *Paradise Lost.*

† Hence the name of the poem.

LITERATURE OF THE SIXTEENTH CENTURY. 147

71. What is Spenser's chief work in prose?
His *View of the State of Ireland.*
72. What may be said of this volume?
To the author of the *Fairy Queen* it is a disgrace. It might have come from the pen of the ruthless Cromwell.

"The admiration with which Shakspeare regarded Spenser, and the care with which he imitated him in his lyrical and idyllic poems, are circumstances of themselves sufficient to make us study, with the liveliest interest, the poem of the *Fairy Queen.*"— *F. Schlegel.*

"There is something in Spenser that pleases one as strongly in one's old age as it did in one's youth. I read the *Fairy Queen* when I was about twelve with a vast deal of delight, and I think it gave me as much when I read it over about a year or two ago."— *Pope.*

LESSON VIII.

THOMAS SACKVILLE, LORD BUCKHURST.   DIED 1608.

Chief works: (1) *Gorboduc.*
(2) *The Mirror for Magistrates.*

73. Where was Sackville born and educated?
He was born in Sussex, England; and studied at both Oxford and Cambridge, taking his M.A. at the latter university.
74. For what profession did he study?
The law.
75. While still a student at the Temple,* what play did he write?
A play entitled *Gorboduc.*†

---

* The Temple is an edifice in London once occupied by the Order of Knights Templars, and now appropriated to the chambers of two inns of court. They are called the *inner* and the *middle temple.*
† Sometimes called *Ferrex and Porrex.*

76. Is *Gorboduc* a *tragedy* or a *comedy*, and what is remarkable about its history?

Gorboduc is a tragedy. It is the *first* instance in which *blank-verse* became the language of an English dramatic composition.

77. Give the date of its production.

It was first acted with great applause in 1561.

78. What, however, is Sackville's most remarkable work?

A poem entitled *The Mirror for Magistrates.*

79. State the design of this poem.

It was designed to exhibit, in a series of metrical narratives and soliloquies, the calamities of men prominent in the history of England.

80. Is the whole poem from Sackville's pen?

No; the plan is his, but he wrote only the *Induction* and one legend—that on the career of Henry Stafford, Duke of Buckingham. Other duties soon compelled Sackville to commit the completion of the poem to two inferior poets.

81. What honors and digni ies were heaped on Sackville, the duties of which transferred his mind from literature to politics?

Soon after writing *Gorboduc* Elizabeth created him Lord Buckhurst; and in 1598 he became Lord Treasurer of England, an office which he held up to the date of his death.

82. What may be s id of the merits of that part of *The Mirror for Magistrates* written by Sackville?

Though it contains but a few hundred lines, yet these are sufficient to place Sackville high on the list of British poets.*

---

* Speaking of the *Mirror for Magistrates*, Craik says that it "must be considered as forming the connecting link between the *Canterbury Tales* and the *Fairy Queen*." It should be remembered that the *Mirror for Magistrates* was written in 1558, when Spenser was but *five* years of age.

LESSON IX.

SIR THOMAS MORE. DIED 1535.

Chief works: (1) *Utopia.*
(2) *History of the Life and Reign of Edward V.*
(3) *Theological Writings.*
(4) *Letters.*

83. Who is the earliest and most distinguished among the English prose-writers of the sixteenth century?

Sir Thomas More, one of the most shining and illustrious names in the history of England.

84. Where and when was More born?

At London in 1480. He was the only son of Sir John More, a judge of the court of King's Bench.

85. After a course of private study, where was he placed in his fifteenth year?

As a page in the household of *Cardinal Morton,* Archbishop of Canterbury. Here he mingled in the society of the most learned and celebrated men of the times. "This child here waiting at the table," the Cardinal used to say, "whoever shall live to see it, will prove a marvellous man."

86. What did Dean Colet of St. Paul's remark of young More's keen sense and ready wit?

"There is but one wit in England, and that is young Thomas More."

87. At which of the universities did More study?

At Oxford, where he gained the friendship of the famous *Erasmus,* and greatly distinguished himself as a scholar.*

---

* It is said, among other things, that More wrote many English poems of much merit during his university career.

88. Give a short account of his public career.

He became a lawyer, and rose rapidly in his profession. At twenty-one he was a member of the English Parliament. He was employed in negotiations with various European powers, was appointed Treasurer of the Exchequer, became Speaker of the House of Commons, and, on the fall of Wolsey, he was raised to the office of Lord High Chancellor of England.*

89. How did he discharge the duties of this high and perilous office?

With a singular purity and manly integrity that were the admiration of a corrupt age.

90. What was the end of this illustrious man?

He fell a victim to the tyranny of Henry VIII. Because More, as a faithful Catholic, refused to acknowledge the royal apostate as head of the Church of God in England, he was condemned to death, and cheerfully gave up his life for the true faith.†

---

* For many years Henry VIII. had been the bosom-friend of More, upon whom he lavished every mark of esteem. The King often ran up to the Chancellor's quiet home at Chelsea to enjoy the wit, learning, and delightful society of the author of *Utopia*. It is said, however, that More always felt a secret distrust as to the disinterested sincerity of Henry's friendship; and time, unhappily, proved the depth of his keen insight into human character.

† More's death, like his life, was lit up with the joy of a pure conscience and the beautiful brightness of Christian heroism. On the way to execution he was met by his favorite daughter, Margaret, and the scene was most touching. As he climbed up the shaky scaffold, he gayly remarked to the lieutenant, "Pray see me safely up; and for my coming down let me shift for myself." He embraced the headsman, and forgave him, saying, "You are to do me the greatest benefit that I can receive; pluck up your spirit, man, and be not afraid to do your work." A moment passed, the cruel axe fell, and the wisest, most learned, and most venerable head in England was severed from the body; and thus died for truth, and justice, and the Catholic faith, the great Sir Thomas More.

"More," writes Charles Butler, "was one of the greatest promoters of classical learning. The letters which passed between him and Erasmus are elegant and interesting; those in which the latter

LESSON X.

SIR THOMAS MORE, CONTINUED.

91. What is More's best-known work?

The *Utopia*, which he wrote in Latin.* It was soon translated into English.

92. What is the meaning of the word Utopia?

The word Utopia is derived from the Greek, and literally signifies *nowhere*. The island of Utopia was the *land of nowhere*.

93. What is the nature of the book to which this odd name is given?

It is a political romance in which More pictures a model republic on an imaginary island named Utopia.† Here all the laws and all the customs of society were marked by wisdom and goodness.

94. What was the object of this strange book?

It was clearly a satire on the society of the sixteenth century. In the imaginary island of Utopia, English vices, follies, errors, and blunders were carefully shunned.‡

95. Mention some of the laws and customs that ruled in Utopia.

All those model islanders learn agriculture. All have trades at which they work six hours a day and

---

relates his tragical end and records his great and amiable virtues are pathetic and beautiful in the highest degree."—*Historical Memoirs*, Vol. I.

* It was published in 1516.

† Hence our adjective *utopian*, meaning foolish, fanciful, or impossible.

‡ To More must be given the credit of originating that peculiar kind of composition which we may style *political romance*. Among his distinguished followers in the same field was Dean Swift. *Utopia*, no doubt, suggested *Gulliver's Travels*.

no more. War is unknown, and religious persecution unheard of. There are no taverns, no ever-changing fashions, few laws, and no lawyers.*

96. What can you say of More's *History of the Life and Reign of Edward V.?*

It is the earliest historical work in our language; and it has been warmly praised for its beauty of diction and for the ease and spirit of the narrative.

97. Did More produce anything on religious subjects?

He did. In his day the religious question agitated Europe, and the ancient faith had no braver defender than the learned and brilliant author of *Utopia.*

98. Mention some of his religious writings.

(1) His answer to Luther's attack on the King of England; (2) his Dialogue on Heresies; and (3) His explanation of the Passion † of our Blessed Lord, with a beautiful prayer.‡

99. What may be said of More's *Letters?*

They are the earliest specimens of simple, charming, and dignified epistolary correspondence in the English language.§

---

* When the Utopia of Sir Thomas More was first published, it occasioned a pleasant mistake. This political romance represents a perfect but visionary republic, in an island supposed to have been newly discovered in America. "As this was the age of discovery," says Granger, "the learned Budeus, and others, took it for a genuine history; and considered it as highly expedient that missionaries should be sent thither in order to convert so wise a nation to Christianity."

† This volume on the Passion was More's last. It remains unfinished. On the last page the ancient editor adds these touching words: "Sir Thomas More wrote no more of this woorke: for when he had written this farre, he was in prison kept so streyght, that all his bokes and penne and ynke and paper was taken from hym, and sone after he was putte to death."

‡ It can be seen at page 315, *Garden of the Soul.*

§ The Life and Letters of Sir Thomas More, by Miss Agnes L. Stewart, has recently been published in England.

LITERATURE OF THE SIXTEENTH CENTURY. 153

100. Had he much reputation as an orator?
His speeches have not come down to us; but tradition assigns to Sir Thomas More the *earliest* place on the glorious roll of English parliamentary orators.§

LESSON XI.
ASCHAM, SIDNEY, HOOKER.

ROGER ASCHAM. DIED 1569.
(1) *Toxophilus.* (2) *The Schoolmaster.*

SIR PHILIP SIDNEY. DIED 1586.
(1) *The Arcadia.* (2) *The Defence of Poesie.**

RICHARD HOOKER. DIED 1600.
The Laws of Ecclesiastical Polity.

101. Who was Roger Ascham?
He was the tutor of Queen Elizabeth, and one of the most elegant and scholarly prose-writers of the sixteenth century.

---

§ The months of June and July, 1535, are remarkable ones in English history. On the 6th of July Sir Thomas More was beheaded. On the 22d of June—fourteen days previously—the venerable John Fisher, Bishop of Rochester, perished on the scaffold. He was born in England in 1459. A stainless and beautiful life of 76 years had made him worthy to die a martyr. He denied that Henry VIII. could be head of the Church of Christ, and in those unhappy days such a denial was high treason—a crime to be punished at the block. He was seized and cast into the Tower. As the venerable bishop lay in prison, the Pope sent him a cardinal's hat. " Ha!" exclaimed the royal monster, "Paul may send him a hat, but I will leave him never a head to wear it!" He was as good as his word, and on the 22d of June the holy, learned, and eloquent John Fisher gave his manly head for the truth. More and Fisher were devoted friends. Of these two great men we can truly say—illustrious in life, they were sublime in death.

Fisher merits a place in English literature on account of his eloquent sermons, which were the *earliest* specimens of classical pulpit oratory in our language.—See *The Life of John Fisher, Cardinal-Bishop of Rochester; with an Appendix containing his Funeral Sermons and Letters,* by Miss Agnes L. Stewart.

* " Poesie," i.e., *Poetry.*

102. What is his *Toxophilus?*†

It is a treatise on archery, in which he advocates the use of the bow and arrow as a pastime.

103. Of what does his *Schoolmaster* treat?

It is a work on education, in many ways remarkable for its keenness and good sense.

104. Who was Sir Philip Sidney?

He was one of the most gifted young Englishmen of the reign of Elizabeth, as a soldier, statesman, and writer.

105. What is the nature of his work entitled *Arcadia?*

It is a tedious pastoral romance.

106. Which is Sidney's chief production?

The Defence of Poesie. On this work rests his reputation as an English classic prose-writer.

107. What is the *Defence of Poesie?*

The title suggests the nature of the work. The grim Puritans of that day attacked poetry. Sidney became its vindicator, and in his book, which is quite short, proves the high uses of poetry to man, and shows that it is the brightest flower in the field of literature.†

108. Who was Richard Hooker?

He was a minister of the Anglican Church, and one of the ablest advocates of that institution.

109. Which is his principal work?

The Laws of Ecclesiastical Polity.

110. What is the object of this treatise?

Its general object was to defend the English Pro-

---

* *Toxophilus* is from the Greek, and signifies *a lover of archery.*
† Sidney was killed at the battle of Zutphen, aged 32. In his own time he was in high repute as a poet, but is now little known as such.

LITERATURE OF THE SIXTEENTH CENTURY. 155

testant Church, its laws, rites, and ceremonies, from the attacks of the Puritans or Calvinists.

111. What are the merits of this work in a literary point of view?

It was an important addition to the English prose literature of the sixteenth century. The style is marked by much grace and dignity.

SUMMARY OF CHAPTER III., BOOK II.

1. The sixteenth century is the most eventful in English history. It carries us through the reigns of Henry VIII., Edward VI., Mary, and Elizabeth.

2. It was in this age that Luther began the so-called Reformation in Germany.

3. The corrupt, tyrannical Henry VIII. withdrew his kingdom from the Catholic Church, and proclaimed himself head of the English Church.

4. Elizabeth continued the work of irreligious change. Monasteries were destroyed, libraries burned, and Catholics persecuted like wild beasts.

5. The Reformation reached Scotland, and that kingdom became a prey to mobs and factions. Mary Queen of Scots fled to England, was cast into prison by Elizabeth, and, after eighteen years' imprisonment, was cruelly beheaded.

6. The chief agents that influenced the literature of the sixteenth century were: (*a*) the printing-press; (*b*) the mature condition of the English language, which had reached its full stature; (*c*) the study of the Latin and Greek classics and the poetry of Italy;

(*d*) the growth of schools and colleges and the spread of education; (*e*) the rise of the people in the scale of social and political importance; (*f*) the discovery of America and the circumnavigation of the globe.

7. The Reformation hindered the progress of sound thought and pure, healthy literature. At first it showed itself an enemy to art, science, literature, and education. English letters, learning, and civilization owe nothing to the so-called Reformation.

8. The English drama dates from the middle of the sixteenth century. It reached its highest eminence in the plays of Shakspeare.

9. *Gavin Douglas*, Catholic Bishop of Dunkeld, was the *first* to translate a Latin classic into English.

10. *William Dunbar* was the *greatest* of the old Scottish poets.

11. *Henry Howard*, Earl of Surrey, introduced the *sonnet* and *blank-verse* into English literature.

12. *Christopher Marlowe* wrote the *first historical play* in English.

13. *Robert Southwell*, S.J., was the *founder* of the modern religious poetry of England.

14. *Edmund Spenser* is one of the great poets of English literature. The *Fairy Queen* is his masterpiece.

15. *Sackville's Gorboduc* is the *first* English drama of any kind written in blank-verse.

16. *More's* best-known work is his *Utopia*.

17. He is the *first* person in British history distinguished by the faculty of public speaking, and remarkable for the successful employment of it in Parliament.

LITERATURE OF THE SIXTEENTH CENTURY.

18. More was the originator of *political romance.* He wrote the *earliest historical work* in our language, and was one of the great, heroic men of all time.

19. *Bishop Fisher's Sermons* may be considered the *first* productions of classical pulpit oratory in English.

20. Ascham's *Schoolmaster* is the *earliest* important work on education written in English.

21. *Sidney's Defence of Poesie* is the *earliest* work in the department of English literary criticism.

22. *Hooker* wrote English in a style of much elegance and dignity; but he has often been censured for the great length of his sentences.

23. *Bird's-eye view* of the *chief British writers and works* of the *sixteenth century:*

POETS:

Gavin Douglas, *The Palace of Honor.*
William Dunbar, *The Dance of the Seven Deadly Sins.*
Henry Howard, *Songs and Sonnets.*
Christopher Marlowe, *The Life of Edward II.*
Robert Southwell, *Poems.*
Thomas Sackville, *The Mirror of Magistrates.*
Edmund Spenser, *The Fairy Queen.*

PROSE WRITERS:

Sir Thomas More, *Utopia.*
Roger Ascham, *Toxophilus.*
Sir Philip Sidney, *The Defence of Poesie.*
Richard Hooker, *The Laws of Ecclesiastical Polity.*

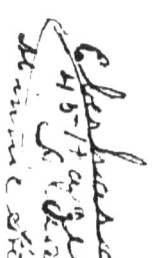

CHAPTER IV.

THE ENGLISH LITERATURE OF THE SEVENTEENTH CENTURY.

A.D. 1600 to 1700.

The Age of Shakspeare, Milton, and Dryden.

HISTORICAL INTRODUCTION.

1. Glances at Great Britain in the Seventeenth Century.—To Great Britain the seventeenth century was an age of political revolutions. The occupants of the English throne were *James I., Charles I., Charles II., James II.,* and *William III.* Of these, one lost his head at the block, and another was forced to fly from his kingdom.

In 1603 began the reign of James I., the son of Mary Queen of Scots, and the first of the Stuart line that ascended the throne of England. Since that day England and Scotland have had a common ruler. James was but a year old when crowned King of Scotland; and he was thirty-seven when he became monarch of England.

His arrogance and silly notions in relation to the royal power and prerogative added to the difficulties of his reign. The "divine right" of kings to govern without control was a theme ever in his mouth. He

LITERATURE OF SEVENTEENTH CENTURY. 159

fawned on favorites, and despised the nation at large. Even the terrible *Gunpowder Plot** neither opened his eyes nor added wisdom or justice to his character. The Catholics were persecuted with fiendish ferocity,† and unhappy Ireland bled and groaned under his infamous rule.

James was desirous to be thought learned; but he was at best a vain, loquacious pedagogue. He wrote books against witches and the use of tobacco. During his life, flatterers styled him the " British Solomon." The Duke of Sully, however, declared that the royal Scotchman was " the wisest fool in Europe." It was during this reign that the Protestant version of the Scriptures known as *King James's Bible* was translated and published.‡

On the death of James, in 1625, his son, Charles I., ascended the throne. He married a Catholic princess, but to please the Puritans he persecuted the Catholics. The penal laws were enforced with great cruelty. But other difficulties soon arose. Charles had imbibed the arbitrary principles of his father.

---

* The Gunpowder Plot was the scheme of a few desperate men to blow up the king and the two Houses of Parliament. It was discovered just in time to prevent the catastrophe. Two hogsheads and over thirty barrels of gunpowder had been stowed away in the cellar of the Parliament House. *Guy Fawkes* was the desperado appointed to fire the mine, and when asked by a Scottish nobleman why he had collected so much explosive material, the reply was. " To blow the Scottish beggars back to their native mountains."

† It was at the bidding of James I. that Catholics and all others who did not conform to the Anglican Protestant Church as by law established were excluded from the universities of Oxford and Cambridge. Laws were framed to that effect, and they were enforced till our own day. " An immortality of mischief," says Mackenzie, " seemed to have been conferred on that foolish king. Two centuries and a half after he was in his grave he had not yet ceased from troubling. His senseless and intolerant edicts still provoked strife among the English people."

‡ The translation was begun in 1607, and was completed and published in 1611. It was the work of forty-seven persons.

It has been remarked with some truth that

> "He never said a foolish thing,
> And never did a wise one."

Parliament refused to grant him the necessary supplies to carry on a war against France and Spain; and Charles resolved to rule without their aid and to levy money without their authority. Thus began a conflict that led to that most direful of national calamities—a civil war. Both the king and the parliament appealed to the sword. The royalists were named *Cavaliers;** while the parliamentary forces were called *Roundheads.*† The war raged for nearly five years. One battle followed another, until finally the royal standard went down at Naseby before the desperate charges of *Oliver Cromwell* and his famous *Ironsides.*‡ Charles surrendered himself to the Scottish army, by which he was basely delivered into the hands of the Parliament for the sum of $2,000,000. He was tried, condemned, and beheaded in 1649.

The moment the head of this royal victim fell on the scaffold at Whitehall, a proclamation was read in Cheapside, declaring it treason to give to any person the title of king without the authority of Parliament; and, at the same time, it was published that the supreme authority in the nation resided in the people's representatives. In a few days the House of Lords and the office of king were abolished. A republican form of government was established. The House

---

* They were so named on account of the gayety of their dress, manners, etc., as contrasted with the gloomy austerity of the Roundheads, or adherents of the Parliament.
† This nickname was given to the Puritans, or parliamentary party, because they were accustomed to wear their hair cut close to the head. They were so called in opposition to the Cavaliers, who wore their hair in long ringlets.
‡ A term applied to Cromwell's cavalry.

of Commons ordered a new *Great Seal* to be made, bearing the words, "On the first year of freedom, by God's blessing, restored, 1648." The king's statue in the Exchange was thrown down, and on the pedestal was inscribed, *Exit tyrannus, Regum ultimus*— the tyrant is gone, the last of the kings!

The people of Ireland and Scotland, however, were still faithful in their allegiance to the fallen monarch. Cromwell was appointed commander-in-chief to carry on the war against the Irish and Scottish royalists. He landed in Ireland. His course was marked by scenes of blood, butchery, and barbarous massacres; and the unfortunate country was speedily obliged to submit to his fanatical authority. He next directed his steps to Scotland, and, after several sanguinary conflicts, he routed the royalists, and completely established the rule of the Parliament.

Cromwell, the desperate fanatic and master-tyrant of his age, now wielded immense power. He dissolved the Long Parliament, and, after three months, assembled what is known as the *Barebones' Parliament.** It was composed of a body of out-and-out fanatics. It conferred the title of *Lord Protector of the Commonwealth of England* on Cromwell, clothed him with supreme authority, and was soon after dissolved. The Protector's rule, it must be said, advanced the military glory of England. Abroad, his fleets and armies were victorious; he obliged the Dutch to sue for peace, and he humbled the power of Spain. But the fanatical despot was far from happy. Well he knew that he was despised by the nation, when death called him away in 1658.

---

* So named from one of its members, *Praise-God Barebones*. He was a London leather-dealer.

In less than two years the Stuart line was restored in the person of Charles II., eldest son of Charles I.* The young king was welcomed with joy, but he proved to be one of the most worthless and arbitrary monarchs that had ever ruled England. He soon plunged into a life of licentiousness. His example exercised the most pernicious influence on the morals of the higher classes of his subjects; and his court became a school of vice in which the restraints of decency were laughed to scorn.

During this reign London was visited with a plague which carried off 90,000 of its inhabitants; and in the following year† occurred the great fire by which 13,200 houses in the metropolis were reduced to ashes. Wars and plots were numerous, and the Catholics were persecuted and calumniated with all the fury of insane fanaticism. One of the venerable victims was *Oliver Plunkett*, the saintly Archbishop of Armagh. When, however, the last hour of the weak and erring monarch arrived, he became a Catholic; and a good priest, at much risk, received him into the Church of ages, heard his confession, and gave the Holy Communion to the last of the Charles that occupied the throne of England.‡

---

* From the reign of Charles I. to the beginning of the reign of Charles II. was the great period of *pamphlet literature* in England. "Nearly 30,000 pamphlets," says Shepherd, "were published between the close of the year 1640 and the Restoration, 1660." They were the growth of strife and dissension.

† 1666.

‡ By law, the reconciliation of any person to the Catholic Church was an act of high treason. No priest could be privately introduced to the king for that purpose, while the room was crowded with lords, bishops, and medical attendants; and to remove them without a plausible reason could only provoke suspicion and inquiry. Having motioned the company to withdraw to the other end of the apartment, James—the Duke of York and the king's brother—knelt down by the pillow of the sick monarch, and asked if he might send for a Catholic priest. "For God's sake do!" was

As the late king died without leaving any legitimate children, he was succeeded by his brother, James II., in 1685. James was a Catholic. He "wished," says Cobbett, "to put an end to the penal code; he wished for general toleration; he issued a proclamation, suspending all penal laws relating to religion, and granting a general liberty of conscience to *all* his subjects. This was his offence. For this he and his family were set aside forever!"

Bigotry at once became alarmed. Six bishops of the Anglican Church sounded the tocsin of intolerance. As time passed the trouble increased. James became unpopular, and without being suspected, his bitter enemies prepared the kingdom for a general revolt. They secretly applied for aid to William, the Protestant Prince of Orange and son-in-law of James,* and offered him the throne.

There was little delay. In November, 1688, William sailed from Holland in pursuit of the English crown. The invader, in a few days, was joined by the greater part of the English army; and James suddenly found himself deserted, even by those who owed all to his bounty. Among others who left him in this hour of dark distress was his favorite daughter *Anne*, who secretly withdrew to join the standard of the man who had pushed himself into the dominions

---

the reply; but he immediately added, "Will it not expose you to danger?" James replied that he cared not for the danger; and, having despatched a trusty messenger in search of a priest, stated aloud that the king required all present to quit the apartment, with the exception of the Earl of Bath, Lord of the Bed-chamber, and the Earl of Feversham, Captain of the Guard. In a short time, Hudleston, a priest, was led through the queen's apartments to a private door on the right hand of the bed; and James introduced him to the king with these words: "Sir, this worthy man comes to save your soul."—*Lingard.*

* He was married to James's daughter, the Princess Mary.

of her father and was about to snatch the crown from his brow.

The unhappy king was unnerved by this ungrateful conduct, and exclaimed, "God help me! My own children have forsaken me in my utmost need." James and his queen fled to France. William and Mary were proclaimed sovereigns.* On the fatal banks of the Boyne James saw his last hopes vanish; and as we pass into the eighteenth century William III., an intruding Dutchman, sits securely on the throne of Alfred the Great.

2. REMARKS ON THE BRITISH LITERATURE OF THIS AGE.—The British literature of the seventeenth century reflects the eventful history of that age. Its chief representative names are SHAKSPEARE, JONSON, MASSINGER, MILTON, BUTLER, DRYDEN, BACON, CLARENDON, and WALTON.

The immortal genius of Shakspeare made him the poet "not of an age but of all time." Milton is the Puritan poet of the Commonwealth, and Clarendon is the royalist historian of the Great Rebellion. The contempt of the royalists for the Puritans was hearty, and it found full expression in Butler's *Hudibras.*

The gloomy morals and grim fanaticism of the Commonwealth, when the theatres were closed† and amusement branded as a crime, were succeeded by the unbridled license of Charles II. and his court. Nor does English letters fail to reflect the new condition of things. The most remarkable illustration of this is to be found in the works of John Dryden.

---

* It was then settled that the English sovereign *must* be a Protestant. Even in the present state of things, an English king or queen would forfeit the crown by becoming a Catholic.
† They were closed from 1643, when the Puritans became masters of London, until the Restoration in 1660.

Every great event of the time, social, political, and religious, is mirrored in his poems; while unhappily he panders in his plays to the moral degeneracy of the court and the nobility. But his last years were so redeeming, that we may well forget the errors of the Restoration dramatist in the glory of an old age grand and religious.

New religious sects, bigoted, jealous, and warring, sprung up like mushrooms, each loudly claiming liberty of conscience, and all united in hating and persecuting the unfortunate Catholics. The followers of the ancient faith were not to be tolerated, and thus, in the words of Arnold, they " became an obscure and persecuted minority, which for a hundred years almost disappears from the public gaze and from the page of history."*

But in spite of its revolutions, follies, and fanaticism, the seventeenth century was *the* great age of

---

* During the reign of Charles I. and the rule of diabolical fanaticism that followed, the Catholics lost nearly everything which had escaped the destroying hand of the Reformation. Anything bearing the marks of the Catholic religion—be it book, statue, or picture—was burned by the Puritans. "The scarcity of books concerning the Catholics in this country" (England), writes I. D'Israeli, "is owing to two circumstances; the destruction of Catholic books and documents by the pursuivants in the reign of Charles I., and the destruction of them by the Catholics themselves from the dread of the heavy penalties in which their mere possession involved their owners." An impious wretch named Dowsing placed himself at the head of a mob of image-breakers. He kept a diary. "At Sunbury," he grimly writes, "we brake down ten mighty great angels in glass. At Barham, brake down the twelve apostles in the chancel, and six superstitious pictures more there; and eight in the church—one a lamb with cross (†) on the back." At another place they destroyed "six hundred superstitious pictures, eight Holy Ghosts, and three of the Son." And thus this destroying fiend and his party passed over one hundred and fifty parishes. Well did the poet write:

"There might you see an impious clown
Breaking our Saviour's image down;
And there you might behold another
Tearing the picture of Christ's mother.'

English literature. The English language reached the full meridian of its splendor in the *Plays* of Shakspeare.* Bacon's *Essays* raised English prose to the pinnacle of condensation and beauty of expression. In *Paradise Lost* Milton gave us our greatest epic, and the genius of Dryden exhibited the riches, force, and flexibility of our speech in such a manner as to place him forever among the great masters of style.

LESSON I.

WILLIAM SHAKSPEARE.† DIED 1616.

Chief works: *Thirty-five Plays.*

1. Which is the greatest name in English literature?

William Shakspeare.

2. Where and when was he born?

At Stratford-on-Avon, England, in 1564. His parents were *John Shakspeare* and *Mary Arden.*

3. Do we know much about his life?

No; it is shrouded in obscurity.

4. State the chief facts which have come down to us in relation to Shakspeare's career.

He was educated at the grammar-school of his native place; married at the age of eighteen; went to London three years later; became an actor, playwriter, and part-owner of the Globe Theatre; and,

---

* Shakspeare wrote some of his *Plays* as early as 1592, but it is pretty well settled that all his great masterpieces—as *Hamlet, King Lear, Macbeth, Othello, Julius Cæsar*—were written between the year 1600 and his death in 1616.

† Variously has the name of the great dramatist been spelled. It is *Shakspeare* in the body of his will. He himself writes it two different ways—*Shakspeare* and *Shakspere.*

finally, retired to Stratford a few years before his death.* This, in brief, is the sum of all that is really known of Shakspeare's personal life.†

5. What is the date of his death?

1616.

6. Did Shakspeare before his death collect and publish his plays?

No; but some years after his death this was done by Heming and Condell, two of his professional friends.

7. How are his thirty-five *Plays* classed?

They are commonly classed according to their nature into *tragedies*, *comedies*, and *histories*.

8. How many of them are tragedies?

Eleven.

9. How many are comedies?

Fourteen.

10. How many are histories?

Ten.

---

* About the year 1610 he retired permanently to Stratford, though he continued to write plays for the company with which he was connected.—*Whipple.*

† Shakspeare, the recorded incidents of whose outward career were so few and trifling, lived a more various life—a life more crowded with ideas, passions, volitions, and events—than any potentate the world has ever seen. Compared with his experience, the experience of Alexander or Hannibal, of Cæsar or Napoleon, was narrow and one-sided. He had projected himself into almost all the varieties of human character, and, in imagination, had intensely realized and *lived* the life of each. From the throne of the monarch to the bench of the village alehouse, there were few positions in which he had not placed himself, and which he had not for a time identified with his own. No other man had ever seen nature and human life from so many points of view, for he had looked upon them through the eyes of *Master Slender* and *Hamlet*, of *Caliban* and *Othello*, of *Dogberry* and *Mark Antony*, of *Ancient Pistol* and *Julius Cæsar*, of *Mistress Tearsheet* and *Imogen*, of *Dame Quickly* and *Lady Macbeth*, of *Robin Goodfellow* and *Titania*, of *Hecate* and *Ariel*. . . . Capable of *being* all that he actually or imaginatively *sees*, he enters at will, and abandons at will, the passions that brand or blast other natures.—*Whipple.*

LESSON II.

SHAKSPEARE, CONTINUED.

11. Name the five great tragedies of Shakspeare.

Hamlet, Macbeth, Othello, King Lear, and *Romeo and Juliet.*

12. Mention some of his best comedies.

The Merchant of Venice, As You Like It, and *The Midsummer-Night's Dream.*

13. Name a few of the most remarkable of his historical plays.

Julius Cæsar, Richard the Third, Henry the Eighth, and *Coriolanus.**

14. Are the plays of Shakspeare well known to other nations?

They have been translated into every language of Europe and into some of the Asiatic tongues.

15. What, it may be asked, is the true secret of Shakspeare's power and universal fame?

His wonderful insight into human nature, the human soul, and the philosophy of life; his unrivalled power in the creation and delineation of character; the boundless reach of his exquisite imagination; and his magic mastery over language. He was poet, dramatist, moralist, and philosopher in one.†

---

* The above-named twelve plays show Shakspeare, perhaps, in his finest vein; but the student who would know him thoroughly must read him from cover to cover.

† He dissects the human mind in all its conditions. He displays its workings as it lives and throbs. He divines the secret impulses of all ages and characters—childhood, boyhood, manhood, girlhood, and womanhood; men of peace and men of war; clowns, nobles, and kings. His large heart was sympathetic with all, and even most so with the lowly and suffering; he shows us ourselves, and enables us to use that knowledge for our profit. All the vir-

16. What may be said of him as a word-painter?

When Shakspeare describes anything, you more than see it—you feel it too.

17. What can you say of his style?

In the art of writing well Shakspeare arrived at a perfection which places him above all other poets. It resembles no other style. But his language is most simple and natural. He had the happy gift of saying much in a few words, and his bright, pithy sentences often bend under a load of wit or wisdom.

18. Why is Shakspeare, perhaps, more frequently quoted than any other writer?

Because nearly every one of his pages sparkle with gems of thought, where some happy word or phrase conveys to us a whole train of ideas condensed, so to speak, into a single luminous point. Thus it is that writers and orators give point and dignity to their own periods by quoting Shakspeare.*

---

tues are held up to our imitation and praise, and all the vices are scourged and rendered odious in our sight. To read Shakspeare aright is of the nature of honest self-examination—that most difficult and most necessary of duties.—*Coppée.*

* In reading Shakspeare we feel pleasure in stumbling upon such phrases and sayings as "trumpet-tongued"; "single-blessedness"; "food for gunpowder"; "to the manner born"; "the live-long day"; "as firm as faith"; "the observed of all observers"; "to take arms against a sea of troubles"; "Brevity is the soul of wit"; "Be just, and fear not"; "Dressed in a little brief authority"; "Seeking the bubble reputation even in the cannon's mouth"; "The poet's eye in a fine frenzy rolling"; "Upon his brow shame is ashamed to sit"; "The undiscovered country from whose bourne no traveller returns"; "It is a custom more honored in the breach than the observance"; "Beggar that I am, I am poor even in thanks"; "The evil that men do lives after them"; "I am constant as the northern star"; "The valiant never taste of death but once"; "Cowards die many times before their deaths"; "This was the noblest Roman of them all."

"Poor Brutus, with himself at war,
Forgets the shows of love to other men."

"He who filches from me my good name,
Robs me of that which not enriches him,
And makes me poor indeed."

19. What did Shakspeare write besides his thirty-five plays?

One hundred and fifty-four sonnets and some poems of considerable length.

20. Is our language much indebted to Shakspeare?

It is; it may be said that he moulded the elements of English for the first time into one harmonious whole.*

21. What may be considered the chief defects of Shakspeare's plays?

The style has been criticised for occasional obscurity, flatness, and bombast; some passages are justly accused of immodest coarseness;† and the ending of some of the plots is hurried and imperfect.

22. Was Shakespeare a Catholic?

Nothing absolutely conclusive is known on this point, but it can be truly affirmed that in numberless passages of his plays he gives abundant proof that he

---

"There is a tide in the affairs of men,
Which, taken at the flood, leads on to fortune;
Omitted, all the voyage of their lives
Is bound in shallows and in miseries."

It has been said that many of the sayings of Shakspeare drop upon the mind "like a splendor out of heaven."

* There are three men in the annals of poetry who may be said to have created, or rather *fixed*, not merely the literature but also the language of their several countries. These three are *Homer*, *Dante*, and *Shakspeare*, and of the three the last is not the least.—*Hart*

† Shakspeare is often immodest but never sensual, as the learned Cardinal Newman remarks. We must not forget that he lived in an age of great coarseness and corruption. He held "the mirror up to nature"—or rather depraved nature—and it is not surprising that we see reflected in his bright and sparkling pages many a sad truth, over which the pure mind instinctively hurries. It remembers frail humanity. It is charitable. It is prudent. It looks up to heaven. It passes on without shock or fright. In comparison, however, with the other dramatists of his time, Shakspeare is remarkably pure.

held the doctrines and practices of the Catholic Church in tender and reverential regard.*

"He was the man who, of all modern and perhaps ancient poets, had the largest and most comprehensive soul."—*John Dryden.*
"I profess myself one of Shakspeare's enthusiastic admirers. His language is the purest and best, his verses the most flowing and rich; and as for his sentiments, it would be difficult without the command of his own language to characterize them. No other writer has ever given such periods of sententious wisdom."—*Cardinal Wiseman.*
"Shakspeare is, by the common consent of mankind, the greatest dramatist, and in the opinion of a large and growing number of critics the greatest writer, that the world has ever produced. His writings created an era in literature, and constitute of themselves a special and most important study."—*Dr. J. S. Hart.*
"The name of Shakspeare is the greatest in our literature. It is the greatest in all literature. No man ever came near him in the creative powers of the mind; no man ever had such strength, at once, and such variety of imagination."—*Henry Hallam.*
"A whole world is unfolded in the works of Shakspeare. He who has once comprehended this, and been penetrated with its spirit, will not easily allow the effect to be diminished by the form, or listen to the cavils of those who are incapable of understanding the import of what they would criticise. The form of Shakspeare's writings will rather appear to him good and excellent, because in it his spirit is expressed and clothed, as it were, in a convenient garment."—*F. Schlegel.*

---

* We know so very little about his personal life that, in any inquiry into his religious opinions, we are forced to fall back upon his works; and it is pretty certain that a careful perusal of his plays—always bearing in mind that they were penned in the barbarously intolerant reigns of Elizabeth and James I.—will leave little doubt as to Shakspeare's having been in his soul a sincere Catholic. In vain may we search his historical plays for a single passage containing a sneer or hostile reflection on the *doctrines* or *ceremonies* of the Catholic Church. It is true that he has few compliments for some of his high ecclesiastical personages. But though the Religious Orders were especially odious to the early Protestant reformers, Shakspeare invariably draws the characters of nuns and the regular clergy with a hand that seems both kind and Catholic. To his gifted mind grim Puritanism was a thing utterly repulsive. He raises the laugh at it in many a passage. In one place he makes a gay good-humored fellow say:

"Let me play the fool;
With mirth and laughter let old wrinkles come.
Why should a man whose blood is warm within,
Sit like his grandsire cut in alabaster?
There are a sort of men whose visages
Do cream and mantle like a standing pond.

LESSON III.

BEN JONSON. DIED 1637.

Chief works: *Forty-six Plays.**

23. Who was Ben Jonson?

He was one of the greatest of the English dramatists. Jonson is generally considered as second only to Shakspeare.

24. Give a short account of his early life.

It was rough and varied. The sturdy young fellow was by turns a school-boy, a hod-carrier, a soldier shouldering his pike, and a student at Cambridge. The frowns of fortune induced him to become an actor, and at the age of twenty-two he produced his first comedy.

25. What is the name of Jonson's first comedy, and what are its merits?

It is called *Every Man in his Humor*, and is commonly ranked among the best of his productions. Jonson, however, had little real fun, wit, or imagination, and the characters in his play pass before us more like shadows than live flesh-and-blood personages.

26. Which is the most remarkable character in *Every Man in his Humor?*

Captain Bobadil, a great coward and bouncing braggart.†

"And do a wilful stillness entertain,
With purpose to be dressed up in an opinion
Of wisdom, gravity, profound conceit;
As who should say, I am Sir Oracle;
And when I ope my lips, let no dog bark!"

* Two of these are tragedies, eleven are comedies, three are comical satires, one is a pastoral drama, and twenty-eight are masques or other court entertainments.

† "Bobadil, especially," says Whipple, "is one of Ben's master-

27. To what office was Jonson appointed in 1616—the year that Shakspeare died?

He was appointed poet-laureate.

28. Which are his finest comedies?

Every Man in his Humor, *Volpone*, and *The Alchemist*.

29. Name his two tragedies.

Catiline and *Sejanus*, which are founded on two of the darkest pages in Roman history.

30. Where was Jonson buried?

In Westminster Abbey, where the inscription on his tombstone—"*O Rare Ben Jonson*"—can be seen to this day.

31. How may Jonson's chief characteristics as a writer be summed up?

With much learning, little imagination, and a great deal of vanity, he was one of the most moral play-writers of his time, and, next to Shakspeare, the most original.

"His pieces are in general deficient in soul, in that nameless something which never ceases to attract and enchant us even because it is indefinable."—*A. W. Schlegel.*

"Jonson possessed all the learning that was wanting to Shakspeare, and wanted all the genius which the other possessed."—*Hume*

"He is 'Saxon' England in epitome—John Bull passing from a name into a man—a proud, strong, tough, solid, domineering individual, whose intellect and personality cannot be severed, even in thought, from his body and personal appearance."—*Whipple.*

---

pieces. He is the most colossal coward and braggart of the comic stage. He can swear by nothing less terrible than *by the body of Cæsar*, or *by the foot of Pharaoh*, when his oath is not something more terrific still, namely, *by my valor!* Every school-boy knows the celebrated passage in which the boasting Captain offers to settle the affairs of Europe by associating with himself twenty other Bobadils, as 'cunning in the fence' as himself, and challenging an army of 40,000 men, twenty at a time, and killing the whole in a certain number of days. Leaving out the cowardice, we may say there was something of Bobadil in Jonson himself."—*Literature of the Age of Elizabeth.*

LESSON IV.

PHILIP MASSINGER. DIED 1640.

Chief works: *Eighteen Plays* *

32. What is known of Mas inger's personal life?

Almost nothing, but that he was the son of a gentleman, that he studied for a year or two at Oxford, that he became a play-writer, and finally died in poverty and obscurity.†

33. How many of his plays do we possess?

Eighteen.

34. Which of Massinger's famous comedies still keeps the stage?

A New Way to Pay Old Debts; it keeps possession of the stage for the sake of the finely drawn character, *Sir Giles Overreach.*

35. What may be considered his chief tragedy?

The Virgin Martyr; it has telling situations, and was extremely popular in its day. The martyr is Dorothea, a Christian maiden of the age of Diocletian.

---

* Six tragedies, eight comedies, and four tragi-comedies. "He wrote *thirty-eight* plays," says Whipple, "twenty of which have perished. Eleven of them, in manuscript, were in the possession of a Mr. Warburton, whose cook, desirous of saving what she considered better paper, used them in the kindling of fires and the basting of turkeys, and would doubtless have treated the manuscript of the *Fairy Queen* and the *Novum Organum* in the same way had Providence seen fit to commit them to her master's custody."—*Literature of the Age of Elizabeth.*

† "His death and burial were in harmony with the loneliness of his life. We are told that, on the 16th of March, 1640, he went to bed seemingly in good health, and was found dead in the morning. In the parish register of the Church of St. Saviour's, under the date of March 20th, we read: '*Buried, Philip Massinger, a stranger.*' No stone indicates where in the churchyard he was laid."—*Whipple.*

36. What may be said of Massinger's style?
His style charms by its ease, clearness, dignity, elegance, and flexibility.*

"Massinger is by some critics ranked next after Shakspeare. Assuredly his skill in the representation of character is superior to that of any of the secondary dramatists except Jonson."--*Spalding.*
"The English drama never suffered a greater loss than in the havoc which time and negligence have committed among the works of Massinger; for of thirty-eight plays attributed to his pen, only eighteen have been preserved."--*Drake.*
"In expressing the dignity of virtue, and in showing greatness of soul rising superior to circumstance and fate, Massinger exhibits so peculiar a vigor and felicity that it is impossible not to conceive such delineations--in which the poet delighted--to be a reflection of his own proud and patient soul, and perhaps, too, but too true a memorial of ' the rich man's scorn, the proud man's contumely,' which he had himself undergone."--*Shaw.*

---

* In spite of their occasional coarseness—which is to be referred rather to the manners of the time than to the author—the plays of Massinger abound in noble passages like the following:

'When good men pursue
The path marked out by virtue, the blest saints
With joy look on it, and seraphic angels
Clap their celestial wings in heavenly plaudits.'

'As you have
A soul moulded from heaven, and do desire
To have it made a star there, make the means
Of your ascent to that celestial height
Virtue winged with brave action; they draw near
The nature and the essence of the gods
Who imitate their goodness.''

LESSON V.

JOHN MILTON. DIED 1674.

Chief works: (1) *Paradise Lost.*
(2) *Paradise Regained.*
(3) *Comus.*
(4) *Samson Agonistes.*
(5) *Ode on the Nativity.*
(6) *Lycidas.*
(7) *L'Allegro.*
(8) *Il Penseroso.*
} Poems.

(9) *Areopagitica.* } Prose.

37. Who was John Milton?

He was the greatest epic poet of English literature.

38. Give a brief account of his early life.

Young Milton was a native of London, and a handsome, studious boy, who grew up under Puritan influences.* He completed his studies at the University of Cambridge, and after some years made a tour through France and Italy.

39. What appointment did he receive under the iron rule of Cromwell?

That of Latin or Foreign Secretary.†

40. What became of Milton on the restoration of Charles II.?

The restoration brought gloom and terror to the house of the great Puritan poet. He hid himself for a time, and lived in retirement till his death in 1674.‡

41. What ode did Milton compose in his twenty-first year?

The magnificent *Ode on the Morning of Christ's Nativity.* It is the earliest of the great English odes, and ranks among the finest specimens of lyric poetry in our language.

---

* The poet's grandfather was a strict Catholic, but his father became a Protestant.
† Latin was then the language of diplomacy.
‡ Milton was totally blind for the last twenty years of his life.

42. What is the *Allegro?*

It is a poem of mirth, in which we see

"Sport that wrinkled Care derides,
And Laughter holding both his sides."

43. What is the nature of *Il Penseroso?*

It is a poetical tribute to Melancholy, represented as a

"Pensive nun devout and pure,
Sober, steadfast, and demure,
All in a robe of darkest grain,
Flowing with majestic train."

44. Are the *Allegro* and *Il Penseroso* popular poems?

These two gems are perhaps the best known and most appreciated of all Milton's works.

45. What is *Comus?*

Comus, though written as a *mask*,* is a noble poem in the form of a drama.† It exhibits the power and glory of Chastity.‡

46. What is *Lycidas?*

It is a poem on the loss of a friend named King.§

---

* A mask, or masque, is a dramatic performance written in a tragic style, without attention to rules of composition or probability, and introducing such characters that the actors must be masked.

† "Of Milton's early poems," says Henry Reid, "the most beautiful is the exquisite *Masque of Comus*, one of the last and loveliest radiations of the dramatic spirit, which seemed almost to live its life out in about half a century of English literature, beginning in the times of Queen Elizabeth, and ending in those of Charles I."— *Lectures on English Literature.*

‡ The following beautiful lines are often quoted:

"So dear to Heaven is saintly Chastity,
That, when a soul is sincerely so,
A thousand liveried angels lackey her,
Driving far off each thing of sin and guilt."

§ *Lycidas* was written to commemorate the death of a college friend, Mr. King, who was drowned on the passage from England to Ireland. But Milton's grief sets him thinking; and, in this remarkable poem, the monotone of a deep sorrow is replaced by the linked musings of a mind which, once set in motion by grief, pours forth abundantly the treasures of thought and imagination stored up within it.—*T. Arnold.*

Critics say that the enjoyment of *Lycidas* is a good test of a real feeling for what is peculiarly called poetry. It contains the oft-quoted line,

" To scorn delights, and live laborious days."

47. What is Milton's *Samson Agonistes?*

It is a drama constructed on the model of a Greek tragedy.

48. Was Milton a noted prose-writer?

He was; he left behind him eleven works, on various subjects, written in prose.

49. Which is usually considered his best work in prose?

The *Areopagitica*, an appeal for the freedom of the press.

LESSON VI.

MILTON, CONTINUED.

50. What celebrated epic has given Milton such an exalted rank in our literature?

His *Paradise Lost*, at which he labored seven years.*

51. How is the great poem divided?

It is divided into twelve books.†

---

* From 1658 to 1665. It had to wait two years for a publisher. "Milton's great poem," says Hart, "after its completion had to wait two years before it could find a publisher, and even then its way to fame was very slow. The whole amount received by him and his family from the copyright of it was only £28."

† There can scarcely be any doubt that, in the plan and details of his great epic, Milton received much aid from the poems of the venerable monk Cædmon. They were first printed in 1655, just *three years before* Milton began the composition of *Paradise Lost*. "Milton's Satan," says Taine, "already existed in Cædmon's as the picture exists in the sketch."

52. Of what does the first book treat?

Book first treats briefly of the fall of man and the loss of paradise; the evil power that had led him to disobey the Almighty; and the revolt and overthrow of Satan and his rebel angels.*

53. What do the third and fourth books describe?

They describe the steps by which Satan proceeded on his mission to tempt our first parents.

54. In which book are Adam and Eve first introduced?

In the fourth book.

55. What takes up a great part of the fifth, sixth, and seventh books?

The story of the war in heaven between the good and the bad angels, the overthrow and expulsion of the wicked spirits, and the creation of the earth and of Adam and Eve. All this is related to Adam by the archangel Raphael.

56. What does the ninth book relate?

It contains an account of the transgression of our first parents by eating the forbidden fruit.

"Earth felt the wound, and Nature from her seat,
Sighing, through all her works gave signs of woe
That all was lost."

57. What do we find in the eleventh and twelfth books?

The last two books are chiefly taken up with the recital of the future fortunes of the human race, which is related to Adam by Michael the archangel.

---

* It is in the first book that Milton describes hell, which he makes a place curiously vast and vague:
"A dungeon horrible on all sides round,
As one great furnace, flamed; yet from those flames
No light, but rather darkness visible
Served only to discover sights of woe,
Regions of sorrow—doleful shades."

58. How does the poem end?
With the expulsion of our first parents from paradise.
"Some natural tears they dropt, but wiped them soon;
The world was all before them, where to choose
Their place of rest, and Providence their guide:
They, hand in hand, with wandering steps and slow
Through Eden took their solitary way." *

59. Considered from a religious standpoint, what may be said of *Paradise Lost?*
Its character, in a religious point of view, is very questionable for two reasons: (1) The false picture of Satan presented to us by Milton. Satan seems to be the hero of the poem, and he certainly does not pass before us as the vile ruler of hell and hateful spirit of wickedness.† (2) Milton lacked due reverence in handling the sacred mysteries of religion, and especially the Divine Nature.‡

---

* To be understood, Milton's *Paradise Lost* must be read. No brief explanation can assist the student much in comprehending the great poem.
† Milton thus describes Satan, when marshalling the hosts of hell:
"He, above the rest
In shape and gesture proudly eminent,
Stood like a tower: his form had not yet lost
All its original brightness, nor appeared
Less than archangel ruined, and the excess
Of glory obscured; as when the sun new risen
Looks through the horizontal misty air,
Shorn of his beams; or from behind the moon,
In dim eclipse, disastrous twilight sheds
On half the nations, and with fear of change
Perplexes monarchs. Darkened so yet shone
Above them all the archangel."

This may be sublime, but it is a sublimity that owes little to truth. "The finest thing," writes Taine, "in connection with this paradise is hell; and in this history of God the chief part is taken by the devil. The ridiculous devil of the Middle Ages, a dirty jester, a petty and mischievous ape, band-leader to a rabble of old women, has become a giant and a hero. Like a conquered and vanished Cromwell, he remains admired and obeyed by those whom he has drawn into the abyss."
‡ "The dialogues in heaven," says Thomas Arnold, "to say nothing of the undisguised Arianism which disfigures them, are either

60. What may be said of the *unity* of the poem, and the manner in which it is worked out?

Paradise Lost forms one connected whole, and it is worked out with great care and vigor.

61. Is the language of *Paradise Lost* worthy of high praise?

It is often rough, harsh, and sometimes ungrammatical, but in many passages it rolls along with unsurpassed splendor and sublimity.

62. But aside from all its imperfections, what must be said of the merits of the poem?

It is the greatest epic in English literature, and one of the three great epics of all time.

63. What did Milton write at the suggestion of a friend who remarked, that as he had written of Paradise Lost, what had he t say of Paradise Found?

He wrote *Paradise Regained*, an epic poem in four books. Though much inferior to *Paradise Lost*, it is superior to any epic that has since made its appearance.

"Milton is as great a writer in prose as in verse. Prose conferred celebrity on him during his life, poetry after his death; but the renown of the prose-writer is lost in the glory of the poet."—*Chateaubriand.*

"Three poets in three distant ages born,
Greece, Italy, and England did adorn:
The first * in loftiness of thought surpassed;
The next † in majesty; in both the last.‡
The force of nature could no further go—
To make a third she joined the other two."
                                    Dryden.

"*Paradise Lost* partakes in all those difficulties and defects which, as I have already said, attend all Christian poems which attempt to make the mysteries of religion the subjects of their fic-

painful or simply absurd, according as one regards them seriously or not."

"Milton," says Chateaubriand, "never speaks of the Trinity. The Son, according to him, is not begotten from eternity. The poet even places His creation after that of the angels. Milton is Arian, if he is anything."

* Homer.   † Dante.   ‡ Milton.

tion. It is strange that Milton did not observe that the loss of paradise forms in itself no complete whole, but is only the first act of the great Christian history of man, wherein the *Creation*, the *Fall*, and the *Redemption* are all equally necessary parts of one mighty drama. It is true that he sought afterwards to remove this main defect by the addition of the *Paradise Regained;* but this poem is too insignificant in its purpose and size to be worthy of forming the keystone to the great work. When compared with the Catholic poets, *Dante* and *Tasso*, who were his models, Milton, as a Protestant, labored under considerable disadvantages by being entirely denied the use of a great many symbolical representations, histories, and traditions, which were in their hands the most graceful ornaments of Christian poetry. He was sensible of this, and attempted to make amends for the defect by adopting fables and allegories out of the *Koran* and the *Talmud*, such as are extremely unfit for the use of a serious Christian poet. The excellence of his epic work consists, therefore, not in the plan of the whole, so much as in particular beauties and passages, and, in general, in the perfection of the high language of poetry."—*F. Schlegel.*

LESSON VII.

SAMUEL BUTLER. DIED 1680.

Chief work: *Hudibras.*

64. Who was Samuel Butler?

He was a humorous writer of great celebrity.

65. What do you know of his early life?

He was the son of a farmer in Worcestershire, England; received his education at a grammar-school; and was knocked about from one employment to another, so that by his very misfortunes he acquired that rare and varied knowledge of human life which is so admirably displayed in his *Hudibras.*

66. When was *Hudibras* published?

In 1663, when Butler was over fifty years of age.*

67. What was the object of *Hudibras?*

The object of this poem was to ridicule the Puritans.

---

* *Hudibras* was published in three parts—the first in 1663, the second in 1664, and the third in 1678.

68. Who are the chief characters in this poem?

*Hudibras,** a fanatical Presbyterian justice of the peace, from whom the poem takes its name, and his squire, *Ralph*, a cross-grained, dogmatic fellow.

69. Give some idea of the plot in *Hudibras*.

Hudibras and his man Ralph sally forth to correct abuses, and especially to enforce the observance of the oppressive laws lately made by the Rump Parliament against the sports and amusements of the people. Their ridiculous appearance and adventures are given in detail. The plot, however, is rambling and disconnected, but Butler contrives to go over the whole ground of English history in his matchless burlesque.†

70. Mention the divisions, metre, and length of *Hudibras*.

The poem is divided into three parts, each containing three cantos. It is written in eight-syllable rhyming couplets, and is about 11,000 lines in length.‡

---

* The title of the poem, which is also the name of its hero, is taken from the old romances of chivalry, *Sir Hugh de Bras* being the appellation of one of the knights—an Englishman, too, according to the legend—of Arthur's fabulous Round Table.—*Shaw*.

† Butler thus describes the learning of Hudibras:

" He was in logic a great critic,
Profoundly skilled in analytic;
He could distinguish and divide
A hair 'twixt south and southwest side;
On either which he would dispute,
Confute, change hands, and still confute;
He'd undertake to prove by force
Of argument a man's no horse;
He'd prove a buzzard is no fowl,
And that a lord may be an owl —
A calf, an alderman—a goose, a justice—
And rooks, committeemen and trustees.
He'd run in debt by disputation,
And pay with ratiocination;
And this by syllogism, true
In mood and figure, he would do."

‡ *Hudibras* was doubtless suggested by the famous Spanish novel of *Don Quixote*.

71. What are the merits of Hudibras as a burlesque poem? It is considered the best burlesque poem in the English language, but in our day few persons have the patience to read it through.

72. What was the end of the unhappy Butler? After living in poverty and obscurity, he died in a wretched lodging in London. He was even indebted to the charity of a friend for a grave in the churchyard, but some time after his death a monument was erected in his honor.*

"*Hudibras* is the very prince of *burlesques;* it stands alone of its kind, and still retains its popularity."—*Coppée.*

"The political importance of the poem was great. It turned the laugh against those terrible Puritans, a handful of whom had so long held the nation down, and defeated more effectually than cannon-balls or arguments could have done 'the stubborn crew of errant saints'—

> 'Who build their faith upon
> The holy text of pike and gun,
> Decide all controversies by
> Infallible artillery,
> And prove their doctrine orthodox
> By apostolic blows and knocks.'"

T. Arnold.

---

* It is said that this sadly slow recognition of Butler's merit and genius gave origin to one of the keenest epigrams in the English language:

> "Whilst Butler, needy wretch, was yet alive,
> No generous patron would a dinner give:
> See him, when starved to death and turned to dust,
> Presented with a monumental bust.
> The poet's fate is here in emblem shown—
> *He asked for bread, and he received a stone.*"

LESSON VIII.

JOHN DRYDEN. DIED 1700.

Chief works: (1) *Ode in Honor of St. Cecilia's Day.*
(2) *Absalom and Achitophel.*
(3) *The Hind and Panther.*
(4) *Essay on Dramatic Poetry.*
(5) *Translation of Virgil's Æneid.*
(6) *Twenty eight Plays.*

73. Who was John Dryden?

He was the most prominent figure in the literary history of the latter part of the seventeenth century.

74. Give a short account of his early life.

He belonged to an ancient English family, grew up to manhood under Puritan influences, completed his education at the University of Cambridge, taking the degree of M.A., and did not write anything remarkable till after the age of thirty.

75. What branch of literature did Dryden first cultivate as a means of livelihood?

The drama.

76. How many plays did he write, and what can you say of them?

Dryden produced twenty-eight plays.* They contain some excellent passages here and there, but are all stained with immorality.

77. What office of honor was conferred upon him in 1670?

He was appointed poet-laureate.

78. What famous poem did he write in 1687, after becoming a Catholic?

The Hind and Panther.

---

* *Twelve* of these were tragedies, *four* tragi-comedies, *eight* comedies, *three* operas, and *one* a masque. Of all Dryden's plays, *Don Sebastian* and *The Conquest of Granada* are the finest.

79. Is the *Hind and Panther* a long poem, and what is its nature?

The *Hind and Panther* is in three books, making in all about 2000 lines in length. It is a controversial poem in which two animals—the Hind and the Panther—are represented as engaged in a lengthy argument concerning the churches which they symbolize. The Catholic Church is represented by a "milk-white Hind," * and the Anglican Church by a "spotted Panther."†

80. What is your opinion of the merits of this singular poem?

The *Hind and Panther* is a remarkable union of wit, logic, and poetry. It is the greatest controversial poem in English, or perhaps in any language. Hallam says "it is the energy of Bossuet in verse."

81. What happened to Dryden at the Revolution?

He was dismissed from his office of poet-laureate, and thus, in old age, was thrown on his own resources.

82. What can you say of the last years of Dryden's life?

They were his purest, brightest, and most happy

---

* "A milk-white *Hind*, immortal and unchanged,
Fed on the lawns, and in the forest ranged;
Without unspotted, innocent within,
She feared no danger, for she knew no sin."

† "The *Panther*, sure the noblest, next the Hind,
And fairest creature of the spotted kind;
Oh, could her inborn stains be washed away,
She were too good to be a beast of prey!"

The various Protestant sects play their parts as hares, boars, bears, wolves, and other animals. The Calvinists are wolves:

"More haughty than the rest, the wolfish race
Appears, with belly gaunt and famished face—
Never was so deformed a beast of grace.
His ragged tail betwixt his legs he wears,
Close-clapped for shame, but his rough crest he rears,
And pricks up his predestinating ears!"

LITERATURE OF SEVENTEENTH CENTURY. 187

years. He was a good, faithful Catholic.* His mind grew to the last; and the vigor of his intellect enabled him to make head against the spite of fortune.
83. When did he die?
In the year 1700.
84. What is *Absalom and Achitophel?*
It is the most perfect and powerful satirical poem in our language.†
85. What is the *Essay on Dramatic Poetry?*
It is the work by which Dryden is chiefly known

---

* He educated his two sons in the true faith. One of them entered a Religious Order, and the other was usher of the Papal Palace under Pope Clement XI. Writing to them both in 1697, Dryden says: "I do not flatter myself with any manner of hopes, but to do my duty and suffer for God's sake, being assured beforehand never to be rewarded, even though the times should alter. . . . Remember me to poor Harry, whose prayers I earnestly desire. . . . I never can repent of my constancy, since I am thoroughly persuaded of the justice of the cause for which I suffer."

† "The occasion of the satire," says Arnold, " was furnished by a plot, matured by the busy brain of Shaftesbury, for placing on the throne at the king's death his natural son, the Duke of Monmouth, to the exclusion of his brother, the Duke of York. The story of Absalom's rebellion supplied a parallel, singularly close in some respects, of which Dryden availed himself to the utmost. Absalom is the Duke of Monmouth; Achitophel, his crafty adviser. is the Earl of Shaftesbury; David stands for Charles II.; Zimri for the Duke of Buckingham, etc."

Shaftesbury is thus described:

"Of these the false *Achitophel* was first,
A name to all succeeding ages cursed;
For close designs and crooked counsels fit,
Sagacious, bold, and turbulent of wit,
Restless, unfixed in principles and place,
In power unpleased, impatient of disgrace—
A fiery soul which, working out its way,
Fretted the pygmy body to decay,
And o'erinformed its tenement of clay."

Buckingham (*Zimri*) is thus described:

" A man so various that he seemed to be
Not one, but all mankind's epitome:
Stiff in opinions, always in the wrong—
Was everything by starts and nothing long;
But in the course of one revolving moon,
Was chemist, fiddler, statesman, and buffoon."

as a prose-writer, and is the earliest attempt in our language to systematize the laws of poetry.

86. What can you say of *Alexander's Feast, an Ode in Honor of St. Cecilia's Day?*

This famous *Ode* is a tribute of Dryden's devotion to the beautiful St. Cecilia, patroness of music, and is one of the very finest lyrics in the English language. It is, indeed, a masterpiece of art and rapture.

87. Which is the best known of Dryden's translations?

The *Æneid* of Virgil, which is rendered into English verse.*

"The matchless prose of Dryden is rich, various, natural, animated, pointed, lending itself to the logical as well as the narrative and pcturesque—never balking, never cloying, never wearying. Nothing can surpass Dryden."—*Brougham.*

"Without either creative imagination or any power of pathos, he is in argument, in satire, and in declamatory magnificence the greatest of our poets. His poetry, indeed, is not the highest kind of poetry, but in that kind he stands unrivalled and unapproached."—*Craik.*

"If I could be guilty of the absurdity of recommending to a young man any author on whom to form his style, I should tell him that, next to having something that will not stay unsaid, he could find no safer guide than Dryden."—*Lowell.*

---

* We string together a few of the many pithy sayings that dropped from Dryden's pen:

1 "The greatest argument for love is love."
2 "Few know the value of life before it is past."
3 "Forgiveness to the injured does belong.
   But they ne'er pardon who have done the wrong."
4 "Men are but children of a larger growth."
5 "That bad thing, gold, buys all good things."
6 "The cause of love can never be assigned;
   'Tis in no face, but in the lover's mind."

LESSON IX.

LORD BACON. DIED 1626.

Chief works: (1) *Essays.*
(2) *Advancement of Learning.*
(3) *Instauratio Magna.* (In Latin.)

88. Who was Lord Bacon?

He was a celebrated English prose-writer, philosopher, and statesman.

89. Give a brief account of his early life.

Francis Bacon was born at London in the first years of the reign of Elizabeth, was educated at Cambridge, studied law, and rose rapidly in his profession.

90. What high position did he finally reach under King James I.?

That of Lord High Chancellor of England.

91. How did he dishonor his exalted office, and what was the result?

He received bribes and gave false judgments for money. Being impeached and convicted, he was sentenced to pay over $200,000, and to be imprisoned in the Tower during the king's pleasure.*

92. How did the degraded chancellor spend the last years of his life?

Chiefly with his books in the retirement of the country. Bacon died of a fever in 1626, and thus passed away what Pope styled " the wisest, brightest, meanest of mankind."†

---

* King James remitted the fine, and set Bacon free in two days.
† The story of his death is curious. Driving in his carriage one snowy day, the thought struck him that flesh might be preserved as well by snow as by salt. At once he stopped, went into a cottage by the road, bought a fowl, and with his own hands stuffed it full of snow. Feeling chilly and too unwell to go home, he went to the house of the Earl of Arundel, which was near. There he was

93. Which is Lord Bacon's best known and most popular work?

His *Essays*.

94. How many Essays are there, and over what kind of subjects do they range?

The *Essays* are fifty-eight in number, and, to use Bacon's own words, they touch on subjects that " come home to men's business and bosoms." *

95. What may be said of the value and style of Bacon's Essays?

They contain much that is wise, suggestive, and practical. As to style, they combine the greatest brevity with the greatest beauty of expression.†

---

put into a damp bed; fever ensued; and in a few days he was no more.—*Collier*.

* Bacon's *Essays* were first published in 1597, and were but ten in number. He retouched them and added to their number at various times. The last edition, issued under his supervision, appeared in 1625. It contained 58 Essays. It may be interesting to note briefly some changes in English grammar, spelling, and punctuation since the days of Bacon—about two centuries and a half ago. Our remarks are based on the *last* edition of his *Essays*.

(1) He writes nearly every noun and verb of importance with a capital; as, " It is Heaven upon Earth to have a Mans Minde Move in Charitie, Rest in Providence, and Turne upon the Poles of Truth."

(2) He writes connectives immediately following colons and semicolons with capitals; as, " In taking Revenge, a Man is but even with his Enemy; But in passing it over, he is superior: For it is a Princes part to Pardon."

(3) It will be noticed in the two examples just given that Bacon did not use the apostrophe (') to mark the possessive case.

(4) The use of *a* instead of *an* before words beginning with *h* was not at all uniform in Bacon's time. He writes " an hill," " an habit," " an high speech."

(5) He sometimes makes use of expressions that would not be sanctioned by the English grammars of our day; as, " between them two," " sixteene foot."

(6) From the following samples of Bacon's spelling, the student will notice that many changes, such as dropping the *final e*, has taken place in English orthography since the seventeenth century: *daye*, *minde*, *poore*, *gor*, *hee*, *sinne*, *selfe*, *foole*, *bloud* (blood), *limme* (limb), *shal*, *troth* (truth), *alwaies* (always), *fift* (fifth), *sixt* (sixth), etc.

† We give a few sayings from his *Essays*:

" God never wrought a miracle to convince atheists, because His ordinary works convince it "; " A little philosophy inclines man's

96. Of what does the *Advancement of Learning* treat?
It takes a survey of the whole field of human knowledge with the object of showing its actual state, and of noting omissions and deficiencies.

97. On what work do s Bacon's fame as a philosopher chiefly rest?
On his *Instauratio Magna*, or Great Restoration. It is written in Latin, and consists of six parts, some of which are unfinished.

"Bacon's *Essays* show him to be the greatest master of English prose in his day, and to have had a deep insight into human nature."—*Coppée*.

"He had the sound, distinct, comprehensive knowledge of Aristotle, with all the beautiful lights, graces, and embellishments of Cicero."—*Addison*.

"Bacon is misunderstood by two classes of men. One regards him as the creator of a new and previously unknown method, to which modern science is indebted for all its triumphs. This is an impossibility. He could not change the intellect. He could not give man another faculty distinct from those he already possessed. Intelligence works now exactly as it worked prior to my Lord Bacon. The sum and substance of his philosophy is this: 'Leave scholastic disputations. You have talked enough over words. Turn to things. Interpret nature. Experiment. Be careful of the biases of your mind. Be not over-hasty in your inferences. Look to facts. Wait. Read the lessons of nature as it is, and not as you think it ought to be.' This simple piece of advice constitutes his title to immortality and our gratitude. And though it is a good one, there is nothing in it that had not at all times occurred to the careful man in the experiences of his every-day life. Bacon added no real truth to any of the sciences. He enforced his views generally by the crudest facts and by childish illustrations. He invented no new method. He only called attention to that which men should follow in investigating the laws of nature."—*Brother Azarias*.

---

mind to atheism; but depth in philosophy brings men's minds about to religion"; "There is nothing makes a man suspect much, more than to know little"; "Discretion of speech is more than eloquence"; "Reading makes a full man, conference a ready man, and writing an exact man."

LESSON X.

EDWARD HYDE, EARL OF CLARENDON. DIED 1673.
History of the Great Rebellion.

ISAAC WALTON. DIED 1683.
The Complete Angler.

98. Who was Edward Hyde, Earl of Clarendon?

He was an eminent English writer and statesman of the time of Charles I. and Charles II.

99. After many ups and downs in life, what position did he finally reach?

That of Lord High Chancellor of England, and for seven years he was the ruling spirit of English politics.*

100. What was his end?

The nation grew to hate him, he lost the royal favor, fled from England, and died in exile.

101. What is Clarendon's chief literary production?

The *History of the Great Rebellion*, that is of the civil war connected with the expulsion and restoration of the Stuarts.†

102. What is the sadly suggestive story of this famous book?

Clarendon began it in exile as the faithful servant

---

* Forming the door-posts of a stable-yard, there stand, or stood a short time since, two old defaced Corinthian pillars, chipped, weather-stained, drab-painted, and bearing upon their faded acanthus crowns the sign-board of the livery stables. Ostlers lounge and smoke there; passers-by give no heed to the poor relics of a dead grandeur; and the brown London mud bespatters them pitilessly from capital to base, as rattling wheels jolt past over the uneven pavement. These pillars are all that remain of a splendid palace which was reared upon that site by the famous Edward Hyde, Earl of Clarendon and Lord High Chancellor of England.—*Collier.*

† It is a large work usually printed in 6 or 7 vols. 8vo.

of a dethroned prince; and many years after he ended it in exile as the cast-off servant of an ungrateful monarch.*

103. What may be said of the style of this work?

The style is offhand and careless, and is rather that of a speaker than of a writer.

104. What is the chief merit of the *History of the Great Rebellion?*

It is an invaluable key to the knowledge of English life during the Rebellion, and just after the Restoration.†

105. In what does Clarendon especially excel?

As a great painter of character. His book abounds in minute and complete descriptions of public men.

106. What are the shortcomings of this *History?*

It is neither impartial nor entirely trustworthy. Clarendon was a warm royalist and a bitter Protestant, and both his political opponents and the much-persecuted Catholics get small justice at his hands.

107. Who was Isaac Walton?

He was an English linen-draper who, after retiring from business, wielded both pen and fishing-rod for many a year with equal love and skill.

108. Which is his best known and most popular work?

The Complete Angler, a pleasant book that still finds many readers.

---

* Clarendon was the companion of Charles II. in exile, and began his famous *History* in 1646; when Charles returned to England and mounted the English throne, he made him his Prime Minister, and the book remained unfinished till the author's second and last exile.

† " A checkered reputation on the page of history, and two old pillars in Piccadilly," says Collier, " might have been all that remained of the great lawyer's life-work, had nót his brilliant pen raised a monument of eloquence, imperishable while the English language lives."

17

Summary of Chapter IV., Book II.

1. Five monarchs—*James I., Charles I., Charles II., James II.,* and *William III.*—reigned during the seventeenth century. It was an age of changes and political revolutions.

2. *Charles I.* was beheaded, and the Commonwealth established, with *Cromwell* as Lord Protector.

3. Puritanism ruled during the Commonwealth.

4. Monarchy and the Stuart line were restored in 1660. This is called the *Restoration*.

5. *James II.* was forced to fly from his kingdom, and *William Prince of Orange*, a foreigner, was placed on the throne, 1689.

6. The *Penal Laws* were enforced, and the Catholics cruelly persecuted.

7. The seventeenth century was the golden age of English literature.

8. *Bird's-eye view of the chief British writers and works of the seventeenth century:*

POETS AND DRAMATISTS:

William Shakspeare,* *Hamlet.*
Ben Jonson, *Every Man in His Humor.*
Philip Massinger, *A New Way to Pay Old Debts.*
John Milton,† *Paradise Lost.*
Samuel Butler, *Hudibras.*
John Dryden, *Absalom and Achitophel.*

---

* It is stated that Shakspeare uses about 15,000 words, or, perhaps *one third* of the whole English vocabulary of the seventeenth century.
† Milton employs about 8000 words.

LITERATURE OF SEVENTEENTH CENTURY. 195

PROSE-WRITERS:

Lord Bacon, *Essays*.*
Lord Clarendon, *History of the Great Rebellion*.
Isaac Walton, *The Complete Angler*.

For the other writers of the seventeenth century most worthy of mention—namely, *Edmund Waller, Abraham Cowley, Richard Crawshaw, Sir William Davenant, Sir Walter Raleigh, Sir Thomas Browne, M.D., Jeremy Taylor, D.D., John Bunyan,* and *John Locke*—see the SHORT DICTIONARY at the close of the volume.

---

* The *Essays* may be considered Bacon's chief contribution to *English literature*, though not his chief contribution to *science* and *philosophy*.

CHAPTER V.

THE BRITISH LITERATURE OF THE EIGHTEENTH CENTURY.

A.D. 1700 to 1800.

THE AGE OF POPE, ADDISON, AND JOHNSON.

HISTORICAL INTRODUCTION.

1. GREAT BRITAIN IN THE EIGHTEENTH CENTURY. —For England the eighteenth century was a period of comparative repose and internal stability, though she engaged in fierce conflicts both in Europe and America. Four sovereigns reigned—*Anne, George I., George II.*, and *George III.*

Queen Anne, the undutiful daughter of James II., succeeded to the throne on the death of William III. in 1702. The famous fortress of Gibraltar was captured,* and the victories of *Marlborough* over the French increas d the glory and prestige of England. But the greatest event of this reign was the *union* of England and Scotland. This measure was carried by threats and bribery in 1707, and the two countries were united under the title of GREAT BRITAIN.

Queen Anne died 1714, and George, the *first* British sovereign of the *House of Brunswick*, a dull man, destitute of wit or wisdom, grasped the reins

---

* By an English fleet under Rooke and Shovel, in 1704.

of government. His reign was far from brilliant. It was chiefly marked by an unsuccessful insurrection in Scotland in favor of the son of James II., and the wild commercial delusion known as the *South Sea Bubble*. George I. "was an unamiable man who could hardly speak the language of the people he ruled, who quarrelled with his wife and his son, was of gross tastes, and naturally preferred his fatherland to the home of his adoption."

He was succeeded in 1727 by his son George II., whose reign was made notable by several military enterprises that have passed into general history. In the contest known as the war of the *Austrian Succession*, England took the side of *Maria Teresa*. The French were defeated at Dettingen; but, soon after, the English got severely punished at Fontenoy. This last victory was gained by the brilliant charge of the *Irish Brigade*.

"'Push on my Household Cavalry!' King Louis madly cried;
To death they rush, but rude their shock—not unrevenged they died.
On through the camp the column* trod; King Louis turns his rein.
'Not yet, my liege,' Saxe† interposed; '*the Irish yet remain.*'
And Fontenoy, famed Fontenoy, had been a Waterloo,
Were not these exiles ready then, fresh, vehement, and true."

Prince Charles Edward, the grandson of James II., made a last effort to regain the throne of his ancestors. Landing in Scotland, he placed himself at the head of an army, and gained the battle of Prestonpans. But brief were his successes. The famous battle of Culloden was fought in 1746, and Charles was signally defeated by the royal forces under the Duke of Cumberland. This gave the final blow to

---

* A column of 6000 English veterans.
† Marshal Saxe, the commander-in-chief of the French forces.

17*

his hopes, and, after many adventures,* he escaped to France.

It was in 1752 that the *Calendar*, as corrected by *Pope Gregory XIII.* in 1582, was adopted by act of Parliament. At first England would not accept the ten days' correction. Rather than agree with the Pope, that bigoted nation stupidly fought against the sun and stars for nearly two hundred years.

In 1755 a new conflict broke out between France and England. It is known as the *Seven Years' War.* It arose in consequence of disputes which took place on the subject of the boundary line of their North American colonies. For several years the genius of Montcalm brought disaster to British arms; but the victory gained by Wolfe on the Plains of Abraham in 1759 added *Canada* to the possessions of England.†

George III., the first English-born sovereign of the House of Brunswick, came to the throne in 1760. Nine years later appeared the famous *Letters of Junius.*‡ A course of unjust and oppressive measures

---

* £30,000 was offered for his capture.
† Canada was ceded to England by the treaty of Paris, 1763.
‡ These *Letters* appeared in the *Public Advertiser* of London. The first is dated January 21, 1769, and the last January 21, 1772. They number 69, the majority of them being signed "Junius." The letters are addressed to various personages, high and low; but it is especially the Duke of Grafton and his colleagues that Junius attacks with cutting satire and merciless severity. The Duke was Premier of England, and to him eleven of the letters are addressed. The thirty-fifth letter was addressed to the king. It concludes with these bold words: "The prince who imitates their (the Stuarts) conduct should be warned by their example; and, while he plumes himself upon the security of his title to the crown, should remember that as it was acquired by one revolution it may be lost by another."

The *Letters of Junius* hold the rank of a classic in English literature. But who was Junius? It is now commonly agreed that Junius was Sir Philip Francis. Still, these letters have been attributed to *forty* different persons, and over *one hundred* books have been written on the subject of their authorship.

LITERATURE OF EIGHTEENTH CENTURY. 199

towards the British possessions in North America aroused the hardy colonists. They were driven into rebellion. On the 4th of July, 1776, the "Declaration of Independence" was announced to the world. Two years later France acknowledged the independence of the United States, and became the ally of the Americans; and the obstinate tyrant, George III., was compelled to acknowledge American independence in 1783. The last events worthy of note in this century were the *French Revolution* and the *Irish Rebellion*.*

2. REMARKS ON THE LITERATURE OF THE EIGHTEENTH CENTURY.—The seventeenth century was a great creative period in English letters, but the eighteenth brings us to an age with less creation and more criticism. This was to be expected. "Criticism," as Bascom well remarks, "follows invention, completes it, and makes its gains permanent in rules and principles."

The chief names in the British literature of this century were: POPE, its greatest poet; ADDISON, ARBUTHNOT, DE FOE, RICHARDSON, FIELDING, SMOLLETT, BUTLER, CHALLONER, HUME, ROBERTSON, GIBBON, JOHNSON, BURNS, and COWPER.

Great Britain produced no great dramatist during this period.† The classic drama of France had reached

---

* It may be noted that it was in the reign of George III. that the first step was taken towards mitigating some of the odious Penal Laws against Catholics. This movement proceeded from motives of fear rather than justice. But it fanned the slumbering fires of fury and fanaticism. Protestant riots occurred in Edinburgh. A London mob destroyed Catholic churches and residences, and it took the strong arm of the militia to put down the savage rioters.

† Mere mention is, perhaps, more than the British dramatists of this age deserve here. Of these writers, the four most conspicuous in the early part of the century were *Congreve, Wycherley, Vanbrugh,* and *Farquhar*. But most of their plays are stenches of

the zenith of its splendor; and English writers modelled their plays after the French pattern. ·This is the case with Addison's famous tragedy of *Cato*.

3. THE ORIGIN OF NEWSPAPERS.—As it was Catholics who invented printing and raised it to an art, so it was Catholics who originated the first newspaper. This was the *Gazette* of Venice, issued in 1563, during the war with the Turks. It received its name from a small coin called *gazetta*—the price charged for the privilege of reading it. *The News* * *of the Present Week* was established in 1622, during the Thirty Years' War. This may be considered the *first regular English newspaper*. It contained only foreign news. The fierce struggle between Charles I. and his Parliament called out a host of small sheets. Each party had several organs, and a furious paper war kept pace with the stern conflict and the crash of arms. Defoe's *Review* began in 1704, and was, strictly speaking, the first English serial; but our periodical literature may be said to date from Steele's *Tatler*, which began in 1709. This was succeeded, at varying intervals, by the *Spectator*, the *Guardian*, the *Rambler*, and the *Idler*. The *Gentleman's Magazine* dates from 1731. The *Public Advertiser* gave the *Letters of Junius* to the world between 1769 and 1772. The London *Morning Post* was started in 1772, and the London *Times* in 1788. These peri-

---

immorality, written in defiance of good sense and Christian decency.
"Immodest words admit of no defence,
For want of decency is want of sense."
Garrick, *Foote*, and *Colman* belong to the latter part of the century.
* Although the word *news* is significant enough, many persons considered it as made up of the initial letters representing the cardinal points of the compass. N. E. W. S., from which the curious people looked for satisfying intelligence.--*Coppée*.

odicals took the place of the drama in literary influence.

4. PROSE PUSHES AHEAD. THE NOVEL AND THE HISTORY.—Poetry and prose were each well represented in the early part of this century. But after the death of Pope a change came. Poetry waned. Prose pushed ahead, rapidly developed, and took possession of new fields. " Everything has its day," wrote Dr. Johnson. " Through the reigns of William and Anne no prosperous event passed undignified by poetry. In the last war,* when France was disgraced and overpowered in every quarter of the globe, when Spain, coming to her assistance, only shared her calamities, and the name of an Englishman was reverenced through Europe, no poet was heard amidst the general acclamation ; the fame of our councillors and heroes was intrusted to the gazetter."

Internal peace and security prolonged through many years, while adding enormously to the national wealth, occasioned the rise of that large class of readers to whom so much of modern literature is addressed—persons having leisure to read and money to buy books, but who demand from literature amusement rather than instruction, and care less for being excited to think than for being made to enjoy. This new demand was to have a supply. It arose in the form of the modern novel. *Defoe* led the way. *Richardson, Fielding,* and *Smollett* worked on at the mine which Defoe had opened. " The novel," says Bascom, " is the last stage of prose in its progress towards poetry."

Some of the best known historical productions in our literature date from this period. A new group

---

* The Seven Years' War, 1755 to 1762.

of historians appeared in *Hume, Robertson*, and *Gibbon*, who carried that highest branch of prose composition to much perfection.

A good portion of the last half of the eighteenth century acknowledged the rule of *Johnson*. It was the reign of King Samuel. There is nothing quite like it in our literature. Great minds had come and gone, but none of them had held such absolute authority—such quiet, undisputed supremacy. This was due to the fact that the period was one of criticism. It prepared the way for immediate and personal control on the part of any one pre-eminent in this art; and Johnson's ability and dogmatic character soon raised him to the rank of a great literary dictator.

Johnson passed away, and the last fifteen years of this period gave us two poets who struck at a fresh pathway in the domain of poetry and were the pioneers of a new school. The gentle mind of Cowper broke loose from the trammels of an over-refined art, and his productions gave a healthy impulse to deep genuine poetry. The genius of *Burns* shed a dazzling glow over the literature of Scotland, where no truely original poet had appeared since the days of Dunbar.

But, on the whole, the writers of the eighteenth century have been overestimated. Its literature, though occupying a large space to our eyes at the present day, from the proximity of time and the want of other thinkers who have taken up the ground more satisfactorily, is for the most part essentially of the fugitive sort. In future ages it will probably be considered as *not having treated with true depth and appreciation one single subject which it has handled.**

---

* T. Arnold.

LESSON I.
ALEXANDER POPE. DIED 1744.

Chief works: (1) *Essay on Criticism.*
(2) *Rape of the Lock.*
(3) *Essay on Man.*
(4) *The Dunciad.*
(5) *Translation of Homer.*
(6) *Letters.*

1. Which is the greatest name in the British literature of the eighteenth century?

Alexander Pope.

2. Where was Pope born?

He was born at London, of well-to-do Catholic parents, but passed a large part of his life at Twickenham, where he possessed a villa.

3. Give a short account of his early life.

Being a Catholic, the doors of the bigoted public schools and the universities were closed to the gifted boy, and he received his education chiefly at home from an aunt and several priests. But he soon took the work into his own hands. He was a self-taught man. His poetic power showed itself at an early age, for he says:

"As yet a child, and all unknown to fame,
I lisped in numbers, for the numbers came."

4. What was the earliest production of the young poet that we now possess?

An *Ode to Solitude*, written before Pope was twelve years old. Dr. Johnson considers it "a perfect masterpiece" from one so young.*

---

* The *Ode to Solitude* consists of five four-lined stanzas, of which the following is the opening one:

"Happy the man whose wish and care
A few paternal acres bound,
Content to breath his native air
In his own ground."

5. How did Pope chiefly spend his whole life?

In retirement, study, and literary labor.

6. What is the first of his remarkable poems in the order of time?

The *Essay on Criticism*, which is, perhaps, unparalleled as the composition of a young man of twenty.* In it Pope lays down the laws of just criticism, and the causes which prevent it.

7. Which is, perhaps, the happiest and most original of all Pope's poems?

The *Rape of the Lock*, which is commonly considered the best and most charming specimen of the mock-heroic to be found in English literature.

8. Which is now, perhaps, the most widely known of his poems?

The famous *Essay on Man;* it is remarkable for

---

* It is the kind of a poem a man might write at the end of his career, when he has handled all modes of writing, and has grown gray in criticism; and in this subject, whose treatment demands the experience of a whole literary life, he was in an instant as ripe as Boileau.—*Taine*.

The *Essay on Criticism* contains many often-quoted passages, as:

    "Of all the causes which conspire to blind
    Man's erring judgment, and misguide the mind,
    What the weak head with strongest bias rules,
    Is Pride--the never-failing vice of fools."

    "Good nature and good sense must ever join;
    To err is human; to forgive, divine."

    "A little learning is a dangerous thing;
    Drink deep, or touch not the Pierian spring."

    "Nay, fly to altars; there they'll talk you dead,
    For fools rush in where angels fear to tread."

    "'Tis not enough no harshness gives offence;
    The sound must seem an echo to the sense."

    "True ease in writing comes from art, not chance,
    As those move easiest who have learned to dance."

    "Some positive, persisting fops we know,
    Who, if once wrong, will needs be always so;
    But you with pleasure own your errors past,
    And make each day a critic on the last."

wise sayings, poor theology, and beautiful versification. No poem in English has furnished so many proverbs.*

9. What is the *Dunciad?*

The Dunciad, or epic of the dunces, is a satirical poem in which Pope revenged himself on a number of obscure poets and feeble critics by whom he had been attacked and libelled.†

10. How is the poem divided, and what are its merits and defects?

It is divided into four books, containing in all about 1750 lines. *The Dunciad* is the most sweeping, fierce, and brilliant satirical poem in English, but it

---

* Here are a few detached specimens:
"Know thou thyself, presume not God to scan;
The proper study of mankind is man."

"A wit's a feather, and a chief's a rod:
An honest man's the noblest work of God."

"Hope springs eternal in the human breast;
Man never *is*, but always *to be*, blest."

"Lo, the poor Indian, whose untutored mind
Sees God in clouds, or hears Him in the wind."

"Honor and shame from no condition rise;
Act well your part—there all the honor lies."

"Worth makes the man, and want of it the fellow;
The rest is all but leather or prunella."

"What can ennoble sots or slaves or cowards?
Alas! not all the blood of all the Howards."

"All nature is but art unknown to thee—
All chance, direction, which thou canst not see."

† The publication of Pope's *Miscellanies* (1727-8), in which Swift also took a share, brought round the heads of the offending authors an angry swarm of scribblers, buzzing like wasps whose nest has been rashly invaded. Then the real power of the crippled poet flashed out in full lustre. Seizing each wretched insect with the firm yet delicate hold of a skilful entomologist, he ruthlessly pinned it, in the full gaze of the world's scorn, on the sheets of the immortal *Dunciad*. There the unfortunate creatures still hang and wriggle; and there, while English books are read, they shall remain —*Collier.*

18

sometimes blazes and flashes with a bitterness that cannot be defended on any grounds.

11. What translation gave Pope both fame and money?

His translation of Homer's *Iliad* and *Odyssey* into English verse.*

12. What branch of prose literature was enriched by the pen of this poet?

Letters, whose chief defect is want of simplicity: but Pope lived in an artificial age.

13. Do you know anything about his personal appearance?

He was small and deformed in person, and was always in delicate health.†

14. What was one of the most noble traits in Pope's character?

His great affection for his father and mother.‡

15. Was his death edifying?

It was truly so; whatever may have been the er-

---

* Milton and his family got but £28 for the greatest English epic; Pope received more than £8000 for his translation of Homer

† Through all his fifty-six years Pope was very frail and delicate. It is a wonder that soul and body kept together so long. When the poor little man got up in the morning, he had to be sewed into stiff canvas stays, without which he could scarcely stand erect. Fur and flannel were wrapped around his thin body, and it required three pairs of stockings to give his meagre legs a respectable appearance. "He was," says Sir Joshua Reynolds, "about four feet six inches high, very humpbacked and deformed. He wore a black coat, and, according to the fashion of that time, had on a little sword. He had a large and very fine eye, and a long, handsome nose; his mouth had those peculiar marks which are always found in the mouths of crooked persons, and the muscles which run across the cheek were so strongly marked that they seemed like small cords."

‡ The following feeling and beautiful lines refer to the poet's mother:
"Oh, friend, may each domestic bliss be thine!
Be no unpleasing melancholy mine!
Me let the tender office long engage
To rock the cradle of declining age;
With lenient arts extend a mother's breath—
Make languor smile, and smooth the bed of death,
Explore the thought, explain the asking eye,
And keep at least one parent from the sky."

rors of Pope's life, its closing scene was one of faith and pious resignation.*

"If Pope must yield to other poets in point of fertility of fancy, yet in point of propriety, clearness and elegance of diction he can yield to none."—*Warton.*
"This great man is allowed to have been one of the first rank amongst the poets of our nation, and to acknowledge the superiority of none but Shakspeare, Milton, and Dryden."—*Dr Johnson.*
"The most striking characteristics of his poetry are lucid arrangement of matter, closeness of argument, marvellous condensation of thought and expression, brilliancy of fancy ever supplying the aptest illustrations, and language elaborately finished almost beyond example."—*Dyce.*

LESSON II.

ROBERT BURNS.   DIED 1796.
(1) *Poems.*   (2) *Songs.*

WILLIAM COWPER.   DIED 1800.
(1) *Poems.*   (2) *Letters.*   (3) *Translation of Homer.*

16. Who was Robert Burns?

He was the greatest and most original of the British song-writers.

17. Can you give a short account of his humble life?

Burns was a poor Scottish ploughboy, with no advantages but those of a country school. His career was sad. It seems that his life was one continued struggle with poverty, strong passions, and a poorly balanced character. But the many faults of the man

---

* The priest who administered the consolations of our holy religion "came out from the dying man, . . . penetrated to the last degree with the state of mind in which he found his penitent—resigned and wrapt up in the love of God and man."—Carruther's *Life of Pope.*

are almost forgotten in the glory of the poet. He died at the age of thirty-seven.*

18. Mention some of his best poems.

Tam o' Shanter, his most famous poem; *The Cotter's Saturday Night;* and *To a Mountain Daisy*. They are all short productions.

19. What is it that makes the memory of Burns especially dear to his countrymen?

His *Songs*, which are at once tender, manly, soul-stirring, and patriotic.

20. Name a few of his best known songs.

Bruce's Address to his Troops at Bannockburn, Honest Poverty,† The Banks of Doon, and *To Mary in Heaven.*

21. Who was the special poet of the domestic affections in the eighteenth century?

William Cowper.

---

* Burns was a strong, fine-looking man, and, in the words of Sir Walter Scott, " his manners were rustic, not clownish; a sort of dignified plainness and simplicity which received part of its effect perhaps from one's knowledge of his extraordinary talents. . . . I never saw such another eye in human head, though I have seen the most distinguished men in my time."

It was his delight to wander along the banks of the Ayr, and to listen to the song of the blackbird at the close of the summer's day. But still greater was his pleasure, as he himself informs us, in walking on the sheltered side of a wood, in a cloudy winter, and hearing the storm rave among the trees; and more elevated still his delight to ascend some eminence during the agitations of nature, to stride along its summit while the lightning flashed around him, and, amid the howlings of the tempest, to apostrophize the spirit of the storm. Such situations he declares most favorable to devotion—" Rapt in enthusiasm, I seemed to ascend towards Him *who walks on the wings of the wind.*"—*Hudson.*

† HONEST POVERTY.

" Is there, for honest poverty,
That hangs his head and a' that?
The coward-slave we pass him by,
We dare be poor for a' that!
For a' that, and a' that,
Our toil's obscure and a' that;
The rank is but the guinea-stamp,
The man's the gowd for a' that.

LITERATURE OF EIGHTEENTH CENTURY.

22. Do you know anything concerning his life?

It was most unhappy. Cowper was a native of England. He was a gentle, melancholy character—and at times a maniac—who turned to poetry, like Saul to the harper, for relief in his sufferings.

> "What though on hamely fare we dine,
> Wear hodden grey, and a' that;
> Gie fools their silks, and knaves their wine,
> A man's a man for a' that!
> For a' that, and that.
> Their tinsel show and a' that;
> The honest man, though e'er sae poor,
> Is king o' men for a' that.
>
> "Ye see yon birkie, ca'd a lord,
> Wha struts, and stares, and a' that;
> Though hundreds worship at his word,
> He's but a coof for a' that,
> For a' that, and a' that;
> His riband, star, and a' that.
> The man of independent mind,
> He looks and laughs at a' that.
>
> "A king can mak' a belted knight,
> A marquis, duke, and a' that;
> But an honest man's aboon his might—
> Guid faith, he maunna fa' that!
> For a' that, and a' that,
> Their dignities and a' that.
> The pith o' sense and pride o' worth
> Are higher ranks than a' that.
>
> "Then let us pray that come it may,
> As come it will for a' that,
> That sense and worth, o'er a' the Earth,
> May bear the gree, and a' that;
> For a' that, and a' that.
> It's coming yet, for a' that,
> That man to man, the world o'er,
> Shall brothers be for a' that."

The student must remember that Burns wrote in the dialect of the Scottish Lowlands. The following explanation of a few words may assist him in better comprehending *Honest Poverty:*

a'................................all
gowd............................gold
hamely..........................homely
gie..............................give
sae..............................so
o'...............................of
birkie...........................a conceited fellow

23. Which is Cowper's greatest poem?

The Task, a didactic work in six books.*

24. Name his two best known short poems.

John Gilpin and *Alexander Selkirk*.

25. What may be said of Cowper's *Letters?*

They are among the best in our literature.

26. What ancient poet did he give to England in a new translation?

Homer; it was the work of seven years.

---

ca'd	called
wha	who
coof	a dunce
mak'	make
aboon	above
guid	good
maunna	must not
fa'	to fall
gree	to agree

* Cowper was but six years old when his mother died. More than fifty years after that sad day—it was sad for him—an old man bent over the never-forgotten image of that kindest of earthly friends, and penned the following beautiful *Lines to his Mother's Picture ;* they are from *The Task :*

> "My mother! when I learned that thou wast dead,
> Say, wast thou conscious of the tears I shed?
> Hovered thy spirit o'er thy sorrowing son,
> Wretch even then—life's journey just begun?
> Perhaps thou gav'st me, though unfelt, a kiss;
> Perhaps a tear, if souls can weep in bliss:
> Ah, that maternal smile! it answers, Yes.
> I heard the bell tolled on thy burial-day,
> I saw the hearse that bore thee slow away,
> And turning from my nursery-window, drew
> A long, long sigh, and wept a last adieu!
> But was it such?—It was.—Where thou art gone
> Adieus and farewells are a sound unknown.
> May I but meet thee on that peaceful shore,
> The parting words shall pass my lips no more!"

LITERATURE OF EIGHTEENTH CENTURY. 211

LESSON III.

JOSEPH ADDISON. DIED 1719.
(1) *Essays in The Spectator.* (2) *Cato, a Tragedy.*

JOHN ARBUTHNOT, M.D. DIED 1735.
The History of John Bull.

27. Give a short account of Addison's career.

He was born in England, educated at Oxford, raised himself to political position by penning a few timely poems, and to high literary fame by his ability as an essayist and master of pure, elegant prose.*

28. By what productions is he best known?

By his essays in *The Spectator.*†

29. What is Addison's *Cato?*

It is a tragedy in the strictly classical form; but time has greatly diminished its early reputation.

---

* Not many years ago it was very generally the custom. I remember, for every young person, male and female, to go through a course of reading of the papers of *The Spectator.* This has fallen quite into disuse nowadays, and I do not know that it is much to be regretted. *The Spectator* contains, undoubtedly, much sensible and sound morality; but it is not a very high order of Christian ethics. It contains much judicious criticism, but certainly not comparable to the deeper philosophy of criticism which has entered into English literature in the present century. Those papers will always have a semi-historical interest, as picturing the habits and manners of the times—a moral value, as a kindly, good-natured censorship of those manners. In one respect *The Spectator* stands unrivalled to this day—I allude to the exquisite humor in those numbers in which Sir Roger de Coverley figures. If any one desire to form a just notion of what is meant by that very indefinable quality called "humor," he cannot more agreeably inform himself than by selecting the Sir Roger de Coverley papers and reading them in series.—*Henry Reed.*

† *The Spectator*, which was owned and edited by *Sir Richard Steele,* was issued daily. The first number is dated March 1, 1711; the last December 20, 1714—in all 635 numbers, 274 of which were written by Addison.

30. **Who was Dr. John Arbuthnot?**

He was a native of Scotland, an amiable man, a learned physician, and one of the most witty and brilliant writers of the eighteenth century.

31. **Which is his most famous work?**

A curious volume entitled the *History of John Bull*, which, according to Lord Macaulay, is "the most ingenious and humorous political satire in our language."

32. **Give some idea of the nature of the work.**

It was intended to ridicule the Duke of Marlborough. The great war in which Europe was involved was represented as a lawsuit carried on by *John Bull* against *Lord Strutt*.* *Nicholas Frog* † and *Esquire South* ‡ were parties to the suit on one side—John Bull paying their expenses. *Louis Baboon* § was on the other side. John Bull's attorney, *Humphrey Hocus*,∥ manages the suit in such a way as to plunge John into a bottomless gulf of expense.

33. **What was one result brought about by Arbuthnot's amusing burlesque?**

It first stamped and fixed the popular ideal of *John Bull*, as the embodiment of English peculiarities.¶

---

* Spain.   † Holland.   ‡ Austria.   § France.
∥ The Duke of Marlborough.
¶ Of Arbuthnot, Swift said: "He has more wit than we all have, and his humanity is equal to his wit." Pope wrote: "His good morals were equal to any man's, but his wit and humor superior to all mankind."

LITERATURE OF EIGHTEENTH CENTURY. 213

LESSON IV.

DANIEL DE FOE. DIED 1731.

Life and Adventures of Robinson Crusoe.

34. Who was Daniel De Foe?

He was the *first* of the English novelists.

35. At what age did he write his world-renowned book?

When nearly sixty years of age, after a long and busy career as a political writer, he tried his hand at prose fiction, and gave the world his famous *Robinson Crusoe.**

36. What can you say of *Robinson Crusoe?*

It is the earliest work of its class in English, and to this day it remains unrivalled.

37. What did Dr. Johnson remark of the book?

That "nobody ever laid it down without wishing it were longer."†

---

* De Foe's works number over 200. Many were the ups and downs of his life. He wrote:
  "No man hath tasted differing fortunes more;
   As thirteen times I have been rich and poor."

† Alexander Selkirk, the sailing-master of an English privateer, who set ashore in 1704, at his own request, on the uninhabited island of Juan ernandez, which lies several hundred miles from the coast of Chili, in the Pacific Ocean. He was supplied with clothing and arms, and remained there alone for four years and four months. It is supposed that his adventures suggested the work. It is also likely that De Foe had read the journal of Peter Serrano, who, in the sixteenth century, had been *marooned* in like manner on a desolate island lying off the mouth of the Orinoco. The latter locality was adopted by De Foe. But it is not the fact or the adventures which give power to *Robinson Crusoe*. It is the manner of treating what might occur to any fancy, even the dullest. The charm consists in the simplicity and the verisimilitude of the narrative, the rare adaptation of the common man to his circumstances, his projects and failures, the birth of religion in his soul, his conflicting hopes and fears, his occasional despair. We

LESSON V.

SAMUEL RICHARDSON. DIED 1767.
Pamela.

HENRY FIELDING. DIED 1754.
Tom Jones.

TOBIAS SMOLLETT. DIED 1771.
Humphrey Clinker.

38. Who are usually classed together as the three most famous British novelists of the eighteenth century?

Richardson, Fielding, and *Smollett.*

39. Which of these write s com s first in the order of time?

Samuel Richardson.

40. Do you know anything of his life?

It was a common one. He was a prudent and successful English tradesman.

41. In what branch of fiction did Richardson lead the way?

He was the pioneer in that branch of fiction which describes *the common events of life.*

42. Which was his earliest production?

*Pamela, or Virtue Rewarded.**

43. Who next followed in the new path struck out by Richardson?

Henry Fielding, an English lawyer of great genius and loose morals, who jeered at the virtue pictured

---

see in him a brother, and a suffering one. We live his life on the island; we share his terrible fear at the discovery of the footprint, his courage in destroying the cannibal savages and rescuing the victim. Where is there in fiction another man *Friday?* From the beginning of his misfortunes until he is again sailing for England— after nearly thirty years of captivity—he holds us spell-bound by the reality, the simplicity, and the pathos of his narrative.— *Coppée.*

* Richardson's other works are *Clarissa Harlowe* and *Sir Charles Grandison.*

by Richardson in *Pamela*, and wrote a novel* to make the wicked jeer more lasting.

44. Which is his greatest work?

Tom Jones.

45. How did Fielding particularly excel?

As a most skilled delineator of human life—often in its most degraded forms.

46. For what do his productions deserve severe condemnation?

For their coarseness and gross indelicacy. It is no excuse to say that his tainted pages are but real pictures of English life in his day.

47. Who was Tobias Smollett?

He was a physician, a native of Scotland, and stood third among the old masters of English fiction.

48. Which was the last and best effort of his genius?

Humphrey Clinker, the finest and most humorous of his works.

49. Are Smollett's novels open to censure on the score of immorality?

They are, and justly so. He even exceeds Fielding in vile coarseness, and many of his chapters are shockingly obscene.

50. Sum up the chief points in which Richardson, Fielding, and Smollett each excel.

Richardson is noted for passion and sentimentality; Fielding, for unrivalled humor, satire, freshness, and skill in picturing human nature; and Smollett, for broad humor and comic incidents.† Of the three, Fielding was much the greatest genius.

---

* *Joseph Andrews.*
† Each of those authors wrote three noted works of fiction.

"Richardson always wrote with a moral purpose, which the other two had not; though that does not hinder much that he wrote from being of an objectionable tendency."—*T. Arnold.*

"Richardson, marked according to our standard, might be set down as licentious As compared with Fielding, however, and others of his age, his works appear to great advantage, and show a distinct moral tendency. Richardson himself probably never dreamed but that he was furthering the cause of good morals; and the favor with which *Pamela* and *Clarissa* were read and recommended by the best and wisest of the day shows us how careful we must be in our estimates of writers of works of imagination."— *Hart.*

LESSON VI.

ALBAN BUTLER. DIED 1773.
Lives of the Saints.

RICHARD CHALLONER. DIED 1781.
(1) *Memoirs of Missionary Priests and other Catholics.*
(2) *The Catholic Christian Instructed.*
(3) *Revision of the Douay Bible.*

51. Who was Alban Butler?

A native of England and a pious and learned Catholic priest, he was for many years president of the English college at St. Omer, France.

52. Which is his chief work?

The Lives of the Saints.

53. What does this work comprise?

It comprises the lives of the Apostles, Doctors, Fathers, Martyrs, and other principal Saints from the foundation of the Church down to the writer's own time.*

---

* *The Lives of the Saints* is divided into 12 volumes—sometimes published in 4—corresponding to the months of the year. Each volume contains about 120 lives, together with many notes, critical, historical, literary, and explanatory. The work is truly a vast storehouse of curious learning both secular and ecclesiastical. It was translated into French, Spanish, and Italian.

54. What are its merits?

It is an incomparable production—the result of a life of unwearied piety, labor, and learning. Even Gibbon pronounced it "a work of merit"; and we risk nothing in saying that it is the greatest storehouse of Catholic biography in the English language.*

55. Who was Bishop Challoner?

The Right Rev. Richard Challoner was one of the most learned and best known English Catholic writers of the eighteenth century.

56. What subjects were chiefly enriched by his pen?

Devotional, religious, and controversial subjects.

57. What is his *Memoirs of Missionary Priests and other Catholics?* †

It is a most interesting series of sketches of Catholic missionaries and other faithful men and women who lived, labored, and suffered death in England during the time of the barbarous Penal Laws. An account is given of 180 martyrs who suffered in the reign of Elizabeth alone.

58. Which is the most popular of all Dr. Challoner's works?

The Catholic Christian Instructed, which was first published in 1737. It is in the form of question and answer, and is one of the very best and shortest works on the *Sacraments, Holy Mass, Festivals, Ceremonies,* and *Observances of the Catholic Church.*

---

* It is to be regretted that Butler's notices of the *Irish Saints* are so extremely meagre and imperfect. Even such illustrious personages as St. Patrick, St. Bridget, and St. Columbkille are dismissed in short, dry sketches that can barely claim the merit of accuracy.

† First published in 1741. The full title is *Memoirs of Missionary Priests and other Catholics of both Sexes who suffered Death in England on Religious Accounts*, 1577 to 1684. A new edition has recently been issued.

59. What was his chief Scriptural labor?

A much-esteemed revision of the Douay version of the Catholic Bible.*

60. What may be said of the style of Butler and Challoner?

They both wrote in pure, calm, elegant English.

LESSON VII.

DAVID HUME.   DIED 1776.

(1) *Essays.*   (2) *History of England.*

WILLIAM ROBERTSON.   DIED 1793.

(1) *History of Scotland.*
(2) *History of Charles V.*
(3) *History of America.*

61. Who were the British historians of the eighteenth century?

Hume, Robertson, and *Gibbon.*

62. Do you know anything of Hume's career?

He was a native of Edinburgh, and led a studious and retired life.

---

† It is commonly called the *Douay Bible*, because it was first published at Douay, in France. The English college at Douay was established in 1568 by the famous *Cardinal Allen* and other learned Catholic professors who had been banished from Oxford and Cambridge by the fanatics of the English Reformation. The translation of the whole Sacred Volume was completed in 1582, and the New Testament was printed at Rheims in that year. This is why the English Catholic Bible is sometimes called the *Rheims Douay Bible.* Owing to want of funds, however, the Old Testament was not published until 1609, in which year it was issued at Douay. The burden of translation fell mainly upon *Dr. Gregory Martin*, renowned as one of the greatest Greek and Hebrew scholars of that age; and his work was revised by *Cardinal Allen, Dr. Richard Bristow,* and *Dr. William Reynolds.* The notes to the New Testament were from the pen of Dr. Bristow, and the notes to the Old Testament were the work of *Dr. Thomas Worthington.* This version has the approval of the Faculties of the Universities of Rheims and Douay, but it has never received a Roman approbation. The *Douay Bible* is a direct translation from the Latin Vulgate of St. Jerome. The first edition of Challoner's revision is dated 1750.

63. Which were the first works he gave to the world?

Essays on various moral, political, and philosophical subjects.

64. To what dangerous class of thinkers did Hume belong?

He was a free-thinker and a thorough-going infidel, who sneered at the Christian religion.

65. What period does his *History of England* cover?

From the earliest period to 1688.

66. What may be said of the style of this work?

The style is flowing and graceful, but is very far from being idiomatic. Hume was a Scotchman, and this, together with his French studies, gave a wrong turn to his phraseology.

67. How is this once-lauded History now estimated by the best scholars?

It is acknowledged to be weak, one-sided, and untrustworthy. Hume was a careless, dishonest, bigoted, and superficial writer. He is no longer an authority on English history.*

68. Who was William Robertson?

He was a native of Scotland, a Presbyterian minister, and for some time head of the University of Edinburgh.

---

* Speaking of the historical writers of the eighteenth century, Henry Reed says: "Of these historians *Gibbon* is the only one whose history preserves to this day its authority, on the score of such extensive research and deep learning as were required by his large theme. With regard to *Hume* and *Robertson*—the two most popular historians—the labors of later students of history have demonstrated that their works are of that indolent and superficial character which destroys their authority as trustworthy chroniclers. I do not suppose that any careful and conscientious inquirer after historic truth would at the present day consider a question of history determined by a statement in the Histories of either Hume or Robertson."—*Lectures on English Literature.*

"One object, always uppermost with *Hume*, is to malign the Catholic religion."—*Cobbett.*

69. Name his chief works.

(See list at the beginning of the Lesson.)

70. Which of these do you consider Robertson's most important work?

The History of America.

71. What does it contain?

The History of America, in eight books, contains an account of the discovery of the New World and of the progress of the Spanish arms and colonies on its shores down to the latter part of the eighteenth century. It covers the most splendid portion of early American history.*

72. What may be said of the once-admired style of this writer?

His style, though stately and elegant, is too cold, wordy, affected, and rhetorical.

73. What, perhaps, prevented Robertson from being a g eat historian?

He was bigoted, frigid in feeling, and careless in research.† He lacked that industry, that deep love of truth, that absorbing interest in his subject, and that marvellous life-giving power which are the property of true genius, and the real secret of success in the work of historical composition.

---

* Robinson's work does not touch the French or British colonies in America. Mexico and Peru receive the largest share of attention

† Here is one instance out of many. Robertson, while engaged in writing his *History of Scotland*, had consulted Hume about the trial of Mary Queen of Scots. The bigoted, easy going Hume sent him a version which was at once used. But in the mean time a gentleman who went more deeply into such things showed the historian of England* that his version was false. It was too late. Robertson's work had just gone to press, and the publisher refused to have any changes or corrections made. And thus, says a late writer, "the blind led the blind, and *The History of Scotland*— whole sheets of which ought to have been re-written, and scattered passages founded upon theory erased—was given to the world because the printer refused to disturb the press and the author was disinclined to demolish such a fair creation!"

LESSON VIII.

EDWARD GIBBON. DIED 1794.

Chief works: (1) *The Decline and Fall of the Roman Empire.* (2) *Autobiography.*

74. Who was Edward Gibbon?

He was the greatest British historian of the eighteenth century.

75. n a few words, tell us something of his career.

He was a native of England, studied for a time at Oxford,* then in Switzerland, and at the age of twenty-eight, while on a visit to Rome, he conceived the idea of writing his famous history.† He died six years after its completion.

76. What period of time is embraced in *The Decline and Fall of the Roman Empire?*

It begins with the reign of Trajan, A.D. 98, and ends with the fall of the Eastern Empire, A.D. 1453.

---

* It was while at Oxford that Gibbon became a Catholic. He was led to this step by a careful reading of the works of Bossuet and Parsons. His displeased father at once sent the young student to Lausanne in Switzerland, to be under the training of a Protestant minister. With such influences brought to bear upon him, the unstable Gibbon soon ceased to be a Catholic. But he did not return to Protestantism. He became an unbeliever. Speaking of the famous work that had most to do in directing his course toward the Catholic Church—*Bossuet's History of the Variations of the Protestant Churches*—he says: " In the *History of the Varia-'tions,* an attack equally vigorous and well-directed, Bossuet shows, by a happy mixture of reasoning and narration, the errors, mistakes, uncertainties, and contradictions of our first Reformers, whose variations, as he learnedly maintains, bear the marks of error; while the uninterrupted unity of the Catholic Church is a sign and testimony of infallible truth. I read, approved, and believed."—*Gibbon's Memoirs.*

† "It was at Rome," he writes, " on the 15th of October, 1764, as I sat musing amidst the ruins of the Capitol, while the Barefooted Friars were singing Vespers in the temple of Jupiter, that the idea of writing the decline and fall of the City first started to my mind."

77. **What is your opinion of the** *style* **in which** *The Decline and Fall* **is written?**

It is elegant and powerful, but in Gibbon's style we miss the charm of simplicity. All is pompous and elaborate. He can say nothing in plain terms. He is always trying to shine.

78. **Is this famous History, then, a work of great merit?**

It is, in many respects, a great historical composition. Sweeping over a vast field in the annals of the world, it exhibits astonishing industry, and wide and varied learning skilfully handled. But in spite of its many merits, it must be said that it is a very dangerous and offensive work.

79. **How so?**

Gibbon was destitute of moral feeling and nobility of sentiment. He was dead to the moral grandeur of the Catholic Church. And though nowhere professing unbelief, he takes care on every occasion to mock at the beauty, power, and purity of the Christian religion. He has praises only for paganism. He cannot be just, because he will not believe.*

80. **Is there any other feature that is especially offensive in** *The Decline and Fall?*

There is; its pages are often stained by that wo-

---

* The very fact that Gibbon could not appreciate the heavenly action of the Catholic Church on those peoples which she converted, civilized, educated into national greatness, and stimulated to all kinds of noble and heroic deeds, is in itself a proof conclusive that he was wholly wanting in the very first qualification essential to the historian of the long, eventful period covered by the *Decline and Fall of the Roman Empire.* Gibbon had no spiritual aspirations himself, and he could neither appreciate nor understand them in others. His soul was contracted, his heart deprived of feeling, his moral nature stunted, and his mental eyesight dimmed by the cold, withering influence of infidelity. Those who wish to know more about the fallacy of Gibbon's arguments, and the true history of the rise of Christianity, may consult Morison's *Life of Gibbon,* Cardinal Newman's *Grammar of Assent,* and Father Thébaud's *Church and the Gentile World.*

ful depravity of imagination which delights in the description of scenes disgusting and licentious.

81. What is Gibbon's *Autobiography*?
As the title indicates, it is his life written by himself. It is one of the most interesting autobiographies in our language.

"When a Christian bishop or doctor, or a religious king, comes before his field of vision, it is not in Gibbon to be just; he cannot or will not believe that such a man was anything more than a compound of enthusiasm and superstition, in whom morality was always ready to give way to ecclesiastical considerations; and his sneering cavils seem to leave their trail upon the purest virtue, the most exalted heroism, which the times that he writes of produced for the instruction of mankind. He is in thorough sympathy with no one except Julian the Apostate!"--*Thomas Arnold.*

"Gibbon is a writer full of thoughts. In general, his language is powerful and exquisite; but it has, to great excess, the faults of elaboration, pomposity, and monotony. His style is full of Latin and French words and phrases. That elaborate and half-Latin manner of writing by which Gibbon is distinguished had before him been brought very much into fashion by the example of the critic Johnson; in principle at least the English have now departed from it, and speak of it as a false kind, and one hostile to the spirit of their language. The work of Gibbon, however instructive and fascinating it may be, is nevertheless at bottom an offensive one, on account of his propensity to the infidel opinions and impious mockeries of Voltaire."--*F. Schlegel.*

LESSON IX.

SAMUEL JOHNSON. DIED 1784.

Chief works: (1) *Dictionary of the English Language.*
(2) *Lives of the English Poets.*
(3) *Rasselas, a Tale.*
(4) *The Rambler, and The Idler.*
(5) *Journey to the Hebrides.*

82. Who was Dr. Samuel Johnson?
He was an English poet, critic, essayist, novelist, dramatist, and lexicographer, who holds a central

place among the writers of the second half of the eighteenth century.

83. Tell us something of his life.

It was a life of many ups and downs. In youth he had a hard battle with poverty and disease. He was nearly fifty before he became well known.* But care and industry raised him from the condition of a hungry, penniless wanderer to the rank of Great Mogul of English letters.

84. What was Johnson's most important contribution to English letters?

His great *Dictionary of the English Language*, which was published in 1755.†

85. What d es the volume on the *Lives of the English Poets* comprise?

It comprises the lives of *fifty-two poets* and *thirteen eminent persons*. He begins with Cowley, and writes of the leading poets down to his own day. The work gives us Johnson's estimate of many of the names in English literature, and is the last important volume that came from his pen.

86. What story did Johnson write during the evenings of

---

* In his poem called *London*, Johnson thus gives expression to his own long struggles:

"This mournful truth is everywhere confessed—
Slow rises worth by poverty depressed."

† The *first* English dictionary was John Bullokar's *English Expositor of Hard Words*. It was published in 1616, the very year that Shakspeare died, and contained about 5000 words. Johnson's *Dictionary* contained about 43,000 words. Since that time, great advances have been made in English lexicography.

Webster's *Unabridged Dictionary* (edition of 1880) contains 118,000 words. Worcester's *Dictionary* (edition of 1881) contains 116,000 words. Ogilvie's *Imperial Dictionary* (edition of 1881) contains 130,000 words.

But the greatest of all English dictionaries—only a portion of which has yet been published—is the *New English Dictionary on Historical Principles*, edited by Dr. James A. H. Murray.

one week, in 1759, in order to defray the expenses of his mother's funeral?

Rasselas, Prince of Abyssinia.

87. What were *The Rambler* and *The Idler?*

They were periodicals from Johnson's pen somewhat on the plan of *The Spectator.* Each lived about two years.

88. What was the origin of his famous *Journey to the Hebrides?*

During a tour through the western islands of Scotland, Johnson gave charming descriptions in a series of letters to a lady-friend, which he afterwards prepared for publication. The work has many eloquent passages.*

89. What may be said of Johnson's style?

It was neither simple nor natural. It was a style marked by "words of learned length and thundering sound." But it seems there was some strange sympathy between Johnson's bulky frame † and the ponderous terms that fell from his pen.

---

* Here is one. It exhibits Johnson's style at his best. It is his reflections on landing at Iona, which had been blessed by the life and labors of St. Columbkille:
"We are now treading," says Johnson, "that illustrious island which was once the luminary of the Caledonian regions, whence savage clans and roving barbarians derived the benefits of knowledge and the blessings of religion. To abstract the mind from all local emotion would be impossible if it were endeavored, and would be foolish if it were possible. Whatever withdraws us from the power of our senses, whatever makes the past, the distant, or the future predominate over the present, advances us in the dignity of thinking beings. Far from me and my friends be such frigid philosophy as may conduct us indifferent and unmoved over any ground which has been dignified by wisdom, bravery, or virtue. That man is little to be envied whose patriotism would not gain force on the plains of Marathon, or whose piety would not grow warm among the ruins of Iona."

† A huge and slovenly figure, clad in a greasy brown coat and coarse black worsted stockings, wearing a gray wig with scorched foretop, rolls in his arm-chair long past midnight, holding in a dirty hand his nineteenth cup of tea. As he pauses to utter one of his terrible growls of argument, or rather of dogmatic assertion,

90. What celebrated work has done much to spread the name of Johnson and to immortalize his fame?
Boswell's *Life of Johnson.**

"In massive force of understanding, multifarious knowledge, sagacity, and moral intrepidity, no writer of the eighteenth century surpassed Dr. Samuel Johnson. His various works, with their sententious morality and high-sounding sonorous periods—his manly character and appearance—his great virtues and strong prejudices —his early and severe struggles—his love of argument and society, into which he poured the treasures of a rich and full mind—his wit, repartee, and brow-beating—his rough manners and kind heart—his curious household in which were congregated the lame, the blind, and the despised—his very looks, gesticulations, and dress—have all been brought so vividly before us by his biographer, Boswell, that to readers of every class Johnson is as well known as a member of their own family."—*Chambers.*

SUMMARY OF CHAPTER V., BOOK II.

1. Four English sovereigns reigned during the eighteenth century—*Anne, George I., George II.,* and *George III.*

2. The union of England and Scotland took place in 1707.

3. France ceded Canada to England in 1763.

4. The American colonists achieved their independ-

---

commencing invariably with a thunderous "Sir," we have leisure to note the bitten nails the scars of king's evil that mark his swollen face, and the convulsive workings of the muscles round mouth and eyes which accompany the puffs and snorts foreboding a coming storm of ponderous English talk. Such was the famous Dr. Samuel Johnson in his old age, when he had climbed from the most squalid cellars of Grub Street to the dictatorial throne of English criticism—such the man who wrote *Rasselas* and *London,* who compiled the great *English Dictionary,* and composed the majestically moral pages of *The Rambler.—Collier.*

* "Homer," says Lord Macaulay, "is not more decidedly the first of heroic poets. Shakspeare is not more decidedly the first of dramatists. Demosthenes is not more decidedly the first of orators, than *Boswell* is the first of biographers."

ence and founded this Republic between 1776 and 1783.

5. Prose developed in this century, and took possession of new fields in fiction, history, and periodical literature.

6. English fiction, newspapers, and periodical literature date from this age.

7. Great Britain produced no great dramatist during the eighteenth century.

8. Pope is the most famous name in the literature of this period. He is one of the great refiners of our language.

9. Burns stands at the head of the song-writers of Scotland, and, indeed, of Great Britain.

10. Addison is among the greatest English prose-writers of this century.

11. De Foe's *Robinson Crusoe* may be called the *first* English novel.

12. De Foe was followed in the field of fiction by *Richardson*, *Fielding*, and *Smollett*.

13. *Butler* and *Challoner* were the principal Catholic prose-writers of this age.

14. The British historians of the eighteenth century are *Hume*, *Robertson*, and *Gibbon*. Robertson was a Presbyterian minister. Hume and Gibbon were infidels.

15. Dr. Samuel Johnson is one of the most famous names in our literature. The English language is indebted to him for its *first* great dictionary.

16. His style of writing has received the name of *Johnsonese.* It is marked by "words of learned length and thundering sound."

17. Boswell's *Life of Johnson* holds the first place among English personal biographies.

18. *Bird's-eye view of the chief British writers and works of the eighteenth century:*

POETS:

Alexander Pope, *Essay on Man.*
Robert Burns, *Songs.*
William Cowper, *Poems.*

PROSE-WRITERS:

Joseph Addison, *Essays in The Spectator.*
John Arbuthnot, M.D., *The History of John Bull.*
Daniel De Foe, *Robinson Crusoe.*
Samuel Richardson, *Pamela.*
Henry Fielding, *Tom Jones.*
Tobias Smollett, M.D., *Humphrey Clinker.*
Alban Butler, *Lives of the Saints.*
Richard Challoner, D.D., *Memoirs of Missionary Priests.*
David Hume, *History of England.*
William Robertson, D.D., *History of America.*
Edward Gibbon, *Decline and Fall of the Roman Empire.*
Samuel Johnson, LL.D., *Dictionary of the English Language.*

19. For the other British writers of the eighteenth century most worthy of mention—namely, *Matthew Prior, John Gay, Ambrose Philips, Thomas Gray, James Thomson, William Collins, Mark Akenside, M.D., Allan Ramsay, Edward Young, James Beattie, Sir Isaac Newton, Joseph Butler, D.D., Lady Montagu, Charles Dodd, James Boswell, James Macpherson, Hannah More, William Paley, D.D., Adam Smith,* and *Sir William Blackstone*—see SHORT DICTIONARY at the close of the volume.

CHAPTER VI.

THE BRITISH LITERATURE OF THE NINETEENTH CENTURY.

A.D. 1800 to 1880.

THE AGE OF SCOTT, NEWMAN, AND TENNYSON.

HISTORICAL INTRODUCTION.

1. GREAT BRITAIN IN THE NINETEENTH CENTURY. —The nineteenth century is our own age, and is, perhaps, too near to write its history. But we may glance at some of the most important events that influenced British literature. Since the year 1800, four rulers have occupied the English throne— *George III., George IV., William IV.*, and *Queen Victoria.*

Towards the close of the last century the *French Revolution* led to a dreadful social, irreligious, and political upheaval. It rocked France like an earthquake. The shock was felt in England and throughout Europe. It involved France in war with the other great powers, and raised up the most brilliant military genius of modern times. For years the gentle voice of peace was drowned by the tramp of armies and the thunder of artillery. Again and again England and her allies grappled with *Napoleon,** and

---

* Born 1769, died 1821.

were made to bite the dust. Britannia, indeed, "ruled the wave"; but on the land France was supreme. In 1810 George III. lost the little reason he ever had, and his son, the Prince of Wales,* was appointed Regent. The extraordinary career of Napoleon was also drawing to a close. Flushed with triumph, this soldier of fortune grew dizzy in his elevation, and forgot to be just and religious. His treatment of the Vicar of Christ was shameful. The bubble of success burst. Disaster frowned on his arms, and, in 1815, his last hopes were buried on the blood-stained field of Waterloo. England and her allies rejoiced in the hard-won victory.

The insane George III. died in 1820, and was succeeded by his son George IV., who for ten years had acted as Regent. His short reign was full of political excitement. Its most glorious event, however, was the emancipation of the much-oppressed Catholics in 1829,† which was brought about chiefly by the manly, persevering exertions of *Daniel O'Connell*, the fearless and eloquent champion of civil and religious liberty. George IV. was called "the first gentleman in Europe," but he dabbled in scandal, quarrelled with his wife, swore like a jockey, and made anything but a clean reputation. He was a worn-out voluptuary. He had some ability but no virtue.

George IV. died in 1830, and his brother William IV. came to the throne. His reign of seven years would be a complete blank except for the passage of

---

* Afterwards George IV.
† Many years before this, William Pitt had given the Catholics a pledge that he would relieve them from their disabilities. But old George III.—fanatic that he was—was hopelessly obstinate in his anti-Catholic feeling. He even intimated that he should regard every man as his personal enemy who would urge the claims of the Catholics to emancipation.

the *Reform Bill.** William had little brains, and was rough and boorish in behavior. He had been an unmanageable naval officer before being clothed with regal power; but, certainly, he was better fitted by nature to walk a quarter-deck than to guide the destinies of a great kingdom.

The crown passed to the youthful Victoria, daughter of the Duke of Kent,† in 1837, and her already long reign has been marked by many historic events. In 1840 she was married to her German cousin, *Prince Albert.* About this time an extraordinary movement began in the *Anglican Church*—the Protestant Church of England as by law established—which has gone on increasing, and which must at no distant period lead to its destruction. The days of savage fanaticism were passing. A spirit of honest inquiry led some of the best and brightest minds of England to study Christian antiquity and the claims of the Catholic Church. A new world of truth was revealed. The scales of prejudice and ignorance fell from their eyes. Grace completed the work. Many of these noble and gifted men sacrificed every earthly consideration, and returned to that ancient faith from which their fathers had apostatized in the reigns of Henry VIII. and Elizabeth. The leader in this glorious movement was the learned *John Henry New-*

---

* The Reform Act (passed in 1832) bestowed the privilege of the franchise in towns upon occupants who paid a rental of ten pounds; in counties upon those who paid a rental of forty pounds. It gave the people some influence over a corrupt representative government. At the beginning of the present century, fully two thirds of the members of the House of Commons were appointed by peers or other influential persons. Seats in the House were openly sold, and amongst the buyers and bribers of members was the king himself, George III.

† The Duke of Kent was the fourth son of George III. Queen Victoria was born in 1819.

man* of Oxford University. He became a Catholic in 1845. "I am this night," he wrote to some friends on October 8th, "expecting Father Dominic, the Passionist. . . . He is a simple, holy man; and withal gifted with remarkable powers. He does not know of my intention; but I mean to ask of him admission into the One Fold of Christ."† *Faber, Manning, Digby, Ward, Allies, Marshall, Dalgairns,* the *Marquis of Bute,* and other eminent men followed his example; and during the last thirty-five years over 2000 of the master-intellects and the highest nobility of England have sought peace and truth in the One Fold so happily reached by Newman.

The gaunt figure of famine visited Ireland in 1846, and in a few years over two millions of that faithful and sorely tried people took their way to the silent tomb, or were scattered over the wide world. The great O'Connell died in 1847. Three years later Pope Pius IX. re-established the Catholic hierarchy in England, with *Cardinal Wiseman* at its head. "Catholic England," wrote the new Archbishop, "has been restored to its orbit in the ecclesiastical firmament from which its light had long vanished, and begins anew its course of regularly adjusted action round the centre of unity, the source of jurisdiction, of light, and of vigor." Protestant bigotry shouted itself hoarse; and the boundless fanaticism and big lungs of the Briton became the laughing-stock of the world. Parliament, in a fit of insanity, passed an act forbidding Catholic bishops to take titles from their sees, but it was never put in force. Nobody troubled about it, and many years after (1871) it was quietly re-

---

* Now Cardinal Newman.   † *Apologia.*

pealed. The attack on Russia, known as the *Crimean War*, lasted nearly two years (1854–1856), and England retired from the contest with little glory and less reward. The manner in which disaffected portions of the British Empire are "governed" even in this age was well represented in 1857, in the treatment of the rebellious Sepoys of India, who, when captured, were hung in groups upon any convenient tree, or were fastened to the muzzles of cannon whose discharge shattered their bodies into fragments. The Anglican Church in Ireland was disestablished in 1869; and ten years later Leo XIII. re-established the Catholic hierarchy in Scotland. Thus the great English apostacy of the sixteenth century has proved in our own day that it is a mere thing of time—the work of man, and like him subject to change, decay, and dissolution.

2. THE NINETEENTH CENTURY AS AN "AGE OF PROGRESS" IN GREAT BRITAIN.—The nineteenth century has really been an "age of progress" in Great Britain. In the early part of the century the social, religious, and political condition of the people was lamentable. They were crushed by taxation. Bread was taxed. The light of heaven was taxed. Windows were taxed, and rather than pay it people shut out the sunlight to the great injury of health and comfort. Newspapers were taxed about seven cents a copy, in order, it seems, to render such reading too costly a luxury for the workingman. The high price of soap from taxation made filth inevitable. Even salt was taxed to the extent of forty times its cost, and it was with much difficulty the toiling millions could obtain it. At the beginning of the century, it was estimated that a poor mechanic paid nearly *half*

his scanty income to the government in direct and indirect taxation. One by one, however, those crying abuses were swept away by a progressive legislation.

The British criminal laws were savage, and were administered with brutal ferocity. Eighty years ago the law recognized *two hundred and twenty-three capital crimes.** Every rogue, great or small, was put to death. If a man thoughtlessly shot a rabbit, or cut down young trees, he was hanged: his punishment was the same as that of the murderer or the highway robber. But these needless cruelties were gradually abolished. In 1837 the list of capital offences was reduced to *seven*.

A general coarseness of manners prevailed. Profane swearing was the constant practice of gentlemen. Even ladies swore orally and in their letters. The Protestant chaplain cursed the sailors, because it seemed to make them more attentive to his sermon. Lawyers swore at the bar. Judges swore on the bench. The king swore incessantly. Thus when the "head of the Anglican Church" and the "first gentleman in Europe" wished to express approval of the weather, of a handsome horse, or of a dinner which he had enjoyed, he supported his royal word by a profane oath. Among high and low, this coarseness was deplorable. Conversation was stained with wickedness, and society clothed itself with cursing as with a garment. The ordinary manners at the courts of George IV. and William IV. were such in truth as could not be seen in a decent bar-room of the present day. The accession of Queen Victoria, however, brought about a much-needed change; and both manners and conversation have since greatly improved.

---

* Among these was the "terrible crime" of being a Catholic.

England had fallen into an abyss of ignorance in spite of the boasted "Reformation." Education was as far advanced in the reign of Henry VIII. as in that of George III. At the beginning of the present century, England had only about 3300 public and private schools. Fifty years later they numbered 45,000; but it was only in 1870 that the work of public instruction began with real earnestness. In 1837 there were only 58 persons in every 100 who were able to sign their names to the marriage-register; in 1876 the number had risen to 81 in every 100, and is steadily growing.

It was only in 1807 that gas was first used to light the streets of London. When the battle of Waterloo was fought it took the despatches three days to reach the English capital. But soon the *steamboat*,* the *railway*,† and the *telegraph* ‡ came, and the world moved as it never did before. At the beginning of the century the *printing-press* was still a rude machine able to throw off no more than 150 copies an hour.§ To-day a machine, driven by steam, is fed with huge rolls of paper, and gives out newspapers, cut and folded, at the rate of 25,000 copies an hour. The postage-stamp dates from 1840.

At the beginning of the century the human hand performed all the work that was done, and performed

---

* First successfully used in 1807 by Robert Fulton on the Hudson River, and soon after introduced into Great Britain.
† A railway from Liverpool to Manchester was formally opened for traffic in 1830.
‡ Morse's telegraph came into practical use in 1844. The first successful submarine cable was laid between Dover and Calais in 1851. The first successful Atlantic cable, connecting the Old and New Worlds, was laid in 1858.
§ From the date of the invention of printing down to the close of 1814 there had been almost no improvement made on the printing-press.

it badly. Now machinery sews our clothing, reaps the fields, thrashes the grains, moves the steam-locomotive at a mile a minute, and drives the majestic steamer across the Atlantic in a week. *Chemistry, physiology, medicine,* and all the natural and physical sciences have made magnificent advances.

"One cannot but feel how fortunate," says Henry Reed, "how providential it was that the wonderful results of physical science which this century has witnessed were not accomplished in the last century, at a time when a low state of religious opinion was prevailing, when scepticism was dominant in literature; for at such a time the victories of science over the powers of the material universe, instead of raising our sense of the Creator's power, and inspiring that humility which true science ever cherishes, the more deeply at every advance it makes—instead of this, an age of unbelief, whose literature had divorced itself from revelation, would have been ready to use the results of science to decoy men into that insidious atheism which substitutes Nature for God, and would have entangled our spiritual nature in the meshes of materialism.

"The truest cultivation of science and the truest cultivation of literature in our day have shown this harmony, that alike for the scientific and the literary study of man and nature—for the naturalist, for instance, and the poet—there is needed the same humble, willing, dutiful inquiry, a power of recipiency as well as of search. The man of science, and the poet, equally, will miss the truth, if either the one or the other grows to deal boldly with nature, instead of reverently following her guidance; if he seals his heart against her secret influences; if he has a theory to maintain, a solution which shall not be disturbed; and once possessed of this false cipher, he reads amiss all the golden letters around him." *

3. THE ENGLISH LITERATURE OF THE NINETEENTH CENTURY, AND SOME OF THE AGENTS THAT INFLUENCED IT.—The nineteenth century has greatly enriched English literature. It has been a period of noted intellectual activity and bold, original investigation in Great Britain. Its history, of course, throws much light on its literature. In its early years we trace the dark, stormy influence of the French Revolution and the conquering career of Napoleon—events that stirred the mind of Europe and left their impression on English letters. The poetry of *Byron*—the "Napoleon of the realms of rhyme"—is a true reflection of that wild and warlike period. Much that was then written is unhappily tinged by the prevailing coarseness, skepticism, and indelicacy of the times. The efforts that finally produced Catholic emancipation gave birth to the fiery, splendid, and powerful eloquence of *Grattan*, *Shiel*, *O'Connell*,† and others, and aroused the strong genius of *Bishop Doyle*, and the keen, witty mind of *Sydney Smith*. For better or worse, German literature, more than that of any other nation, has greatly influenced the British intellect of the present century. This influence is most distinctly traceable in the writings of *Coleridge*, and especially those of *Thomas Carlyle*. The religious movement which gave *Newman*, *Faber*, *Manning*, and so many bright, noble spirits to the Catholic Church has a rich literature of its own.

---

* *Lectures on English Literature.*
† The productions of those Irish writers are noticed in Book III.

But infidelity and materialism have profanely invaded the domain of both science and literature. The ant, snail, frog, and ape are as eagerly studied and misread as if each had a boon or a revelation to confer upon the whole human race. The soul of man is neglected, but his body is honored with patient and minute investigation. God is ignored. The earth is asked to bear false witness against its Almighty Creator. We have such an abundance of profound babble, "scientific" lies, and blasphemous nonsense, that it has grown unfashionable to "read sermons in stones," or express a belief in everlasting punishment. Such gifted men as *Darwin*, *Huxley*, *Tyndall*, and *Spencer* have set themselves to the work of teaching a false philosophy, degrading to man and hostile to God and the Christian religion. The same false and pernicious principles have been carried into general literature by such able writers as *Mill, Buckle, Lecky*, and "*George Eliot*." English literature is cursed with a growing pagan element. This is an age of intellectual pride, but the repulsive pride which attacks truth inspires no kind feeling. It is the spirit of Lucifer. It deserves nothing but scorn and punishment. "I believe," says Ruskin, "the first test of a truly great man is humility." But humility is a virtue almost unknown in English letters, which for over three centuries have been pride-stricken, filled with falsehood, and in a state of revolt against the truth.

Another feature is quite noteworthy. British bigotry and anti-Catholic fanaticism, it need hardly be said, have largely found expression in print. Nor is the present century an exception. During its early portion England was overflowing with intolerance, and every branch of literature was pervaded by an ignorant and malignant spirit of hatred towards the Catholic Religion. Even the school-books on grammar, history, geography, logic, and rhetoric were pressed into the service of falsehood and fanaticism. Picking up a school-dictionary, issued about sixty years ago, we turn over a few leaves and read: "*Anti-Christ*, one who opposes Christ—*the Pope.*" Nor was this miserable teaching without its fruits. " When 1 was young," says Cardinal Newman, " and after I was grown up, I thought the Pope to be antichrist. At Christmas, 1824–5, I preached a sermon to that effect." * Pulpits rang with abuse of the Pope from one end of the year to the other. The blind led the blind, and England was full of brutal, blinding bigotry. Even such men as Sir Walter Scott in his *Waverley Novels*, Macaulay and Hallam in their *Histories* † and other works, and Archbishop Whately in his *Elements of Logic* could not rise above the narrow spirit of anti-Catholic intolerance. Happily, there is now less to complain of. The doors of the Universities of Oxford and Cambridge were opened to Catholics in 1871; and, on the whole, English letters are marked by a more just and generous spirit towards the ancient faith.

The first thirty or forty years of the present century constitute one of the great creative periods in

---

* *Apologia.*
† It may be stated, once for all, that there is not a single British Protestant historian who does not in some way bear false witness against Catholics and the Catholic Church; but whether this systematic injustice is to be attributed to invincible ignorance or invincible intolerance in the writers it would indeed be hard to conjecture. English history is crammed with falsehood, and Cobbett has bluntly said that it contains more lies than that of all the other books in the world.

English literature; and, as is usual during such periods, poetry rose in popularity, and held the supremacy. It was a time of transition from the cold, artificial formalism of the eighteenth century to something more warm, hearty, and natural. The names of *Scott*, *Byron*, *Moore*, *Coleridge*, *Campbell*, and *Wordsworth* belong to this period. Later years can claim no such array of poetic genius. Our own day may be represented by *Mrs. Browning*, *Miss Procter*, *Robert Browning*, and *Alfred Tennyson*.

The present century has witnessed the decline of the British drama even below the point at which it stood one hundred years ago. Why this is so it would not be easy to explain; but there is no doubt as to the fact that the plays written by men of genius within the last sixty or seventy years have generally proved ill adapted for the stage, while the authors of the successful plays have not been men of genius.*

Prose has had a growth that is truly marvellous. It covers immense fields in fiction and periodical literature, not to mention other departments of letters. Scott's *Waverley Novels* and the works of Dickens, Thackeray, and other writers of fiction would, in themselves, make a large library.

As to British periodical literature, it may be said that its size and variety baffle description. At its two extremes stand the *quarterly* and the *daily*. The *Edinburgh Review*, the oldest of the quarterlies, was started in 1802 by Sydney Smith, Francis Jeffrey, and a few able young men. It was followed by *The Quarterly Review* (1809), *The Westminster Review* (1824), *The Dublin Review* † (1836), and some others.

---

* Thomas Arnold.
† The chief organ of the Catholics of Great Britain.

Among the chief monthlies are the *Gentleman's Magazine* (1731), the oldest of its class; *Blackwood's Magazine* (1817), *Frazer's Magazine* (1830); and of later growth are *The Cornhill*, *Macmillan's Magazine*, *The Month*,* *The Fortnightly Review*, *The Contemporary Review*, and *The Nineteenth Century*. Among the most prominent of the British *weeklies* are *The Saturday Review*, *The Athenæum*, *The Spectator*, and *The Tablet*;* while among the principal *dailies* we may note *The Times*, *The Daily News*, and *The Daily Telegraph*—all published in London and having a large circulation.†

The present age has produced the greatest historians in English literature. No other century can point to such men as *Lingard*, *Hallam*, *Macaulay*, *Alison*, *Grote*, *Carlyle*, *Stubbs*, *Green*, and *Freeman*. The fields of art, science, criticism, politics, philosophy, biography, and theology have all been ably and ardently cultivated. The chief names in this connection are *Ruskin*, *Brewster*, *Hamilton*, *Faraday*, *Whewell*, *Darwin*, *Huxley*, *Tyndall*, *Spencer*, *Mivart*, *Jeffrey*, *Sydney Smith*, *Cobbett*, *Lockhart*, *Wiseman*, *Faber*, *Newman*, *Manning*, *Marshall*, *Dalgairns*, *Ward*, and *Harper*.

English letters, in Great Britain, seem to be drifting into a period of decline. The old masters are rapidly passing away, and their places remain unfilled. Nor can much hope be gathered from the intellectual condition of the nation at large. While a taste for reading of some sort is daily increasing, the taste for serious study of any kind is diminishing among the

---

* Catholic.
† The *Times* has a reputed circulation of 100,000 copies a day; the *Daily News*, 160,000 copies; and the *Daily Telegraph*, 220,000 copies.

great mass of the English people. It is the age of rapid living and rapid reading. Books are devoured, but few study.* "A true student," says a recent English writer, "will soon be as rare as the dodo, and a true *littérateur* be as old-fashioned a spectacle as a true scholar is to-day."

LESSON I.

LORD BYRON. DIED 1824.

(1) *Childe Harold's Pilgrimage.*   (2) *The Prisoner of Chillon.*
(3) *Don Juan.*   (4) *Dramas.*

SAMUEL T. COLERIDGE. DIED 1834.

(1) *Rime of the Ancient Mariner.*   (2) *Christabel.*
(3) *Lectures on Shakspeare.*   (4) *Biographia Literaria.*

1. Who was Lord Byron?

Lord Byron,† the first English poet of his day, was an erratic genius of great energy, originality, and depth of feeling.

2. Tell us something of his career.

Byron was born at London, and had the misfortune of belonging to a bad family.‡ He derived little benefit from his stay at Cambridge, for he was a careless, headstrong student. After being a member of

---

* During the year 1880 there were published in England 5708 new books and new editions. There is really a superabundance of cheap manuals, boiled-down biography, trashy fiction, poor poetry, and ready-made criticism on the most abstruse subjects.
† His full name was *George Gordon Byron.*
‡ His father was a villain; his grand-uncle a murderer; his mother a woman of violent temper; and himself, with all this legacy, a man of powerful passions. If evil is in any degree to be palliated because it is hereditary, those who most condemn it in the abstract, may still look with compassionate leniency upon the career of Lord Byron.—*Coppée.*

the House of Lords for some years, he left England in 1816—never to see it again. The close of his wild, unhappy life, however, is gilded by a ray of sunset glory. He went to aid the struggling Greeks, and died in the land of Homer and Demosthenes.

3. Which is his chief poem?

Childe * *Harold's Pilgrimage.*

4. In what does this work abound?

It abounds in exquisite photographs of man, art, nature, and society.† It was inspired by the poet's travels.

5. Mention one of the best of his many short poems?

The Prisoner of Chillon, a painful story of touching tenderness.

6. Did not Byron try his pen at dramatic writing?

He did, but without much success. Byron had not the power of *going out of himself,* and his dramas are only dramas *in form.*‡

7. What was the last famous work that came from his pen, and how must it be judged?

The poem of *Don Juan.* It exhibits fine descrip— ... that ... the ... and awaited the achievements of this gifted man?

He lacked *steadiness of purpose* and *manly industry,* without which nothing really great can be achieved.† Coleridge was a magnificent dreamer.

---

* "The *Ancient Mariner,*" writes Dice, "was founded on a strange dream which a friend of Coleridge had, who fancied that he saw a skeleton ship, with figures in it."

"The fair breeze blew, the white foam flew,
The furrow followed free;
We were the first that ever burst
Into that silent sea."

† "No amount of genius," says Lacordaire, "will go far unbacked by work. Work is the key to eloquence and knowledge, as well as to virtue."—*Letters to Young Men.*

21*

tive power and a wonderful mastery over language; but, in spite of all its beauties, it is grossly immoral, and the most dangerous of Byron's productions.

8. What may be said of Byron as a teacher?

He was, unhappily, a bad teacher, who wrote some of the worst lessons contained in poetry. So long as truth is beautiful and virtue precious, so long must the warning finger of condemnation be raised against the writings of Lord Byron. Danger lurks under the leaves of his works.*

9. What has been observed of his style and merits as a literary artist?

He possesses a style of remarkable vigor and great felicity of expression; but the beauty and sublimity of his poems *are confined to passages.* Judged as a whole, none of them can be called a finished work of art.

10. What other most remarkable personage figured in the literary world during the time of Lord Byron?

Samuel Taylor Coleridge, a native of England, and an eccentric genius of rare powers but no industry.

Byron was born at London, and had the misfortune of belonging to a bad family.‡ He derived little benefit from his stay at Cambridge, for he was a careless, headstrong student. After being a member of

---

* During the year 1880 there were published in England 5708 new books and new editions. There is really a superabundance of cheap manuals, boiled-down biography, trashy fiction, poor poetry, and ready-made criticism on the most abstruse subjects.
† His full name was *George Gordon Byron.*
‡ His father was a villain; his grand-uncle a murderer; his mother a woman of violent temper; and himself, with all this legacy, a man of powerful passions. If evil is in any degree to be palliated because it is hereditary, those who most condemn it in the abstract, may still look with compassionate leniency upon the career of Lord Byron.—*Coppée.*

11. Which is Coleridge's chief and best known poem?

The Rime of the Ancient Mariner, a weird sea-tale told in the simple style of the old ballad.*

12. What is *Christabel?*

It is a noble fragment of a poem, wild and mystic in character. Its diction is delightful, and it glitters with exquisite imagery.

13. What merit belo gs to Coleridge's *Lectures on Shakspeare?*

They were the *first* masterly criticism, in English, on the genius of Shakspeare.

14. What is the *Biographia Literaria?*

It is a collection of valuable sketches of men of letters, and is written with rare critical power.

15. What has been remarked of Coleridge's mastery over language?

He was a consummate master of prose and verse. His verse, especially, breathes all sounds and melodies:

> "For now 'tis like all instruments,
> Now like a lovely flute;
> And now it is an angel's song.
> That makes the heavens be mute."

16. What radical defect marred the charact r and dwarfed the achievements of this gifted man?

He lacked *steadiness of purpose* and *manly industry*, without which nothing really great can be achieved.† Coleridge was a magnificent dreamer.

---

* "The *Ancient Mariner*," writes Dice, "was founded on a strange dream which a friend of Coleridge had, who fancied that he saw a skeleton ship, with figures in it."

> "The fair breeze blew, the white foam flew,
> The furrow followed free;
> We were the first that ever burst
> Into that silent sea."

† "No amount of genius," says Lacordaire, "will go far unbacked by work. Work is the key to eloquence and knowledge, as well as to virtue."—*Letters to Young Men.*

21*

He scarcely finished anything but his sentences. We know him only by fragments. He was a giant in conception, but a dwarf in execution.

LESSON II.

THOMAS CAMPBELL. DIED 1844.
(1) *The Pleasures of Hope.* (2) *Gertrude of Wyoming.*
(3) *Songs.*

WILLIAM WORDSWORTH. DIED 1850.
(1) *The Excursion.* (2) *The Prelude.*
(3) *Sonnets and Short Poems.*

17. Who may be considered the greatest British lyric poet of this century?

Thomas Campbell.

18. Give a brief outline of his career.

Campbell was born at Glasgow, Scotland, and educated in the university of that city.* His first poem made him famous. He travelled for a time, but his life was otherwise quiet and uneventful. He was one of the founders of the London University.

19. What was his first poem?

The Pleasures of Hope, which was given to the world before Campbell was twenty-two years of age. It is a brilliant production, exquisite in language, and lovely and sublime in the subjects selected.†

---

* Campbell, though born in Glasgow, was a Highlander both in blood and nature; and his genius is most attractive in those poems in which his loving Celtic nature has free play.—*Arnold.*

† Among others it contains the often-quoted lines,
  "Like angel-visits, few and far between,"
and
  " 'Tis distance lends enchantment to the view."

20. What is *Gertrude of Wyoming?*

It is a beautiful poem, written in the Spenserian stanza, and embodying a sad, touching tale ; but it is neither true to the nature of the country nor the Indian character.*

21. In what branch of poetry has Campbell attained the highest excellence?

As a lyric poet.

22. Name some of his most noted lyrics and short poems.

The Exile of Erin†, *Ye Mariners of England*,‡

---

* The scenes, characters, and incidents of this poem, as is well known, are laid in the ill-fated Valley of Wyoming. on the Susquehanna, opposite the present town of Wilkesbarre, in Pennsylvania. The savage massacre that suggested it took place during the American Revolution in the summer of 1778, and was the work of Tories and Indians, commanded by Colonel Butler and the Indian chief Brant. "Colonel Butler," writes Hassard, " defeated the small body of soldiers which attempted to oppose him (July 3), and compelled the rest of the people who had taken refuge in Fort Wyoming to surrender, on promise of security to life and property. Butler, however, was unable to control his savage allies. They massacred about 400 prisoners and civilians, burned the houses, and destroyed the crops; and the survivors, mostly women and children, fled to the mountains, where many of them perished."—*History of the United States.*

† It is said that he wrote this touching poem at Hamburg, after meeting a number of brave Irish exiles, who had fled from the hapless rebellion of 1798. *The Exile of Erin* consists of five stanzas, of which the following is the first:

" There came to the beach a poor exile of Erin,
 The dew on his thin robe was heavy and chill;
For his country he sighed, when at twilight repairing
 To wander alone by the wind-beaten hill.
But the day-star attracted his eye's sad devotion,
For it rose o'er his own native isle of the ocean,
Where once, in the fire of his youthful emotion,
 He sang the bold anthem of *Erin go bragh!*'"

‡ *Ye Mariners of England* is in four stanzas. We give the first:

" Ye mariners of England!
 That guard our native seas;
Whose flag has braved, a thousand years,
 The battle and the breeze!
Your glorious standard launch again,
 To match another foe!
And sweep through the deep,
 While the stormy tempests blow;
While the battle rages loud and long,
 And the stormy tempests blow."

The Battle of the Baltic, Hohenlinden,* O'Connor's Child, and *Lord Ullin's Daughter.*

23. Sum up Campbell's good qualities as a poet.

Campbell had the true poetic fire. He possessed, in the highest degree, what we call beauty of style.† He did not write much, but the exquisite finish of his poems is admirable, and some of his lyrics seem to be absolutely perfect.

24. Who was acknowledged to be one of the great chiefs of English le ters about the middle of the present century?

William Wordsworth. From 1840 to 1850 he was considered the greatest living poet in England.

25. Is there anything remarkable about his life?

No; he was born in the extreme northwest of England, and took his degree at Cambridge. Some

---

* While travelling in Europe in 1800, Campbell witnessed the battle of Hohenlinden from the tower of a Bavarian monastery. His lines on the event form a ringing battle-song.

"By torch and trumpet fast arrayed,
Each horseman drew his battle-blade,
And furious every charger neighed
To join the dreadful revelry.

"Then shook the hills with thunder riven,
Then rushed the steed to battle driven,
And, louder than the bolts of heaven,
Far flashed the red artillery.
. . . . . .
"Few, few shall part where many meet!
The snow shall be their winding-sheet,
And every turf beneath their feet
Shall be a soldier's sepulchre."

† As an instance take his first two stanzas "To the Rainbow":

"Triumphal arch, that fill'st the sky
When storms prepare to part,
I ask not proud Philosophy
To teach me what thou art.

"Still seem, as to my childhood's sight,
A midway station given
For happy spirits to alight
Betwixt the earth and heaven."

travelling and the labors of a studious and literary career filled up the remainder of his long life. He became poet-laureate in 1843.

26. Which is Wordsworth's chief poem?

The Excursion, a long unfinished poem—the fragment of a great moral epic. It is written in blank-verse, and in its present form consists of nine books.

27. Of what topics does *The Excursion* treat, and what are its merits and defects?

It discusses the deepest questions concerning *God*, *man*, *nature*, and *society*. The poem contains many sublime passages, but it has too much flat, wearisome reflection and philosophy to be all poetry. Few ever read it through, and it is only the *thinking few* who can appreciate it. But, in spite of its faults and dulness, it is a grand composition.

28. What is *The Prelude?*

It is a long autobiographical poem in fourteen books.*

29. What praise has been given to Wordsworth's *Sonnets?*

The very highest; he has written some of the finest sonnets† in our language.

---

* The full title is, *The Prelude, or Growth of a Poet's Mind*. It was begun as a preparation for his other works.
† The one entitled *Scorn not the Sonnet* is a happy and suggestive effort:

"Scorn not the Sonnet! Critic, you have frowned,
Mindless of its just honors. With this key
Shakspeare unlocked his heart; the melody
Of this small lute gave ease to Petrarch's wound;
A thousand times this pipe did Tasso sound;
With it Camoëns soothed an exile's grief;
The Sonnet glittered a gay myrtle-leaf
Amid the cypress with which Dante crowned
His visionary brow; a glow-worm lamp,
It cheered mild Spenser, called from fairy-land
To struggle through dark ways; and when a damp
Fell round the path of Milton, in his hand
The thing became a trumpet, whence he blew
Soul-animating strains,—alas! too few."

30. What verdict may be fairly passed on Wordsworth and his poems?

Wordsworth was a poet, deep, thoughtful, and religious; but he was wanting in the fire and force of high genius. He is true to nature. His style is simple and often vigorous. But notwithstanding many merits and beauties, his longer poems are nearly devoid of living interest and are frequently flat, lifeless, and commonplace.* He will soon be read only in a volume of "beauties," containing one twentieth of his writings.

LESSON III.

MRS. E. B. BROWNING. DIED 1861.
(1) *Aurora Leigh*, and other Poems.
(2) *Sonnets from the Portuguese.*

ADELAIDE A. PROCTER. DIED 1864.
Poems and Lyrics.

31. Who has been pronounced the greatest English poetess of the nineteenth century?

Elizabeth Barrett Browning, who was born at London, and whose genius was aided by a very superior education. She was a thorough Latin and Greek scholar.

32. Which is her chief work?

Aurora Leigh, a long narrative poem in nine books. It recounts the life and thoughts of the poetess herself. It is "the autobiography of a heart and intellect."

---

* "His longer poems," writes Lowell, "are Egyptian sand-wastes, with here and there an oasis of exquisite greenery, a grand image, sphynx-like, half buried in drifting commonplaces, or the solitary Pompey's Pillar of some towering thought."—*Among my Books.*

33. How does she rank as a writer of sonnets?

Her *Sonnets from the Portuguese* are among the very finest in the language.

34. What defects mar the writings of this gifted woman?

She is sometimes obscure in thought, and turgid and faulty in language; while, here and there, in her poems we catch the echoes of that false philosophy which is the curse of our age.

35. Who was Adelaide Anne Procter?

She was the accomplished daughter of the poet Procter,* a native of London, and one of the best and sweetest singers of this age.

36. What are the chief characteristics of her poetry?

Simplicity, purity, Christian tenderness, and a faultless finish and felicity of expression.†

---

* Bryan Waller Procter, better known as "Barry Cornwall," who died in 1868.

† Thirteen years before her happy death Miss Procter became a Catholic. The true faith—as it ever does—added new force and beauty to her genius. Her poetry had its roots in her own lovely character, at once so pure, cheerful, rounded, and full of charity. After a lingering illness, she died of consumption. "At midnight," writes Charles Dickens, "on the 2d of February, 1864, she turned down a leaf of a little book she was reading, and shut it up. And she quietly asked, as the clock was on the stroke of one, 'Do you think I am dying, mamma?'

"'I think you are very, very ill to-night, my dear.'

"'Send for my sister. My feet are so cold. Lift me up!'

"Her sister entering as they raised her, she said, 'It has come at last!' and, with a bright and happy smile, looked upward and departed."

The following is from her little poem called *Now*:

"Rise! for the day is passing,
 And you lie dreaming on;
The others have buckled their armor,
 And forth to the fight are gone.
A place in the ranks awaits you;
 Each man has some part to play:
The Past and the Future are nothing
 In the face of the stern To-day."

LESSON IV.

ALFRED TENNYSON.

Chief works: (1) *The Princess.*
(2) *In Memoriam.*
(3) *The Idylls of the King.*
(4) *Locksley Hall*, and other Poems.
(5) *Queen Mary*, and *Harold.* (Dramas.)

37. Who stands at the head of the living poets of Great Britain?

Alfred Tennyson, the poet-laureate of England.

38. Give a brief outline of his life.

He was born in England, educated at Cambridge, and, on the death of Wordsworth, in 1850, was created poet-laureate. His life has been passed in study and retirement.

39. What is *The Princess*, and when was it first published?

The Princess is a pleasant poem which touches the subject of higher female education, and through every page of which there runs a golden thread of delicate playfulness, or suggestive wisdom. It was published in 1847.*

---

* Among the exquisite songs introduced here and there in *The Princess* is *The Bugle Song*:

"The splendor falls on castle walls
 And snowy summits old in story;
The long light shakes across the lakes
 And the wild cataract leaps in glory.
Blow, bugle, blow, set the wild echoes flying,
Blow, bugle,—answer, echoes, dying, dying, dying.

"O hark, O hear! how thin and clear,
 And thinner, clearer, farther going!
O sweet and far from cliff and scar
 The horns of Elfland faintly blowing!
Blow, let us hear the purple glens replying;
Blow, bugle,—answer, echoes, dying, dying, dying.

"O Love, they die in yon rich sky,
 They faint on hill or field or river;

40. What remarkable poem did Tennyson write to commemorate the untimely death of his friend, Arthur Henry Hallam, son of the famous historian?

In Memoriam.

41. What are its length and merits?

In Memoriam contains 129 four-lined stanzas,* but it is rather a group of elegies than a single poem. It is considered one of Tennyson's most famous and finished productions.

42. On what work will Tennyson's fame, however, most likely pass down to posterity as a poet?

The Idylls† of the King, in which he has revived with great success the old legends of King Arthur, and made them a part of the living literature of England.

43. Where, also, is much of this poet's excellence to be found?

In *Locksley Hall,* and many of his short pieces,

Our echoes roll from soul to soul,
And grow forever and forever.
Blow, bugle, blow, set the wild echoes flying,
And answer, echoes, answer, dying, dying, dying."

* The following stanza is often quoted:

"I hold it true whate'er befall;
I feel it when I sorrow most;
'Tis better to have loved and lost
Than never to have loved at all."

† An Idyll, in the sense used by Tennyson, is a narrative poem, written in an elevated and highly refined style. Few are aware how very considerable a portion of Tennyson's poems is deliberate rendering into pure melodious verse of what has already existed in another form. All poets, indeed, avail themselves of the heritage of the past, and there are few poems of any length which do not owe their origin to some story, event, or other circumstance outside of their author's brain. The whole of the *Idylls of the King* are poetic renderings of the old prose Arthurian legends, in great part from the *History of King Arthur* by Sir Thomas Malory, from Lady Schreiber's version of the *Mabinogion*, and in part from less known sources. Touches are brought from other books, and it is curious that passages even from Crofton Croker's *Irish Legends* are adapted, and made to fit into the story of King Arthur.

which are exquisite gems. The *Charge of the Light Brigade*, for instance, is a fine battle lyric.

44. Has not Tennyson recently tried his hand at dramatic writing?

Yes; he has given to the world *Queen Mary* and *Harold*, two dramas which, however, are *not real dramas*. They are mere poems in dramatic form, and are far from adding to Tennyson's reputation, being untrue to history, and pervaded with a narrow, anti-Catholic spirit.

45. What do you think of his style as exhibited in his best poems?

While wanting in vigor and deep, warm, expressive feeling, at the same time, no poet has more finished beauty of style and exquisite charm of melody than Tennyson.*

LESSON V.

JOHN LINGARD. DIED 1851.

(1) *History of England.*
(2) *Antiquities of the Anglo-Saxon Church.*

LORD MACAULAY. DIED 1859.

(1) *Critical and Historical Essays.*   (2) *History of England.*
(3) *Lays of Ancient Rome.*

HENRY HALLAM. DIED 1859.

(1) *Introduction to the Literature of Europe in the 15th, 16th, and 17th Centuries.*
(2) *View of Europe During the Middle Ages.*
(3) *Constitutional History of England.*

46. Who was Dr. John Lingard?

He was a learned Catholic priest, a native of England who was educated at Douay in France, and spent

---

* It has been well said that the secret of Tennyson's success is, *he is in perfect harmony with his age.* His artificial turn suits this pretentious century. His poetry, indeed, enchants the ear and

the last forty years of his life at the secluded mission of Hornby in Lincolnshire.

47. Which is his chief work?

A History of England, from the First Invasion of the Romans to the Accession of William and Mary in 1688. The last edition, as revised by the author, is in ten octavo volumes.*

48. Mention some of the many admirable qualities of this masterly production?

It possesses all the higher qualities which should adorn a great history—deep research, fulness of detail, lucid arrangement, and an impartiality that is truly admirable. Among the crowd of works on English history it stands alone—unrivalled.

49. What may be said of the style in which it is written?

The style is one of classic purity. It is calm, concise, vigorous, and idiomatic. It is a style which, while avoiding their defects, seems to unite the beauties of Hume, Robertson, and Gibbon.

50. Which was Lingard's earliest production, the pioneer, indeed, of his great *History?*

The Antiquities of the Anglo-Saxon Church, a work of great merit, which treats of the establishment of the faith among the Anglo-Saxons, and of the customs, laws, learning, and literature of early Christian England.

51. Who was one of the most brilliant writers of this century, especially in the field of historical criticism?

Thomas Babington Macaulay, a native of England

---

plays with the fancy, but it seldom stirs the heart or penetrates the soul.

* In recognition of Lingard's great services to religion and literature, Pope Pius VII. conferred upon him the degrees of Doctor of Divinity and of Canon and Civil Law, in 1821. At one time it was rumored that he was to be raised to the dignity of Cardinal, but the learned priest remonstrated, as it would interfere with the completion of his *History.*

who, as a student at Cambridge had won high honors, and while still a young man had become famous by his essays in the *Edinburgh Review.*

52. Which is his greatest historical work, and what period of time does it cover?

His *History of England from the Accession of James II.* It begins with the reign of James II., and covers a period of little more than fifteen years. It is only a brilliant fragment.*

53. What are Macaulay's chief defects as an historian?

He was a man of strong prejudices. He is always either a warm partisan or a bitter enemy, and is thus unfitted to hold the balance of justice. He paints James II. in the blackest colors, but his over-praise of William of Orange is false and fulsome. He is brilliant, but not always reliable.

54. What may be said of his poetry?

He wrote little, but that little is delightful in its way. In the *Lays of Ancient Rome,* he chants some of the daring deeds which adorn the pages of early Roman history.

55. Which, on the whole, may be considered the best among the works of this learned and most versatile genius?

His *Critical and Historical Essays.*

56. Is Macaulay's style remarkable?

It is; he usually expresses himself in short, pithy sentences. His diction is remarkably clear, lively, pointed, forcible, and brilliant. He was, indeed, a distinguished master of English prose.

---

* "I purpose," said Macaulay, "to write the history of England from the accession of James the Second down to a time which is within the memory of men still living." But when death came, he had only completed a fraction of his self-imposed task.

57. What other English historian greatly enriched our literature with productions of permanent value during the present century?

Henry Hallam, who was one of the very ablest and most distinguished of the critical historians of modern times.

58. By what famous work did he enrich English criticism in 1837?

By his *Introduction to the Literature of Europe in the Fifteenth, Sixteenth, and Seventeenth Centuries*, a most valuable work of which the sagacity and calmness are well matched with the profound erudition.

59. Which was the first of Hallam's productions, in the order of time?

A View of the State of Europe in the Middle Ages, which was first published in 1818. It is an elegant, highly finished, and solid production.

60. What other remarkable historical work did he publish in 1827?

The Constitutional History of England from the accession of Henry VII. to the death of George II., a work which Macaulay pronounced the most impartial book he ever read.

61. In what way do Hallam's works rebuke such careless historical writers as Robertson, Hume, and Froude?

Besides deep and varied learning and exhaustive research, Hallam brought to his tasks a wonderfully earnest, truth-loving, and impartial mind.*

---

* It is worthy of note, however, that one exception must be made —his occasional treatment of Catholics and their religion. But in making this exception we do not mean to impeach either the candor or the honesty of Hallam. He was a Dean's son, a graduate of Oxford, and a Protestant Englishman; and knowing this, we must make due allowance for his "color-blindness" and other shortcomings in regard to the Catholic Church.

LESSON VI.

SIR WALTER SCOTT. DIED 1832.

Chief works: (1) *Poems.*
(2) *The Waverley Novels.*

62. Who was Sir Walter Scott?

He was one of the greatest literary geniuses of the nineteenth century—a man whose pen added to the riches of English poetry, and who stands unsurpassed in the field of prose fiction.

63. Give an outline of his early life.

He was born at Edinburgh, passed a delicate boyhood surrounded by picturesque ruins and historic localities—famous in war and verse—which failed not to leave an enduring impression on his mind. He finished his education at the university of his native city, and was admitted to the bar, but he soon abandoned the legal profession.

64. How did Scott first become famous in letters—as a poet or as a novelist?

As a poet.

65. Which was his first great poem?

The Lay of the Last Minstrel, published in 1805. It was the first of a series of enchanting tales in verse.

66. Of all Scott's poems, mention the three that may be considered his best.

The Lay of the Last Minstrel, *Marmion*, and *The Lady of the Lake.**

67. In what new department of literature—which he may

---

* "The *Lay* is generally considered as the most natural and original, *Marmion* as the most powerful and splendid, and *The Lady of the Lake* as the most interesting, romantic, picturesque and graceful."—*Lockhart.*

be said to have discovered or created—did Scott begin to labor in 1814?*

- Historical romance.

68. Which was the pioneer of the new works that now came from his busy, fertile pen?

Waverley, a tale of the romantic rising of the Scottish clans for Prince Charles Edward in 1745.

69. What followed during the next seventeen years?

Twenty-eight other works of varied degrees of excellence. They are called the *Waverley Novels* from the name of the first number of the series.

70. Into what two classes may the *Waverley Novels* be divided?

The *historical* and the *personal*. The first picture some real persons and events of history—chiefly Scottish or English. The second deals principally with private life or family legends.

71. Had Scott the true idea of historic fiction?

He had; his genius happily called up in living array, not merely the names, but the character, manners, thoughts, and passions of past ages.

72. What misfortune befell this gifted man in the financial panic of 1825?

He suddenly found that, through the failure of two publishing houses, he was a bankrupt to the amount of over half a million dollars.

73. What did he now do?

He bore himself bravely in the midst of this utter ruin; and, though fifty-five years of age, he at once set to work with his well-worn pen to pay off the vast debt. He nearly succeeded, but the effort killed him.

---

* Some years after this, he wrote to a friend: "In truth, I have given up poetry. . . . I felt the prudence of giving way before the more forcible and powerful genius of Byron." But in the new path which he struck out, Scott stood alone—head and shoulders above all.

74. What is your opinion of his style?

Though easy and animated, it cannot be said that Scott is always careful and correct in his language. He is too diffuse. But he is a master of the picturesque—a great painter in words.*

"In the historical novel, Sir Walter Scott—the inventor of the style—remains unapproached."—*Thomas Arnold.*

"It is the fashion, among writers of a certain class, to speak of Scott as superseded by Thackeray and Dickens. In a measure this is true; every writer, no matter how great, is crowded out more or less by his successors. Not even Shakspeare, Dante, and Goethe have been exceptions to this rule. But it may well be pondered, whether, years from now, when the final muster-roll of English novelists is called, Scott's name will not head the list."—*J. S. Hart.*

"Scott's fame as a poet was eclipsed by his reputation as a novelist; and the appearance of a star of greater magnitude drew from him, by degrees, the popularity he had so long engrossed. Yet we venture to hazard an opinion, that if it be possible for either to be forgotten, his poems will outlive his prose; and that *Waverley* and *Ivanhoe* will perish before *Marmion* and *The Lady of the Lake.* We can find no rare and valuable quality in the former that we may not find in the latter. A deeply interesting and exciting story, glorious and true pictures of scenery, fine and accurate portraits of character, clear and impressive accounts of ancient customs, details of battles—satisfying to the fancy, yet capable of enduring the sternest test of truth—are to be found in the one class as well as in the other."—*S. C. Hall.*

LESSON VII.

SYDNEY SMITH. DIED 1845.
(1) *Essays.* (2) *Letters of Peter Plymly.*

LORD JEFFREY. DIED 1850.
Essays.

75. Who was Sydney Smith?

He was a gifted and witty Protestant clergyman, a native of England, and one of the founders and the first editor of the *Edinburgh Review.*

---

* It must be added with regret, however, that Scott was not above the religious bigotry of his time and country; for his treatment of Catholics and their religion is sometimes very far from being just and generous.

76. Where did most of his *Essays* first appear, and on what subjects did he usually write?

Most of his *Essays* first appeared in the *Edinburgh Review*. He commonly wrote on politics, literature, and philosophy.

77. Which is his most celebrated series of writings?

His *Letters on the Subject of the Catholics*. He wrote under the name of "Peter Plymly," and the *Letters* were addressed to "my brother Abraham who lives in the country." They are a fine example of wit used as a political weapon.

78. When were these *Letters* published, and what was their object?

They were published in 1807, and their object was to hasten the emancipation of the Catholics. Smith's warm, manly sympathy was given to the oppressed Catholics of Ireland, and his exertions in their behalf should never be forgotten.

79. For what are his writings especially marked?

For hearty wit, solid reasoning, and keen common sense. Indeed, for pure wit, Sydney Smith stands unrivalled among the British prose-writers. Many of his bright sayings have passed into proverbs.*

80. Who was Lord Jeffrey?

Francis Jeffrey was a native of Scotland, a lawyer,

---

* Only two years before his death, in answer to the inquiries of a French journalist, Smith wrote the following It is a good specimen of his style: "I am 74 years of age; and being a Canon of St. Paul's in London, and Rector of a parish in the country, my time is equally divided between town and country. I am living amid the best society in the metropolis; am at ease in my circumstances; in tolerable health; a mild whig; a tolerating churchman; and much given to talking, laughing, and noise. I dine with the rich in London, and physic the poor in the country; passing from the sauces of Dives to the sores of Lazarus. I am, upon the whole, a happy man; have found the world an entertaining world, and am heartily thankful to Providence for the part allotted to me in it."

edited the *Edinburgh Review* for twenty-six years, and finally rose to be Lord-Advocate.

81. **What are his chief published works?**

Essays, which are in four volumes, and consist of a selection of *seventy-nine* of his best articles from the *Edinburgh Review*.

82. **What may be said of his standing as a critic, writer, and reviewer?**

Jeffrey was a distinguished critic, and a writer of great vigor and elegance. He stands at the head of modern English reviewers.

LESSON VIII.

FREDERICK WILLIAM FABER.   DIED 1863.
(1) *All for Jesus.*   (2) *The Blessed Sacrament.*
(3) *The Creator and the Creature.*   (4) *Spiritual Conferences.*
(5) *Poems.*

NICHOLAS PATRICK WISEMAN.   DIED 1865.
(1) *Lectures on the Connection between Science and Revealed Religion.*
(2) *Lectures on the Principal Doctrines and Practices of the Catholic Church.*
(3) *Recollections of the Last Four Popes.*
(4) *Essays on Various Subjects.*
(5) *Fabiola, or the Church of the Catacombs.*

83. **Who was Father Faber?**

Frederick William Faber, D.D., a native of England, was educated at Oxford, became a convert* to

---

* In 1845, four years *before* his conversion, during a tour through Europe, he wrote the following. It is a fair specimen of his style: "As we ascended the river (Enns) from this mountain pass, the valley opened out into a wet and sterile and forlorn basin. In the midst of this stands the spacious Benedictine monastery, Ad Montes. It was founded by Gebhard, Bishop of Salzburg, in 1074. The pile of building is immense. There are ninety monks in it, who have theological pupils under them, and also instruct the poor of the parishes on their estates in agriculture and domestic arts. The usual indomitable energy of the monks has done much to

the Catholic faith, and for nearly twenty years was one of the most prominent priests and popular spiritual writers in Europe.

84. Name some of his principal works.

(See the list at the head of the lesson.)

85. What may be said of his spiritual writings?

They are very popular. Faber is a writer of great unction. He is attractive.* He often conveys truth in short, epigrammatic sentences, full of practical wisdom and the spirit of holy kindness. His volumes abound in literary beauties.

86. How may his personal and literary merits be summed up?

He was an apostolic man, an eloquent preacher, a writer of exquisite prose, and a poet of rare excellence.†

---

cover this bleak basin with cultivation; but, like an imperfect garment, it only calls attention to the nakedness it would fain conceal. Yet I saw phalanxes of wheat-sheaves along the river side, and many unpromising spots upon the steeps were fragrant with red clover. Almost every Englishman, in books, letters, and conversation, is ready with the hack phrases to which a few Whig historians of the seventeenth and eighteenth centuries have tuned us, such as 'lazy monks,' 'drones of monasteries,' 'fatteners on the poor,' and the like. Yet, if men, who would or could think, were to wander, as I have done, up river-courses, threading sequestered valleys, and tracing hill-born brooks, and exploring deserted woodlands, not for any such purpose as to gather evidence in behalf of monks, but merely to foster and strengthen meditative power, they would see how, under the toiling hands of the old monks, green grass and yellow corn encroached upon the black heath and unhealthy fen—how lordly and precious woods rose upon unproductive steeps—how waters became a blessing where they had been a curse, irrigating the lands which once they ravaged—how poor communities were held together by their alms in unhopeful places for years, till the constrained earth yielded her reluctant fruits—and cities are *now* where the struggling tenant villages of the kind monks were, as the monks' salt-pans are now the princely Munich."

* "I want to make piety bright and happy," he writes in the preface to his *All for Jesus*.

† Faber was a great admirer of Wordsworth. Indeed, it seems the admiration was reciprocal. "If it were not for Frederick Faber's devoting himself so much to his sacred calling," said Wordsworth on one occasion, "he would be *the* poet of his age."

87. Who was Cardinal Wiseman?

He was a native of Spain, of Irish and English descent, was educated * chiefly at Rome, filled various important offices, was one of the founders of the *Dublin Review*, and in 1850 was created Cardinal, and first Archbishop of Westminster.

88. Which of his works is best known to the general literary world?

His famous *Lectures on the Connection between Science and Revealed Religion*. They exhibit deep, sound and varied learning, and a diction rich and brilliant.

89. Name his other chief works.

(See the list at the head of the lesson.)

90. What is Fabiola?

Fabiola is a charming story—an exact, graceful, and entertaining picture of Roman life in the early ages of Christianity.†

91. What may be said of this celebrated man as a scholar and ecclesiastic?

Cardinal Wiseman was one of the most accomplished scholars, linguists, and theologians of this century; and his is one of the great names destined to shine with undimmed splendor in the annals of the Catholic Church of England.

92. What do you think of his style?

It is graceful and vigorous, and fitly adorns thoughts often strikingly rich, suggestive and beautiful.‡

---

* Wiseman was brought to Ireland in his childhood, and received his first education at Waterford.

† *Fabiola*, said Dr. Brownson, "is the first work of the kind that we have read in any language in which truly pious and devout sentiment, and the loftiest and richest imagination are so blended, so fused together, that one never jars on the other."

‡ Cardinal Wiseman's last literary effort was an unfinished essay on Shakspeare, of whom he was a sincere admirer.

LESSON IX.

W. M. THACKERAY. DIED 1863.
(1) *Vanity Fair.* (2) *Arthur Pendennis.* (3) *The Newcomes.*
(4) *Lectures on the English Humorists of the Eighteenth Century*

CHARLES DICKENS. DIED 1870.
(1) *The Pickwick Papers.* (2) *Nicholas Nickleby.*
(3) *The Old Curiosity Shop.* (4) *David Copperfield.*

93. Which are, perhaps, the two greatest British novelists that have appeared since the days of Scott?

Thackeray and Dickens.

94. Give a short account of William Makepeace Thackeray.

He was born at Calcutta, of English parents; was educated at Cambridge; studied law; but devoted his life to art and literature.

95. Which was his first famous work?

Vanity Fair, a novel of great power and originality.

96. Mention three of his other most remarkable productions.

(See the list at the head of the lesson.)

97. What have you to observe of Thackeray's pictures of human character?

He describes people as he finds them; but his individuals are generally types of classes.

98. What may be said of his style and general merits as a writer?

Thackeray was a prince of satire—a master of fresh, sparkling, idiomatic English. He applied the lash to shams, snobs, humbugs, and hypocrites; and in a certain way proved himself a moralist and reformer. At times, however, his cynicism is annoying.*

99. Give a brief outline of the early career of Charles Dickens.

He was a native of England, passed his youth in poverty, but finally discovered the ladder to fame and fortune when he became a newspaper reporter. His training on the press prepared his genius for a higher sphere in literature.†

100. Name four of his principal works.

(See foregoing list for the answer.)

101. Which of these is generally considered his finest production?

David Copperfield, which is in some respects an autobiography, describing the struggles of his own youth.

102. Has not Dickens been charged with making his low characters nearly always *vulgar?*

He has indeed, and justly so. Some of his characters are not the best of company for anybody; they are very vulgar in speech, and coarse and clownish in manners.

---

* "In a moral point of view, Thackeray's writings are open to serious objection. The fundamental principle which underlies them is the total depravity of human nature, rendering virtue an impossibility, and religious practice a sham. As Catholics, we know that the human power for good has been weakened,—not destroyed,—and that the grace of Christ may yet raise men to the sublimest virtue."—*Fr Jenkins.*

Among the many fine, sensible passages from Thackeray's pen, we have room for one only: "Might I give counsel to any young hearer, I would say to him, Try to frequent the company of your betters. In books and life, that is the most wholesome society; learn to admire rightly; the great pleasure of life is that. Note what great men admired; they admired great things. Narrow spirits admire basely and worship meanly."

† Only two years before his death Dickens is reported to have said: "To the wholesome training of severe newspaper work, when I was a very young man, I constantly refer my first successes."

103. What is your opinion of the merits and defects of this famous writer?

Dickens was a moral writer, who exposed and scourged many of the crying evils of his time, but he was ignorant of the true foundations of Christian virtue and morality.* He had great dramatic power, and his stories are always humorous and interesting, though often overloaded with minute details. It seems he had little real knowledge of character. He was, indeed, quick to notice the eccentricities of human nature; and nearly all his creations are caricatures and exaggerations.

"Dickens gives us real characters in the garb of fiction; but Thackeray uses fiction as the vehicle of social philosophy. Dickens is eminently dramatic; Thackeray has nothing dramatic—neither scene nor personage. He is Democritus the laughing philosopher, or Jupiter the thunderer; he arraigns vice, pats virtue on the shoulder, shouts for muscular Christianity, uncovers shams —his personages are only names. Dickens describes individuals; Thackeray only classes. His men and women are representatives, and, with but few exceptions, they excite our sense of justice, but not our sympathy; the principal exception is *Colonel Newcome*, a real individual creation upon whom Thackeray exhausted his genius."—*Coppée*.

LESSON X.

THOMAS CARLYLE. DIED 1881.
(1) *Sartor Resartus.*   (2) *The French Revolution.*
(3) *Life of Frederick the Great.*   (4) *Reminiscences.*

JOHN RUSKIN.
(1) *Modern Painters.*   (2) *The Seven Lamps of Architecture.*
(3) *The Stones of Venice.*

104. Who was Thomas Carlyle?

Thomas Carlyle, an eccentric genius of strong, inflexible character, was a farmer's son, and a native of

---

* His standard of moral philosophy is false, and cannot be approved by Catholics. The Christian religion is not a matter of im-

Scotland. He was educated at the University of Edinburgh, and devoted his life to literature.

105. Which was his first work of marked power?

A mixture of farce and indignation, entitled *Sartor Resartus*,* which is one of the most curious productions in English.

106. Which is Carlyle's most popular work?

The French Revolution, which has well been called "a history in flashes of lightning." But it is a fiery, historical drama, rather than a real history. It is a series of lurid pictures, unmatched for vivid power, in which the figures of such wild sons of earth as Danton and Mirabeau loom up gigantic and terrible as the glare of a volcanic eruption. With all its defects, however, this is a fine book, and is perhaps the best specimen of Carlyle's odd, rugged, and picturesque style, and of his powerful and melancholy eloquence.

107. Mention one of his most important biographical works.

The Life of Frederick the Great of Prussia—a work stuffed with unmerited admiration for a successful soldier but despotic monarch, who was really little in intellect, immoral in life, and nothing in virtue.

108. Which was Carlyle's last production?

Reminiscences, a volume of some interest, published after his death.

109. How do you estimate Carlyle as a thinker and writer?

Carlyle was a bold, arrogant, and original thinker. He had a ridiculous veneration for force—even brute

---

pulse or sentiment; yet Dickens's best characters act from impulse rather than virtue or high principle. He knows nothing of the supernatural. The moral miseries of mankind cannot be cured by the quack nostrums which are so lauded in his witty pages.

* That is, *The Patcher Repatched*.

force.* He disliked shams and infidels, but lashed the bulk of mankind as a crowd of boobies and blockheads, who had no mercy to expect from a grim, gloomy, sour dyspeptic.† He was crammed with violent prejudices.‡ But his pages are lighted up, here and there, with flashes of humor. He abounds in German § ideas and modes of expression, and twists English into an odd style of his own, which is vivid, uncouth, turgid, and powerful.

110. Who is the acknowledged chief of English writers on art and art-criticism?

John Ruskin, a native of London and a graduate of the University of Oxford. He has devoted his life to the study of art.

111. Which was Ruskin's first work?

Modern Painters, a book that immediately established his reputation.

112. What other production soon followed?

The Seven Lamps of Architecture; that is, the seven moral principles of architecture.

---

* Witness how he sings the praises of Frederick the Great and Oliver Cromwell.

† Carlyle suffered for the greater part of his long life from chronic dyspepsia.

‡ On one occasion the grievances of Ireland were discussed at an after-dinner company. Carlyle and an Irish gentleman being present. "Ye see the Irish," said the grim old sage, "may have their grievances; but I tell you, sirs, before I'd listen to one word from them, I'd just, with sword and gun, shoot and cut and hew them all until I had taught them to respect human life, and give up murder. Then I'd listen to them." The Irish gentleman did not agree with this fanatical, bulldog doctrine, so worthy of Cromwell. "Then, what would ye propose, sir? There is no remedy," sneered Carlyle. "Yes," said the gentleman, "the British can go away—go home." "We'll cut all your throats first!" cried the savage old Scotchman. The anecdote is characteristic of a man who was so full of pugnacity and violence that he had little room for justice and charity.

§ Carlyle's knowledge of German literature was unequalled by that of any English writer of our age. He was as German as the Germans themselves.

113. Which is commonly considered his greatest work?

The Stones of Venice.

114. What may be said of the style of this famous writer?

Ruskin's style possesses much that is eccentric but beautiful. It is marked by force, animation, suggestiveness, and a certain wild loveliness. He has wonderful powers of description.

LESSON XI.

JOHN HENRY NEWMAN.

(1) *Apologia.* (2) *Grammar of Assent.* (3) *Idea of a University.* (4) *Callista.* (5) *Poems.**

HENRY EDWARD MANNING.

(1) *The Four Chief Evils of the Day.*
(2) *The True Story of the Vatican Council.*
(3) *The Vatican Decrees in their Bearing on Civil Allegiance.*
(4) *Miscellanies.*
(5) *Sermons.*

115. Who is considered the greatest living master of the English tongue?

Cardinal Newman.

116. Give a short outline of his life.

John Henry Newman, the son of a banker, was born at London in 1801. He was educated at the University of Oxford, where he rose rapidly to be a leader of thought. At the age of forty-four he became a Catholic; and seven years later he was appointed first Rector of the new Catholic University at Dublin. He was elevated to the dignity of cardinal in 1879.

---

* These five are only representative works; we have 36 volumes in all from the pen of Cardinal Newman. Some of his best thoughts are collected in a handy volume of well-chosen extracts entitled *Characteristics from the Writings of John Henry Newman*, arranged and edited by W. S. Lilly.

117. What is the *Apologia?*

It is a history of Newman's religious opinions until he happily found his way into the Catholic Church; and it has been well said that "he who wishes to know the sterling pithy English that cleaves straight to the core of its subject, will give his days and nights to the *Apologia.*"

118. Which is the most deeply philosophical of this great man's works?

The *Grammar of Assent,* which restates, brings together, and harmonizes the philosophical principles discussed in many of his other productions.

119. What is the *Idea of a University?*

It is a collection of discourses and essays as to the scope and work of a model university.

120. Of what does the story of *Callista* treat?

It is a vivid picture of Christianity and paganism as they existed in Africa in the days of Saint Cyprian.

121. What is to be said of the merit, rank, and variety of Newman's writings?

Cardinal Newman's writings are great both in quality and quantity. He addresses all classes. He is at once a poet, novelist, essayist, historian, sacred orator, philosopher, and theologian; and he has stamped the seal of beauty and solidity on everything that felt the touch of his wonderful genius.

122. What is your opinion of his style?

It is a style that combines, in the highest degree, grace, strength, beauty, and simplicity. The language is as clear as light.

123. Who is Cardinal Manning?

Henry Edward Manning, born in 1808, is a native of England and a graduate of Oxford. At the time of his conversion to the Catholic faith he was forty-three years of age, and was one of the most gifted, learned, and honored dignitaries of the Anglican Church. He succeeded Cardinal Wiseman, as Archbishop of Westminster, fourteen years later. This venerable man was a prominent member of the Vatican Council, and in 1875 was created cardinal.

124. What is Cardinal Manning's rank in the world of letters?

He is one of the real masters of English prose. As early as 1850, Henry Reed mentions "the sermons of Manning" as among the most polished and artistic writings of the age.

125. Mention some of his chief works.

(See list at the head of the lesson.)

Summary of Chapter VI., Book II.

1. The English rulers of the nineteenth century were *George III., George IV., William IV.*, and the present sovereign, *Queen Victoria.*

2. The nineteenth century has been an age of vast progress in Great Britain.

3. The act of *Catholic Emancipation* became a law in 1829.

4. Inventions, education, manners, just laws, literature, medicine, and all the natural and physical sciences, have made great advances.

5. Among the chief agents that influenced the British literature of this century were: (1) *The French Revolution;* (2) *Catholic Emancipation;* (3) *German Literature;* (4) *Anti-Catholic bigotry;* (5) *The re-*

ligious movement headed by *Newman;* and (6) *The profane spirit of materialism which now so widely prevails.*

6. The first third of the present age constitutes one of the great creative periods of English literature.

7. Of late, works of fiction and periodical literature have grown to immense proportions.

8. The English dramatic writings of this century are so trivial and devoid of original merit as to be almost unworthy of mention.

9. The present has been rich as an age of great historians.

10. The signs of the times seem to point to a period of decline in nearly every department of letters.

11. *Byron,* though perhaps the most brilliant British poet of the nineteenth century, is a very unsafe teacher.

12. *Thomas Campbell* stands at the head of the British lyric poets of this age.

13. Among the female poets, the first place is doubtless due to *Mrs. E. B. Browning.*

14. *Tennyson,* the present poet-laureate of England, seems to reign without a rival at home.

15. *Lingard's History of England* justly claims the first place on that subject. Green's *History of the English People* is a work of much merit.

16. As great reviewers *Lord Macaulay* and *Lord Jeffrey* hold undisputed rank; while for keen, hearty wit *Sydney Smith* remains unrivalled.

17. English criticism reached its highest standard of excellence in Hallam's *Introduction to the Literature of Europe.* Craik's *History of the English Lite-*

rature and Language, Chambers's *Cyclopædia of English Literature*, and Matthew Arnold's *Essays in Criticism* and *Study of Celtic Literature* deserve honorable mention.

18. Among the few biographical works of real interest and classic excellence are Lockhart's *Life of Sir Walter Scott* and Trevelyan's *Life and Letters of Lord Macaulay*.

19. Though Sir Walter Scott wrote soul-stirring poems, his Waverley series proclaim him the prince of British novelists.

20. Father Faber was among the most popular of the Catholic religious writers of Great Britain. His *All for Jesus* is a book as beautiful as it is good.

21. Cardinal Wiseman was one of the most charming and accomplished writers of this century; and he has permanently enriched English letters in his admirable *Lectures on the Connection between Science and Revealed Religion*.

22. Thackeray's ablest and most original work is *Vanity Fair*, but *The Newcomes* is his most popular production.

23. Dickens's masterpiece is *David Copperfield*.

24. The eccentric genius of Carlyle can perhaps best be seen in his *French Revolution*.

25. *The Stones of Venice* is regarded as Ruskin's finest production.

26. Cardinal Newman, who has been styled the greatest living master of the English language, is a writer, thinker, and philosopher of the very highest order. His *Apologia* is the best mirror of his mind and style, and it is a masterpiece.

27. Another of the real masters of English prose is Cardinal Manning.

28. *Bird's-eye view of the chief British writers and works of the nineteenth century:*

POETS:

Lord Byron, *Childe Harold.*
S. T. Coleridge, *Christabel.*
Thomas Campbell, *The Pleasures of Hope.*
William Wordsworth, *The Excursion.*
Mrs. E. B. Browning, *Aurora Leigh.*
Miss A. A. Procter, *Poems*
Alfred Tennyson, *Idylls of the King.*

PROSE-WRITERS:

Sir Walter Scott, *Ivanhoe.*
Sydney Smith, *Essays.*
Lord Jeffrey, *Essays.*
John Lingard, *History of England.*
Henry Hallam, *Introduction to the Literature of Europe.*
Lord Macaulay, *History of England.*
F. W. Faber, *All for Jesus.*
Cardinal Wiseman, *Connection between Science and Religion.*
W. M. Thackeray, *Vanity Fair.*
Charles Dickens, *David Copperfield.*
Thomas Carlyle, *The French Revolution.*
John Ruskin, *The Stones of Venice.*
Cardinal Newman, *Apologia.*
Cardinal Manning, *The Four Great Evils of the Day.*

29. See *Short Dictionary* for the other British writers of the nineteenth century most worthy of mention; namely, *Robert Southey, P. B. Shelley, John Keats, Robert Browning, Kenelm H. Digby, William G. Ward, T. W. Allies, T. W. M. Marshall, Thomas Harper, S.J., St. George Mivart, J. B. Dalgairns, " George Eliot," John Tyndall, Herbert Spencer, Thomas Huxley, Charles Darwin, J. S. Mill, Thomas Buckle, I. Disraeli, B. Disraeli, Bulwer Lytton, John R. Green, William Stubbs, Sir Henry Sumner Maine, J. A. Froude, Edward A. Freeman, Charles Lamb, Thomas de Quincey, William Morris, Charles Reade, Thomas Hughes, Jane Austen, Lady Fullerton, William Cobbett, Sir William Hamilton,* and *William Whewell.*

BOOK III.

THE LITERATURE OF IRELAND.

CHAPTER I.
THE IRISH OR CELTIC LITERATURE OF IRELAND.
A.D. 432 to 1700.

HISTORICAL INTRODUCTION.

"In no nation in the world are there found so many old histories, annals, chronicles, etc., as among the Irish; and that fact alone suffices to prove that in periods most ancient they were truly a civilized nation, since they attached such importance to the records of events then taking place among them."—*Thébaud.*

1. A BIRD'S-EYE VIEW OF ANCIENT IRISH HISTORY.—Some idea of ancient Ireland is necessary in order to have a better understanding of its Celtic literature, and of the unhappy Ireland of the eighteenth century and that of our own age. It is only quite recently that English has become the speech of the majority of the Irish people—a people whose history, language, and literature are the most ancient in Europe.

2. PAGAN IRELAND.—Ireland is a beautiful island on the western extremity of Europe. It is 306 miles long and 182 miles broad, and its area is about 32,-

700 square miles. Thirteen centuries before Christ an expedition of Celts from Spain, led by the sons of Milesius, approached this island.

 "They came from a land beyond the sea,
   And now o'er the western main
 Set sail, in their good ships, gallantly,
   From the sunny land of Spain.
 'Oh, where's the Isle we've seen in dreams,
   Our destined home or grave?'
 Thus sung they as, by the morning's beams,
   They swept the Atlantic wave."

They landed, conquered the country, and identified themselves so completely with their new possessions that they have come to be regarded as the true type of the Irish race. The Milesians were the Normans of that age—a brave, trained, enlightened people. They did not destroy the natives, but reduced them to subjection. After the conquest the island was named *Scotia*,* and was divided between *Heber* and *Heremon*, the sons of Milesius, to one or other of whom all the native families of ancient blood delight to trace their pedigree; and to this day the favorite name for an Irishman in poetry and romance is a Milesian.†

---

* It was so called, it is said, after Scota, the mother of Heber and Heremon; and her grave is still pointed out in the county of Kerry. Ireland was named at various times *Erin*, *Hibernia*, and *Scotia*. It has been called *Ireland* since the English invasion. It is the true Scotia, and the Irish are the true Scots of antiquity. *The name Scotia was applied exclusively to Ireland until the eleventh century*, when it was transferred to Scotland, called *Alba*, *Scotia Minor*—and sometimes *Caledonia*—before that period. As early as the third century the ancient Irish or Scots established colonies in Alba, or Scotland; and in course of time their descendants became the kings of North Britain, and called their country Scotia Minor, or Lesser Scotia, after the mother-country Ireland, or greater Scotia. When the term Ireland supplanted that of Scotia, Scotia Minor alone retained the name, which finally became Scotland. The MacDonalds, Campbells, and other Highland clans are lineal descendants of the ancient Irish who conquered and colonized North Britain.

† Sir C. G. Duffy.

The rule of the Milesians over Ireland continued unbroken down to the English invasion in the twelfth century—a period of over 2400 years. Among the most noted in a long line of pagan monarchs, most of whom pass before us like shadows in a dream, were *Ollamh* Fola, Connary the Great, Conn of the Hundred Battles,* and *Cormac MacArt.*

Ollamh Fola, who began to reign 918 B.C., was a famous legislator. It is said he established a national assembly or congress which met at Tara every third year. This representative body was composed of the druids, bards, brehons, princes, and the four provincial kings, and was presided over by the supreme monarch in person.† It regulated the public affairs of the whole island. Connary the Great reigned when our Blessed Redeemer came into this sin-stained world. Conn of the Hundred Battles was a warrior of renown who died A.D. 183.

But the greatest of the pagan monarchs was the Irish Solomon, Cormac MacArt, who came to the throne in A.D. 244, and reigned for twenty-three years. He revised, purified, and condensed the ancient laws of the nation and formed them into a code of jurisprudence—the *Brehon Laws*—which remained in force for more than a thousand years.‡ He had the annals of the country from the earliest period collected into a work called the *Psalter of Tara.* He encouraged learning by establishing a military academy and two colleges—one for the study of law, and another for history. He reconstructed the famed pa-

---

* Pronounced *ollāve*.
† Ireland was anciently divided into five states or kingdoms. The supreme monarch was styled *Ard-ri* in the Irish language.
‡ In some parts of Ireland it regulated the dealings between man and man as late as the reign of James I. of England.

lace at Tara, and just before his death this wise and brilliant man wrote an *Advice to Princes*, a work addressed to his son and successor. To this day the reign of Cormac remains in the Irish mind as a beautiful memory; and the intelligent peasant, in contrasting it with his own unhappy time, will give a snatch from an old poem the first stanza of which begins—

> "In the reign of Cormac, the son of Art,
> A life of joy and plenty cheered each heart;
> For ninescore nuts in a fair cluster grew,
> And with ninescore clusters the branch bent too."

3. CHRISTIAN IRELAND.—But the most important event in the early history of Ireland is the introduction of the Christian religion in A.D. 432 by the great St. Patrick. Years before he had been a shepherd on the hills of Antrim, but now he came as an apostle with the staff of Jesus in his hand. He was sent to the Irish by Pope St. Celestine, just as, over a century and a half later, St. Augustine was sent to the Anglo-Saxons by Pope Gregory the Great. St. Patrick's mission was blessed with marvellous success. The nation cast away its heathen prejudices. King and prince, bard and brehon, bowed to the cross. It was a peaceful and glorious revolution that placed Ireland on the road to true greatness. Countless churches and monasteries sprang up, schools and colleges were founded, and in less than a century after the death of St. Patrick Ireland was known as the light of Europe, "the holy isle of saints and sages."

The Irish golden age covered the sixth, seventh, and eighth centuries. "It has been said," says the Count de Montalembert, "and cannot be sufficiently repeated, that Ireland was then regarded by all Christian Europe as the principal centre of knowledge and piety. In the shelter of its numberless monasteries a crowd of missionaries, doctors, and preachers were educated for the service of the Church and the propagation of the faith in all Christian countries. A vast and continual development of literary and religious effect is there apparent, superior to anything that could be seen in any other country of Europe."

4. THE IRISH SCHOOLS.—The most celebrated of the Irish schools were Armagh, Clonard, Derry, Durrow, Clonmacnoise, Lismore, Clonfert, and Bangor. The last-named school had 3000 students. Armagh at one time could boast of 7000 students. And Clonard, the *alma mater* of St. Columbkille, was the famous monastic school of which Ussher, the learned Protestant, wrote, "that saints came out of it in as great numbers as Greeks of old from the sides of the horse of Troy." "The science and Biblical knowledge which fled from the continent," says the English historian Green, "took refuge in famous schools which made Durrow and Armagh the universities of the West."

The Irish monastic schools were open to all. The poor and the rich, the slave as well as the freeman, the child as well as the old man, had free access and paid nothing. In them " were trained an entire population of philosophers, writers, architects, carvers, painters, caligraphers, musicians, poets, and historians; but above all, of missionaries and preachers, destined to spread the light of the Gospel and of Christian education, not only in all the Celtic countries, of which Ireland was always the nursing mother, but throughout Europe, among all the Teutonic races— among the Franks and Burgundians, who were already masters of France, as well as amid the dwellers of the Rhine and Danube, and up to the frontiers of Italy."*

5. THE EARLY IRISH MISSIONARIES.—Among the famous Irishmen who carried the light of the Gospel and the blessings of Christian education and civilization over Europe were *St. Columbkille, St. Columbanus, St. Gall, St. Aidan, St. Maildulph, St. Cuthbert, St. Killian,* and *St. Donatus.* St. Columbkille, the great abbot of Iona,† was the apostle of Scotland. St. Columbanus became the apostle of eastern France, where he founded the famous monastery of Luxeuil. He afterwards passed to Italy, and established the monastery of Bobbio, where he died. St. Gall converted Switzerland, and his name yet blesses a Canton. St. Aidan founded the great monastery of Lindisfarne, and with his monks converted northern England. St. Maildulph established the celebrated Abbey of Glastonbury, where he taught St. Aldhelm, the first of the Anglo-Saxons, it will be remembered, that wrote in Latin. St. Cuthbert was an apostolic light in northern England. St. Killian died for the faith in Germany. He is honored as the apostle of Bavaria. St. Donatus became bishop of Fiesole in Italy. In short, the early Irish missionary traversed sea and land, carrying with him the sacred torch of religion. Germany honors one hundred and fifty-six Irish saints, thirty-six of whom were martyrs, who labored, lived, and died there. Forty-five Irish saints find a place in the calendar of France. Forty-four Irish saints are venerated in England. Belgium honors thirty Irish saints; Italy, thirteen; Norway and Iceland, eight—the last all martyrs.

---

* Montalembert.
† See quotation from Johnson about Iona, p. 225.

6. A Picture of Ireland in the Seventh Century.—Ireland was then a happy, prosperous, and independent nation. It was the school of Europe. It was the *insula sanctorum*. Students flocked to it from all parts. "The Anglo-Saxons," says Camden, "went in those times to Ireland, as if to a fair, to purchase knowledge, and we often find, in our authors, that if a person were absent, it was generally said of him, by way of a proverb, that he was sent to Ireland to receive his education."* The best picture of Ireland in those bright ages has been left us by a royal Saxon student, Prince Alfred, who became king of Northumbria in 685. He spent several years in the schools of Ireland, studying philosophy and the sciences, and in travelling through the country; and he then wrote a famous poem in fifteen four-lined stanzas, giving an account of what he saw.† The folowing is a translation:

> "I found in Innisfail the fair,
> In Ireland, while in exile there,
> Women of worth, both grave and gay men,
> Many clerics and many laymen.
>
> "I travelled its fruitful provinces round,
> And in every one of the five I found,
> Alike in church and in palace-hall,
> Abundant apparel and food for all.
>
> "Gold and silver I found, and money,
> Plenty of wheat and plenty of honey;
> I found God's people rich in pity,
> Found many a feast and many a city.
>
> "I found in Armagh, the splendid,
> Meekness, wisdom, and prudence blended,
> Fasting as Christ hath recommended,
> And noble counsellors untranscended.

---

* Among those who were thus sent to Ireland was *Alfred the Great*.
† Alfred wrote his poem in Irish. It was first translated into English by the illustrious Irish scholar, Dr. John O'Donovan, in 1832. The foregoing version is a later one by James Clarence Mangan.

IRISH OR CELTIC LITERATURE OF IRELAND. 283

"I found in each great church moreo'er,
Whether on island or on shore,
Piety, learning, fond affection,
Holy welcome and kind protection.

"I found the good lay monks and brothers
Ever beseeching help for others,
And in their keeping the holy word
Pure as it came from Jesus the Lord.

"I found in Munster unfettered of any,
Kings, and queens, and poets so many—
Poets well skilled in music and measure,
Prosperous doings, mirth and pleasure.

"I found in Connaught the just, redundance
Of riches, milk in lavish abundance;
Hospitality, vigor, fame,
In Cruachan's land of heroic name.

"I found in Ulster, from hill to glen,
Hardy warriors—resolute men;
Beauty that bloomed when youth was gone,
And strength transmitted from sire to son.

"I found in Leinster the smooth and sleek,
From Dublin to Slewmargy's peak—
Flourishing pastures, valor, health,
Long-living worthies, commerce, wealth.

"I found in Meath's fair principality,
Virtue, vigor, and hospitality;
Candor, joyfulness, bravery, purity—
Ireland's bulwark and security.

"I found strict morals in age and youth,
I found historians recording truth;
The things I sing of in verse unsmooth,
I found them all—I have written sooth."

7. THE DANISH INVASION.—The beauty of this matchless picture of peace and piety was soon to be sadly marred. Ireland was the only nation in Europe whose soil had never been pressed by the foot of a Roman soldier. But a wilder race of warriors were now roving the seas. About the year 800 the Danes made their appearance. Those barbarous new-comers burned monasteries, destroyed libraries, sacked churches, murdered women and priests, and obtained

a foothold on the sea-coasts. They were demons of destruction. At Bangor, for instance, they pillaged the celebrated abbey, and murdered the bishop and 900 monks. Before the dangers and troubles of a long period of such merciless warfare, the School of the West of Europe, the abode of learning and sanctity, dwindled away; and it had fallen into complete decay before *Brian Boru*, on Good Friday in the year 1014, finally subdued the Danish invaders, at the famous battle of Clontarf.*

Brian the Brave holds the same place in the memory of his nation that Alfred the Great won in England by similar services; and even to-day wherever enterprise and industry seek new homes—among the cities of New York or Pennsylvania, on the banks of the Mississippi, or among the gold-fields of Australia—you can recognize a settlement of Irish by the rude effigy of a royal warrior carrying in one hand a cross, and in the other the sword which scattered the northern pirates.†

8. THE ORIGIN OF IRISH SIRNAMES.—In ancient times there were no *sirnames*. But to preserve the more correctly the history and genealogy of the different clans, Brian Boru made a law that every family in Ireland should adopt a particular sirname. Each family was at liberty to select a sirname from some particular ancestor, and commonly chose for the pur-

---

* About 20 supreme monarchs reigned in Ireland from the introduction of the Christian religion to the battle of Clontarf. Many of them were true kings—men of worth, learning, and piety. Donald III. and Neill II. died monks at Iona. Six monarchs had the name of Hugh.

† Sir C. G. Duffy.—It is worthy of note that the English king Ethelred fled to Normandy in despair, and that the Danes took possession of England the very year that Brian Boru crushed their barbarous power in Ireland.

pose a chief of their race famous for his valor, wisdom, or piety. Some prefixed *Mac*, which means *son*, as MacMahon—that is, the son of Mahon; while others selected *Ua*, which has been Anglicized *O'*, and signifies *grandson* or *descendant*, as O'Neill—that is, the grandson or descendant of Neill. Thus, according to the old verse, the Irish have no sirnames without the Mac and the O':

> "By Mac and O' you'll always know
> True Irishmen, they say;
> But when they lack the O and Mac
> No Irishmen are they." *

9. THE ANGLO-NORMAN INVASION.—Centuries of warfare with the Danes had, it is said to say, demoralized Ireland; and its political system had by degrees lost all cohesion. The idea of a common national interest or a central national authority came to be wholly discarded. Each provincial king fought for his own hand. The post of supreme monarch was claimed by various competitors in reckless and exhausting contests that bathed the island in blood.

As we have already learned in Book I., the Normans had become masters of England, and by the middle of the twelfth century they had consolidated their new kingdom, while Ireland had been steadily falling into fragments. At this very time, unhappily, an event occurred that presented an opportunity for English interference. A nation is like a house; and every house divided against itself shall fall. *Dermot MacMurrough*, the worthless king of Leinster, having been expelled from the country for his crimes and tyranny, fled to the king of England for assistance. The traitor threw himself at the feet of Henry II.,

---

* O'Hart.

and offered to hold his dominions as a vassal of the English crown if the needed aid were furnished for his restoration. Henry, who was then in France, gladly accepted the proffered fealty, and gave the Irish prince letters-patent to raise forces. Dermot beat up recruits. He was soon surrounded by a large band of needy Norman adventurers. The chief of these was *Richard de Clare*, Earl of Pembroke, commonly known as *Strongbow;* and to him Dermot promised his daughter Eva in marriage, on condition that he would raise an efficient body of troops and transport them into Ireland. It was done. Scenes of blood, butchery, and desecration followed. Waterford, Dublin, and other important places fell into the hands of the English.*

A few years later, in 1171, Henry II. followed with a large fleet and army. The Irish were divided among themselves. *Rory O'Conor*, the last supreme monarch of Ireland, was a brave man but a poor leader. He lacked clear-headed vigor and promptitude of action. Besides, many of the Irish princes imagined that Henry was irresistible; and without a master-spirit to subdue their tribal jealousies, to arouse their patriotism, and to cement the discordant elements together, united resistance was impossible.

---

* The death of the *first* Irish traitor is thus recorded in the *Annals of the Four Masters:* "A.D. 1171. Dermot MacMurrough, King of Leinster, by whom a trembling sod was made of all Ireland—after having brought over the Saxons, after having done extensive injuries to the Irish, after plundering and burning many churches—died before the end of a year of an insufferable and unknown disease: for he became putrid while living through the miracle of God, Columbkille, Finnian, and other saints of Ireland, whose churches he had profaned and burned some time before; and he died at Fearnamor without making a will, without penance, without the Body of Christ, without unction—as his evil deeds deserved."

The Munster princes and chiefs were the first to pay homage to the English king. O'Conor retired behind the Shannon. The Ulster princes would have no dealings with the royal new-comer.

The authority established by Henry was acknowledged in Dublin—where he fixed the seat of his government—and in a limited territory beyond it known as the *Pale:* which, as the name implies, was a rudely fortified camp on a large scale, whose boundary shifted with circumstances. Beyond the English Pale, however, there was little change. The native prince ruled his principality, and the native chief ruled his clan, as of old.

10. THE BEGINNING OF ENGLISH MISRULE.—The English had now a foothold in Ireland. Henry II., the murderer of St. Thomas à Becket, was one of the most unscrupulous ruffians that ever wore a crown. He introduced the feudal system—a handy system for royal robbers.* To it we may trace the origin of the "Land Question"—that unhappy question which has proved a stumbling-block to the peace of Ireland for over seven hundred years. He generously parcelled out the whole island—to which he had no more right than he had to the moon—among his prominent followers. He conferred Meath on Hugh

---

* The theory of the feudal system was that all the soil belonged to the king, who had accordingly the right to make grants of tracts of land in his discretion to his followers, to be held by them upon condition of their rendering him the services of themselves and their retainers in the field whenever he should require them. . . . This system could not be applied to Ireland, where the tribal system prevailed, without revolutionizing the whole structure of society; and its application was, in the eyes of the Irish, nothing but a high-handed invasion of the rights of property, and an act of shameful injustice.—*C. G. Walpole.*

"Under the Celtic tenure," says Sir Charles Gavan Duffy, "a chief was only joint owner with the clan."

de Lacy. He gave all Connaught to William Fitzaldhelm de Burgo. He presented Ulster to John de Courcy, if he could take it;* and, finally, he made the magnificent grant of all Ireland to his worthless son John. And thus opens the sad story of English misrule and robbery in the land of St. Patrick—the once famous *insula sanctorum*.†

Henceforth the state of Ireland was more or less one of chronic wretchedness. The seeds of discord were sown broadcast. There was constant warfare between the Irish and the Anglo-Norman settlers, and often between the Irish princes themselves. But slow was the progress of conquest. One hundred years after the English invasion scarcely a third of the island was in the hands of the invaders. The Irish, as is the case with all superior races, had the magic power of absorbing and assimilating the new-comers to themselves. The Anglo-Norman lords and their followers intermarried with the natives, adopted their language, laws, and customs; and, in the course of time, their descendants, it is said, became " more Irish than the Irish themselves."

11. THE STATUTE OF KILKENNY.—The English authorities resolved to crush out such a promising state of things. It was dangerous to their amiable " divide-and-conquer" policy in Ireland; and the infamous

---

* This John de Courcy thought he would try his fortune in Ulster in 1178, and the Irish annals tell the result: "John and his English were defeated with great slaughter, but he himself escaped, and arrived in Dublin covered with wounds." Later on, however, he had better success.

† The death of *Strongbow* is thus recorded in the *Annals of the Four Masters:* "A.D. 1176. The English Earl, Richard, died of an ulcer that broke out on his foot. This was attributed to the miracles of St. Bridget and St. Columbkille, and of the other saints whose churches he had plundered, and he was heard to say that he saw St. Bridget killing him."

code known as the *Statute of Kilkenny* became a law in 1367. Among its enactments were: (1) Any alliance with the Irish by marriage was to be punished as an act of high treason; (2) Any Englishman taking an Irish name, or using the Irish dress or language, should forfeit all his land; (3) The English were forbidden to admit any Irish into their convents and monasteries. The result of this unchristian code was to fill Ireland with hatred, riots, and civil war. The "mere Irishman" was to be dealt with as one who had no rights in his own country. He was to be exterminated.*

But while the Irish might be insulted, they could neither be conquered nor exterminated. Several Irish princes led their hardy legions to victory, and punished the bigoted, brutal creatures who had enacted the Statute of Kilkenny. Years passed on. English power diminished. Castle after castle and town after town, as Sir Charles Gavan Duffy well remarks, pulled down the banner of St. George. When Henry VIII. was jousting in the Field of the Cloth of Gold within the English Pale in France, the English Pale in Ireland, which had once embraced six counties and stretched its offshoots deep into the South and deep into the North, was a territory which might be conveniently inspected in a morning's ride from Dublin Castle.

12. THE PROTESTANT REFORMATION.—The blackest clouds of misfortune arose, so to speak, from the

---

* Donald O'Neill, King of Ulster, and other Irish princes, bore witness to the truth of the following in 1318:
"They [the English] heretically maintain, not their laymen or seculars merely, but even some of their ecclesiastics, that it is no greater sin to kill an Irishman than a dog or any other brute beast."

sea of religious corruption in England, and their fateful shadows fell upon Ireland. The so-called Reformation came. But Henry VIII. utterly failed to introduce *his* new religion into the land of St. Columbkille and Brian Boru. In 1535, however, he appointed George Brown, an apostate priest, *first* Protestant Archbishop of Dublin. The royal robber seized many abbeys, convents, and monasteries; but the faithful Irish regarded his irreligious schemes with horror.*

The religious quarrel now added a new element of bitterness and brutality to English misrule in Ireland. One of the first acts of Elizabeth was to order all persons, under pain of fine and imprisonment, to attend Protestant places of worship. This was a high-handed outrage on the faith and freedom of the Irish people. It was manfully resented. The outcome was rebellion, massacre, and a series of wars unparalleled for barbarity in the annals of history. Shane O'Neill, of Ulster, was crushed, and his territory confiscated. The old plan of planting the country with English settlers was revived. The Earl of Desmond was easily goaded into rebellion, and then defeated by an appalling system of armed ferocity. The southern portion of the island was reduced to a wilderness. Fire and sword left nothing untouched or undestroyed. Half a million acres of land were confiscated, and handed over to needy English adventurers.†
The soldiers of Elizabeth spared no human being. "Many women," says Lombard, "were found hang-

---

* It was the apostate Brown that burned the most celebrated religious relic in Ireland—the crozier of St. Patrick, known as the Staff of Jesus.

† Among these were Edmund Spenser, the poet, who got 3000 acres; and Sir Walter Raleigh, who got 42,000 acres.

ing on trees with their children at their breasts, strangled by the mother's hair." Nor did this murderous warfare cease during the whole reign. O'Neill, O'Donnell, O'Kane, Maguire, and other princes of Ulster—the last stronghold of Irish independence—made a noble stand, and battled with the heroism of true patriots for their faith and fatherland. In short, the reign of Elizabeth was one long effort to root out the Catholic religion and to exterminate the Irish race. Did she succeed? It is true that thousands of Irish perished. The island was drenched in the blood of its best and bravest sons; but at the death of Elizabeth, " after nearly one hundred years of Protestantism, only *sixty* Irishmen of all classes had received the new religion." *

James I., it must be said, governed Ireland like a Turk, and like a true Turk he attempted to ram the odious new creed down the throats of the Irish people at the point of the sword. He laid the hand of a robber on the soil. He confiscated six counties in Ulster, containing 3,800,000 acres. The land was thus stolen from the original Irish proprietors, who had been there since the Redemption of man, and given to a horde of hungry thieves, Scotch and English, who were " well affected in religion." † One of the king's chief agents in this gigantic piece of iniquity was Sir Arthur Chichester, the scoundrel that wrote: " It is famine that must consume the Irish, as

---

* Not one of the sixty "converts" was a clansman—all belonged to the titled classes, or were ecclesiastics.
† Those Scotch and English colonists were styled "undertakers," and the name was very appropriate, as they were anxious to make a national funeral and bury the Irish race.
"The colonists in Ulster," says Walpole, "were in a great measure the *scum* of both nations—debtors, bankrupts, and fugitives from justice."

our swords and other endeavors work not that *speedy* effect which is expected."

Charles I. continued the work of plunder and persecution. The Catholics were hunted down like wolves, and Protestant new-comers were planted in their homes. Cromwell passed over Ireland like a demon of destruction. After butchering over 3000 persons at Drogheda, this merciless fanatic writes to England that it was done by "the spirit of God." The work of uprooting and exterminating the native inhabitants was continued with unspeakable ferocity. By an act of the English Parliament, the people of Ulster, Leinster, and Munster were ordered, under the penalty of death, to cross the Shannon and "go to h ll or Connaught" before May 1, 1654. "The order," says Walpole, "was proclaimed by beat of drum in the middle of harvest." The Irish were to be plucked out of the soil root and branch. Over 15,500,000 acres, or three-fourths of the island, were confiscated.* It is well known how the unfortunate James II. added to the calamities of Ireland. Then came William III. of Boyne celebrity, the violated Treaty of Limerick, the exile of the flower of Irish manhood, and the woful exhaustion of a crushed and hapless nation.

13. REMARKS ON THE IRISH LANGUAGE.—What we term the Celtic Period of Literature in Ireland extends from the introduction of Christianity to the year 1700; and from the dawn of history to the year 1700 there was but *one* national language, and that was the Irish language.

"The language which grows up with a people,"

---

* Ireland contains 20,800,000 acres.

says Thomas Davis, "is conformed to their organs, descriptive of their climate, constitution, and manners, mingled inseparably with their history and their soil, and is fitted beyond any other language to express their prevalent thoughts in the most natural and efficient way."

"The Saxon and Norman colonists," continues the same writer, "melted down into the Irish and adopted all their ways and language. For centuries upon centuries Irish was spoken by men of all bloods in Ireland, and English was unknown, save to a few citizens and nobles of the Pale."

The following record in the *Annals of the Four Masters* is suggestive, as it refers to the head of a famous Anglo-Norman house: "A.D. 1398. Gerald, Earl of Desmond, a cheerful, polite man, who had excelled all the English of Ireland, and many of the Irish, *in his knowledge of the Irish language, poetry, and history*, and also in all the other literature of which he was possessed, died after the victory of penance."

In those times, and even at a later period, according to Stanihurst, the Irish held the unformed English tongue in contempt. They are unwilling, he adds, as they say in derision, "to distort their chins by speaking English." When *Shane O'Neill* visited the court of Elizabeth, his interpreter was asked by a citizen of London why the Irish prince did not speak English. "Think you," he replied, "it would become the O'Neill to twist his mouth with such a barbarous jargon!"

The Irish language, however, suffered immensely with the decay of national independence. English law made it a crime to speak Irish. We have seen how it was proscribed in 1367, under Edward II., by the Statute of Kilkenny. Another hostile law was framed against it in 1537, under Henry VIII. By destroying the Irish schools and monasteries, the ruffians of the Reformation drove it from the seats of learning. When the last of the Irish princes perished it was left without a patron; and thus the most ancient and venerable language of Europe sought refuge in the souls of a brave, faithful, and persecuted people.

An acquaintance with the following short list of Irish words will prove useful:

MAC, *son;* as, *MacDonald,* that is, the son of Donald.
UA, anglicized O'. *grandson*, and by an extension of meaning any descendant; as, *O'Brien,* that is, the grandson of Brien.
MÓR (more), *great;* as, *Dunmore,* the great fort.
BEAG (beg). *small, little;* as, *Ardbeg,* the little height.
ARD, *high,* a *height;* as, *Ardmore,* great height.
CLANN, *children, descendants, race;* as, *Clann-na-Gael,* or the race of Gael—the Irish race.
RI (ree), *king;* as, *Ard-ri,* high king.
LIS, *habitation;* as, *Lismore,* the great habitation.
BAILE (bally), a *town;* as, *Ballymore,* the great town; *Ballykillbey,* the town of the little church.*
GAEL (gail), an Irish Celt, or a Scottish Highlander of Celtic origin.
GAELIC (gā'-lik), the Celtic language of the Irish and the Highland Scotch.†

---

* The plural of *baile* is *bailte* (pronounced *balty*); now, we find in the two Irish words *bailte* and *mór* the key to the meaning of the name of one of our famous cities—*Baltimore*—that is, *great towns.* Sir George Calvert derived his title of Lord Baltimore from the little seaport of Baltimore, in the south of Ireland. It has been rendered famous by Davis in his *Sack of Baltimore,* when

"The yell of *Allah* broke above the prayer, and shriek, and roar—
Oh, blessed God! the Algerine is lord of Baltimore!"

† The *Irish* language may also be called the *Gaelic* language and the *Celtic* language. The term Celtic, however, has commonly a wider meaning than Irish or Gaelic. The Celtic language is divided into the *Irish* and the *British* branches. The Irish is subdivided into three dialects—(*a*) the Irish proper, (*b*) the Scottish Gaelic, and (*c*) the Manx, or Irish dialect spoken in the Isle of Man. The British branch is divided into three dialects—(*a*) the Welsh, (*b*) the Cornish, and (*c*) the Armoric, or language of Brittany. The Irish of

CILL (kill), a *church*, a *cloister;* as, *Kilpatrick*, or Patrick's church; *Kilmore*, the great church
DUN, a *fort*, a *fortified residence;* as, *Dunmore*, the great fort.
CLON, a *plain*, a *meadow;* as, *Clonard*, the high plain; *Clonmel*, the vale or plain of honey.
CNOC (knoc), a *hill;* as, *Knocklayd*, the broad hill.
TIR or TYR, a *territory;* as, Tyrone, or Owen's territory.*
LEABHAR (lëv'ar), a *book;* as, *Leabhar Breac*, the Speckled Book.
BARD, a poet.
BRE'HON, a judge, a professor of law.

14. REMARKS ON ANCIENT IRISH LITERATURE, A.D. 432 TO A.D. 1700.—The Irish possessed a peculiar literature, art, music, and poetry in which their very soul is portrayed, and which belongs exclusively to them. The literature was a perfect expression of the social state of the people. Each clan had its historian to record the most minute details of every-day history, as well as every fact of importance to the whole clan, and even to the nation at large; and thus we may see how literature with them grew naturally out of their social system. Each clan also had its bard and its brehon.† History, poetry, and music entwined themselves about everything in ancient Ireland.‡

The golden age of Irish literature opens with the introduction of the Christian religion, and closes with the Danish invasion. Then began a decline. The fearful struggle with the fierce northern pirates covered a period of over two hundred years. " The

---

Ireland is the oldest and purest form of the Celtic. Irish proper and Scottish Gaelic are practically the same language; and an Irishman and a Scottish Highlander find no difficulty in conversing together in Celtic. But it is different when we come to the British branches. A Welshman cannot understand a Highlander or an Irishman. The Welsh language has an extensive literature.

* The names of places in Ireland "are purely Celtic, with the exception of a thirteenth part, which are English and mostly of recent introduction."—*Joyce, Irish Names of Places.*

† Bardism and Brehonism, like many other offices in Ireland, were hereditary in certain families; and each of the kings, princes, and chiefs had his own bards and brehons.—*O'Hart.*

‡ Thébaud, *The Irish Race.*

Danes," says O'Curry, "made it a special part of their savage warfare to tear, burn, and *drown*—as it is expressed—all books and records that came into their hands, in the sacking of churches and monasteries, and the plundering of the habitations of the chiefs and nobles."

Armagh, the renowned ecclesiastical capital of Ireland, was burned and sacked fully a dozen times between the year 800 and the battle of Clontarf. The great schools of Clonfert and Clonmacnoise bore four or five such terrible visitations during the same stormy period; in short, every distinguished monastic town in Ireland was plundered and burned by the Danes. The destruction of Irish literature must have been immense.

It is said misfortune never comes alone, and the proverb finds a sad illustration in the history of Irish letters. The Anglo-Norman invasion followed soon after the expulsion of the Danes. "The protracted conflicts between the natives and their invaders," remarks Prof. O'Curry, "were fatal not only to the vigorous resumption of the study of our language, but also to the very existence of a great part of our ancient literature. The old practice of reproducing our ancient books, and adding to them a record of such events as had occurred from the period of their first compilation, as well as the composition of new and independent works, was almost altogether suspended. And thus our national literature received a fatal check at the most important period of its development, and at a time when the mind of Europe was beginning to expand under the influence of new impulses." *

---

* *Lectures on the Manuscript Materials of Ancient Irish History.*

But the crowning calamity for Irish literature was the Protestant Reformation and the diabolical penal laws that followed. The monasteries and their precious libraries were ruthlessly destroyed. The Irish bards were hunted like wild beasts in the reign of Elizabeth, because they were true to their faith and their country. They could neither be bribed nor bought by English gold. That was their crime. They sang the hopes of Ireland in strains of misty song which the circumstances and shrewdness of the people rendered transparent. When the sword of O'Neill was broken, the minstrelsy which had made it start from its scabbard still lived and moved the pulse of the nation. The warrior's strength dies with him; but the poet's power ever stirs like an immortal prophecy. The days of the bards, however, were numbered. And thus when Shakspeare was stamping the seal of his bright genius on the English language and literature, the language and literature of unhappy Ireland were withering away under the deadly shade of persecution.

The destruction of Irish literature in the seventeenth century was truly lamentable. "Precious manuscripts," says Father Thébaud, "were every day given to the flames and wantonly destroyed, seemingly for the mere pleasure of the destruction. A very few years would have sufficed to render the former history of the country a perfect blank. In no spot of the same size on earth had so many interesting books ever been written and treasured up."

But at this period the hand of God raised up a race of learned and patriotic Irishmen, who toiled like giants to save the scattered remains of Irish literature from wholly perishing in the wreck of ages and by the hand of persecution. *Brother Michael O'Clery* and his companions gathered the old annals around them, and then wrote the famous *Annals of the Four Masters;* Father John Colgan compiled the *Lives of the Irish Saints* at Louvain, in Belgium; Rev. Dr. Geoffrey Keating prepared his *History of Ireland* "among the caves and woods of Tipperary, to which the proscription of Protestant persecution had driven the Catholic priest;" and the learned *Duald MacFirbis,* though dogged by the penal laws, compiled the *Chronicum Scotorum,* the *Book of Pedigrees,* and other valuable works. MacFirbis was the *last* regularly educated Irish antiquary and historian. All those writers flourished between A.D. 1620 and 1670.

15. THE LOST BOOKS, AND THE REMAINS OF IRISH LITERATURE.—From the Danish invasion down to the dark days of the English penal laws—a period of over one thousand years—the destruction of Irish literature scarcely ever ceased. It is a wonder that it did not all perish. Prof. O'Curry in his excellent work on *The Manuscript Materials of Ancient Irish History* devotes the greater portion of the first lecture to the subject of the *lost books*. Three of these, whose names have come down to us, were works of great antiquity—*The Cuilmenn, The Psalter of Tara,* and *The Psalter of Cashel.*

The *Cuilmenn* was, it seems, the greatest literary treasure of ancient Ireland before the introduction of the Christian religion. The *Psalter of Tara* was a cyclopædia of Irish history prepared by King Cormac MacArt and his bards, brehons, and historians in the third century.

The *Psalter of Cashel* was from the pen of the

venerable *Cormac MacCullinan*, archbishop of Cashel, who died in the year 903. It seems to have been an historical and genealogical compilation of large size and great diversity.

But in spite of all destructive processes, the *remains* of Irish literature exhibit gigantic proportions. The quality, quantity, and variety astonish the scholars of our age. "Of Irish literature," says Matthew Arnold, "the stock, printed and manuscript, is truly vast." Professor O'Curry's estimate is noteworthy. He takes the *quarto page* of Dr. O'Donovan's *Annals of the Four Masters* as the standard of measurement. Let us hear an English writer on the result. " Eugene O'Curry says," continues Matthew Arnold, " that the great vellum* manuscript books belonging to Trinity College, Dublin, and to the Royal Irish Academy— books with fascinating titles—the *Book of the Dun Cow*, the *Book of Leinster*, the *Book of Ballymote*, the *Speckled Book*, the *Book of Lecain*, the *Yellow Book of Lecain*—have, among them, matter enough to fill 11,400 of these pages; the other vellum manuscripts in the library of Trinity College, Dublin, have matter enough to fill 8200 pages more; and the paper manuscripts of Trinity College and the Royal Irish Academy together would fill, he says, 30,000 pages more. The ancient laws of Ireland, the so-called Brehon laws, which a commission is now publishing, were not as yet completely transcribed when O'Curry wrote; but what had even then been transscribed was sufficient, he says, to fill nearly 8000 of Dr. O'Donovan's pages." †

---

* *Vellum* is a fine kind of parchment or skin rendered clear and white for writing.
† *The Study of Celtic Literature.*

It was stated on good authority, in 1875, that there were *one thousand volumes* of unpublished Irish manuscripts in the libraries of Trinity College and the Royal Irish Academy, Dublin.* In short, the number of Irish books containing the *Historic Tales* alone is "so great that the authentic list of them far surpasses in length what has been preserved of the old Greek and Latin writers."

The contents of those Irish manuscripts may be classified as follows: 1. Grammars and glossaries; 2. Annals, genealogies, and pedigrees; 3. Histories, in prose and verse; 4. Mythological and other imaginative tales; 5. Lyric poetry; 6. Satire; 7. Religious literature, including lives of the saints; 8. Law; 9. The sciences, including medicine; 10. Miscellaneous works, and translations from other languages.

Among existing Irish manuscripts are some of the most remarkable illuminated books in Europe, such as the *Book of Kells*, which is considered to be the work of St. Columbkille. These precious works are to be found chiefly in the old libraries of Italy, Switzerland, France, Belgium, and Germany.

LESSON I.
THE IRISH LANGUAGE.

1. What name is given by philologists of the present day to the primitive language of man?

The *Aryan language*. The word *Aryan* means *high, noble, illustrious*.

---

* The greater portion of the most valuable MS. Irish books in existence are to be found in four libraries—the Royal Irish Academy, Dublin; Trinity College, Dublin; the Bodleian Library, Oxford; and the British Museum, London. The collection in the Royal Irish Academy is the largest of all.

2. What relation does the Irish language bear to the Aryan?

It is a branch or dialect of the Aryan language. This is proved by comparative philology.*

3. Which is the most ancient living language in Europe?

The Irish language.

4. How is that known?

So far as history and philology can pronounce definitely on a question that carries us back to the very dawn of ages, we learn that the Celts were the *first* of the human family that entered Europe, and the Irish language is the oldest and purest dialect of the Celtic.†

5. Mention some of the chief characteristics of the Irish language.

The Irish is a language of rare grace, vigor, and soul-touching tenderness. It is expressive and beautiful. "If you plead for your life, plead in Irish," is a well-known saying. An old English writer confesses that it "abounds in grandeur of words, harmony of diction, and acuteness of expression."

6. What may be remarked of this ancient language in relation to poetry and music?

The Irish language is soft, lively, and melodious, and, according to an eminent musical authority, those qualities make it admirably suited "for poetical and musical compositions—far superior either to the Latin or any of the modern tongues."

---

* All the languages of Europe, India, and Persia have, like branches from a parent trunk, sprouted forth from that ancient tree of prehistoric speech—the Aryan. See the *Introduction* to Chapter I., Book I.

† The Celts seem to have been the *first* of the Aryans to arrive in Europe. The pressure of subsequent migrations, particularly of Teutonic tribes, has driven them towards the westernmost parts, and latterly from Ireland across the Atlantic.—*Max. Müller.*

Moore says that the Celtic language was "the vehicle of the first knowledge that dawned upon Europe."

7. What may be said of the Irish language as a literary instrument?

This venerable language has been the polished medium of every form of literary composition from the simple tale to the exquisite productions of the poet and the sententious wisdom of the philosopher.

8. Of what practical val e would a knowledge of the Irish language be to the scholar of our day?

It would greatly aid in the labor of acquiring other languages. The Irish is a *primitive tongue*, and, as such, *it is the key to a host of others.**

9. What does Sir William Betham say of its value in the study of philology?

" The Irish language," says Sir William Betham, " is a mine of philological wealth—a guide that will explain most of the difficulties which have hitherto so much obscured the history of the ancient people and languages of Europe."

10. Which two members of the Aryan family most resemble each other?

The Irish and the Latin.†

11. Of the three ancien European languages, Irish, Latin, and Greek, which is the lon est in Europe?

The Irish, as it was the *first* to arrive in Europe.‡

---

* I think it a great pity that Irish is not more studied as a key to Greek and Latin and the modern dialects of Latin. One who knows Irish well will readily master Latin, French, Spanish, Italian, and Portuguese.—*P. MacMahon, M. P.*

I would give a thousand dollars to be able to hear confessions in the language of my fathers.—*Bishop Lynch, of Charleston, S. C.*

† Many Latin words retain only secondary meanings where the primary ones are manifest in the Celtic. Thus *monile*, a necklace, is from the Irish *muineal*.—*Newman* in his *Regal Rome*.

‡ Irish is an older language than either the Latin or the Greek. " Comparative philology," says Canon Bourke. " furnishes abundant reasons to show that Irish is an older language than that in which Homer and Sappho or Virgil and Horace wove their wreaths of deathless song and story."

12. In point of age and value, what is the *rank* of the Irish language as a member of the Aryan family?

Irish is one of the oldest members of the Aryan family. It is the sister of Sanskrit, Latin, and Greek. In the field of philology its usefulness is admitted to be equal to that of Sanskrit.*

13. In what language are the most ancient existing manuscripts in Europe written?

The Irish. Sir William Betham truly says: "It is a singular fact, not generally known, that the most ancient European manuscripts now existing are in the Irish language, and that the most ancient Latin manuscripts in Europe were written by Irishmen."

LESSON II.

THE IRISH BARDS.

14. What branch of Irish literature has suffered most from tyranny and destruction?

Poetry. The Irish annals record the names of scores of famous bards not one of whose poems has come down to our day.†

15. Who was Ossian (ŏsh'an)?

Ossian was a famous warrior-poet, son of the celebrated Finn MacCumhaill,‡ and he is supposed to

---

* In order to obtain anything like a correct notion of philology, and to be skilled in any fair way in comparative grammar, the student must learn either Sanskrit or Irish. He must learn some primitive language—one of those two.—*Canon Bourke, M.R.I.A.*

† The monk Columbkille was a poet. After Ossian, he opens the series of 200 *Irish poets*, whose memories and names, in default of their works, have remained dear to Ireland.—*Montalembert.*

‡ Pronounced *Finn MacCoole*. He was the son-in-law of King Cormac MacArt, and, according to the *Annals of the Four Masters*, died A.D. 283.

have flourished about A.D. 300. He is commonly credited with the authorship of the *Fenian Poems;* but unhappily his works have come down to us only in fragments.*

16. Who was the greatest poet of the early Christian period in Ireland?

The illustrious St. Columbkille, who was at once prince and poet, monk and missionary.

17. Mention some of his best known hymns and poems.

The *Altus,* in twenty-three six-lined stanzas, the *Noli Pater,* and the *In Te Christe*—three Latin hymns. The *Altus* is a magnificent composition. The *Song of Trust,* the *Praise of St. Bridget,* and other poems are written in the Irish language.†

18. Mention an Irish poet of the ninth cent'ry who became Bishop of Fiesole in Italy?

St. Donatus, who died about the year 863. One of this saint's poems contains the following beautiful stanza:

> "Far westward lies an isle of ancient fame,
> By nature blessed, and Scotia ‡ is her name;
> An island rich—exhaustless is her store
> Of veiny silver and of golden ore.
> Her fruitful soil forever teems with wealth.
> With gems her waters, and her air with health.
> Her verdant fields with milk and honey flow,
> While woolly fleeces vie with virgin snow."

---

* The poems of Ossian—*Fin'gal* and *Temora*—which were published in 1762 and 1763 by James Macpherson, a Scotchman, as translations from Scottish Gaelic manuscripts as old as the fourth century, are now regarded as clever literary forgeries.

† It is stated that St. Columbkille left 300 copies of the *New Testament* for his various churches, written by his own hand.

A precious collection of ancient Irish hymns, by various authors, is the *Liber Hymnorum.* "This beautiful manuscript," says Rev. Dr. Todd, "which cannot be assigned to a later date than the ninth or tenth century, may safely be pronounced one of the most venerable monuments of Christian antiquity now remaining in Europe."

‡ The ancient name of Ireland.

19. Who was Brian Boru's chief Bard?

MacLaig, many of whose poems are still in existence.

20. Mention one of the most popular of MacLaig's poems?

Kinkora, a touching lament for the fallen condition of Brian's famous palace of that name, after the monarch's death. It stood on the banks of the Shannon.* The second stanza runs thus:

"Oh, where, Kinkora! are thy valorous lords?
Oh, where, thou Hospitable! are they gone?
Oh, where are the Dalcassians † of the golden swords?
And where are the warriors Brian led on?"

21. What battle, fought in 1260, was the cause of two rare Irish poems still in existence?

The battle of Downpatrick, fought between Brian O'Neill, King of Ulster, and the English. O'Neill and the flower of his army were slain.

22. What two Irish poets commemorate that event in verse?

MacNamee, Brian O'Neill's chief bard, and *MacWard*, the bard of Tirconnell. MacNamee principally deplores the death of O'Neill, whose virtues and heroism are praised at length.

23. What is the burden of MacWard's poem?

He chiefly laments the loss of his foster-brother, *Manus O'Kane*, head of the famous Ulster family of that name.

"If Brian was not in the slaughter,
There would be no loss like O'Kane." ‡

---

* Moore has a beautiful reference to Kinkora:
"Remember the glories of Brian the Brave,
Though the days of the hero are o'er;
Though lost to Mononia, and cold in the grave,
He returns to Kinkora no more!"

† The Dalcassians were Brian's body-guard.

‡ In recording the battle of Downpatrick, the *Annals of the Four Masters* say: "Fifteen chiefs of the family of *O'Kane* were slain on the field."

24. Who was John O'Duggan?

John O'Duggan, the chief bard of O'Kelly, was the author of a lengthy, valuable *Topographical* and *Historical Poem* which is still extant, and which has been translated into English. O'Duggan died A.D. 1372.

25. What remarkable Irish poem of the seventeenth century, written by the last bard of Tirconnell, Owen Roe Mac-Ward, do we still possess?

The *Lament for the Princes*—an elegy on the death of O'Neill and O'Donnell. It was addressed to O'Donnell's sister, Nuala. Lord Jeffrey, the British critic, was a great admirer of this famous poem, the first stanza of which, as translated by Mangan, opens thus:

"O, woman of the piercing wail,
Who mournest o'er yon mound of clay
With sigh and groan,
Would God thou wert among the Gael!
Thou wouldst not then from day to day
Weep thus alone."

26. Mention another eminent Irish bard of the seventeenth century.

Rory Dall O'Kane.*

27. Who is commonly considered the last and greatest of the Irish bards?

Tirlogh O'Carolan, who was justly celebrated for his musical and poetical genius. As he felt the end approaching, he called for his harp and played his famous *Farewell to Music* in a strain of tenderness that drew tears from the listeners. He then breathed a prayer, and died in 1737.

---

* Rory Dall O'Kane, a celebrated minstrel and author of some of the most beautiful strains that ever sounded on the harp of Ireland, was a member of the ancient sept of the O'Kanes of Kienachta (in Derry). He is the same person who is so famous in Scotland under the name of Rory Dall Morrison, and who Sir Walter Scott, with his usual skill in employing facts for the illustration of his tales, introduces as the musical instructor of Annot Lyle in the *Legend of Montrose.*—Rev. J. S. Porter, *Ulster Journal of Archæology*, Vol. IV.

LESSON III.
IRISH ANNALS AND HISTORIES.

(1) *The Wars of the Danes with the Irish.**
(2) *The Annals of Tighernach* (nearly *teer'nah*).
(3) *The Annals of Innisfallen.*
(4) *The Annals of Ulster.**
(5) *The Annals of Loch Cé* (key).*
(6) *Keating's History of Ireland.**
(7) *MacFirbis's Chronicle of the Irish.**
(8) *MacFirbis's Book of Genealogies.**
(9) *Lynch's Cambrensis Overthrown.**
(10) *The Annals of the Four Masters.**

28. Give a brief description of the contents of the work entitled *The Wars of the Danes with the Irish.*

It is an ample account of the dreadful warfare that covers the long unhappy period of the Danish invasions, and the final and complete overthrow of the fierce Northmen. It was written in the twelfth century.

29. Who was Tighernach (teer'nah)?

Tighernach O'Breen, a gifted, holy, and learned abbot of the celebrated monastery of Clonmacnoise, was one of the very greatest of the Irish annalists. He died in the year 1088.

30. What period do the *Annals of Tighernach* cover?

The *Annals of Tighernach* sweep over the history of Ireland, and many other countries, from the earliest times down to the days of the venerable author, and form the most important historical composition of Ireland in the middle ages.

31. What is the *Annals of Innisfallen?*

The *Annals of Innisfallen* is a short general history of the world down to the introduction of the Christian religion into Ireland; and from that to the year

---
* There is an English translation.

1318, when it ends, it is a brief chronicle of Irish affairs.

32. Describe the work called the *Annals of Ulster*.

The *Annals of Ulster*, a great body of Irish national records, is so called because it was written in Ulster, and relates more to the affairs of Ulster than to that of any other portion of Ireland. It begins at A.D. 444, and is carried down to the sixteenth century. The author was Charles Maguire, a learned and saintly priest, who died in 1498.

33. Give a brief account of the *Annals of Loch Cé* (key).

The *Annals of Loch Cé* is a chronicle of Irish affairs from the battle of Clontarf, A.D. 1014 to A.D. 1590. The account of the battle of Clontarf contains many interesting details not to be found in any of the other Annals now in existence.

34. Who was Keating and when did he write his *History of Ireland?*

Dr. Geoffrey Keating was a learned and patriotic Irish priest who wrote a valuable *History of Ireland* among the hills of Tipperary, about the year 1625. It was written in the common Irish of the seventeenth century.

35. Give a brief description of the *Chronicle of the Irish** and the *Book of Genealogies* by MacFirbis.

The first is a chronicle of Irish affairs from the earliest times to A.D. 1135; and the second is a vast work, giving the pedigrees of all the Celtic Irish families.

36. What is the nature of the work entitled *Cambrensis Overthrown*, and who wrote t?

Cambrensis Overthrown is a triumphant refutation

---

* Called in the original the *Chronicum Scotorum*.

IRISH OR CELTIC LITERATURE OF IRELAND. 309

of the shameful works of Giraldus Cambrensis on Ireland. Cambrensis, the foul, malicious libeller of the Irish, was a British ecclesiastic who wrote shortly after the English invasion. The author of *Cambrensis Overthrown*[*] was John Lynch, a learned and patriotic Irish bishop of the seventeenth century.

37. Which is the greatest and most comprehensive of all the Irish annals?

The *Annals of the Four Masters*, which begins at the earliest period and comes down year by year to A D. 1616. The last record is the death of the illustrious Hugh O'Neill.

38. Why is this great work called the *Annals of the Four Masters?*

Because it was written by four eminent Irish historians, masters in antiquarian lore—*Michael O'Clery, Conary O'Clery, Peregrine O'Clery*, and *Ferfeasa O'Mulconary*. The chief of these was Michael O'Clery. The *Annals of the Four Masters* was finished in 1636.

39. Which is the best English translation of the *Annals of the Four Masters?*

That by Dr. John O'Donovan, in seven large quarto volumes, first published in 1851.[†]

---

[*] It was written in Latin, and the original title is *Cambrensis Eversus*.
[†] "We regard the *Annals of the Four Masters* as the largest collection of national, civil, military, and family history ever brought together in this or perhaps any other country."—*Prof. O'Curry*.

LESSON IV.

ANCIENT IRISH BIOGRAPHY.

(1) *The Confession of St. Patrick.*
(2) St. Fiacc's *Metrical Life of St. Patrick.*
(3) St. Evin's *Tripartite Life of St. Patrick.*
(4) St. Adamnan's *Life of St. Columbkille.*
(5) Colgan's *Lives of the Irish Saints.*

40. What is the *Confession of St. Patrick?*

It may be described as a brief, humble autobiography of the great Apostle of Ireland, who died A.D. 465.

41. Who was St. Fiacc?

St. Fiacc, a famous bard, was converted by St. Patrick, and afterwards became first Bishop of Leinster. He was the father of Christian biography in Ireland.

42. What is his *Metrical Life of St. Patrick?*

It is a brief eulogistic sketch of the Apostle of Ireland in thirty-four four-lined rhyming stanzas. The twelfth stanza runs thus:

> "Renowned was St. Patrick through life,
> And of error he was a dire foe;
> Hence forever his name shall be grand
> Among the nations, as ages shall flow." *

43. What can you say of St. Evin's *Tripartite Life of St. Patrick*, and why was it so named?

The *Tripartite Life* is one of the most remarkable literary monuments of ancient Irish Church history. The book derives its name from the fact that it is divided into *three parts*. The author, St. Evin, wrote in the sixth century.

---

* As this was written 1400 years ago, the last two lines are truly prophetic.

IRISH OR CELTIC LITERATURE OF IRELAND. 311

44. Is the life of St. Columbkille by St. Adamnan a valuable work?

It is a work of great value—an inestimable literary relic of the ancient Irish Church. St. Adamnan was the cousin and ninth successor of St. Columbkille, as abbot of Iona. He died in 704.

45. Who was Father John Colgan?

He was a learned and patriotic Franciscan who has forever made Irish literature his debtor by his *Lives of the Irish Saints*. Colgan died in the year 1658.

LESSON V.

MISCELLANEOUS ANCIENT IRISH BOOKS.

(1) *The Book of the Dun Cow.**
(2) *The Book of Leinster.*
(3) *The Book of Armagh.*
(4) *The Book of Ballymote.*
(5) *The Speckled Book.*
(6) *The Yellow Book of Lecain.*
(7) *The Cattle Spoil of Cooley.**

46. What is the *Book of the Dun Cow?*

The *Book of the Dun Cow* is the most ancient work existing in the Irish language, but only a splendid fragment of it remains. It is a precious collection of tales, poetry, and history. It was written by Maelmuiri, who died in 1106.

47. Give a brief description of the contents of the *Book of Leinster.*

The *Book of Leinster* is a collection of historical tracts, tales, poems, genealogies, and pictures of social life in ancient Ireland. The author was Finn MacGorman, Bishop of Kildare, who died in the year 1160.

---

* There is an English translation.

48. What is the *Book of Armagh?*

The *Book of Armagh* is a religious work, containing the life of St. Patrick, the Confession of St. Patrick, the life of St. Martin of Tours, and a large portion of the New Testament. It was compiled by Ferdomnach in the year 807.

49. What is the *Book of Ballymote?*

The *Book of Ballymote* is a large historical, biographical, and genealogical compilation, and is the work of several hands. Portions of it were written about the year 1590.*

50. What is the *Speckled Book?*

According to Dr. Petrie, the *Speckled Book* is the oldest and best Irish manuscript relating to church history now preserved.†

---

* "The Book of Ballymote," says Professor Eugene O'Curry, "begins with an imperfect copy of the ancient *Leabhar Gabhála,* or Book of Invasions of Erin, differing in a few details from other copies of the same tract. This is followed by a series of ancient chronological, historical, and genealogical pieces in prose and verse. Then follow the pedigrees of Irish saints; the history and pedigrees of all the great families of the Milesian race, with the various minor tribes and families which have branched off from them in the succession of ages; so that there scarcely exists an O' or a Mac at the present day who may not find in this book the name of the particular remote ancestor whose name he bears as a sirname, as well as the time at which he lived, what he was, and from what ancient line he was descended. These genealogies may appear unimportant to ordinary readers; but those who have essayed to illustrate any branch of the ancient history of this country, and who could have availed themselves of them, have found in them the most authentic, accurate, and important auxiliaries—in fact, a history which has remained so long unwritten as that of ancient Erin could never be satisfactorily compiled at all without them."— *Lectures on the Manuscript Materials of Ancient Irish History.*

† This venerable book is thus described by Professor O'Curry: "The volume is written in a most beautiful style of penmanship, on fine large folio vellum. The contents are all, with one exception, of a religious character, and all, or nearly all, in the purest style of Gaelic. Many of the tracts are translations and narratives from the Latin. Among these are found a Scripture narrative from the creation to Solomon; the birth, life, passion, and resurrection of our Lord; and the lives and manner of death of several of the apostles; various versions of the finding of the Cross, etc.

51. What is the *Yellow Book of Lecain?*

The *Yellow Book of Lecain* is a great work, a portion of which has perished. In its original form it seems to have been a valuable collection of ancient historical pieces, civil and ecclesiastical, in prose and verse.

52. What is the *Cattle Spoil of Cooley?**

The *Cattle Spoil of Cooley* is a famous historic tale which has been styled the great epic of Ireland. The wild events described in it took place about A.D. 39.†

There are besides these several pieces, ancient sermons or homilies for certain days and periods of the year—such as sermons for Lent, Palm-Sunday, Easter-Sunday, Pentecost, on the institution of the Holy Eucharist, and others of a similar kind. In these sermons the Scripture text is always given in Latin, and then freely and copiously expounded and commented on in pure Gaelic; and in the course of these expositions various commentators are often mentioned and quoted. Besides these sermons, there are many small tracts on moral subjects, illustrative of the divine teachings of our Lord. St. Sechnall's *Hymn,* in praise of his uncle St. Patrick, is also to be found there, as well as the celebrated *Altus* of St. Columbkille, etc., etc."—*Lectures.*

* The title in the original Irish is *Táin Bo Chuailgné.*

† I am not acquainted with any tale in the whole range of our literature in which the student will find more of valuable details concerning general and local history—more of description of the manners and customs of the people—of the druidical and fairy influence supposed to be exercised in the affairs of men—of the laws of Irish chivalry and honor—of the standards of beauty, morality, valor, truth, and fidelity recognized by the people of old - of the regal power and dignity of the monarch and the provincial kings, as well as much concerning the division of the country into its local dependencies lists of its chieftains and chieftainesses—many valuable topographical names, the names and kinds of articles of dress and ornament, of military weapons, of horses, chariots and trappings, of leechcraft and of medicinal plants and springs, as well as instances of, perhaps, every occurrence that could be supposed to happen in ancient Irish life.—*O'Curry.*

Summary of Chapter I., Book III.

1. The Celts were the *first* inhabitants of Europe after the Deluge.

2. Ireland was inhabited at a very early period.

3. Thirteen centuries before Christ Ireland was invaded by the Milesians, who became the ruling race.

4. Scotia and Hibernia were the ancient names of Ireland.

5. The most famous of the Milesian monarchs, before the introduction of Christianity, was Cormac MacArt, who died A.D. 267.

6. In A.D. 432 St. Patrick began to preach in Ireland.

7. Ireland became the school of Europe during the sixth, seventh, and eighth centuries, which constitute the golden age of Irish history.

8. The early Irish missionaries traversed Europe, and became the apostles of Scotland, Northern England, Eastern France, Belgium, Switzerland, Germany, Norway, and Iceland.

9. Prince Alfred of Northumbria has left us in his poem a glowing picture of Ireland in the seventh century.

10. In A.D. 795 the Danes first appeared on the coasts of Ireland.

11. The celebrated Irish monarch, Brian Boru, utterly crushed the power of the Danes at the battle of Clontarf, A.D. 1014.

12. Irish sirnames, which were always preceded by *O'* or *Mac*, originated in the tenth century.

IRISH OR CELTIC LITERATURE OF IRELAND. 315

13. We may date the Anglo-Norman invasion from the arrival of Henry II. in Ireland A.D. 1171.

14. Rory O'Conor was the last *ard-ri*, or supreme monarch, of Ireland.

15. The infamous statute of Kilkenny became a law A.D. 1367.

16. Ulster was the last stronghold of Irish independence, and O'Neill, O'Donnell, O'Kane, Maguire, and other princes of the North, battled for years against the armies of Elizabeth.

17. The shameful process of *confiscation*, which gradually outlawed the whole Irish nation and deprived the Irish people of the soil, went on with unspeakable barbarity from the so-called Reformation to the end of the present chapter, A.D. 1700, and later still.

18. From the earliest period of history down to A.D. 1700, Ireland had but one national language— the *Irish language*.

19. Irish literature was a perfect expression of the social state of the Irish people. Every king, prince, and chief had his own bard, brehon, and historian.

20. The golden age of Irish literature opens A.D. 432, and closes A.D. 800.

21. The ancient literature of Ireland suffered immensely from the Danish invasion and the Anglo-Norman invasion; but the crowning stroke of misfortune for it was the Protestant Reformation and the savage penal laws that followed.

22. The remains of Irish literature, however, that have escaped the destroying hand of Dane, Norman, and Saxon, and the action of time, are of truly gigan-

tic proportions. Over 60,000 quarto pages of ancient Irish manuscripts can be found in the libraries of the Royal Irish Academy and Trinity College, Dublin.

23. The Irish language is the most ancient in Europe.

24. *Ossian, St. Columbkille, St. Donatus, Mac Laig, O'Duggan, Mac Ward, O'Kane,* and *O'Carolan* are a few of the names of Irish bards some of whose works have come down to us.

25. *Tighernach O'Breen,* abbot of Clonmacnoise, and *Brother Michael O'Clery, O.S.F.,* were the greatest of the Irish annalists.

26. *Duald MacFirbis* was the last regularly educated Irish antiquary and historian; and *Tirlogh O'Carolan* was the last of the Irish bards.

27. The *Annals of the Four Masters* is the greatest and most comprehensive of the Irish annals.

28. *St. Fiacc,* author of the *Metrical Life of St. Patrick,* was the father of Irish biography.

29. The most ancient work existing in the Irish language is the *Book of the Dun Cow.*

30. The *Táin Bo Chuailgné* is the epic of ancient Ireland.

31. See *Short Dictionary* for the other Irish writers of this period most worthy of mention; namely, *John Scotus Erigena, James* **Ussher,** **Sir James Ware,** and *Roderick O'Flaherty.**

---

* For a fuller account of ancient Irish literature and the Irish language, see Prof. O'Curry's *Lectures on the MS. Materials of Ancient Irish History,* Canon Bourke's *Aryan Origin of the Gaelic Race and Language,* and Matthew Arnold's *Study of Celtic Literature.*

CHAPTER II.

THE ENGLISH LITERATURE OF IRELAND.

A.D. 1700 to 1800.

THE AGE OF SWIFT, GOLDSMITH, AND BURKE.

HISTORICAL INTRODUCTION.

1. GLIMPSES AT IRELAND IN THE EIGHTEENTH CENTURY.—The eighteenth century carries us through the reigns of Anne and the first three Georges, and during this mournful period Ireland was the most wretched and misgoverned nation on the round earth. It was in the reign of Queen Anne (1702–1714) that the penal laws against Catholics were brought to what Edmund Burke calls a " vicious perfection."

2. THE PENAL LAWS.—Let us glance at some of these horrid enactments. Every Catholic in Ireland was disarmed, and forbidden the use of a gun. Every officeholder, from a clerk to an archbishop, and all professional men, were obliged to swear against the Catholic doctrine of the Holy Eucharist. A Catholic could not sit in Parliament, could not hold any office under the crown, could not enter the army or navy, could not vote at an election, could not be a lawyer, a physician, a sheriff, or even a gamekeeper. A Catholic was not permitted to own a horse of greater value than $25; and if he owned a fine horse he was bound to sell it for that sum to any Protestant who was disposed to buy. Catholics were fined $300

a month for absence from the Protestant form of worship, and they were forbidden to travel five miles from their houses. No Catholic could go near a walled city—especially Galway and Limerick. "In order," writes John Mitchel, "that they might be sure not to get near a walled town, they were to remain several miles away, as if they were lepers whose presence would contaminate their select and pampered Protestant fellow-citizens." If a younger brother turned Protestant, he supplanted the elder in his birthright. A Protestant lawyer who married a Catholic lady was disqualified to continue the practice of his profession. Marriages of Protestants and Catholics, if performed by a priest, were annulled, and the priest was liable to be hanged. A Catholic could educate his children neither at home nor abroad. Catholic schools were closed, and all Catholics were forbidden to teach. The doors of the only university in Ireland* were closed to Catholics. A reward of $50 was offered for the discovery of each Catholic schoolmaster. Catholics who went abroad to be educated were disinherited of all their property. If a Catholic entertained a priest or a bishop, he was fined $100; for a second offence of the kind he was fined $200; and for a third offence he forfeited his whole estate. The exercise of the Catholic religion was forbidden; its churches were closed or stolen; its priests were banished, and hanged if they returned home.† Rewards, varying according to the rank of the victim, were

---

* Trinity College, Dublin.
† For instance, 424 priests were banished from Ireland in the year 1698. "Some few," says an Irish historian, "disabled by age and infirmities sought shelter in caves, or implored and received concealment and protection of Protestants whose humane feelings were superior to their prejudices."

offered for the discovery of Catholic clergymen. At one period, the same price was offered for the head of a priest and that of a wolf. Even Jews came from Portugal to hunt down Catholic priests in the Emerald Isle of the sea, and found it a profitable business. The fierce Mohawk, ranging the ancient forests of New York, was not more eager and skilful on the trail of an enemy than was the ferocious and barbarous government of England in its rage after Catholic ecclesiastics. Bribes were offered to all who would betray Catholics. Truly has Davis written:

> "They bribed the flock, they bribed the son,
>   To sell the priest and rob the sire;
> Their dogs were taught alike to run
>   Upon the scent of wolf and friar.
>   Among the poor,
>   Or on the moor,
>   Were hid the pious and the true;
>   While traitor knave,
>   And recreant slave,
>   Had riches, rank, and retinue."

A Catholic could neither purchase land nor dispose of it by will. Pilgrimages to Lough Derg, to shrines of the saints, or to holy wells were forbidden under severe penalties; and magistrates were ordered to destroy all crosses and religious pictures and inscriptions.*

---

* The language of those brutal enactments is painfully offensive. A Catholic is never termed a Catholic, but a "Papist," and his religion is nicknamed "Popery." The vulgar words "Popish," "Romish," "Romanist," and "Romanism" can also be met. I have already remarked in one of my books that "the same malignant and uncultured spirit which produced the penal laws gave the world this mongrel brood of ragged, boorish words. It is said that 'Papist' was first used as a nickname for Catholics by Martin Luther; the others had their disgraceful origin in England. But no educated speaker or writer of our day can use such outcasts; they are literary eyesores, forbidden alike by politeness, good sense, and elegance of diction. Things and persons should be called by their right names."

Is it any wonder that Montesquieu exclaimed with indignation: "This horrid code was conceived by devils, written in human gore, and registered in hell"?

"The Irish," says Edmund Burke, 'have been more harassed for religion than any people under the sun."

"I have read," declares the famous Dr. Doyle, "of the persecutions of Nero, Domitian, Genseric, and Attila, with all the barbarities of the sixteenth century. I have compared them with those inflicted on my own country, and protest to God that the latter, in my opinion, have exceeded in duration, extent, and intensity all that has ever been endured by mankind for justice's sake."

The spirit of the Catholics was crushed and broken under the weight of such enormous oppression. The wealthy were ruined, and the poor became poorer. "The poor people of Ireland," said Lord Chesterfield, "are worse used than negroes." Ireland was not for the Irish, but for the Protestant English colony, or the Protestant garrison, as they called themselves.

The members of this insolent minority filled all the public offices, ruled the island, and formed the corrupt body falsely known as the "Irish Parliament." But this so-called Irish parliament was Irish only in name. It did not represent the Irish Catholics who composed the great body of the nation, but who were not recognized by the law, and who were still spoken of as "the common enemy." * It merely represented a faction of intolerant upstarts—the persecuting English Protestant colony in Ireland. It was this sham "Irish" par-

---

* Chief-Justice Robinson, interpreting the law, declared: "*It appears plain that the law does not suppose any such person to exist as an Irish Catholic.*"

liament that passed and sanctioned most of the shameful enactments of which I have given a summary.

The Catholics formed nine-tenths of the nation, but for them the door was closed to every ennobling impulse. They were doomed to ignorance and social degradation. There was no way out of obscurity; no promise of worldly success; no scope for energy and enterprise, except at the awful price of surrendering their hopes of Heaven and turning their backs on the dear old faith of St. Patrick. But this noble people sacrificed everything earthly for the sake of their religion, "accounting all things as dross that they might gain Christ;" and in the words of the Holy Book, "Blessed are they that suffer persecution for justice's sake, for theirs is the kingdom of Heaven."

3. HEARING MASS.—What dangers were braved to hear and celebrate Mass! The Holy Sacrifice was secretly offered up in caves, secluded valleys, and mountain-gorges.* The fear, however, created in

---

* William Carleton, in one of his novels, gives a vivid pen-picture of Mass in a mountain-cave. It is full of interest and sublimity. "The day was stormy in the extreme," he writes. "It was a hard frost, and the snow, besides, falling heavily—the wind strong and raging in hollow gusts about the place. The position of the altar-table, however, saved the bishop and the chalice and the other things necessary for the performance of worship from the direct fury of the blast, but not altogether: for occasionally a whirlwind would come up, and toss over the leaves of the *Missal* in such a way, and with such violence, that the bishop, who was now trembling from cold, was obliged to lose some time in finding out the proper passages. It was a solemn sight to see two or three hundred persons kneeling, and bent in prostrate and heartfelt adoration in the pious worship of that God who sends and withholds the storm—bareheaded, too, under the piercing drift of the thick-falling snow, and thinking of nothing but their own sins, and that gladsome opportunity of approaching the forbidden altar of God, now doubly dear to them that it was forbidden. The bishop was getting on to that portion of the sacred rite where the consecration and elevation of the Host are necessary, and it was observed by all that an extraordinary and sudden lull took place, and that the

England by the Scottish Rebellion of 1745 served slightly to relax some of the penal laws against Catholic worship. In a *Tour through Ireland* by two English travellers, written in 1748, we read: "The poorer sort of Irish natives are mostly Catholics, who make no scruple to assemble in the open fields. As we passed yesterday, in a by-road, we saw a priest under a tree, with a large assembly about him, celebrating Mass in his proper habit; and though at a great distance from us, we heard him distinctly. This sort of people seem to be very solemn and sincere in their devotions." Later on Catholics were permitted to build a little chapel here and there, but with the humiliating condition that it should have neither bell nor steeple.

4. THE CHANGES MADE BY A QUARTER OF A CENTURY.—As the trouble with the American colonies became more serious, the galled and goaded followers of the ancient faith were to experience another taste of English generosity. But what was it? In 1771 the magnificent concession was made to them of permission to hold long leases of fifty acres of *bog for reclamation*, provided it was not within a mile of any city or town! In 1782, after England had been beaten to her knees in America, the Irish Catholics were allowed to purchase, inherit, and dispose of land; and ten years later, when the French Revolution was shaking Europe, the professions were opened to them, and they were permitted to keep schools. St. Patrick's College, Maynooth, an institution for the

---

rage of the storm had altogether ceased. He proceeded and had consecrated the Host—*Hoc est Corpus Meum*—when a cry of terror arose from the affrighted congregation.
"'My lord, fly and save yourself! Captain Smellpriest and his gang are upon us!'"—*Willy Reilly*, chap. xiii.

education of the Catholic clergy, was opened in 1795. But no people can be satisfied while wickedly cheated out of their rights. Discontent filled the air. The unhappy people were driven into premature rebellion in 1798. A swarm of Scotch, English, and German ruffians, misnamed soldiers, were let loose on the country, and crimes the most horrible were committed. The pitch-cap, whipping, half-hanging, burning off the hair, and other unspeakable barbarities were sanctioned by the English authorities.*

5. REMARKS ON THE ENGLISH LITERATURE OF IRELAND IN THE EIGHTEENTH CENTURY.—The English penal laws explain why not one Catholic author of distinction appeared in Ireland during the eighteenth century. The nation was inhumanly gagged. It was reduced to a sad silence. Ignorance was compulsory. To master the multiplication-table was a crime; to learn to read was a crime; to learn to write was, perhaps, a greater one.† It was dangerous to own a Catholic book, and many a family was ruined by the possession of an Irish manuscript. The faithful priest and the worthy hedge-schoolmaster kept, however, the lamp of knowledge dimly burning among a people who love and honor true knowledge above any race in the world. What was a hedge-school? It is aptly described by Carleton in his *Willy Reilly*. "Father Maguire," he writes, " previous to his receiv-

---

* Lord Cornwallis was so sickened at the condition of things that he wrote from Dublin Castle to a friend: "The conversation even at my table, where you will suppose I do all I can to prevent it, always turns on hanging, shooting, burning, etc.; and if a priest has been put to death, the greatest joy is expressed by the whole company."

† The woful "laws" were so rigorously enforced that, according to a writer in the *Ulster Journal of Archæology*, there were probably not 200 persons in Ireland who could *read and write* their native Irish at the close of the eighteenth century.

ing orders, had been a schoolmaster, and exercised his functions in that capacity in holes and corners; sometimes on the sheltery or sunny side of a hedge, as the case might be, and on other occasions when and where he could. In his magisterial capacity 'the accomplishment' of whistling was absolutely necessary to him, because it often happened that, in stealing in the morning from his retreat during the preceding night, he knew no more where to meet his little flock of scholars than they did where to meet him; the truth being that he seldom found it safe to teach two days successively in the same place. Having selected the locality for instruction during the day, he put his forefinger and thumb into his mouth and emitted a whistle that went over half the country. Having thus given the signal three times, his scholars began gradually and cautiously to make their appearance, coming towards him from all directions; reminding one of a hen in a farm-yard, which having fallen upon some wholesome crumbs, she utters that peculiar sound which immediately collects her eager little flock about her, in order to dispense among them the good things she has to give."

Sir Charles Gavan Duffy, in his *Young Ireland*, has a very suggestive passage on this mournful period. "Among the Catholics," he says, "there was no national literature; no books of any kind indeed except a few pamphlets written by Irish priests or exiles on the Continent and smuggled into the country. But an injured people have a long memory. By the fireside on a wintry night, at fairs and markets, the old legends and traditions were a favorite recreation. The wandering harpers and pipers kept them alive; the hedge-schoolmaster taught them with more unction than the rudiments. Nurses and seamstresses, the tailor who carried his lapboard and shears from house to house and from district to district, the peddler who came from the capital with shawls and ribbons, the tinker who paid for his supper and shelter with a song or a story, were always ready with tales of the wars and the persecution. A recent historian * cannot repress his disdain that in those times—for this was 'the Augustan age of Queen Anne'—no great drama or epic poem or masterpiece of art was produced in Ireland; but it is not on the jailers in this penal settlement, but on their prisoners, that the critic's reproaches fall."

The chief names in the English literature of Ireland in the eighteenth century are *Sir Richard Steele, Jonathan Swift, Oliver Goldsmith, Edmund Burke, Richard Brinsley Sheridan, John Philpot Curran, Henry Grattan,* and *William Drennan*—all non-Catholics. Let us glance at the attitude of each towards Ireland and his shamefully oppressed Catholic countrymen. It will throw much light on nobility of character and the love of fair play and civil and religious liberty. Steele lived most of his life in England, and I am not aware that he ever uttered a word in favor of Ireland. Swift was a Protestant clergyman. He spent most of his life in Ireland. He has been falsely called an Irish patriot; but his narrow patriotism never extended beyond the English colony in Ireland. He was at heart an English snob, and was ashamed to be taken for an Irishman. " I no more consider myself an Irishman," he writes, " because I happened to be born in Ireland, than an Englishman chancing to be born in Calcutta would con-

---

* Lord Macaulay.

sider himself a Hindoo." He scoffs at the Catholics as "the savage old Irish." He has no word of sympathy for their worse than wolfish treatment by the English, but speaks with disdain and aversion of the very people who gave him his bread and butter. It is worthy of notice that Goldsmith has no reference to Ireland in any of his writings. Burke was a great man and a true Irishman. He loved his native isle, and, though he spent most of his life in England, he never ceased by tongue and pen to demand justice for his oppressed Catholic countrymen. Sheridan had many failings, but he never lost his affection for his native land. Among the last words he uttered in the English House of Commons were the following: "Be just to Ireland. I will never give my vote to any administration that opposes the question of Catholic emancipation." Grattan was the soul of Irish chivalry, and an intense lover of justice. "So long," he exclaimed, "as we exclude Catholics from natural liberty and the common rights of man we are not a people." Curran was a genuine Irishman and an earnest advocate of religious freedom. Drennan was the patriotic poet of the Irish Rebellion. He was the first to give the title of the Emerald Isle to Ireland in his poem *Erin:*

"When Erin first rose from the dark swelling flood,
God blessed the green island, and saw it was good;
The *emerald* of Europe, it sparkled and shone,
In the ring of the world the most precious stone."

LESSON I.

SIR RICHARD STEELE. DIED 1729.

(1) *Essays.*   (2) *Comedies.*   (3) *Letters.*

JONATHAN SWIFT. DIED 1745.

(1) *Tale of a Tub.*   (3) *Gulliver's Travels.*
(2) *Drapier Letters.*   (4) *Poems.*

1. Who was Sir Richard Steele?

Sir Richard Steele, *the founder of English periodical literature*, was one of the most original and brilliant writers of the eighteenth century.

2. Tell us something of his career.

Steele was born at Dublin. His father was an Englishman, but his mother was Irish, and from her he seems to have inherited his bright fancy, tenderness, and impulsive ardor. He studied at Oxford, became a captain in the Horse Guards, then a member of the English Parliament, and died in poverty.

3. Where did his *Essays* first appear?

In his papers—the *Tatler*, *Spectator*, and *Guardian*.*

4. Which was the first English periodical?

The Tatler.

5. When did Steele begin *The Tatler?*

In 1709.

6. Of the three periodicals, which was the most celebrated?

The Spectator, a daily paper, which to this day ranks as one of the most famous publications in the history of British periodical literature. It is an Eng-

---

* "The *Tatler, Spectator,* and *Guardian* were all of them Steele's journals, begun and ended by him at his sole discretion. In these three he wrote 510 papers; Addison, 369."—*Henry Morley*

lish classic. The best essays written by Steele and Addison appeared in its pages.*

7. By what other works is Steele chiefly known?

By his *Comedies*, and *Letters* to his wife.

8. Which is his best comedy, and what should be remembered to his honor?

The *Conscious Lovers* is his best comedy. Steele was the first dramatist after the Restoration to introduce virtue on the English stage.

9. Who was one of the most original writers of the eighteenth century?

Jonathan Swift, "the greatest wit of all time," and one of the greatest masters of the English language.

10. Give a short account of his life.

Swift was born at Dublin, was left an orphan, studied at Trinity College, and, after many ups and downs, became Dean of St. Patrick's Church † in his native city. He was insane during the last three years of his life, and died at the age of 78.

11. In what line of thought did the ambitious Swift first make his mark as a writer?

He plunged into politics, and used his pen as the lever by which he meant to raise himself to the pinnacle of clerical and political greatness.‡

---

* It must be remembered that Steele published his famous papers in England, not in Ireland. "It was through the *Tatlers*," writes Henry Morley, "and the daily *Spectators* which succeeded them, that the people of England really learned to read."—*English Writers*.

The first number of *The Spectator* is dated March 1, 1711; the last, December 20, 1714—in all, 635 numbers.

† It was stolen from the Catholics. Swift, as has been already stated, was a Protestant clergyman.

‡ "Against all comers he stood the Goliath of pamphleteers in the reign of Queen Anne, and there arose no David who could slay him."—*Coppée.*

12. Which was his first work of marked power and originality?

The *Tale of a Tub*, which was published in 1704. It is the coarsest, wildest, and wittiest of all his polemical works.

13. What caused Swift to write the *Drapier Letters?*

In 1724 an Englishman named Wood obtained a patent from the government empowering him to coin over half a million dollars' worth of copper money for circulation in Ireland. Swift opposed the measure in a series of public letters, marked by a bold, simple, and hardy eloquence, and signed "M. B. Drapier." The blow crushed Wood and his odious patent.

14. Which was Swift's most popular and original work?

Gulliver's Travels, which he made the vehicle of his contempt and hatred of mankind. The gross indecency of certain portions of the work merit severe condemnation.

"Immodest words admit of no defence,
For want of decency is want of sense."

15. What is your opinion of his poems?

Swift was a poet, but the less said in praise of his poetry the better.

"I am far from wishing to depreciate Addison's talents, but I am anxious to do justice to Steele, who was, I think, upon the whole, a less artificial and more original writer."—*William Hazlitt.*

"Swift knew, almost beyond any man, the purity, the extent, and the precision of the English language."—*Blair.*

LESSON II.

OLIVER GOLDSMITH. DIED 1774.

Chief works: (1) *Poems.*
(2) *Plays.*
(3) *Essays.*
(4) *The Vicar of Wakefield.*

16. Who was Oliver Goldsmith?

He was a gifted, kind-hearted Irishman, " who left scarcely any style of writing untouched, and touched nothing which he did not adorn."

17. Give a brief outline of his career.

Goldsmith was born at Pallas, in the county of Longford; graduated at Trinity College, Dublin; studied medicine; made a tour of Europe with "a guinea in his pocket, a shirt on his back, and a flute in his hand;" and at length, settling in London, he devoted his life to literature.

18. Which are his chief poems?

The Traveller and *The Deserted Village;* but he wrote a number of short poems of great merit.

19. What is *The Traveller?*

It is a didactic poem in which Goldsmith gives his impressions of the scenes and society that he met on his travels through the various countries of Europe. He comes to the conclusion that—

"Still to ourselves in every place consigned,
Our own felicity we make or find."

20. Which is Goldsmith's masterpiece?

The Deserted Village, the most polished, precious, and soul-touching of all his poems. It speaks to the heart. It is full of exquisite pictures of rural life and manners. The diction is simple and beautiful. In short, it is a poem unsurpassed in the whole range of English literature.*

21. What do you know of his comedies?

Goldsmith's comedies are *The Good-Natured Man* and *She Stoops to Conquer*. The former is an agreeable satire on the follies of benevolence, and the latter a laughable burlesque on a very improbable mistake. They still keep the stage.

22. How does Goldsmith rank as an essayist?

As an essayist he ranks with the highest in our language.

23. What merit belongs to him as a writer of fiction?

The great merit of purifying the novel and of raising it above the sensual and obscene. The *Vicar of Wakefield* stands alone in English letters, the matchless story of his own matchless pen.

"Goldsmith, both in prose and verse, was one of the most delightful writers in the language. His verse flows like a limpid stream."—*William Hazlitt.*

"From the excitement of our present literature, whether genuine or spurious, it is a pleasant change to take up the tranquil pages of Goldsmith—to feel the sunny glow of his thoughts upon our hearts. and on our fancies the gentle music of his words."—*Henry Giles.*

---

*The following suggestive lines are often quoted:
 "Ill fares the land, to hastening ills a prey,
  Where wealth accumulates and men decay.
  Princes and lords may flourish or may fade—
  A breath can make them as a breath has made;
  But a bold peasantry, their country's pride,
  When once destroyed, can never be supplied."

LESSON III.

EDMUND BURKE. DIED 1797.

Chief works: (1) *Speeches.*
(2) *Public Letters.*
(3) *Reflections on the Revolution in France.*

24. Which is the greatest name among the Irish writers of the eighteenth century?

Edmund Burke, who was to England and all Europe a new light of political wisdom and moral experience.

25. Tell us something of his career.

Burke was born at Dublin, received his education at Trinity College, entered the English Parliament, and spent a long and spotless life in laboring for the advancement of justice and civil and religious liberty.

26. Which was his earliest original work of marked power?

His *Essay on the Sublime and Beautiful*, a work written in a style of great elegance.

27. What is said of his eloquence?

The eloquence of Burke, though it often flew over the thick heads of those to whom it was addressed, is destined to be the admiration and delight of unborn generations. Lord Macaulay styles him "the greatest master of eloquence," and pronounces him "superior to every orator, ancient or modern."

28. Upon what subjects did he speak and write with most force and fervor?

On the claims of the oppressed Irish Catholics,* on justice to the American colonists, on the impeach-

---

* But a few months before his death, he wrote his last *Letter on the Affairs of Ireland.*

ment of Warren Hastings, and on the French Revolution.

29. Mention his three splendid pieces on the American struggle.

(1) *Speech on American Taxation;*
(2) *Speech on Conciliation with America;*
(3) *Letter to the Sheriffs of Bristol.*

He was ever the friend of America, and his protests against the war will last as long as our literature.

30. What does John Morley remark of those three productions?

It is no exaggeration to say that th y compose the most perfect manual in our literature, or in any literature, for one who approaches the study of public affairs, whether for knowledge or for practice.

31. Which, perhaps, was the grandest oratorical achievement of his life?

The famous impeachment of Warren Hastings in 1788.*

32. What has a famous critic said of his *Letter to a Noble Lord?*

That it is the most splendid repartee in the English language.

33. Which, however, is Burke's masterpiece?

The *Reflections on the Revolution in France*, an incomparable work, that gives the fullest and clearest statement of his political philosophy. It is a treasury of eloquence and political wisdom. It is a Christian book. It shows that without religion true civilization must cease to exist. "We know," says Burke, "and what is better we feel inwardly, that re-

---

* Hastings had been Governor-General of India, and had sadly abused his position.

ligion is the basis of civil society, and the source of all good and of all comfort."

34. What is your opinion of Edmund Burke's rank as a writer?

He is one of the greatest masters of English prose. He united wise solidity of thought to brilliancy of imagination in a degree perhaps never possessed by any other writer of our language.

"Burke is among the greatest of those who have wrought marvels in the prose of our English tongue."—*John Morley.*

"Shakspeare and Burke are, if I may venture the expression, above talent. Burke's works contain an ampler store of political and moral wisdom than can be found in any other writer whatever."—*Sir James Mackintosh.*

"He was a prodigy of nature and of acquisition. He read everything—he saw everything. His knowledge of history amounted to a power of foretelling; and when he perceived the wild work that was doing in France, that great political physician, cognizant of symptoms, distinguished between the access of fever and the force of health, and what others conceived to be the vigor of her constitution he knew to be the paroxysm of her madness; and thus prophet-like, he pronounced the destinies of France, and, in his prophetic fury, admonished nations."—*Henry Grattan.*

LESSON IV.

RICHARD BRINSLEY SHERIDAN. DIED 1816.

Chief works: (1) *Plays.* (2) *Speeches.*

35. Who was Richard Brinsley Sheridan?

He was the greatest dramatist and one of the most brilliant orators of the eighteenth century. As a dramatist he is second to Shakspeare only.

36. Give a short outline of his life.

Sheridan, the son of very gifted parents, was born at Dublin, in 1751. After an imperfect education, he began life as a literary adventurer, and grasped at position, fame, and fortune as if they were his birthright. He seemed to fail in nothing except virtue and temperance. His career in the English Parliament was brilliant, but he died in poverty and neglect.

37. Name his principal plays.

The School for Scandal, The Rivals, and *The Critic.*

38. What is *The School for Scandal?*

It is a regular comedy, the object of which is to satirize the society of London. The dialogue is one incessant sparkle of the finest and most polished repartee. In spite of some faults, it may safely be pronounced the best comedy in the English language.

39. What is *The Rivals?*

It is an exquisite comedy over which the reader never ceases to laugh. The sketches of character are light and admirable. The blustering Sir Anthony and Mrs. Malaprop with her " parts of speech" can never be forgotten.

40. What is *The Critic?*

It is a witty farce, and has a capital character in Sir Fretful Plagiary.

41. What have you to remark of Sheridan's speeches and parliamentary career?

He never failed to amuse the House, and, when stirred by the trumpet-call of a great occasion, he was capable of rising to heights of noble eloquence. Burke declared that Sheridan's famous speech against Warren Hastings was " the most astonishing effort of eloquence, argument, and wit united of which there is any record or tradition."

" As mere acting plays, those of Sheridan are considered the best in the language."—*Hart.*

" As a dramatic author, Sheridan produced three works which will ever be considered masterpieces in their different styles—the two comedies entitled *The School for Scandal* and *The Rivals,* and the inimitable dramatic caricature *The Critic.*"—*Shaw.*

LESSON V.

HENRY GRATTAN. DIED 1820.

Chief works: *Speeches.*

JOHN PHILPOT CURRAN. DIED 1817.

Chief works: *Speeches.*

42. Who was Henry Grattan?

He was one of the purest and greatest of Irish orators, patriots, and statesmen.

43. Give some of the chief points in his life.

Grattan was born at Dublin, educated at Trinity College, called to the Irish bar, became member of the Irish Parliament, and by the efforts of his genius he procured the legislative independence of Ireland in 1782. After the Union, he entered the British Parliament.

44. Mention a few of his most famous speeches.

The Rights of Ireland, *Philippic against Flood*, *Reply to Corry*, and *Speeches on the Catholic Question.*

45. Can you give an often-quoted passage from the peroration of his great speech on the Rights of Ireland?

Grattan said: "I never will be satisfied so long as the meanest cottager in Ireland has a link of the British chain clanking to his rags. He may be naked—he shall *not* be in irons."

46. What has an eminent critic remarked of Grattan's speeches?

That they are the finest specimens of imaginative eloquence in the English or in any language.

47. Give a short sketch of the eloquent and patriotic John Philpot Curran.

He was born in the county of Cork; received his education at Trinity College, Dublin; was called to the Irish bar; and devoted his life and his genius to the good of his country.

48. Have we complete reports of his speeches?

We have no complete report of Curran's speeches, but only hurried notes, which give us many hints of what the speeches actually spoken must have been.

49. Can you name some of his greatest speeches?

Among his greatest speeches were the following: *On Catholic Emancipation, For Archibald Hamilton Rowan, For Peter Finnerty, For Henry Sheares,* and *For Lady Pamela Fitzgerald and her Children.*

50. What may be said of Curran's eloquence?

Curran's eloquence was rich in feeling, courage, earnestness, exquisite humor, moral simplicity, moral elevation, and the spirit of poetry and patriotism. It glowed with brilliancy, for his soul was lighted with the fire of an impassioned imagination.

"No other orator is so uniformly animated as Grattan. No other orator has brightened the depths of political philosophy with such vivid and lasting light. No writer in the language, except Shakspeare, has so sublime and suggestive a diction."—*Thomas O. Davis.*

"No government ever dismayed Grattan. The world could not bribe him; he thought only of Ireland; lived for no other object; dedicated to her his beautiful fancy, his manly courage, and all the splendor of his astonishing eloquence."—*Sydney Smith.*

"I have met Curran at Holland House. His imagination is beyond human, and his humor is perfect. I never met his equal."—*Lord Byron.*

"No one can read even the meagre reports which we have of Curran's speeches without feeling how profoundly his life was in the cause of Ireland, and how his heart was bowed down under the burden of her calamities. This interest in his country is the central inspiration of his eloquence, and in his day his country was clad in mourning."—*Henry Giles.*

Summary of Chapter II., Book III.

1. The English penal laws were a horrible code framed with one main object in view—*the utter destruction of the Catholic religion in Ireland.*

2. Though subjected to appalling persecution for centuries; though robbed of all human resources—liberty, homes, lands, education, churches, colleges, and religious institutions—the Irish Catholics with a never-to-be-forgotten patience and heroism triumphed, and the so-called Reformation proved a signal failure in Ireland.

3. An insolent Protestant minority misruled the island, and tyrannized over the long-suffering Catholics.

4. The laws were made, not for the protection of the Catholics, but for their inhuman punishment. The cattle that roamed the fields had more legal rights than the royal descendants of Milesius.*

5. The corrupt and persecuting legislative body known as the "Irish Parliament" was Irish in name only.

6. The difficulties of England first forced her to relax the penal code against Catholics.

7. The penal laws made it impossible for one Irish Catholic writer of distinction to exist in the eighteenth century. To learn to read, to write, and to pray were equally acts of treason.

8. Persecuted priests and hedge-schoolmasters kept

---

* "We hold these truths to be self-evident: That all men are created equal; that they are endowed by their Creator with certain inalienable rights; that among these are life, liberty, and the pursuit of happiness."—*The Declaration of Independence.*

the lamp of knowledge dimly burning at the risk of their lives.

9. The Irish writers of the eighteenth century were all non-Catholics.

10. Steele was the founder of English periodical literature, and his *Spectator* is a classic.

11. Swift is one of the most original writers of this period.

12. Goldsmith was the first to purify the novel and make it a teacher of virtue.

13. Burke may be fairly called the prince of English prose-writers. His *Reflections on the Revolution in France* has been styled " the greatest work of the greatest writer of English prose."

14. Sheridan wrote the best and wittiest comedies in our language.

15. The *Speeches* of Burke, Grattan, Curran, and Sheridan are the earliest specimens of true *Irish* eloquence in the English language.

16. *Bird's-eye view of the chief Irish writers and works of the eighteenth century:*

Sir Richard Steele, *Essays in The Spectator*.
Rev. Jonathan Swift, *Gulliver's Travels*.
Oliver Goldsmith, *The Deserted Village*.
Edmund Burke, *Reflections on the Revolution in France*.
Richard Brinsley Sheridan, *The Rivals*.
Henry Grattan, *Speeches*.
John Philpot Curran, *Speeches*.

See *Short Dictionary* for the other Irish writers of the eighteenth century most worthy of mention; namely, *Thomas Parnell, Bishop Berkeley, Laurence Sterne, William Drennan*, and *Rev. Arthur O'Leary.**

---

*For a fuller account of the writers of this period, see *The Prose and Poetry of Ireland*.

CHAPTER III.

THE ENGLISH LITERATURE OF IRELAND.

A.D. 1800 to 1880.

THE AGE OF MOORE, GRIFFIN, AND D. F. MACCARTHY.

HISTORICAL INTRODUCTION.

"Ireland is a land of poetry. It is a country of tradition, of meditation, and of great idealism. Monuments of war, princedom and religion cover the surface of the land. The meanest man lingers under the shadow of piles which tell him that his fathers were not slaves. He toils in the fields with structures before him through which echoes the voice of centuries—to his heart the voice of soldiers, of scholars, and of saints."—*Henry Giles*.

1. GLIMPSES AT IRELAND IN THE NINETEENTH CENTURY.—We have already touched upon some of the chief events in the Irish history of the present age (Book II., Chap. VI.). The political misery of the nation was completed at the very dawn of the century. It was a time of struggle and confusion. Corruption and treachery ruled. The Catholics were powerless. William Pitt spent nearly $10,000,000 in bribing members of the so-called Irish Parliament, and a majority of that corrupt body voted for its destruction. "It sold the birthright of the nation," says Walpole, "for its own selfish ends."* And

---

* It must not be fancied that all the members turned traitors to their country. The Parliament contained such genuine patriots as Henry Grattan, Sir John Parnell, and many others. The iniquitous measure, however, was carried by a majority of forty-three.

thus, in brief, came about the legislative union of Great Britain and Ireland.

Dr. Johnson once remarked to an Irishman : "Do not make a union with us, sir. We should only unite with you to rob you. We should have robbed the Scotch if they had had anything of which we could have robbed them." The truth of this pointed remark is beyond question.

"From the first of January, 1801," writes McGee, "Ireland ceased to have even the semblance of nationality. Her laws in future were to be made in London, in a House of Commons seven-eighths of whose members had never seen Ireland, or knew anything whatever of her resources, trade, commerce, or agriculture ; and in a House of Lords where the ignorant majority was even more anti-Irish and anti-Catholic."

2. CATHOLIC EMANCIPATION.—The Irish Catholics —the great body of the nation—were still white slaves to whom, indeed, a few crumbs from the table of justice had been thrown. They were sunk in gloomy apathy.

> "The peasant scarce had leave to live—
> Above his head
> A ruined shed,
> No tenure but a tyrant's will."

At this critical period a great man appeared. It was Daniel O'Connell—the foremost political figure in Ireland for nearly half a century. His voice was a trumpet-blast that aroused the nation. The pens of Bishop Doyle, Bishop MacHale, Rev. Sydney Smith, and the eloquence of Shiel came to his assistance. O'Connell knocked at the doors of the English Parliament, and forced England to grant the Catholics emancipation, in 1829. At last the atrocious penal laws were erased from the statute-book, after filling the island with misery for centuries. Six millions of Irish Catholics were told that they had the right to live, move, say their prayers, and learn to read, write, and cipher, without being hunted like wild beasts. It was a great step forward.

3. REPEAL, YOUNG IRELAND, AND THE FAMINE.— O'Connell next aimed at the repeal of the Union. He wished Ireland to have her own legislature in Dublin. After years of peaceable agitation, however, the English Government had him arrested, prosecuted, and imprisoned. O'Connell was now an old man. His prestige waned. He was opposed by the "Young Ireland Party;" and, in the midst of these political dissensions, gaunt famine came in all its terrible reality. The potato-crop withered away mysteriously. It was the only food of the poor. A shout of alarm arose, and, in 1847, a doomed people beheld the awful spectre of starvation. It was a stupendous calamity, and the English Government was never "a friend in need" to Ireland. The unhappy people perished— died in thousands by the waysides, and hastened to foreign lands in millions. During the last third of a century fully three millions of Irish have made their homes in this Republic.

The "Young Ireland Party" grew wild at the deplorable condition of the country under English misrule, and rushed heedlessly into a short-lived rebellion. But Ireland wanted food even more than freedom. The outbreak of 1848 was a mad effort at revolution. It was only the sword-flashes of a few gifted, foolish, and fearless young Irishmen.

4. WHAT IS AN EVICTION?—Poverty and starva-

tion were not the only woes that haunted the path of the Irish peasant. He could be evicted at any moment by the merciless landlord. Such a heart-rending scene is thus described by an eye-witness: " Seven hundred human beings," says Dr. Nulty, the venerable Catholic Bishop of Meath, " were driven from their homes on this one day. There was not a shilling of rent due on the estate at the time, except by one man. The sheriff's assistants employed on the occasion to extinguish the hearths and demolish the homes of those honest, industrious men worked away with a will at their awful calling until evening. At length an incident occurred that varied the monotony of the grim and ghastly ruin which they were spreading all around. They stopped suddenly and recoiled, panic-stricken with terror, from two dwellings which they were directed to destroy with the rest. They had just learned that typhus fever held these houses in its grasp and had already brought death to some of their inmates. They therefore supplicated the agent to spare these houses a little longer; but he was inexorable, and insisted that they should come down. He ordered a large winnowing-sheet to be secured over the beds in which the fever-victims lay,—fortunately they happened to be delirious at the time,—and then directed the houses to be unroofed cautiously and slowly. I administered the last Sacrament of the Church to four of these fever-victims next day, and, save the above-mentioned winnowing-sheet, there was not then a roof nearer to me than the canopy of heaven. The scene of that eviction-day I must remember all my life long. The wailing of women, the screams, the terror, the consternation of children, the speechless agony of men, wrung tears of grief from all who saw them. I saw the officers and men of a large police force that were obliged to attend on the occasion cry like children. The heavy rains that usually attend the autumnal equinoxes descended in cold, copious torrents throughout the night, and at once revealed to the houseless sufferers the awful realities of their condition. I visited them next morning, and rode from place to place administering to them all the comfort I could. The landed proprietors in a circle all round, and for many miles in every direction, warned their tenantry against admitting them to even a single night's shelter. Many of these poor people were unable to emigrate. After battling in vain with privation and pestilence, they at last graduated from the workhouse to the tomb, and in little more than three years nearly a fourth of them lay quietly in their graves."*

5. DISESTABLISHMENT OF THE ENGLISH PROTESTANT CHURCH.—From the reign of Elizabeth well into that of Victoria—a period of over 300 years—the Protestant Church as by law established added to the woes of Ireland. It brought not the peace of the Gospel. It filled the land with tears and blood. "The ground was dug as for a grave," says Father Burke, O.P. "The seedling of Protestantism was cast into the soil, and the blood of the Irish nation was poured in to warm it and bring it forth. It

---

*During the last thirty years eviction has been in full swing. Thousands were evicted immediately after the famine of '47. Here are the eviction-figures for the four years preceding the present decade:

 1876.... .... 1200 evictions.
 1877.............. .... over 1300 "
 1878.... .... over 1700 "
 1879 .. .. nearly 4000 "

Is it any wonder that, as a class, the Irish landlords are regarded as merciless tyrants?

never grew; it never bloomed; it never came forth." As early as the year 1700 the Protestant bishops of Ireland—men who had nothing to do—held nearly one million of acres of the best land, or one-nineteenth of the island.* This so-called Church was the fruitful cause of strife, hatred, and heart-burnings. It was the emblem of bitter oppression. The Catholics were obliged to support the odious institution. The poor man often paid out his last shilling, or saw his last cow marched away to pay the tithes of an idle, intruding minister from whom he received nothing in return—except, perhaps, cold contempt.† When Sunday came, the bell of a neat parish church—which had been stolen from the Catholics—often summoned only the parson and his clerk. There was no one else to come; while, not far away, one thousand Catholics were huddled together in a miserable hovel " to render thanks to God for even these blessings, and to tell their woes to Heaven!" " There is no abuse like it," said Sydney Smith, " in all Europe, in all Asia, in all the discovered parts of Africa, and in all we have heard of Timbuctoo." This barren institution, with the curse of innocent blood upon it, was dises-

---

* In 1845 it was ascertained before a parliamentary committee that seven Protestant bishops in Ireland had died, leaving behind them in ready money the enormous sum of *over seven millions of dollars*. And "this," as an historian remarks, "among an ill-fed, ill clothed, ill-educated people—the most miserable in Europe."

† It took an army to collect these unholy tithes. On one occasion a regiment of hussars might be seen driving a flock of geese. Deplorable scenes occurred. In 1831 a dozen men were killed and about twenty wounded by the police at Newton Barry. At Rathcormac, in Cork, a Protestant archdeacon brought a party of military to collect tithes of a family named Ryan. The Ryans were Catholics, and resisted payment. The military fired. Eight persons were killed and thirteen wounded. "Will you pay me now?" roared the brutal archdeacon to Mrs. Ryan, whose son had just been shot before her eyes. Sydney Smith estimated that perhaps a million of lives had been sacrificed to this outrageous collection of tithes in Ireland.

tablished in 1869, and Ireland was thus relieved of another colossal incubus.

6. THE LAND QUESTION AND SOME OTHER QUESTIONS.—The total area of Ireland is a little over twenty millions of acres. At present 744 persons, called landlords, hold nearly ten millions of acres, or one-half of the island; and two-thirds of all Ireland is held by 1942 persons. Thus a few intruding monopolists claim all—or nearly all—the soil, while the nation at large, five millions of people, remain disinherited—ever reminded of their degradation, ever standing on the ragged edge of misery and pauperism. Is it any wonder that the Irish are not satisfied with being cheated? What people would be? The voice of this plundered and suffering nation still appeals to earth and heaven.

England, as we have seen, robbed the Irish people of all that is dear to man in this world—homes, lands, liberty, family greatness, education, churches, schools, colleges, religious institutions, and an independent legislature. What restitution has she made? What adequate compensation has been rendered for this robbery of a nation—this stripping of a people to the bone? Is it such cheap, windy, pen-and-ink favors on parchment—manufactured in the British Parliament—as "Catholic Emancipation," "Church Disestablishment," and badly tinkered "Land Bills"?

No! a thousand times no! "The Irish people," says the present illustrious Pontiff, Leo XIII., "have their rights, and they are allowed strictly to maintain them, and to claim them back."

7. INFLUENCING AGENTS ON THE ENGLISH LITERATURE OF IRELAND IN THE NINETEENTH CENTURY.— The stern and successful struggle of the long-suffering

Catholics for emancipation produced a fiery, eloquent literature which is to be found chiefly in the speeches of O'Connell and Shiel, in the poems of Moore, and in the public letters of Dr. Doyle and Dr. MacHale. Moore was the *first* Irish Catholic who became a master of the English language, and proved it in his writings. Dr. Doyle was the *first* Irish Catholic bishop who, in the same tongue, wielded a pen of immense power.

At the date of emancipation, Ireland—which before the coming of the fierce Dane or the grasping Norman had been the school of Western Europe—was the most ignorant and impoverished Christian country on the face of the earth. The penal code left nearly *four millions* of Irish unable to read or write, and nearly a *million and a half* who could read but could not write.* The present state-school system, anti-Catholic and anti-Irish in its tendency, was established in 1831. A new generation of readers soon grew up. The Jesuit Fathers, the Christian Brothers, the Franciscan Brothers, the Ursuline Nuns, the Ladies of Loretto, and many other religious congregations of men and women have toiled in the great field of education with an energy and success beyond all praise.

What is known as "Young Ireland" was an offshoot of O'Connell's Repeal party. It originated a new and brilliant school of literature. Its chief organ was the Dublin *Nation*, founded in 1842 by three young men—*Charles Gavan Duffy, Thomas Osborne Davis*, and *John Blake Dillon.* "The five volumes of the *Nation*," says a recent writer, "would

---

* Sir Charles G. Duffy.

of themselves, if nothing else of the writings of its contributors remained, form a small library of prose and poetry, more valuable than scores of ordinary books. The massive prose of Duffy, the electric poetry of Davis, the sharp, intense leaders of Mitchel, the solid, practical reports of McGee, the erudite reviews of Reilly, the lighter but exceedingly pleasant sketches of Meagher, and the songs and ballads of most of those and of scores of volunteer contributors, form a cyclopædia of politics, literature, and verse unmatched in the history of journalism." *

The nineteenth century has witnessed a sort of literary resurrection in Ireland. In the dread days of the penal laws, the people either hid their books or destroyed them. Persecuted monks and nuns, when obliged to fly from their quiet, holy abodes, often deposited valuable manuscripts in strong boxes, which were carefully put away in some secluded chamber. They hoped for happier days which, alas! did not come in their time. Many of these precious treasures came to light in our own age. The *Book of Lismore* was discovered in 1814, while repairs were going on in the ancient castle of Lismore. " In the progress of the work, the men having occasion to reopen a doorway that had been closed up with masonry in the interior of the castle, they found a wooden box

---

* Among the occasional contributors to *The Nation* were James Clarence Mangan, Richard Dalton Williams, Denis Florence MacCarthy, and William Carleton.

The first newspaper in Ireland was printed at Dublin in 1685. It was called *The Dublin News Letter*. The *Freeman's Journal* of Dublin, now the most influential daily in Ireland, was founded in 1763. The *Dublin Penny Journal*, a weekly, began its career in 1832; and though it did not live long, a set of the *Journal* is very valuable. The Dublin *Nation* is still an important weekly. Among the best known of the Irish magazines are the *Dublin University Magazine* and the *Irish Monthly Magazine*. The latter is under the able editorship of Rev. Matthew Russell, S.J.

enclosed in the centre of it, which, on being taken out, was found to contain the *Book of Lismore*, as well as a superb old crozier. The manuscript had suffered from damp, and the back, front, and top margin had been gnawed in several places by rats and mice." *

In 1820, on opening the vault where stood the cloister of the old Abbey of Connor, in the county of Antrim, the workmen discovered an oaken chest, the contents of which proved to be a translation of the Bible into Irish, and a collection of the original poems of Ossian, transcribed at Connor, in 1463, by an Irish priest named Terence O'Neill.

About the year 1821, while certain repairs were being made in an apartment of the old ruined Abbey of Bun-na-Margy, on the coast of Antrim, an oaken chest was discovered containing four manuscripts in a state of good preservation. One consisted of a large portion of a theological treatise by St. Thomas Aquinas, written on vellum, and extending to about 600 quarto pages. "It is the finest specimen of penmanship we have ever seen," says Dr. Stuart in the *Gentleman's Magazine* for August, 1822, "and the ink is superior in brilliancy and intenseness of color to any at present manufactured in Europe."

"Many Irish manuscripts," writes Canon Bourke, "were stowed away in the cottages of the peasantry behind what are called the rafters of the house. The present writer has in his possession at this moment two such manuscripts that had lain for years hid behind rafters in the cottages of respectable peasants named Bodkin and Bourke." †

---

* O'Curry.
† *The Aryan Origin of the Gaelic Race and Language.*

The government survey of Ireland led to a careful study of her rich antiquities by such distinguished men as *O'Curry*, *O'Donovan*, *Petrie*, *Wilde*, and *Todd*. The work of examining and cataloguing the vast collections of Irish manuscripts in the libraries of Trinity College and the Royal Irish Academy, Dublin, together with the establishment of chairs of Irish history and literature in Trinity College, the Catholic University, and the Queen's Colleges,* gave, at least, a temporary impulse to the study of the Irish language, Irish history, and Irish antiquities. The best results of this rich, rare, and scholarly labor are to be found chiefly in Dr. O'Donovan's splendid translation of the *Annals of the Four Masters*, and in O'Curry's two excellent works—*Lectures on the Manuscript Materials of Ancient Irish History* and *The Manners, Customs, and Government of the Ancient Irish*.

8. INFLUENCE OF THE IRISH MIND ON ENGLISH LITERATURE.—The French critic Taine professed to find in the writings of *Goldsmith*, *Burke*, *Moore*, and *Sheridan* "a tone of their own—the Irish tone." This was no great discovery, but it was the first time such a difference was ever pointed out in a work on English literature between the product of the Irish mind and that of the Saxon or English mind. The difference is very marked. An old Irish poem says:

"For acuteness and valor, the Greeks;
For excessive pride, the Romans;
For dulness, the creeping Saxons;
For beauty and amorousness, the Gaels."

Some of the well-defined literary traits that distinguish the Celtic Irishman from the Saxon Englishman, and which characterize the former's best mental

---

* The Queen's Colleges no longer have chairs of Celtic.

productions, are lively wit, a spiritual temperament, delicacy of sentiment, brilliancy of imagination, uncommon power of satire, great aptitude for describing the magic of natural scenery, an emotional nature and a quick perception, a reverence and enthusiasm for the good, the pure, and the beautiful, and the gift of style in a wonderful measure.*

"The Celt's quick feeling," says Matthew Arnold, "for what is noble and distinguished gave his poetry style; his indomitable personality gave it pride and passion; his sensibility and nervous exaltation gave it a better gift still—the gift of rendering with wonderful felicity the magical charm of nature. The forest solitude, the bubbling spring, the wild flowers are everywhere in romance. They have a mysterious life and grace there; they are Nature's own children, and utter her secret in a way which make them something quite different from the woods, waters, and plants of Greek and Roman poetry. Now of this delicate magic, Celtic romance is so pre-eminent a mistress that it seems impossible to believe the power did not come into romance from the Celts." †

For over a hundred years Irish genius—the genius of Goldsmith, Burke, Grattan, Moore, Griffin, Davis, Mangan, Williams, MacCarthy, and others—has done a world of exquisite work peculiarly its own in giving

---

* Canon Bourke claims that the hymns of the Church owe much to ancient Irish writers. "There are," he says, "for the past 1400 years, about 150 Latin hymns in the books of devotion in use among the children of the Catholic Church. Nine out of ten of these hymns are written in the same style as that in which the Irish people of the early period wrote their native *duns* or poems." *Aryan Origin of the Gaelic Race and Language*, p. 438.

† *Rhyme*—the most striking characteristic of our modern poetry as distinguished from that of the ancients, and a main source, to our poetry, of its magic and charm, of what we call its romantic element—rhyme itself, all the weight of evidence tends to show, comes into our poetry from the Celts.—*Matthew Arnold*.

the impulse of a new Celtic life, polish, grace, and dignity to the English language and English literature.

9. ANTI-IRISH WRITERS.—But from English writers—who until recently had the ear of the world—the Irish get small credit for their gifts, virtues, or achievements. Such writers, however, deserve to be exposed that the sensible reader may know how to guard himself against their prejudice, contempt, or malignity. The first on the list is *Gerald Barry*, or Geraldus Cambrensis, the lying historian, who wrote shortly after the English invasion. He is a shameful falsifier. Father Burke hit the truth neatly when he stated that if every word of Barry was not a lie, at least every sentence was. *Edmund Spenser*, the polished scoundrel, the famous author of the *Fairy Queen*, points out what, in his opinion, was the best way to make an end of the Irish people. It was kindly to forbid them to till the soil or pasture the cattle for one whole season. The poet felt that that would bring about the following much-to-be-desired result: "The Irish would quickly consume themselves and devour one another." *Samuel Butler* could not finish his *Hudibras* without writing:

"A deep occult philosopher.
As learned as the wild Irish are."

Daniel Defoe, the author of *Robinson Crusoe*, bitterly blames Cromwell for not driving the whole Irish race out of Ireland. *Hume*, in his *History*, shows an intense hatred of Ireland. *Macpherson* tried to make out that Ossian was a Scotchman, and wrote endless falsehoods to prove it. The wretched *De Quincey* cannot pen a note of nine lines without libelling what he terms "the barbarous Celtic blood." Southey states that the opium-eater was a calumniator, and perhaps Carlyle is not too harsh on De Quincey when he describes him as one that " carries a laudanum-bottle in his pocket and the venom of a wasp in his heart." *Macaulay* gloats over the oppression of the Irish Catholics during the dark days of the penal laws; probably this is why the famous Dr. Cahill styled him a " rhetorical fop." *Thackeray*, in some of his stories, seems to take pleasure in ridiculing everything Irish. His drunken " Captain Costigan" is not only a leading character in *Pendennis*, but he is also dragged into *The Newcomes*. His *Irish Sketch-Book* is an elaborate sneer at everything Irish. Carlyle's *Journey to Ireland* is a disgrace to human nature. His brutal hatred breaks forth in a manner that would bring blushes to the cheek of a Malay or a Mohawk. But of all modern English writers on Ireland and the Irish, Froude is the most false and malignant. He is color-blind to the truth of history.

10. THE IRISH AS A RELIGIOUS AND FAITHFUL PEOPLE.—" The Irish," wrote Bishop Doyle in 1824, " are, morally speaking, not only religious, like other nations, but entirely devoted to religion. The geographical position of the country, it soil and climate, as well as the state of society, have a strong influence in forming the natural temperament of the people. The Irish people are more sanguine than the English, less mercurial than the French; they seem to be compounded of both these nations, and more suited than either to seek after and indulge in spiritual affections."

Justin MacCarthy, a keen, impartial observer, wrote in 1880: " The Irish peasant remained through centuries of persecution devotedly faithful to the Catholic Church. Nothing could win or wean him from it. The Irish population of Ireland—there is meaning in the words—were made apparently by nature for the Catholic faith. Hardly any influence on earth could make the genuine Celtic Irishman a Materialist, or what is called in France a Voltairean. For him, as for Schiller's immortal heroine, the kingdom of the spirits is easily opened. Half his thoughts, half his life, belong to a world other than the material world around him. The supernatural becomes almost the natural for him. The streams, the valleys, the hills of his native country are peopled by mystic forms and melancholy legends, which are all but living things for him. Even the railway has not banished from the land his familiar fancies and dreams. The "good people" still linger around the raths and glens. The banshee even yet laments, in dirge-like wailings, the death of the representative of each ancient house. The very superstitions of the Irish peasant take a devotional form. They are never degrading. His piety is not merely sincere: it is even practical. It sustains him against many hard trials, and enables him to bear, in cheerful patience, a life-long trouble. He praises God for everything; not as an act of mere devotional formality, but as by instinct; the praise naturally rising to his lips. Old men and women in Ireland who seem, to the observer, to have lived lives of nothing but privation and suffering, are heard to murmur with their latest breath the fervent declaration that the Lord was good to them always. Assuredly this genuine piety does not always prevent the wild Celtic nature from breaking forth into fierce excesses. Stormy outbursts of passion, gusts of savage revenge, too often sweep away the soul of the Irish peasant from the quiet moorings in which his natural piety and the teachings of his Church would hold it. But deep down in his nature is that faith in the other world and its visible connection and intercourse with this; his reverence for the teaching which shows him a clear title to immortality. For this very reason, when the Irish peasant throws off altogether the guidance of religion, he is apt to rush into worse extravagances and excesses than most other men. He is not made to be a rationalist; he is made to be a believer." *

11. THE DECAY OF THE IRISH LANGUAGE.—In 1851 there were over one million and a half Irish-speaking inhabitants in Ireland. To-day there is, perhaps, scarcely half that number. English is the official language of the country. It is the language of the schools. It is the language of commerce. Ignorant agents and landlords will not listen to Irish. The people have been forced to learn English, which has gradually displaced the venerable language of Columbkille, Brian Boru, and Hugh O'Neill. The following pathetic lines give voice to a sad truth:

" 'Tis fading, oh, 'tis fading, like leaves upon the trees!
In murmuring tone 'tis dying, like the wail upon the breeze!
'Tis swiftly disappearing, as footprints on the shore
Where the Barrow, and the Erne, and Loch Swilly's waters roar—
Where the parting sunbeam kisses Loch Corrib in the west,
And Ocean, like a mother, clasps the Shannon to her breast!
The language of old Erin, of her history and name—
Of her monarchs and her heroes—her glory and her fame—
The sacred shrine where rested, through sunshine and through gloom,
The spirit of her martyrs, as their bodies in the tomb,
The time-wrought shell where murmured, 'mid centuries of wrong,
The secret voice of Freedom, in annal and in song—
Is slowly, surely sinking into silent death at last,
To live but in the memories of those who love the past."

---

* *History of Our Own Times.*

"Every remarkable man," wrote Lacordaire, "has been fond of letters." The same can be said of every remarkable nation. The Irish have always been a literary people. To song and legend and history, they have clung through sunshine and shadow with the same lofty tenacity as to faith and fatherland. No misfortune has been able to dull the Irish mind, however it may check its expression. The memory of the past is kept alive by a national literature more truly popular than any literature of the kind in Europe. To-day there is less ignorance in Ireland than in any other country in the world. This is one of the wonders of history. "Irishmen who return to their country after a few years' absence," says Sir John Pope Hennessy, "cannot fail to see, as one of the most noticeable changes, an extension of popular literature; a great increase in the number of readers, not, however, in the upper or middle classes, but in the lower classes—that is, lower as far as the possession of pounds, shillings, and pence is concerned. In a recent article in the *London Reader*, some statements were quoted from the reports of the United States Bureau of Education, showing the comparative statistics of education in some of the principal countries in the world, wherein *Ireland heads the list*, the United States comes second, Germany third, then Switzerland, then England, then France, etc." *

The future is full of bright promise. "I look," says Cardinal Newman, with prophetic glance, "towards a land both old and young—old in its Christianity, young in its promise of the future; a nation which received grace before the Saxon came to Britain, and which has never quenched it; a Church which com-

---

* *The Nineteenth Century* for June, 1884.

prehends in its history the rise and fall of Canterbury and of York, which Augustine and Paulinus founded, and Pole and Fisher left. I contemplate a people which has had a long night, and will have an inevitable day. I am turning my eyes toward a hundred years to come, and I dimly see the island I am gazing on become the road of passage and union between two hemispheres, and the centre of the world. I see its inhabitants rival Belgium in populousness, France in vigor, and Spain in enthusiasm."

LESSON I.
JOHN LANIGAN.   DIED 1828.
JAMES DOYLE.   DIED 1834.

1. Who were the first Irish Catholic ecclesiastics of the present age that exhibited marked power as writers?

The Rev. Dr. Lanigan, and the Most Rev. Dr. Doyle, Bishop of Kildare and Leighlin.

2. Do you know anything of Dr. Lanigan's career?

He was born at Cashel, in the county of Tipperary, and received his education at Rome and Pavia. He was for many years an honored professor in the University of Pavia. When the French invaded Italy he returned to Ireland, and spent the remainder of his life chiefly at Dublin, devoting himself to literature. Dr. Lanigan was a man of great learning, a fine linguist, a master of theology, and an accomplished general scholar.

3. Which is his chief work?

The Ecclesiastical History of Ireland, which appeared in four volumes in 1822. It was the first great work on the Irish Church, and it is still unrivalled.

4. Give some of the chief points in the life of Bishop Doyle.

Dr. Doyle was born at New Ross, county of Wexford, and received his education at the University of Coimbra, Portugal.* On returning to his native land he became a professor at Carlow College. He was appointed Bishop of Kildare and Leighlin in 1819, and for fourteen years he shone as a great light in Ireland.

5. Mention one of his public acts by which he performed marked services for his native country, and proved his incomparable ability.

His famous examination before the House of Lords on the state of Ireland. "That Doyle," said the Duke of Wellington, "has a prodigious mind; his head is as clear as rock-water."

6. Which is his chief literary work?

The celebrated *Letters on the State of Ireland*, twelve in number, and signed "J. K. L."†

7. Name his other most noted productions.

Vindication of Catholic Principles, Letters in Reply to Dr. Magee, and *Letters to his Friends.* A fine collection of his correspondence is to be found in Fitzpatrick's *Life and Times of Dr. Doyle.*

8. What may be said of Dr. Doyle as a writer?

He is always practical and to the point. His diction, like his intellect, was rich, simple, luminous, and powerful. With greater dignity and more massive strength he possessed all the wit and satire of Junius. Lord Bacon scarcely surpassed J. K. L. in pointed brevity, nor was Edmund Burke more solid and sublime.‡

---

* It will be noticed that Doyle and Lanigan were educated in foreign countries because those watch-dogs of ignorance, the penal laws, were still in force.

† J. K. L. were the initials of his official title—James, Bishop of Kildare and Leighlin.

‡ Of education the great Bishop wrote: "Next to the blessing of

"The most illustrious name on the roll of ecclesiastical historians of Ireland is that of Rev. Dr. John Lanigan. His critical remarks have contributed more than those of any other writer to illustrate the early life of our Apostle."—*Archbishop Moran.*
"Until Dr. Doyle came to show them how to wield a pen, the prelates and priests of Ireland, from the reign of George II., were, with one or two exceptions, singularly feeble writers."—*Fitzpatrick.*

LESSON II.

THOMAS MOORE. DIED 1852.

Chief works: (1) *The Irish Melodies.*
(2) *Lalla Rookh.*
(3) *The Epicurean.*
(4) *Life of Sheridan.*

8. Who was Thomas Moore?

He was the greatest of Irish poets, and a prose-writer of eminence.

9. Give a short account of his life.

Moore was born at Dublin in 1779; was educated at Trinity College; visited America in 1804; and devoted his life to literature as a profession. His last years were unhappily clouded by mental infirmity.

10. Which is his chief work?

The immortal *Irish Melodies*, which he began in 1807, and spent over a quarter of a century in their composition. They number one hundred and twenty-four.

redemption and the graces consequent upon it, there is no gift bestowed by God equal in value to a good education. Other advantages are enjoyed by the body: this belongs entirely to the spirit. Whatever is great, or good, or glorious in the works of man is the fruit of educated minds. Wars, conquests, commerce, all the arts of peace and industry, all the refinements of life, all the social and domestic virtues, all the refinements and delicacies of mutual intercourse; in a word, whatever is estimable amongst men, owes its origin, increase, and perfection to the exercise of those faculties whose improvement is the object of education. Religion herself loses half her beauty and influence when not attended or assisted by education, and her power, splendor, and majesty are never so exalted as when cultivated genius and refined taste become her heralds or her handmaids."

11. How does the poet himself refer to this work in words as true as they are beautiful?

He says:

> "Dear harp of my country, in darkness I found thee,
> The cold chains of silence had hung o'er thee long,
> When proudly, my own island harp, I unbound thee,
> And gave all thy chords to light, freedom, and song."

12. Mention a few of the most popular and beautiful of the Irish Melodies?

The Minstrel Boy, *The Last Rose of Summer*, *The Meeting of the Waters*, *On Music*, *Remember the Glories of Brian the Brave*, and *The Harp that once through Tara's Halls*.*

13. What is *Lalla Rookh*?

It is a charming versified Eastern romance.

14. What is *The Epicurean*?

The Epicurean is a beautiful Egyptian tale of early Christian times. It is written in pure and elegant prose.

15. How should we estimate Moore as a writer of English?

Moore is one of the greatest masters of our language. In the *Irish Melodies* he forces a music out of English words that has never been equalled by any other writer.

---

* "The harp that once through Tara's halls
  The soul of music shed,
Now hangs as mute on Tara's walls
  As if that soul were fled.
So sleeps the pride of former days,
  So glory's thrill is o'er,
And hearts that once beat high for praise
  Now feel that pulse no more.

"No more to chiefs and ladies bright
  The harp of Tara swells;
The chord alone that breaks at night
  Its tale of ruin tells.
Thus Freedom now so seldom wakes—
  The only throb she gives
Is when some heart, indignant breaks,
  To show that still she lives."

"In the quality of a national Irish lyrist Moore stands absolutely alone and unapproachable."—*Shaw.*
"Of all the song-writers that ever warbled or chanted or sung, the best, in our estimation, is verily no other than Thomas Moore."—*Wilson.*
"The *Irish Melodies* must be considered as the most valuable and enduring of all his works; they

'Circle his name with a charm against death,'

and as a writer of song he stands without a rival. Moore found the national music of his country, with very few exceptions, debased by a union with words that were either unseemly or unintelligible. The music of Ireland is now known and appreciated all over the world, and the songs of the Irish poet will endure as long as the country he loves and the glories of which they commemorate."—*S. C. Hall.*

LESSON III.

GERALD GRIFFIN. DIED 1840.

JOHN BANIM. DIED 1842.

16. Who was Gerald Griffin?

Gerald Griffin, the first of Irish novelists and a distinguished poet, was born at Limerick in 1803. After finishing his education he went to London to seek his fortune as a dramatic writer, and had a severe struggle for existence and recognition in the modern Babylon. He returned to his native land, and wrote some of his finest works in his quiet Irish home. He became a Christian Brother in 1838, and, as *Brother Joseph*, the famous author died the death of the just two years later.

17. Mention some of his best productions.

Poems, Tragedy of Gisippus, The Collegians, The Invasion, and *Tales of the Five Senses.* His works are commonly published in ten handy volumes.

18. Which is his masterpiece?

The Collegians, which he wrote at the age of twenty-five. Sydney Smith pronounced it "an admirable novel." It is an original work of the very highest order.

19. What may be said of Griffin's poetry?

It is remarkable for its pure beauty, freshness, and originality, while at the same time it glows with the fire, fancy, and feeling of youth.

20. Name some of his finest pieces of poetry.

*Old Times,** The Sister of Charity, The Isle of Saints, The Shannon's Stream, A Portrait,* and *A Place in Thy Memory, Dearest.*

21. Who was John Banim?

John Banim, a famous novelist and dramatist, and " a bright-hearted, true-souled Irishman," was born at Kilkenny in 1798, and, like Griffin, he early sought fame and fortune in London. After years of brave, successful toil with his pen, an insidious disease made him a cripple, and he came home to die in peace and honor.

22. Who was his literary partner for many years, and what did they jointly produce?

His brother Michael; they jointly wrote the celebrated *Tales of the O'Hara Family.*†

23. What was John Banim's aim as an author?

His aim, it seems, was to do for Ireland what Sir Walter Scott had done for Scotland.

---

* " Old times! old times! the gay old times!
   When I was young and free,
  And heard the merry Easter chimes,
   Under the sally-tree.
" My Sunday palm beside me placed,
   My cross upon my hand,
  A heart at rest within my breast,
   And sunshine on the land."

† Michael Banim was the sole author of *Father Connell, The Croppy, The Ghost-hunter, Crohoore of the Bill-hook,* and some others. The works of the Banim brothers are usually published in ten volumes.

24. How do you estimate his defects and good qualities as a writer of fiction?

Banim had little humor, and his descriptions are often too detailed and elaborate; but, on the other hand, he possessed a vivid fancy, patriotic fervor, and great intellectual vigor. He pictures the peculiarities of Irish character in strong light and shade.

25. Which are his chief plays?

Sylla and *Damon and Pythias.*

26. Mention two of his best novels.

The Boyne Water and *The Nowlans.*

27. What may be said of this author's *Letters* to his family?

They are among the most hearty, direct, and graceful specimens of epistolary correspondence in English literature. There is about them a simplicity, easy dash, and pointed brevity for which we look in vain among the letters of other famous authors.

"There is one praise which the least interesting of Griffin's works may claim,—and it is the highest of all praise,—that not one of them contains a 'line which dying he may wish to blot:' they breathe the purest morality, inculcate the highest principles, and express the deepest religious feeling."—*Dublin Review.*

"Banim's love of country breaks forth in almost every page of his writings. He has vehement indignation for her wrongs, deep sympathy with her sufferings, nor does he shrink from entering into what are sometimes painful and revolting details, when it is necessary to expose the ill-doings of her oppressors."—*Dublin Review.*

LESSON IV.

DANIEL O'CONNELL. DIED 1847.

Chief works: *Speeches.*

RICHARD LALOR SHIEL. DIED 1851.

Chief works: (1) *Speeches.* (2) *Sketches of the Irish Bar.*

28. Who was Daniel O'Connell?

Daniel O'Connell, the unrivalled máster of popular

eloquence, and one of the purest and greatest political geniuses of modern times, is chiefly known as the champion of Catholic emancipation in Ireland.

29. Tell us something of his life.

He belonged to an ancient Irish family; was born in the county of Kerry in 1775; was educated in Belgium and France; studied law and was called to the Irish bar in 1798; obtained Catholic emancipation in 1829; and was the first Catholic for generations that had a seat in the British Parliament.* He died while on his way to Rome. The life of O'Connell is the history of Ireland for nearly half a century.

30. What did O'Connell afterwards remark of his first speech, which was made in January, 1800?

"All the principles of my subsequent political life," he said, "are contained in my very first speech."

31. What were some of the most noted characteristics of this great man?

O'Connell was a man of prodigious energy, with a patient inflexible will before which difficulties disappeared as the mists of the morning. He was deeply religious, and was truly the embodied voice and spirit of Celtic Ireland.

32. What may be said of him as a popular orator?

As a popular orator he has not been approached in modern times; but he never wrote a speech, and he did not often make a set oration.†

---

* Since the days of Sir Thomas More, the English House of Commons had seen no Catholic within its walls so grand and gifted as Daniel O'Connell.
† John Randolph, of Roanoke, who hated an Irishman almost as much as he did a Yankee, when he got to London and heard O'Connell, the old slaveholder held up his hands and said: "This is the man—those are the lips, the most eloquent that speak English in my day." And I think he was right.—*Wendell Phillips.*

33. What eloquent man greatly aided O'Connell in the battle for Catholic emancipation?

Richard Lalor Shiel.

34. Give s me of the chief points in his life.

Shiel was born at Waterford; was educated at Stonyhurst College, England, and Trinity College, Dublin; studied law, and was called to the Irish bar. After Catholic emancipation he held a seat for many years in the British Parliament.

35. What has been said of his tireless devotion in the cause of Catholic emancipation?

In the battle for Catholic emancipation this splendid and impassioned orator was heard everywhere in Ireland shrieking forth the wrongs of his people.

36. Which are his chief works?

Speeches and *Sketches of the Irish Bar.* The far-famed paper on O'Connell, in the *Sketches*, was translated into French, German, Spanish, and Italian. It is an exquisite pen-picture.

"Hannibal is esteemed the greatest of generals, not because he gained victories, but because he made an army. O'Connell, for the same reason, must be considered among the first of legislators, not because he won triumphs, but because he made a people."—*Henry Giles.*

"I have heard all the grand and majestic orators of America, who are singularly famed ou the world's circumference. I know what was the majesty of Webster; I know what it was to melt under the magnetism of Clay; I have seen eloquence in the iron logic of Calhoun; but all these together never surpassed, and no one of them ever equalled, the great Irishman, Daniel O'Connell."—*Wendell Phillips.*

"Shiel—a man who, while our language lasts, will be spoken of as one of the most brilliant orators of Ireland."—*R S. MacKenzie.*

LESSON V.

THREE POETS—DAVIS, MANGAN, WILLIAMS.

37. Who was Thomas Osborne Davis?

He was an eminent poet and journalist, was born at Mallow in the county of Cork, and educated at Trinity College, Dublin. He devoted himself heart and soul to the cause of his country, and died, deeply lamented, in 1845, at the early age of thirty-one.

38. What has been truly remarked of Davis?

That with him "a new soul came into Ireland." He helped to create a national spirit, a national poetry, and a national literature. The burning love of his native land fired his soul as a sacred inspiration. He wrote:

"She's not a dull or cold land;
No! she's a warm and bold land,
Oh! she's a true and old land—
This native land of mine."

39. Which is Davis's chief work?

A volume of *Poems and Essays*—a truly valuable work.

40. Mention some of his most popular poems.

Fontenoy, My Land, Nationality, The Penal Days, The Sack of Baltimore, and *A Nation Once Again.*

41. What is remarkable about Davis as a poet?

Until three years before his death Davis had not written a line of poetry. Yet his glorious quill dashed off poems for the Dublin *Nation* that will endure as long as the English language—poems that will be read and admired as long as there is a true man of the Irish race living. His poetry was the expression of his own manly nature, patriotic heart, and lofty character. It might be more polished, but it came warm from the heart. It finds its way back to the heart. It has the true ring which finds an echo in every bosom that can admire the brave and the beautiful.

42. Who was James Clarence Mangan?

He was the most original poet among the gifted school of writers that shone in the Young Ireland Party. His brief career, however, was full of sorrow, and he died at Dublin, his native city, in 1849.

43. Which is his chief work?

His *Poems*, original and translated, which have been published in two volumes.

44. How does Mangan rank as a translator?

He is inimitable—the very prince of translators. He is among the few writers of any time or country who have succeeded in transfusing into their own language not merely the literal meaning, graces of style, and musical movement of foreign poems, but also their true spirit and suggestiveness. Often his translation far surpasses the original. He was a most accomplished linguist, and translated from the Irish, French, German, Spanish, Italian, Danish, as well as Turkish and other Asiatic tongues.

45. Who was Richard Dalton Williams?

He was a native of Tipperary, studied medicine at Dublin, and belonged to the same school of writers as Davis and Mangan.

46. Name some of his finest poems.

The Dying Girl, The Sister of Charity, A Thought on Calvary, The Munster War-Song, and *The Lament for Clarence Mangan.*

47. What are the chief characteristics of Williams as a poet?

He had an eye for the beautiful in all things, and

his gentle soul glowed with the bright love of faith and country. Some of his religious pieces are the most finished of his compositions. *The Dying Girl* is one of the pure gems of English literature.*

"It was the object of Davis in all his writings to fire the spark of nationality in the breast of each Irishman."—*Dublin Review*.

"Judging him now, a generation after his death, when years and communion with the world have tempered the exaggerations of youthful friendship, I can confidently say that I have not known a man so nobly gifted as Thomas Davis."—*Sir Charles Gavan Duffy*.

"I was but a boy at the time, but I remember with what startled enthusiasm I would arise from reading the *Poems* of Davis; and it would seem to me that before my young eyes I saw the dash of the Brigade at Fontenoy; it would seem to me as if my young ears were filled with the shout that resounded at the Yellow Ford and Benburb—the war-cry of the Red Hand—as the English hosts were swept away and, like snow under the beams of the rising sun, melted before the Irish onset."—*Father Burke, O.P.*

"The man most essentially a poet among the writers of *The Nation* was Clarence Mangan. He was as truly born to sing deathless songs as Keats or Shelley; but he lived and died in a provincialized city, and his voice was drowned for a time in the roar of popular clamor. He was so purely a poet that he shrunk from all other exercise of his intellect."—*Sir C. G. Duffy*.

"The solidity, the strength, the brilliancy, and the impetus of Williams's political ballads strike the sense like the rush of a squadron of cavalry. There is more imagination in this vehement Tipperary singer than would form one hundred of the ordinary rhetoricians who attempt 'the toil divine of verse.' His intellect is robust and vigorous; his passion impetuous and noble; his perceptions of beauty most delicate and enthusiastic; his sympathies take in the whole range of human affection; and his humor is irresistible."—*Dublin Nation*.

---

* This exquisite piece consists of seven stanzas of eight lines each. The first stanza runs thus:

"From a Munster vale they brought her,
 From the pure and balmy air—
An Ormond peasant's daughter
 With blue eyes and golden hair.
They brought her to the city,
 And she slowly faded there:
Consumption has no pity
 For blue eyes and golden hair."

LESSON VI.
EUGENE O'CURRY. DIED 1862.
JOHN O'DONOVAN. DIED 1861.

48. Who were the two most celebrated Irish scholars and antiquaries of the present century?

Prof. Eugene O'Curry and Dr. John O'Donovan— men of fine critical judgment, immense learning, and rare accomplishments.

49. Tell us something of O'Curry.

O'Curry was born in the county of Clare, in 1796, and owed little to schools, being a life-long student. He was connected for some years with the antiquarian department of the government survey of Ireland, and in 1854 he was appointed to the chair of Irish history and literature in the Catholic University, a position that he held till his death.

50. What was the first great service he rendered to Irish literature?

He performed with admirable skill the work of cataloguing and describing the vast stock of Irish manuscript literature contained in the libraries of Trinity College and the Royal Irish Academy, Dublin.

51. What should be ever remembered to his credit in connection with the Brehon Laws?

The Brehon Law manuscripts were in greater part discovered by O'Curry, and he was the first modern scholar able to decipher and explain them.* O'Curry

---

* Charles O'Conor, of Belanagar, the ablest Irish scholar of the last century, acknowledged in a letter, dated 1786, that neither himself "nor any other Irish scholar in this kingdom" understood the language of the Brehon Laws.

and his brother-in-law, O'Donovan, were engaged for years in transcribing and translating these ancient laws of Ireland. Death alone ended their labors.

52. What famous work did he publish in 1860?

Lectures on the Manuscript Materials of Ancient Irish History—a deeply interesting volume, which takes its place among the greatest critical and historical works of modern times.

53. Which was his last work?

Lectures on the Life, Manners, and Customs of the Ancient Irish. It is a *complement* to the *Manuscript Materials.*

54. Give a brief outline of O'Donovan's career.

John O'Donovan was born in the county of Kilkenny, in 1809, and when only fifteen years of age he became Gaelic instructor to General Larcom, the head of the government survey. He was connected with O'Curry, Petrie, and others in the antiquarian department of the survey. He became a Doctor of Laws of Trinity College, and filled the chair of Irish history and literature in Queen's College, Belfast.

55. By what great work is he best known?

By his translation of the *Annals of the Four Masters*, with many learned notes. This unrivalled work was published in 1851, in seven quarto volumes, and it called forth the compliments of such eminent foreigners as Hallam, Guizot, and Jacob Grimm.

56. Name some of his other works.

Grammar of the Irish Language, and an incomparable essay on Irish sirnames in the Introduction to his translation of O'Duggan's *Topographical and Historical Poem.* He did a vast amount of work as an editor and translator.

"Eugene O'Curry belongs to the race of the giants in literary research and industry, a race now almost extinct."—*Matthew Arnold*.

"Without these national records—the *Annals of the Four Masters*—minutely illustrative as they are of an integral portion of the empire, the history of Great Britain could never be regarded as complete."—*London Athenæum*.

LESSON VII.

THREE NOVELISTS—LOVER, CARLETON, LEVER.*

57. Who was Samuel Lover?

He was a native of Dublin, and the author of a number of very popular Irish songs and novels.

58. Which is his best work of fiction?

Rory O'More, a story containing passages of great power. It is full of point, humor, amusing incidents, and well-drawn characters.

59. Which of his songs are, perhaps, the most admired?

The Angel's Whisper,† *Rory O'More*, and *Molly Bawn*.

---

* For dates of death, see *Short Dictionary*.

† THE ANGEL'S WHISPER.

(A beautiful belief prevails in Ireland that when a child smiles in its sleep it is "talking with the angels.")

A baby was sleeping, its mother was weeping,
  For her husband was far on the wild raging sea;
And the tempest was swelling round the fisherman's dwelling,
  And she cried, "Dermot, darling, oh! come back to me."
Her beads while she numbered the baby still slumbered,
  And smiled in her face as she bended her knee.
"Oh! blest be that warning, my child, thy sleep adorning,
  For I know that the angels are whispering with thee.
"And while they are keeping bright watch o'er thy sleeping,
  Oh! pray to them softly, my baby, with me,
And say thou wouldst rather they'd watch o'er thy father—
  For I know that the angels are whispering with thee."
The dawn of the morning saw Dermot returning,
  And the wife wept with joy her babe's father to see;
And, closely caressing her child with a blessing,
  Said, "I knew that the angels were whispering with thee."

60. Who was William Carleton?

He was a native of the county of Tyrone, and one of the greatest of the Irish novelists.

61. What was his first work of marked power?

Traits and Stories of the Irish Peasantry, which was first published in 1830.

62. Name some of his finest productions.

The Poor Scholar, *Valentine McClutchy*, and *Willy Reilly*.

63. Which is his masterpiece?

The Poor Scholar, a story that abounds in beautiful and touching passages. It is an interesting and highly finished work.

64. Give some idea of the other two works.

Valentine McClutchy vividly paints the horrors of landlordism—that blighting curse of modern Ireland. *Willy Reilly* pictures the unhappy state of society during the dark period of the penal laws, and is a work of great power and absorbing interest. It is, perhaps, the most widely read Irish novel ever written.*

65. Who was Charles Lever?

He was a native of Dublin, a physician, and one of the most popular novelists of the century.

66. Name some of his most characteristic works.

Charles O'Malley, *Roland Cashel*, and *Lord Kilgobbin*.

---

* We read Carleton's early works with mingled feelings of pity, sorrow, admiration, and indignation. He perverted talents of a high order to base ends. Though partially educated for the Catholic priesthood, he became a pervert, and some of his early writings are marked by a bitter anti-Catholic spirit. He lived, however, to regret this, and made due amends in his later productions, especially in the three works just noticed.

67. What is the strong point of *Charles O'Malley* as a novel?

As a genial, mirth-provoking book, bubbling over with fun, it is really unmatched.

68. What have you to remark of *Lord Kilgobbin?*

It is Lever's last work, and is rich in brilliant dialogue.

69. How do you estimate Lever as an Irish novelist?

His books sparkle with wit and humor, and as a describer of natural scenery he takes rank next to Sir Walter Scott. At all times he respects purity and modesty, but he never got beyond the mere surface of Irish life. He felt no true sympathy with the people of Ireland.*

LESSON VIII.

JOHN MACHALE. DIED 1881.

Chief works: (1) *Public Letters.* (2) *Translations.*

THOMAS N. BURKE. DIED 1883.

Chief works: *Lectures* and *Sermons*

70. Who was John MacHale?

John MacHale, the most illustrious Irish prelate of the nineteenth century, was for many years Archbishop of Tuam. His golden pen enriched the Irish

---

* There is one class of his countrymen of whom Lever was so entirely ignorant that his attempt to represent them is full of offence, insult, and injustice—the Catholic priesthood. It was, of course, a bid for popularity. It has been well remarked that when Carleton, Lover, and Lever began to write, a large portion of the Irish could not read, and they wrote for Englishmen, Scotchmen, and the horde of Anglo-Irish who throve on the miseries of Ireland. Such clowns could appreciate nothing that did not ridicule the Catholic priest and the Irish people.

and the English languages. The poet T. D. Sullivan writes:

> "In our green isle of old renown,
> From many a by-gone age
> Full pure and clear the fame comes down
> Of soldier, saint, and sage;
> But high amidst those glories bright
> That shine on Innisfail,
> 'Tis ours to write, in lines of light,
> The name of *John MacHale*."

71. What are his chief literary productions?

Public Letters and *Translations*.

72. What period of time is covered by his *Public Letters*, and how do you value them?

The *Public Letters* of Dr. MacHale touch on nearly every important event in Irish history from 1820 to 1846, and are carefully edited by himself. They rank with the letters of Junius and Dr. Doyle. Those describing his travels in Europe are, perhaps, the most interesting, and abound in exquisite passages.

73. What are Archbishop MacHale's principal translations?

He translated Homer's *Iliad*, Moore's *Melodies*,* and the *Pentateuch*, or five books of Moses, into Irish.

---

* The following is Dr. MacHale's elegant translation of *The Harp that Once through Tara's Hall* into Irish verse. The original is on page 360.

An chruit, do rcap énf callaió 'n ṁṡ
Na ṡaeċe ceolca binn',
Cá 'n ballaió Ceaṁna 'noiṛ 'nn a luióe
San feanrad ceoil. no ninn:
Wan rúd cá 'n c-am, cuaió canc, faoi ceo,
Cá ċáil, 'r a clu faoi fuan;
A'r cnoióċe, 'fancuiṡ molca ceo,
Ní ainiṡeann iad ṡo buan).

74. Who was Thomas N. Burke?

Father Thomas N. Burke, the famous Irish Dominican, was styled "the Prince of Preachers" by Pope Pius IX.

75. What is your opinion of his *Lectures* and *Sermons?*

The *Lectures* and *Sermons* of Father Burke are among the most remarkable literary productions of this age. The subjects are interesting and important. The style is clear, simple, and picturesque. The five *Lectures*, in answer to the calumnies of Froude, form an important addition to our historical literature. Father Burke could be grave, humorous, or pathetic at pleasure.

LESSON IX.

MRS. ANNA JAMESON. MISS MARY CUSACK.

76. Who was Mrs. Anna Jameson?

Mrs. Jameson, a native of Dublin and a daughter of Murphy the painter, won a distinguished reputation as a writer on art and literature, and died in 1860. As a writer on art she ranks with Ruskin.

77. Name her chief works on sacred art.

(1) *Sacred and Legendary Art*, containing legends

Ní cluincan cruic na Teaṁra treun
Weargs cruinniúgaḋ ban, no raoi,
Oin fuagnann í beiṫ feacca, paon,
Fuaim bnirce teuḋ 'ra n-oiḋce!
War rúḋ do 'n t-raoinracc, 'r anaṁ tra
A rúrgcan í go deo,
Acc 'nuair a bnircan cnoiḋe 'g a cnaḋaḋ,
Aig foilrúgaḋ í beiṫ beo.

of the Saints and Martyrs, as represented in the Fine Arts. (2) *Legends of the Monastic Orders*, as represented in the Fine Arts. (3) *Legends of the Madonna*, as represented in the Fine Arts. (4) *The History of Our Lord*, as exemplified in works of Art.

78. Mention her other noted works.

Lives of the Early Italian Painters and *The Characteristics of Women*.

79. Who is Miss Cusack?

Miss Mary Cusack, otherwise known as the Nun of Kenmare, is an Irish lady of rare gifts and an eminent writer.

80. Name her principal biographical works.

The Life of St. Patrick and *The Life of Daniel O'Connell*, which are by far the ablest and most exhaustive works on their respective subjects in literature.

81. Which is her chief work on history?

The History of the Irish Nation. Miss Cusack is a lady whose mental grasp, many virtues, and active patriotism shed a bright glory on her native country.

LESSON X.

DENIS F. MACCARTHY.   AUBREY DE VERE.

82. Who was Denis Florence MacCarthy?

Denis Florence MacCarthy, for many years Professor of Poetry in the Catholic University at Dublin, was one of the most gifted and accomplished poets of this century. He was styled the Poet-Laureate of Ireland.

83. Under what two heads may his chief works be enumerated?

Under the heads of *original poems* and *translations*.

84. Name some of his original poems.

The Bell-Founder ; *The Bridal of the Year* ; *The Pillar-Towers of Ireland*,* a descriptive poem full of beauty and music ; *The Voyage of St. Brendan*, an exquisite poem abounding in beautiful imagery ; *Con O'Donnell*, a fine dashing piece, overflowing with fire and energy ; and *An Ode for the O'Connell Centenary*, a poem of rare merit. Of all Irish poets since Moore, MacCarthy is by far the most fluent, versatile, and melodious.

85. Mention his most noted translations.

The *Dramas* and *Autos* of Calderon, † which he translated into pure and beautiful English. Such accomplished American critics as Ticknor and Longfellow are lavish in praising MacCarthy's admirable translations.

86. Who is Aubrey De Vere?

Aubrey De Vere, the third son of the late Sir Aubrey De Vere,‡ is a distinguished Irish writer, both in prose and verse. He became a Catholic in 1851.

87. Can you name some of his best known poems?

Innisfail, *May Carols*, and *Legends of St. Patrick*.

---

* This poem consists of twelve stanzas, of which the following is the first:

" The pillar-towers of Ireland, how wondrously they stand
By the lakes and rushing rivers, through the valleys of our land,
In mystic file, through the isle, they lift their heads sublime,
These gray old pillar temples—these conquerors of time."

† Calderon, the Shakspeare of Spain, died in 1681. He was a pious priest.

‡ Sir Aubrey De Vere was a poet of merit. He wrote choice sonnets, and two dramas—*Julian the Apostate* and *Mary Tudor*.

The spirit of religion and patriotism, tinged with a gentle melancholy, breathe through these fine productions. He has also written some choice sonnets.

88. Name his most noted dramas.

Alexander the Great and *St. Thomas of Canterbury*, two works of distinguished merit.

89. Which are De Vere's best-known prose works?

English Misrule and Irish Misdeeds, and *Picturesque Sketches of Greece and Turkey*.

LESSON XI.

BIOGRAPHERS—MITCHEL,* MADDEN,* GRIFFIN, FITZPATRICK, O'HANLON.

90. What is John Mitchel's chief production as a biographer?

The *Life of Hugh O'Neill*, a clear, animated, and brilliant work.†

91. What valuable series of lives do we owe to the pen of Dr. R. R. Madden?

The *Lives of the United Irishmen*, which contain ample details of the causes that led to the rebellion of 1798. It is a well-written work of much interest.

92. Who wrote the *Life of Gerald Griffin?*

His brother, Dr. Daniel Griffin, a gifted and learned physician. It is an exquisite work.

93. Who may be considered to hold the first rank among Irish biographers?

Dr. William John Fitzpatrick.

---

* For date of death, see *Short Dictionary.*
† Many years after, when an exile in America, Mitchel wrote a *History of Ireland* from the Treaty of Limerick to the present time. It is a continuation of the Abbé MacGeoghegan's *History of Ireland.*

THE ENGLISH LITERATURE OF IRELAND. 379

94. Which is his masterpiece?

The Life and Times of Bishop Doyle, which may safely be pronounced one of the finest biographies in the whole range of modern literature.

95. Mention some of Fitzpatrick's other works.

The Sham Squire, Irish Wits and Worthies, and the *Life of Charles Lever*.

96. Who has been styled the Irish Alban Butler

The Rev. John O'Hanlon, author of an excellent work—the *Lives of the Irish Saints*.

LESSON XII.

HISTORIANS — NAPIER,* O'CALLAGHAN,* PRENDERGAST,* MEEHAN, LECKY, SULLIVAN,* DUFFY, MACCARTHY.

97. What is Sir William Francis Patrick Napier's most remarkable historical work?

History of the War in the Peninsula, which an eminent critic has styled "the greatest military history in the English language."

98. What famous military history do we owe to the pen of John Cornelius O'Callaghan?

History of the Irish Brigades in the Service of France, a splendid work, to the preparation of which the author gave the labor and research of twenty-five years. It ranks with Napier's *History*.

99. What work of rare value and research, covering a mournful period of Irish history, was written by John P. Prendergast?

The Cromwellian Settlement of Ireland.

---

* For date of death, see *Short Dictionary*.

100. What recent work throws much new light on the last years of O'Neill and O'Donnell, the celebrated Irish princes?

The Fate and Fortunes of O'Neill and O'Donnell, by the Rev. C. P. Meehan.

101. Name some of the chief works written by William E. H. Lecky.

History of England in the Eighteenth Century, *History of Rationalism in Europe*, and *The Leaders of Public Opinion in Ireland*.*

102. How does Alexander M. Sullivan rank in the field of letters?

He is an orator and historian of undoubted eminence. His principal works are *The Story of Ireland*, *New Ireland*, and *Speeches and Addresses*.

103. Who has recently told the story of a portion of Irish history in a style of much felicity?

Sir Charles Gavan Duffy, in his *Young Ireland*.

104. What is your opinion of Justin MacCarthy as a writer?

He is one of the most fascinating writers of this age, both as a novelist and historian. His chief work is *The History of Our Own Times*.

SUMMARY OF CHAPTER III., BOOK III.

1. The nineteenth century has been a period of great change in Ireland.

2. Catholic emancipation dates from 1829.

---

* Lecky is a skilled writer, but he belongs to the rationalistic or irreligious school. He is commonly bitter and offensive when speaking of the Catholic Church. He is sometimes even blasphemous, as in his *History of Rationalism*. In the same work he jeers and misrepresents St. Thomas Aquinas.

3. The year 1847 witnessed the death of O'Connell and the starvation of the Irish people.

4. The Protestant Church, which brought such countless woes to Ireland, was disestablished in 1869.

5. During the reign of Queen Victoria, Ireland has been partially depopulated. In 1841 the population of the island was 8,174,000; in 1881 the population was only 5,160,000—a decrease of *over three millions in forty years.*

6. The political rascality of the English Government in its treatment of Ireland may well be summed up in the words of Shakspeare:

> "I clothe my naked villany
> With old odd ends, stolen from Holy Writ;
> And seem a saint, when most I play the devil."

7. The penal laws left *four millions* of Irish unable to read or write, when Catholic emancipation became a fact in 1829.

8. The Irish people love knowledge, and have made marvellous progress in a short time. Ireland is now *the least illiterate country in the world.*

9. Irish genius has done much to enrich English literature.

10. The Irish language, sad to say, is gradually sinking into decay, and English is taking its place.

11. Moore was the *first* Irish Catholic who became a master of the English language.

12. Dr. Doyle was the *first* Irish Catholic bishop who wielded a powerful pen in English.

13. Moore's *Irish Melodies* are among the immortal masterpieces of our literature.

14. The "Young Ireland Party" originated a new

and brilliant school of literature. Among the eminent writers of this school were *Davis, Duffy, Mangan, Williams, McGee,* and *D. F. MacCarthy.*

15. Eugene O'Curry and John O'Donovan were the most eminent Irish scholars and antiquarians of modern times.

16. The principal Irish novelists of the present age were *Griffin, Banim, Carleton, Lover,* and *Lever.*

17. Mrs. Jameson was a most distinguished art-critic.

18. Among Irish biographers, *Fitzpatrick,* author of the incomparable *Life and Times of Dr. Doyle,* ranks first.

19. Ireland has given to English literature its two best military historians—*Sir William Francis Patrick Napier* and *John Cornelius O'Callaghan.*

20. *Bird's-eye view of the chief Irish writers and works of the nineteenth century:*

John Lanigan, *Ecclesiastical History of Ireland.*
Bishop Doyle, *Letters on the State of Ireland.*
Thomas Moore, *Irish Melodies.*
Gerald Griffin, *The Collegians.*
John Banim, *The Boyne Water.*
Daniel O'Connell, *Speeches.*
Richard L. Shiel, *Speeches.*
Thomas O. Davis, *Poems.*
James C. Mangan, *Poems.*
Richard D. Williams, *Poems.*
Eugene O'Curry, *Lectures on the MS. Materials of Ancient Irish History.*
John O'Donovan, *Translation of the Annals of the Four Masters.*
Samuel Lover, *Rory O'More.*
William Carleton, *The Poor Scholar.*
Charles Lever, *Charles O'Malley.*
Archbishop MacHale, *Public Letters.*
Father Burke, O.P., *Lectures and Sermons.*
Mrs. Jameson, *Sacred and Legendary Art.*
Miss Cusack, *Life of Daniel O'Connell.*
Denis Florence MacCarthy, *Poems.*
Aubrey De Vere, *Poems.*

John Mitchel, *Life of Hugh O'Neill.*
R. R. Madden, *Lives of the United Irishmen.*
Daniel Griffin, *Life of Gerald Griffin.*
William J. Fitzpatrick, *Life and Times of Dr. Doyle.*
John O'Hanlon, *Lives of the Irish Saints.*
Sir W. F. P. Napier, *History of the Peninsular War.*
John C. O'Callaghan, *History of the Irish Brigades in France.*
John P. Prendergast, *The Cromwellian Settlement of Ireland.*
C. P. Meehan, *O'Neill and O'Donnell.*
W. E. H. Lecky, *Irish Leaders.*
A. M. Sullivan, *New Ireland.*
Sir C. G. Duffy, *Young Ireland.*
Justin MacCarthy, *History of Our Own Times.*

See *Short Dictionary* for Sir Jonah Barrington, William Maginn, Lady Morgan, Rev. Francis Mahony, John Francis Maguire, Lady Wilde, Mrs. S. C. Hall, Sir Robert Kane, and other Irish writers not noticed in the foregoing lessons.*

---

* For a fuller account of the English Literature of Ireland during the present age, see *The Prose and Poetry of Ireland*, Williams's *Poets and Poetry of Ireland*, Hayes's *Ballads of Ireland*, and Duffy's *Young Ireland.*

BOOK IV.

THE ENGLISH LITERATURE OF AMERICA

CHAPTER I.
THE EIGHTEENTH CENTURY.

A.D. 1700 to 1800.

THE AGE OF FRANKLIN, JEFFERSON, AND HAMILTON.

HISTORICAL INTRODUCTION.

1. THE YOUNG AMERICAN REPUBLIC. — The incomparable *Christopher Columbus* made known to Europe that a New World lay across the Atlantic. Spain, France, England, and other nations were not slow in sending out expeditions for the purpose of further discovery and exploration. Colonization followed. No permanent English settlement, however, was made before the seventeenth century, when a party of colonists stepped ashore on the banks of the James River, Virginia, and began to build Jamestown in 1607. One hundred and two English Puritans landed at Plymouth, Massachusetts, in 1620, and that was the starting-point of New England. The Catholic colony of Maryland—the first home of religious freedom in America—was founded by *Lord Baltimore*, in 1634. The Dutch settled New York, and

in 1626 Manhattan Island was bought from the Indians for twenty-four dollars. Pennsylvania was first colonized by Quakers under *William Penn*, in 1682. Georgia, the last of the thirteen English colonies, was settled in 1733.

The immortal labors of the Catholic missionaries among the Indians form undoubtedly the first and brightest chapter in our history. *White* was the apostle of Maryland ;* *Jogues* toiled among the Iroquois of New York, and gave his life for the true faith ; and while opening heaven to the red man, *Marquette* discovered the Mississippi. The names of these and other illustrious priests are to this day household words.†

The first event that drew the thirteen English colonies closely together, and served to reveal their united power, was the French and Indian war, which began in 1755. The same event gave *George Washington* his early military experience. It was a fierce conflict. For a time, under the skilled leadership of *Montcalm*, fortune seemed to favor the French ; but after battling for seven years, the fleur-de-lis disappeared from Canada. France made over to England all her possessions east of the Mississippi. England was mistress of North America.

Montcalm had the keenness to foresee and to foretell that as soon as the English colonists in America were relieved of the presence of a hostile French neighbor they would feel themselves independent of English protection, and that revolt, sooner or later, would be the result of that feeling. He was right.

---

* Father White set up the *first* printing-press in the English Colonies, but even the historian Bancroft ignores the fact so honorable to the illustrious Jesuit.
† See *The Catholic Pioneers of America*.

England soon began to lord it with a high hand over the Americans. Resistance followed. And fifteen years after the roar of the last cannon fired on the Plains of Abraham at Quebec, had died away, the heroism of brave men made Bunker Hill ever famous in the annals of this Republic. The *Declaration of Independence* became a fact on July 4th, 1776.

The war of the Revolution lasted eight years to a day, and no conflict of modern times has had such happy results. The aid of France was essential to our success. Providence sent that " friend in need" at the right moment. The English flag—emblem of a tyrannical power—disappeared in 1783, from Maine to Georgia, and the *Stars and Stripes* waved gracefully over a new land—" the land of the free and the home of the brave."

In 1787 the *Constitution of the United States* was drawn up at a convention held in Philadelphia, of which Washington was president. After much discussion it was ratified by all the States. Washington was elected first President in 1782, and his two terms of office and that of John Adams carry us to the close of the eighteenth century.

2. SOME OF THE AGENTS THAT INFLUENCED EARLY AMERICAN LITERATURE.—It is not hard to understand that the circumstances which surrounded the first American colonists were quite unfavorable to literary work—especially literary work of a high order. The pen is no doubt a mighty power in old communities, but in new settlements the axe, gun, spade, and plough are the leading instruments of progress. The pioneers of the New World had to subdue a rude, wild continent. Vast forests were to be cut down. New homes had to be erected. The wants of the hour were imperative.

The majority of the early settlers were simply transplanted, Protestant Englishmen; and the books they wrote, the colleges * they founded, the bitter religious intolerance † they exhibited—all go to prove that they were at best clever imitators. There is not a single work in the literature of the whole colonial period that calls for notice in this small volume. Franklin is the *first* truly distinguished name on the roll of American writers. The best minds were stirred to fervent, patriotic action by the Revolution; and the battle of freedom was fought by the pen as well as by the sword.

LESSON I.

BENJAMIN FRANKLIN.   DIED 1790.

Chief works: (1) *Autobiography.*
(2) *Essays.*
(3) *Correspondence.*

1. What author holds a commanding position in the American literature of the eighteenth century?

Benjamin Franklin, who was equally illustrious as a man of letters, statesman, and philosopher.

2. Tell us something of his life.

Franklin was a native of Boston, and had to leave school at the age of ten. He learned the art of printing, went to Philadelphia, and soon became a leader of public opinion. He signed the *Declaration*

---

* The oldest and best known of these are *Harvard* and *Yale.*
† The English penal laws against Catholics were in force in all the colonies down to the Revolution. As I have already remarked in another work, "To the Catholic it mattered little whether he resided on the banks of the Connecticut, the Hudson, or the Savannah: he was still the same unhappy object of religious hatred and persecution." (See *The Popular History of the Catholic Church in the U. S.*)

of Independence, and was one of the great figures in the Revolution.

3. Which is his most exquisite literary production?

An *Autobiography*, which is one of the most charming and instructive works of the kind ever written.

4. What range of subjects do Franklin's *Essays* cover?

Morals, Commerce, Politics, and Political Economy.

5. How are his Letters regarded?

He was an admirable letter-writer, and it has been well said that in his correspondence a perfect picture of Franklin himself is presented.

6. Through what publication did Franklin first become well known?

By his *Poor Richard's Almanac*, an exceedingly popular publication.*

7. Mention one of his most important discoveries in the field of natural science.

Franklin was the first to prove that lightning is electricity, and he invented the lightning-rod.

"This self-taught American is the most rational, perhaps, of all philosophers. He never loses sight of common-sense in any of his speculations; and when his philosophy does not consist entirely in its fair and vigorous application, it is always regulated and controlled by it in its application and results. No individual, perhaps, ever possessed a juster understanding, or was so seldom obstructed in its use by indolence, enthusiasm, or authority. The distinguishing feature of his understanding was great soundness and sa-

---

* Some of the most popular of our proverbs first appeared in the Almanac, as—
Early to bed and early to rise, make a man healthy, wealthy, and wise.
Diligence is the mother of good luck.
Never leave that till to-morrow which you can do to-day.
Want of care does us more damage than want of knowledge.
What maintains one vice would bring up two children.
It is hard for an empty bag to stand upright.
God gives all things to industry.

gacity, combined with extraordinary quickness of penetration. He possessed also a strong and lively imagination, which gave his speculations, as well as his conduct, a singularly original tone. The peculiar charm of his writings, and his great merit also in action, consisted in the clearness with which he saw an object, and the bold and steady pursuit of it by the surest and the shortest road."—*Lord Jeffrey.*

LESSON II.

OTHER NOTED WRITERS OF THE REVOLUTION.

8. Name a few of the other most noted writers of the Revolutionary Era.

Washington, Jefferson, Madison, Hamilton, Freneau, Trumbull, and *Patrick Henry.*

9. What are the chief productions that we possess from the pen of George Washington?

The famous *Farewell Address,** written in 1796, and a collection of interesting *Letters.* The great man who was " first in war, first in peace, and first in the hearts of his countrymen" was master of a clear, manly, dignified style. He wrote as a man of large and luminous views.

10. What work created an imperishable renown for Thomas Jefferson as a writer and patriot ?

The Declaration of Independence.*

11. Who has been styled the ablest political writer of the Revolution?

Alexander Hamilton.

12. What great work do we owe to the joint authorship of Alexander Hamilton and James Madison?

The Federalist.

13. What is *The Federalist?*

It is a small volume containing eighty-five essays,† which were designed to explain the merits of the Con-

---
* The reader should make himself familiar with this production.
† Of the eighty-five essays, Hamilton wrote fifty-one, Madison twenty-nine, and John Jay five.

stitution to the American people. The essays appeared in the interval between the publication and the adoption of the Constitution.

14. Who were the two most noted poets of the Revolutionary Era?

Philip Freneau and *John Trumbull*. Trumbull's *McFingal*, a satirical poem in the style of Butler's *Hudibras*, is still published and read.

15. Who was the greatest orator of the Revolution?

Patrick Henry, whose fiery, trumpet-toned eloquence aroused the Colonies and infused the courage to battle for liberty into the hearts of his timid, hesitating countrymen.

SUMMARY OF CHAPTER I., BOOK IV.

1. Some strong external influence was required to consolidate the thirteen English Colonies, and such an event was *the French and Indian War*.

2. The next great event that drew them together in still closer union was the *American Revolution*, and from this glorious event we date the birth of a new nation.

3. Franklin is the *first* American writer of distinction.

4. *Bird's-eye view of the chief American writers ank works of the eighteenth century :*

Benjamin Franklin, *Autobiography*.
George Washington, *Farewell Address*
Thomas Jefferson, *The Declaration of Independence*.
Alexander Hamilton, *The Federalist* (in part).
James Madison, *The Federalist* (in part).
Philip Freneau, *Poems*.
John Trumbull, *McFingal*.
Patrick Henry, *Speeches*.*

* For a very full account of early American literature, see Tyler's *History of American Literature*.

CHAPTER II.

THE NINETEENTH CENTURY.

A.D. 1800 to 1880.

THE AGE OF IRVING, LONGFELLOW, AND BROWNSON.

HISTORICAL INTRODUCTION.

"The number of good writers truly American, by which we mean all those who are not imitators of foreign modes, might be counted on the fingers of the two hands. In the politer walks of literature we find much grace of style, but very little originality of thought—productions which might as readily be taken for the work of an Englishman as of an American."—*Francis Parkman.*

1. A GLIMPSE AT THE UNITED STATES IN OUR OWN AGE.—The history of this Republic during the present century has been, on the whole, one of peace and marvellous progress. From 1801 to 1881 nineteen Presidents ruled the nation. We had only three wars.* The conflict known as the War of 1812 was caused by the insolent attitude of England and her outrageous claim to search American vessels on the high seas. The war with Mexico, which began in 1845, added a large strip of continent to our territory. The late civil war, however terrible in some aspects, happily settled two momentous questions that had long agitated the country:

(1) It abolished slavery.
(2) It solemnly decided that no State or number of

---

* Most of the European monarchies have had from four to eight wars, or more, during the same period.

States has the right to withdraw from the Union known as the United States.

When the first census of this country was taken in 1790, it showed a population of over three millions of inhabitants. These brave, intelligent people had just commenced the most interesting political experiment in the history of mankind—they had undertaken to govern themselves. Heaven blessed the undertaking. We see its success. The population of the United States in 1880 was over fifty millions. Our territory has grown even more rapidly than our population. The thirteen original States occupied little more than a narrow strip of country along the Atlantic coast, with claims as far west as the Mississippi. By purchase or conquest, the whole country west of the Father of Waters has since been added. This Republic is not merely one nation, but a grand cluster of nations—the most numerous and extensive alliance of States that has ever been known in the history of the world.

2. THE CHIEF AGENTS THAT INFLUENCED THE LITERATURE OF THIS PERIOD.—It has been well remarked that "after the achievement of independence and the establishment of a national government, the American people were too busy in the work of national progress to give much attention to literature and science. There were, indeed, some honorable exceptions to this remark. But, on the whole, the growth of the nation in this direction was by no means equal to its progress in other respects."

In the early years of the century an American book with the stamp of ability on it was such a rare article that the *Edinburgh Review* asked with a sneer, "Who reads an American book?" Time has made a considerable change. The London *Athenæum*, in 1880, declared that "an American book has nearly always something fresh and striking about it to English readers."

It is deeply to be regretted that much of the best American literature of the present age is tinged with anti-Catholic intolerance, or disfigured with calumnies against the Catholic religion. Let us glance at some representative authors. *Irving* is a writer of high character, yet in his *Newstead Abbey* we find the following gross calumny : "One of the parchment scrolls—found in the eagle of molten brass—throws rather an awkward light upon the kind of life led by the friars of Newstead. It is an indulgence granted to them for a certain number of months, in which plenary pardon is assured in advance *for all kinds of crime.*" In 1836, Bishop Clancy, coadjutor of Charleston, in a private letter called the attention of Irving to this passage. The author confessed, in relation to the document cited, that he "*did not examine it particularly,*" and that he had "*written without sufficient circumspection.*" Such are his own words. He promised, however, to investigate the matter, and to correct his blunder in a future edition. About a year later, Dr. Clancy was transferred to the see of Demerara, and on his way through England he visited Newstead Abbey, and made a careful examination of the old parchment mentioned by Irving. And what was it? "So far from being an indulgence," says Dr. Clancy, "to friars from a Pope or Bishop, or any ecclesiastical authority, it is a pardon for civil offences which an English king thought proper to impart to real or imaginary offenders against the forest-laws in Sherwood, county of Nottingham." The offensive passage in *Newstead Abbey* has never been expunged. It can be seen to this day in the latest editions of the book, and it certainly places Irving, and not the friars, in "an awkward light." * "When the world has once got hold of a lie," says Bulwer, "it is astonishing how hard it is to get it out of the world. You beat it about the head until it seems to have given up the ghost, and lo! the next day it is as healthy as ever."

Bancroft is a distinguished historian, but his *History of the United States* contains many things that cannot fail to insult the Catholic reader. In the recent final revision of that work, made by his own hand, he altered nearly every passage which, in fifteen former editions, were complimentary to the Catholic founders of Maryland. He flatly contradicted himself. Bigotry in old age is odious, and Bancroft is eighty-four.

Prescott is a virulent libeller of the Catholic religion in his *History of Ferdinand and Isabella*. Sometimes his ill-breeding shows itself in using the nickname "Romish" for the title Catholic. His cold bigotry even affects translated passages in his works. In *The Conquest of Mexico* he has a long quotation from Bernal Diaz as to the character of Cortés. The old Spaniard states that the great general was "most true in his devotions to the Holy Virgin." Prescott omits the adjective "holy," and writes "Virgin."

The illustrious missionary Father Jogues, S.J., after many hardships, and in the dress of a beggar, landed

---

* The correspondence that passed between Bishop Clancy and Washington Irving in relation to the foregoing affair can be seen in Clarke's *Lives of the Deceased Bishops of the Catholic Church in the U. S*, Vol. II.

on the coast of Brittany early on Christmas morning. He went to Mass and received the Holy Communion, of which he had been deprived for sixteen months. This incident is thus recounted by the eminent historian Parkman, in his fascinating volume *The Jesuits in North America:* "He reached the church in time for evening Mass, and with an unutterable joy knelt before the altar and renewed the Communion of which he had been so long deprived." Who ever heard of "evening Mass" on Christmas Day, or any other day? In another place in the same work, Parkman writes of the martyred Father Garnier, S.J.: "The affections of his sensitive nature, severed from earthly objects, found relief in an ardent *adoration* of the Virgin Mary." Father Garnier and all good Catholics *adore* God alone. The holy Jesuit had an ardent *devotion* to the Blessed Virgin, not *adoration*.

Bryant's longest poem is *The Ages*, and it is pervaded with a spirit bitterly anti-Catholic.

The best Protestant culture and scholarship of New England appears to be so handicapped by an ignorant, ingrained intolerance as to be unable to rise to the height of making itself familiar with the *name, doctrines,* and *practices* of the greatest and most ancient religious institution in the world—the Catholic Church. The ablest non-Catholic writers of that section of our country seem unable ever to rid their vocabulary of the cant words "Romish" and "Popish" —offensive nicknames that belong to the dark period of the penal laws. They seem incapable of ever comprehending the true theological meaning of the word *indulgence,* and that Catholics neither go to "evening Mass" nor "adore" the Most Holy Virgin.

No; these gentlemen continue to write from an ignorance boundless and lamentable—a prejudiced ignorance that will reflect severely upon themselves, mar their future fame, and present them to posterity in a light not to be envied.

America offers a vast field for original literary effort, but it has been very slightly cultivated. A slavish imitation of English models has been too much the fashion. It has served to stifle healthy originality and manly independence of thought. " In respect to every department of active life," says an eminent American writer, " the United States are fully emancipated from their ancient colonial subjection. They can plan, invent, and achieve for themselves, and this, too, with a commanding success. But in all the finer functions of thought, in all matters of literature and taste, we are essentially provincial. England once held us in a state of political dependency. That day is past; but she still holds us in an intellectual dependency far more complete. Her thoughts become our thoughts by a process unconscious but inevitable. She caters for our mind and fancy with a liberal hand. We are spared the labor of self-support; but by the universal law, applicable to nations no less than to individuals, we are weakened by the want of independent exercise. It is a matter of common remark that the most highly educated classes among us are far from being the most efficient in thought or action. The vigorous life of the nation springs from the deep rich soil at the bottom of society. Its men of greatest influence are those who have studied man before they studied books, and who, by hard battling with the world and boldly following out the bent of their native genius, have hewed their own way to wealth, station, or knowledge from the ploughshare or the forecastle. The comparative shortcomings of the best educated among us may be traced to several causes; but, as we are constrained to think, they are mainly owing to the fact that the highest civilization of America is communicated from without, instead of being developed from within, and is therefore nerveless and unproductive." *

LESSON I.

WASHINGTON IRVING. DIED 1859.

Chief works: (1) *Knickerbocker's History of New York*.
(2) *The Sketch-Book*.
(3) *The Life of Columbus*.
(4) *The Conquest of Granada*.
(5) *The Life of Washington*.

1. Who was Washington Irving?

Washington Irving, the Goldsmith of America, was a most distinguished essayist, historian, and biographer. He is perhaps the most popular of all American authors.

2. Give a short account of his life.

He was born and educated in New York City, spent many years in Europe, and was the first American that made literature a profession.

3. What is *Knickerbocker's History of New York?*

It is a burlesque chronicle, written in such a quiet

---

* Periodical literature has had an unparalleled development in the United States. The earliest American newspaper was the *Boston News Letter*, founded in 1704. There are now over 11,000 newspapers, magazines, and reviews in this Republic. Among the best-known magazines and reviews are *The Century Magazine*, *The Catholic World*, *The Atlantic Monthly*, *Harper's Monthly Magazine*, *The North American Review*, and *The American Catholic Quarterly Review*.

vein of comic humor that many a dull person has taken it for true history. Sir Walter Scott said that in reading it he laughed till his sides were sore.

4. What is the *Sketch-Book?*

It is an exquisite collection of light, charming sketches, tales, legends, descriptions, etc. The two most famous pieces are *Rip Van Winkle* and *The Legend of Sleepy Hollow.*

5. What do you think of Irving's *Life of Columbus?*

It is a great work, marred, however, by some serious errors that do much injustice to the shining character of Columbus.*

6. What is *The Conquest of Granada?*

It is a chapter of Spanish history full of interest and romance.

7. Which is his last and largest biographical work?

The *Life of Washington*, the last volume of which was issued only three months before the death of Irving. It is a work truly worthy of the author and the illustrious subject.

"Irving as an historian is subject to one grave criticism. He is too diffuse in his treatment of the subject, and his style is at times altogether too florid."—*Hart.*

"The *Sketch-Book*, on the whole, remains the best example of Irving's powers, combining, as it does, humor, pathos, and a wonderful felicity of description."—*C. F. Richardson.*

"As a writer, Irving may be safely pronounced to be the most popular of all American authors. His works are known and read by every one. Diedrich Knickerbocker. Sleepy Hollow, Dolf Heyliger, Ichabod Crane, and Rip Van Winkle have become household names and forms. No other creations of the imagination have taken such prominence in American literature."—*Hart.*

---

* Irving, adopting a gross error of some of the older and least trustworthy writers says in several places that the relation of Columbus with his second wife was not sanctioned by marriage. The statement is false. It remained for the Count de Lorgues, about the middle of the present century, to give a grand quietus to this shameful slander about the great and holy discoverer of America. The error has not, however, been corrected in Irving's *Life of Columbus.*

THE ENGLISH LITERATURE OF AMERICA. 399

LESSON II.
REPRESENTATIVE NOVELISTS.

8. What two writers may be safely chosen as our representative novelists?

Cooper and *Hawthorne.*

9. Tell us something of Cooper's career.

James Fenimore Cooper was born in New Jersey; studied for a time at Yale College; entered the navy, but devoted a large part of his life to literature. He was the first American writer to obtain a reputation in Europe, and his novels were translated into nearly every European language.

10. Name a few of his most admired productions.

The Spy, *The Pioneers*, and *The Last of the Mohicans*, all works of fiction. *The Spy*, the first successful American novel, was issued in 1821. It is a tale of the Revolution. The second pictures frontier life and glows with descriptions of forest scenery; the last is his most popular Indian tale.

11. Can you point out in a few words some of Cooper's merits and defects?

He is among the most original and truly national of American writers, and his best novels are full of romantic interest. But he is very unequal. He wrote much that is worthless. He has little humor or pathos; his descriptions are often wearisome in detail, and though his style is direct and manly, it is never graceful. His Indian characters are for the most part falsely drawn.

12. Do you know anything about Hawthorne's life?

Nathaniel Hawthorne was born at Salem, Massachusetts, and educated at Bowdoin College, whence he graduated in 1825, with Longfellow as a classmate. He held a number of public offices, but the greater part of his life was passed in quiet seclusion.

13. Name his finest works.

The Scarlet Letter, a powerful romance of early life in New England; *The House of the Seven Gables*, an intense and solemn story, the scene of which is laid in Salem; and *The Marble Faun*, a romance of Italy.

14. Sum up Hawthorne's principal good qualities and defects as a writer.

Most critics place him at the head of American novelists. He was a master of pure idiomatic English. But, on the other hand, his pages are often tinged with gloom and melancholy—too much " sicklied o'er with the pale cast of thought."

"Cooper was American through and through. He did not hesitate, in some of his later stories, to satirize the 'louder' national characteristics; but to him more than to any other author is due the increasing attention to home subjects and heroes. From his writings, undoubtedly, a part of the English public got the impression—which it has with difficulty corrected—that buffaloes and Indians form the most conspicuous features in our civilization."
—*Richardson*.

"Hawthorne's greatest works are unquestionably *The Scarlet Letter*, *The House of the Seven Gables*, and *The Marble Faun*. Each of these is full of passages, long and intense, where the reader feels that every word is a thought or a picture. The characters are wonderfully defined by a succession of clear, delicate strokes, and move in an atmosphere of broadening fancy. One who feels himself strong enough to overcome the spell exerted by Hawthorne's melancholy genius can find no better model for style and expression."—*Hart*.

LESSON III.

HENRY WADSWORTH LONGFELLOW. DIED 1882.

Chief works: (1) *Evangeline, and Other Poems.*
(2) *Prose Works.*
(3) *Translations.*

15. Who was Longfellow?

Henry Wadsworth Longfellow, the most distinguished of American poets, was a native of Portland, Maine. He was educated at Bowdoin College, and for a long time held the chair of rhetoric and literature in Harvard University. He devoted the last twenty-eight years of his life chiefly to letters.

16. Which is his most celebrated poem?

Evangeline, a Catholic tale, pathetic, religious, and beautiful. The choice of subject was very happy.* It is the most exquisite work of the kind in English literature.

17. Name some of his other poems.

The Golden Legend, a picture of civil and monastic life in the middle ages; *The Song of Hiawatha*, which deals in a rather misty manner with Indian life and legends; and the *Tales of a Wayside Inn*, a collection somewhat after the fashion of the *Canterbury Tales*.

---

* The tale of *Evangeline* is founded on a sad chapter of American history. The French were the first settlers of Nova Scotia, and under their rule it was known as *Acadie*, or *Acadia*. In 1755 the English, without any cause, brutally destroyed the French settlements of Acadia, and dispersed 18,000 souls over the other British colonies. The peaceful inhabitants—all Catholics—were compelled to give up their property, the houses and crops were burned before their eyes, and they themselves shipped in such haste that few families or friends remained together. "To this day," writes Hazletine, "the western coast of Nova Scotia, blessed as it is in a mild climate and fertile soil, discovers many traces of the patient industry which made this district a French Eden."

34*

18. Mention a few of his finest and most admired short pieces.

The Psalm of Life,* *Excelsior,* *The Wreck of the Hesperus,* *The Village Blacksmith,* and *The Hanging of the Crane.*

19. Name two of Longfellow's most-admired prose works

Hyperion and *Kavanagh,* two interesting romances.

20. Which is his chief work as a translator?

The Divine Comedy of Dante. He has preserved the spirit as well as the form of the original; and his work has been pronounced the best English rendering of the greatest work in Italian literature.

21. Can you point out some of the most noted merits and defects of Longfellow as a poet?

Longfellow was a trained word-artist, and his style is noted for grace, finish, and felicity, rather than vigor of thought or depth of passion. His characters do not stand before the mind with sufficient clearness. They pass like shadows. A good critic has remarked that *Evangeline,* of all the characters Longfellow has aimed to draw, stands forth in the memory of his readers with some distinctness of outline.

"Coming generations, it is believed, will cherish Longfellow chiefly as a sweet singer. His future fame will rest upon those

---

* Among its often-quoted stanzas are the following:

"Lives of great men all remind us,
  We can make our lives sublime,
And, departing, leave behind us
  Footprints on the sands of time.

"Footprints that perhaps another,
  Sailing o'er life's solemn main,
A forlorn and shipwrecked brother,
  Seeing, may take heart again.

"Let us, then, be up and doing,
  With a heart for any fate;
Still achieving, still pursuing,
  Learn to labor and to wait."

short, exquisitely simple utterances that speak for the weary heart and aching brain of all humanity."—*J. S. Hart.*

"Whatever shortcomings and limitations may be ascribed to Longfellow's genius, it is certain that no contemporary poet—not even Tennyson—has been so universally and cordially welcomed by the English-speaking race."—*Hazletine.*

LESSON IV.
REPRESENTATIVE ORATORS—WEBSTER, EVERETT, PHILLIPS.

22. Who was Daniel Webster?

Daniel Webster, the son of a farmer, was born in New Hampshire, and educated at Dartmouth College. He studied law. He was a member of the United States Senate for eighteen years, was three times Secretary of State, and died in 1852.

23. What is his rank as an orator?

Among American orators it is commonly conceded that Webster holds the first place.

24. What do you remark of his style?

Webster's style is simple and luminous; it is remarkable for great vigor of reasoning and closeness of statement. It is impressive rather than brilliant, and occasionally rises to real grandeur.

25. Name some of his finest speeches.

The *Reply to Hayne*, the *Bunker Hill Monument Discourse*, and the *Eulogy on Adams and Jefferson*.

26. Who was Everett?

Edward Everett, one of the most distinguished of American orators, was born near Boston, educated at Harvard, and filled various public positions, as Secretary of State and U. S. Senator from Massachusetts. He died in 1865.

27. What is his chief literary work?

Orations, in four large volumes.

28. Mention one of the leading characteristics of his *Orations*.

Everett's *Orations* have a finish and symmetry which, on every page, give token of the richly-endowed and thorough scholar. The style is extremely graceful.

29. Who was Wendell Phillips?

Wendell Phillips, whose eloquent voice has been recently stilled in death, was a native of Boston and a graduate of Harvard. He was long an antislavery advocate, and won a high reputation as a lecturer on art and literature. Among his *Orations*, the one on Daniel O'Connell is marked by his best characteristics.

"If Webster is the Michael Angelo of American oratory, Everett is the Raphael."—*Whipple*.

"Many judges rank Phillips above all other American orators in voice, delivery, personal magnetism, and all that constitutes the power of a public speaker."—*Hart*.

LESSON V.

THREE POETS—BRYANT, WHITTIER, HOLMES.

30. Who was Bryant?

William Cullen Bryant, a famous American poet, was born in Massachusetts; educated at Williams College; studied law, and was admitted to the bar. He finally devoted himself to journalism, and was editor of the New York *Evening Post* for over fifty years. He died, aged eighty-four, in 1878.

31. Name some of his most admired poems.

Thanatopsis, To a Waterfall, The Forest Hymn, and *The Planting of the Apple-Tree.* Bryant's poems are neither so varied nor so numerous as those of Longfellow and Whittier.

32. What are some of his leading characteristics as a poet?

His pieces show care, finish, a love of nature, and —it must be added—a puritanical coldness.

33. Who is Whittier?

John Greenleaf Whittier, the most thoroughly American of all our poets, and next to Longfellow the most popular, is a native of Massachusetts, who began life as a farm-hand and shoemaker. The poet early began to edit a newspaper, and he has devoted his life to literature.*

34. Mention some of his most popular poems.

Snow-Bound, *Maud Muller*,† and *Barbara Frietchie*.

35. What does a recent critic say of the first-named poem?

" *Snow-Bound* is a genuine New England idyl, and puts between its covers more of the spirit of the region than any other American book. It will forever remain a national classic."

36. Who is Holmes?

Oliver Wendell Holmes, one of the wisest and wittiest of American writers and an eminent master of prose and verse, was born near Boston, and educated at Harvard. He studied medicine in Europe, and for over a third of a century filled the chair of anatomy in the medical school of Harvard. He has devoted his leisure time to literature.

---

* In some of his poems Whittier, like Bryant, exhibits his ignorant anti-Catholic prejudices.
† *Maud Muller* contains the often-quoted couplet:
   " For of all sad words of tongue or pen,
      The saddest are these: ' It might have been.' "

37. What do you remark of Holmes as a poet?

In neatness and finish he is hardly surpassed by Pope or Moore. He has written no long poem. Some of his best pieces are *The Last Leaf*, *Old Ironsides*, *The One-Horse Shay*, and a number of short lyrics that glitter with gems of thought.

38. In what line of prose-writing has Holmes acquired great fame?

As a writer of magazine articles. An eminent critic remarks that "no living magazinist, English or American, can equal him." *The Autocrat of the Breakfast-Table* has been widely admired.

"Bryant's poetry has truth, delicacy, and correctness, as well as uncommon vigor and richness. He is always faithful to nature; he selects his groups and images with judgment. Nothing is borrowed; nothing artificial; his pictures have an air of freshness and originality which could come from the student of nature alone."—*North American Review*.

"No American poet, it may be said, is so free as Whittier from obligations to English writers. He is eminently original and eminently American."—*Cathcart*.

"The most concise, apt, and effective poet of the school of Pope this country has produced is Oliver Wendell Holmes, a Boston physician. His best lines are a series of rhymed pictures, witticisms, or sentiments, let off with the precision and brilliancy of the scintillations that sometimes illumine the northern horizon."—*Tuckerman*.

LESSON VI.

REPRESENTATIVE HISTORIANS.*

39. What two eminent authors have most prominently identified themselves with the history of the United States?

Hildreth and *Bancroft*.

---

* Dr. David Ramsay was the earliest American historian of note. He died in 1815. His chief work is *A History of the United States*.

THE ENGLISH LITERATURE OF AMERICA. 407

40. Who was Hildreth?

Richard Hildreth was a native of Massachusetts, and a graduate of Harvard University. His life was chiefly devoted to literature. He died in 1865, aged fifty-eight years.

41. Which is his principal work?

The *History of the United States*, from the discovery of America till 1820. It is in six volumes.

42. What are some of the merits and shortcomings of this work?

It is a plain, straightforward narrative, and is evidently the fruit of great care, labor, and research. The style is somewhat dry and cold.

43. Who is Bancroft?

George Bancroft, the most noted historian of the early affairs of this country, is a native of Massachusetts, was educated at Harvard University and in Germany, and held various public positions as Secretary of the Navy and Minister to England and to Germany.

44. To what work has he devoted the b st years of his life?

The *History of the United States*, which begins with Columbus, but only comes down to 1789. The first volume appeared in 1834, and the twelfth and last in 1882.

45. What may be said of the merits and defects of Bancroft's *History?*

As a record of the origin and early growth of the United States, it is undoubtedly the most finished and elaborate history that has yet appeared. But as we pass from volume to volume it is easy to see that the style is neither uniform nor always attractive. It is sometimes graceful and animated, then cold and inflated. Bancroft has cancelled his claims to impartiality in the new revised edition of his work now (1884) in course of publication. He is partisan and anti-Catholic.

LESSON VII.

REPRESENTATIVE HISTORIANS.

46. What distinguished American historian took the romantic story of early Spanish America as a subject for the exhibition of his powers?

Prescott.

47. Tell us something of his life?

William Hickling Prescott, a native of Massachusetts, was educated at Harvard, where the throwing of a crust of bread by a thoughtless companion cost him one of his eyes, and almost led to total blindness. His quiet, uneventful life was chiefly devoted to the preparation of the works that have rendered his name famous. He died in 1859, aged sixty-three.*

48. Which are his principal works?

The History of Ferdinand and Isabella the Catholic, The History of the Conquest of Mexico, and *The History of the Conquest of Peru*.

49. Of these, which is the most finished and interesting production?

The History of the Conquest of Mexico. The wonderful interest of the narrative, the scenic descriptions, and the portraits of Cortés, Montezuma, and other personages, give it all the charm of an effective romance.

---

* The *Life of Prescott*, by George Ticknor, is one of the most admirable works in American biography.

THE ENGLISH LITERATURE OF AMERICA. 409

50. What may be said of Prescott's style?

It is a style marked by clearness, simplicity, and classic excellence.

51. What eminent writer has recounted the discoveries, achievements, and misfortunes of the French in America?

Parkman.

52. Give a brief outline of his life.

Francis Parkman is a native of Boston, a graduate of Harvard, and, like Prescott, is partially blind. Before publishing anything he travelled on the western prairies, with a view of studying the manners and characteristics of the Indians.

53. Which was his first production of marked power?

History of the Conspiracy of Pontiac, published in 1851. It tells the story of one of the most thrilling episodes in American history.

54. Name some of his most noted works on the French in America.

The Pioneers of France in the New World, *The Jesuits in North America*, and *La Salle, or the Discovery of the Great West*. Parkman has issued five works on this subject, and the sixth and last, now (1884) in course of preparation, will close with Montcalm and the last years of French Canada.

55. Of all Parkman's works, which is perhaps the most admired?

The Jesuits in North America, which, in spite of many shortcomings, is the most exquisite volume in the whole range of our historical literature.*

---

* For the purely material facts of the Jesuit missions Parkman is entirely reliable: but, as a Catholic critic has well remarked, "Of the motives which governed the missionaries, of their faith and charity, as well as of their whole interior spiritual life, he understands less than did the untutored Indian."

56. What is your opinion of the style of this author?

It is a style of marvellous vigor, clearness, grace, and beauty. It lends a charm to the narrative. In power of description—of reproducing natural scenery with photographic vividness — Parkman is unapproached by any other American writer.

LESSON VIII.

THREE REPRESENTATIVE CATHOLIC WRITERS.

57. What three American Catholic prelates were especially noted for a clear, vigorous, popular style of writing?

Bishop England and *Archbishops Hughes* and *Spalding.*

58. Tell us something of Bishop England.

John England, first bishop of Charleston, South Carolina, was born, educated, ordained, and consecrated in Ireland. He established the first Catholic newspaper in this Republic.* He was a scholar—an apostle—one of the really great men of this century. He died in 1842, aged fifty-six.

59. Who first collected his works?

His successor, Dr. Reynolds, who had them published in five large octavo volumes. Bishop England's busy pen touched a wide range of subjects, historical and controversial. His chief aim was to present the Catholic Church and her doctrines and practices in their true light before the American people.

60. What is your opinion of his style?

It is clear, direct, witty, and energetic, and pervaded

---

* *The U. S. Catholic Miscellany,* in 1822.

with an Irish intensity of feeling. It is the style of a great intellect.

61. Give a short outline of the career of Archbishop Hughes.

John Hughes, first archbishop of New York, was born in Ireland, but educated in the United States. He was a man of far-reaching views and wonderful energy. He died in 1864, aged sixty-seven.

62. Do you know anything of Dr. Hughes as a writer?

After his death his writings were published in two large volumes which remain a monument of his uncommon power as an able essayist—a skilful and incisive writer. A very busy life, however, prevented Archbishop Hughes from writing a great work on any one subject.

63. Tell us something of Dr. Spalding.

Martin John Spalding, who died archbishop of Baltimore, in 1872, was a native of Kentucky; was educated at Rome, and was one of the most prominent prelates at the General Council of the Vatican.

64. Name his chief works.

History of the Protestant Reformation in Europe, the most comprehensive work on that subject in English literature; *Miscellanea*, a valuable collection of forty-six essays, lectures, and reviews on a wide variety of popular topics; and the *Evidences of Catholicity*, in a series of fourteen eloquent lectures. Dr. Spalding's style is more forcible than finished.*

---

* For a fuller account of the Catholic writers of this Republic, see the *Popular History of the Catholic Church in the U. S.*, Book V. chaps. i.-iii.

LESSON IX.

THREE REPRESENTATIVE ESSAYISTS AND LITERARY CRITICS.

65. What three American writers have prominently identified themselves with literary criticism?

Emerson, *Lowell*, and *Whipple*.

66. Who was Emerson?

Ralph Waldo Emerson, who was "no less distinguished for the rare beauty of his language than the unsoundness of his thoughts," was a native of Boston and a graduate of Harvard. He died, aged seventy-nine, in 1882.

67. Name his principal works.

Essays, *Lectures*, *Representative Men*, and a volume of *Poems*.

68. What cancels the value of Emerson's utterances on many subjects, notwithstanding the marked beauty of his style?

He was color-blind to the spiritual. He ignored the supernatural in man.

69. Who is Lowell?

James Russell Lowell, a noted poet, essayist, and critic, is a native of Massachusetts, and, like Emerson, a graduate of Harvard. He succeeded Longfellow in the chair of polite letters at his Alma Mater. He has for some years held the position of American ambassador to England.

70. Which are his chief works?

Poems, *My Study-Windows*, and *Among My Books*. The last two works give Lowell a high rank as a literary critic.

THE ENGLISH LITERATURE OF AMERICA. 413

71. What is your opinion of his style?

It is a strong, wordy, figurative style, deficient in clearness and simplicity.

72. Who is Whipple?

Edwin Percy Whipple is a native of Massachusetts, and a critic of eminence and popularity.

73. Mention his most important works.

Character and Characteristic Men and *The Literature of the Age of Elizabeth.* The latter is a really able work, marred here and there, however, by a tone of anti-Catholic prejudice. The style is clear, easy, and attractive.*

LESSON X.

ORESTES A. BROWNSON. DIED 1876.

74. Who was Dr. Brownson?

Orestes A. Brownson, the ablest reviewer and most distinguished philosopher that America has produced during the present age, was a native of Vermont. He owed little to schools and was a self-taught man. After years of wandering from one Protestant sect to another, he became a Catholic in 1844, and thenceforth he devoted his pen with manly energy to the cause of the true faith.

75. What famous periodical did he conduct, almost single-handed, from 1844 till 1864?

Brownson's Quarterly Review, which ceased publication in 1864. He revived the *Review* in 1873, and

---

* The late *Henry Reed* was a genial critic, and *Brother Azarias* is a deep, sound thinker on literary matters.

for two years more he sustained it with a vigor and brilliancy unsurpassed at any previous date.

76. Name some of his chief works.

The Spirit-Rapper, The Convert, or Leaves from My Experience, Essays and Reviews, and *The American Republic.* Dr. Brownson's complete works, in eighteen volumes, edited by his son, Henry M. Brownson, are now in course of publication.

77. Which is his masterpiece?

The American Republic, a work of extraordinary merit, in which the Constitution of the United States is explained in a manner never before attempted or approached.

78. What are some of the chief characteristics of Dr. Brownson's writings?

Boldness, originality, gigantic grasp of intellect, and a style of uncommon purity, vigor, and clearness.

"Brownson's ability as a writer and thinker has never been called in question."— *Hart.*

In Brownson's writings can be found "the terse logic of Tertullian, the polemic crash of St. Jerome, the sublime eloquence of Bossuet, all in combination or alternation, with many sweet strains of tenderness and playful flashes of humor. His style has a magnificent Doric beauty seldom surpassed — rarely even equalled."—*Catholic World.*

Summary of Chapter II., Book IV.

1. The growth and material progress of this Republic during the nineteenth century have been marvellous.

2. Among the causes influencing American literature have been the race after wealth and the ma-

terial wants of life, anti-Catholic intolerance, and a slavish imitation of English literary models. Lowell hits the mark neatly when he says, " You steal Englishmen's books and think Englishmen's thoughts."

3. Irving's varied powers and exquisite style are best represented in *The Sketch-Book*.

4. Cooper was the first American novelist that gained a European reputation.

5. It is still safe to say that Longfellow is the most distinguished American poet, and holds the place of honor.

6. As inimitable narrators and writers of classical English, Parkman and Prescott stand at the head of American historians.

7. Lowell is, perhaps, our most able literary critic.

8. Bishop England was the founder of Catholic journalism in this Republic.

9. Archbishop Spalding's *History of the Protestant Reformation* is the most comprehensive work on that subject in English.

10. Dr. Brownson stands at the head of the American reviewers and philosophers of this age.

11. *Bird's-eye view of the American authors and works of the nineteenth century:*

POETS.

Henry W. Longfellow, *Evangeline*.
William Cullen Bryant, *Thanatopsis*.
John Greenleaf Whittier, *Snow-Bound*.
Oliver Wendell Holmes, *The Last Leaf*.

PROSE-WRITERS.

Washington Irving, *The Sketch-Book*.
James Fenimore Cooper, *The Spy*.
Nathaniel Hawthorne, *The Scarlet Letter*.
Daniel Webster, *Speeches*.
Edward Everett, *Orations*.

Wendell Phillips, *Orations*.
George Bancroft, *History of the United States*.
Richard Hildreth, *History of the United States*.
William H. Prescott, *History of the Conquest of Mexico*.
Francis Parkman, *The Jesuits in North America*.
Bishop England, *Essays and Discourses*.
Archbishop Hughes, *Letters and Discourses*.
Archbishop Spalding, *History of the Reformation*.
Ralph Waldo Emerson, *Representative Men*.
James Russell Lowell, *Among My Books*.
Edwin Percy Whipple, *Literature of the Age of Elizabeth*.
Orestes A. Brownson, *The American Republic*.

12. See *Short Dictionary* for David Ramsay, Charles B. Brown, Matthew Carey, Edgar Allan Poe, Fitz-Greene Halleck, Richard Henry Dana, Henry Reed, John G. Saxe, Horace Greeley, Edmund B. O'Callaghan, Jared Sparks, George Ticknor, John G. Shea, Thomas D. McGee, Father Thébaud, S.J., Father Hewitt, C.S.P., Richard H. Clarke, John Savage, Father A. J. Ryan, John R. G. Hassard, J. V. Huntington, George Henry Miles, Father Hecker, C.S.P., Brother Azarias, Rev. Donald X. McLeod, John Boyle O'Reilly, Rev. Bernard O'Reilly, Mrs. Sigourney, Mrs. Sadlier, Mrs. Stowe, J. G. Holland, Alexander H. Stephens, Thomas B. Aldrich, and others not noticed in the foregoing lesson.*

LAST WORDS.

READING AND THE CHOICE OF BOOKS.

The student who has thus far faithfully studied this volume has, I hope, learned something *about* the most noted works in English literature. He should now begin to read *the books themselves*, or at least the

---

* For a fuller account of American literature, the reader is referred to Duyckinck's *Cyclopædia of American Literature* and Tyler's *History of American Literature*.

best of them. "We must confine ourselves to the masterpieces of great names," said one as wise as he was distinguished; "we have not time for the rest." It is very true. Let us examine this matter of *time* and *reading* a little. A person who reads on an average twenty-five pages a day would finish a volume of four hundred pages in sixteen days, and in a year he would complete twenty-two such volumes. At the same rate, it would take him *fifty years* to read 1100 volumes. But Allibone's *Critical Dictionary of English Literature* contains the names of over 46,000 British, Irish, and American authors, some of whom wrote twenty, thirty, or even forty books. It cannot be too often repeated, "We must confine ourselves to the masterpieces; we have no time for the rest." We should likewise write on our bookmarks and engrave in our minds the sublime old motto, *Ad majorem Dei gloriam*—"To the greater glory of God."

"Choose an author as you would a friend."—*Pope.*
"Every remarkable man has been fond of letters."—*Lacordaire.*
"In the best books great men talk to us—with us—and give us their most precious thoughts."—*Channing.*
"The reading of literary masterpieces not only forms the taste, but it keeps the soul in elevated regions and prevents it from sinking down into vulgarity."—*Lacordaire.*
"Reading furnishes the mind only with the materials of knowledge; it is thinking that makes what we read ours."—*Locke.*
"The true method of study is to read little, to select good authors, and to think much."—*Balmes.*
"To *know* one good book well is better than to know something *about* a hundred good books at second hand."—*Richardson.*
"Concentration is the prime and sole element of strength. Learn to sound thoroughly a few lines of an author at a time. *Nothing can be turned to account except what has been ripened by meditation.* A large range of reading dazzles the mind, and may, in the case of him who has a good memory, dazzle others, but it gives neither solidity nor depth. Depth always supposes extent, but extent does not involve depth."—*Lacordaire.*
"It is a great preservative to a high standard in taste and achievement *to take every year some one great book as an especial study,* not only to be read, but to be conned, studied, brooded over; to go

into the country with it, travel with it, be devotedly faithful to it, be without any other book for the time; compel yourself thus to read it again and again. Who can be dull enough to pass long days in the intimate, close, familiar intercourse with some transcendent mind, and not feel the benefit of it when he returns to the common world?"—*Bulwer.*

"True poetry must be studied, not merely read."—*Henry Reed.*

"As you close a book, ask yourself what good it has done you."—*Henry Reed.*

"Keep your reading *well proportioned* in the two great divisions of *prose* and *poetry.*"—*Henry Reed.*

"Literature is to be employed for the culture of character."—*Henry Reed.*

"I never remember anything but what I write *three times* or read over *six times* at least; and if you do the same you will have as good a memory."—*Porson.**

"All else may pass away, but the wisdom of well-digested knowledge and methodical thought remains through sunshine and storm, making the sunshine more beautiful and the storm less severe."—*Brother Azarias.*

"I advise young men to note down in writing and treasure up in a permanent form every piece of valuable information, classical, scientific, and of any other character, which they might now pick up."—*Cardinal Wiseman.*

"What is a man,
If his chief good and market of his time
Be but to sleep and feed? A beast, no more.
Sure He that made us with such large discourse,
Looking before and after, gave us not
That capability and God-like reason
To fust in us unused."—*Shakspeare.*

Bird's-eye View of Some of the Choice Works in English Literature.

1. Poetry.

Longfellow, *Evangeline.*
Moore, *Irish Melodies.*
Tennyson, *Idylls of the King.*
Campbell, *Lyrics.*
Scott, *The Lady of the Lake.*
Burns, *Tam O'Shanter.*
Goldsmith, *The Deserted Village.*
Pope, *Essay on Criticism.*
Dryden, *Ode in Honor of St. Cecilia's Day.*
Milton, *Paradise Lost.*

2. The Drama.

Shakspeare, *Plays.*
Sheridan, *Plays.*

---

* Porson was considered a prodigy of Greek scholarship. It is said he could repeat most of the Greek poets by heart.

3. HISTORY.

MacCarthy, *History of Our Own Times*.
Green, *Short History of the English People*.
Lossing, *Field-Book of the Revolution*.
MacMaster, *History of the People of the United States*.
Parkman, *The Jesuits in North America*.
Walpole, *Short History of Ireland*.
Sullivan, *New Ireland*.
Creasy, *The Twelve Decisive Battles of the World*.
Prescott, *The Conquest of Mexico*.
Cobbett, *History of the Reformation*.
Maine, *Lectures on the Early History of Institutions*.
Adams, *Manual of Historical Literature*.

4. BIOGRAPHY.

Morley, *Life of Burke*.
Trevelyan, *Life and Letters of Lord Macaulay*.
Griffin, *Life of Gerald Griffin*.
Ticknor, *Life of William H. Prescott*.
Boswell, *Life of Dr. Johnson*.
Fitzpatrick, *Life and Times of Dr. Doyle*.
Irving, *Life of Goldsmith*.
Murray, *The Catholic Pioneers of America*.

5. AUTOBIOGRAPHY.

Franklin, *Autobiography*.
Cardinal Newman, *Apologia*.

6. FICTION.

Cooper, *The Spy*.
Hawthorne, *The Scarlet Letter*.
Griffin, *The Collegians*.
Carleton, *The Poor Scholar*.
Wiseman, *Fabiola*.
Dickens, *David Copperfield*.
Thackeray, *The Newcomes*.
Lever, *Charles O'Malley*.
Scott, *Ivanhoe*.
Goldsmith, *The Vicar of Wakefield*.
Defoe, *Robinson Crusoe*.

7. SKETCHES AND ESSAYS.

Irving, *The Sketch-Book*.
Bacon, *Essays*.

8. SPEECHES.

Burke, *Speeches*.
Grattan, *Speeches*.
Webster, *Speeches*.

9. Lectures and Sermons.

Reed, *Lectures on English Literature.*
Giles, *Lectures and Essays.*
Father Burke, O P., *Lectures and Sermons.*

10. Travels.

Dana, *Two Years before the Mast.*
Kinglake, *Eöthen.*
Vetromile, *Travels in Europe and the Holy Land.*

11. Philosophy.

Father Hill, S.J., *Moral Philosophy.*
Father Harper, S J., *The Metaphysics of the Schools.*
Edmund Burke, *Reflections on the Revolution in France.*
Brother Azarias, *Essay on a Philosophy of Literature.*
Herbert Spencer, *The Philosophy of Style.*

12. Popular Science.

St. George Mivart, *Lessons from Nature.*
C F. Devas, *The Groundwork of Economics.*
Cardinal Wiseman, *The Connection between Science and Revealed Religion.*
Father Ronayne, S.J., *Religion and Science.*

13. Miscellaneous.

Gibbons, *The Faith of Our Fathers.*
Lambert, *Notes on Ingersoll.*
Boudreaux, *The Happiness of Heaven.*
Washington, *Farewell Address.*
Brownson, *The American Republic.*

☞ Those who wish to add to their mental wealth by the thorough study of a few great authors cannot do better than to devote their best hours to the earnest reading of the *New Testament, Shakspeare, Edmund Burke, and Cardinal Newman.*

The true student, however, will " never forget that good literature is not an insular affair, bounded by the limits of one country or by the letters of one language." Familiarity with many languages is no longer necessary as a key to open the masterpieces of other times and other countries. We have many excel'ent translations. " A knowledge of ancient literature," says Henry Reed, " gives us a deeper insight into the modern."

Bird's-eye View of Some of the Ancient and Modern Classics.

1. GREEK.—Homer, *The Iliad;* * Thucydides, *History of the Peloponnesian War;* Demosthenes, *Speeches;* Plutarch, *Lives of Celebrated Greeks and Romans.*

2. LATIN.—Virgil, *The Æneid;*† Tacitus, *Annals* and *Histories* ; Cicero, *Orations;* A Kempis, *The Imitation of Christ.*‡

3. FRENCH.—Lacordaire, *Letters to Young Men;* Souvestre, *The Attic Philosopher;* De Tocqueville, *Democracy in America;* Montalembert, *The Monks of the West;* Chateaubriand, *The Genius of Christianity;* St. Pierre, *Paul and Virginia;* Fénelon, *Telemachus;* Bossuet, *Universal History;* St. Francis de Sales, *Introduction to a Devout Life.*

4 GERMAN.—F. Schlegel, *The Philosophy of History* § and *Lectures on the History of Literature;* Moeller, *Symbolism;* A. Humboldt, *The Cosmos;* Schiller, *Poems;* Fouqué, *Undine.*

5. SPANISH.—Balmes, *European Civilization;* ‖ Donoso Cortes, *Essays;* Calderon,¶ *Dramas;* Cervantes, *Don Quixote.*

6. ITALIAN —Pellico, *My Prisons* and *The Duties of Young Men;* Manzoni, *The Betrothed;* Tasso, *Jerusalem Delivered;* Dante, *The Divine Comedy.*

---

* The poet Pope's translation is, on the whole, the best for the general reader.
† There are various popular editions of the poet Dryden's translation.
‡ Bishop Challoner's translation is, perhaps, the best.
§ Robertson's translation is good and faithful.
‖ His *Criterion* and *Fundamental Philosophy* should be carefully read.
¶ D. F. MacCarthy's translation is unrivalled.

A SHORT DICTIONARY

OF

BRITISH, IRISH, AND AMERICAN AUTHORS.

ABBREVIATIONS USED.

I..................Ireland.	C...................Catholic.
E..................England.	P...................Protestant.
S..................Scotland.	Lit.................Literature.
U. S..............United States.	Hist................History.

The letter P. is used for all non-Catholics. The dash in the second column indicates that the author is living.

(1) Poem.   (2) Fiction.   (3) Drama.

NAME.	DATE OF DEATH.	COUNTRY.	RELIGION.	CHIEF WORK.
ADAM'NAN, SAINT......	704	I.	C.	*Life of St. Columbkille.*
ADDIS, REV. W. E......	—	E.	C.	*A Catholic Dictionary.**
ADDISON, JOSEPH	1719	E.	P.	*Essays in the Spectator.*
AKENSIDE, MARK.......	1770	E.	P.	*Pleasures of the Imagination.*¹
ALCUIN (ăl'kwin).......	804	E.	C.	*Letters.*
ALDHELM, SAINT.......	709	E.	C.	*The Praise of Virginity.*
ALDRICH, THOMAS B...	—	U.S.	P.	*Poems.*
ALFRED THE GREAT...	901	E.	C.	*Translations.*
ALISON, ARCHIBALD....	1867	E.	P.	*History of Europe.*
ALLIBONE, S. AUSTIN...	—	U.S.	P.	*Dictionary of Authors.*
ALLIES, THOMAS W....	—	E.	C.	*Formation of Christendom.*
ALLINGHAM, WILLIAM..	—	I.	P.	*Poems.*
ALLSTON, WASHINGTON	1843	U.S.	P.	*Poems.*
AR'BŬTHNOT, JOHN.....	1734	S.	P.	*History of John Bull.*²
ARNOLD, EDWIN........	—	E.	P.	*The Light of Asia.*¹
ARNOLD, REV. THOMAS.	1842	E	P.	*Lectures on Modern Hist.*
ARNOLD, THOMAS......	—	E.	C.	*Manual of English Lit.*
ARNOLD, MATTHEW.....	—	E.	P.	*Essays in Criticism.*
ASCHAM, ROGER........	1569	E.	P.	*The Schoolmaster.*
AUDOBON, J. J..........	1851	U.S.	P.	*Birds of America.*
AUSTEN, JANE	1817	E.	P.	*Pride and Prejudice.*²
AZARI'AS, BROTHER....	—	U.S.	C.	*Development of Eng. Lit.*

*Father Addis and Thomas Arnold are joint authors of the *Catholic Dictionary.*

Name.	Date of Death.	Country.	Religion.	Chief Work.
Bacon, Lord............	1626	E.	P.	Essays.
Bacon, Roger.........	1292	E.	C.	Opus Majus.*
Baillie, Joanna.......	1851	S.	P.	Plays on the Passions.
Bancroft, George....	—	U.S.	P.	Hist. of the United States.
Bancroft, Hubert H.	—	U.S.	P.	Hist. of the Pacific States.
Bán'im, John.........	1842	I.	C.	Father Connell.[2]
Barbour, Rev. John...	1396	S.	C.	The Bruce.[1]
Barrington, Sir J.....	1834	I.	P.	Rise and Fall of the Irish Nation.
Bayley, Archbishop..	1877	U.S.	C.	Life of Bishop Bruté.
Bayly, Thomas H......	1839	E.	P.	Songs.
Beattie, James........	1803	S.	P.	The Minstrel.[1]
Beaumont & Fletcher†	1615	E.	P.	Dramas.
Bède, Saint...........	735	E.	C.	Ecclesiastical History of the English Nation.‡
Berington, Rev. J.....	1827	E.	C.	Literary History of the Middle Ages.
Berkeley, Bishop.....	1753	I.	P.	Principles of Human Knowledge.
Black, William	—	S.	P.	Princess of Thule.[2]
Blackstone, Sir W..	1780	E.	P.	Commentaries on English Law.
Blaine, James G.......	—	U.S.	P.	Twenty Years in Congress.
Blair, Hugh	1800	S.	P.	Lectures on Rhetoric.
Blessington, Lady....	1849	I.	P.	The Repealers.[2]
Boker, George H....	—	U.S.	P.	Dramas.
Boswell, James.......	1795	S.	P.	Life of Dr. Sam'l Johnson.
Bowden, John E......	—	E.	C.	Life and Letters of Father Faber.
Boyce, Rev. John.....	1868	I.	C.	Shandy Maguire.[2]
Boyle, Sir Robert....	1691	I.	P.	Things above Reason.
Brewster, Sir David	1868	S.	P.	Letters on Natural Magic.
Bronte, Charlotte...	1855	I.	P.	Jane Eyre.[2]

* It is written in Latin, as the title implies.
† Francis Beaumont, 1586–1615; John Fletcher, 1576–1625. They were literary partners; hence their names always appear together. They wrote fifty-two plays. Beaumont and Fletcher rank among the famous dramatists of the days of Shakspeare, but their productions bear the marks of vice and grossness.
‡ "Thus much of the Ecclesiastical History of Britain," says the Saint at the end of his great work, "and more especially of the English nation, as far as I could learn from the writings of the ancients, or the traditions of our ancestors, or of my own knowledge, has, with the help of God, been digested by me, Bede, the servant of God and priest of the monastery of the Blessed Apostles Peter and Paul, which is at Wearmouth and Yarrow."

BRITISH, IRISH, AND AMERICAN AUTHORS. 425

NAME.	DATE OF DEATH.	COUNTRY.	RELIGION.	CHIEF WORK.
BROUGHAM (broom). LORD..	1868	S.	P.	*Lives of Men of Letters.*
BROWN, CHARLES B ...	1810	U.S.	P.	*Arthur Mervyn.*[2]
BROWN, THOMAS	1820	S.	P.	*Lectures on Mental Philosophy.*
BROWNE, SIR THOMAS..	1682	E.	P.	*Religio Medici.**
BROWNING, ROBERT ..	—	E.	P.	*The Ring and the Book.*[1]
BROWNING, MRS. E. B..	1861	E.	P.	*Aurora Leigh.*[1]
BROWNSON, ORESTES A.	1876	U.S.	C.	*The American Republic.*
BRYANT, WILLIAM C...	1878	U.S.	P.	*Poems.*
BRYANT, JOHN D..	1877	U.S.	C.	*Pauline Seward.*[2]
BUCKLE, THOMAS H....	1862	E.	P.	*History of Civilization.*†
BULWER-LYTTON	1873	E.	P.	*Last Days of Pompeii.*[2]
BUNYAN, JOHN ‡	1688	E.	P.	*The Pilgrim's Progress*[2]
BURKE, EDMUND........	1797	I.	P.	*Reflections on the Revolution in France.*
BURKE, REV. THOMAS N.	1883	I.	C.	*Lectures and Sermons.*
BURNEY, FRANCES.. ...	1840	E.	P.	*Cecilia.*[2]
BURNS, ROBERT	1796	S.	P.	*Poems.*
BUTLER, REV. ALBAN...	1773	E.	C.	*Lives of the Saints.*
BUTLER, CHARLES......	1832	E.	C.	*Historical Memoirs.*§
BUTLER, JOSEPH‖.......	1752	E.	P.	*The Analogy of Religion.*
BUTLER, SAMUEL	1680	E.	P.	*Hudibras.*[1]
BURTON, ROBERT.......	1640	E.	P.	*Anatomy of Melancholy.*
BYRON, LORD	1824	E.	P.	*Poems.*
CABLE, GEORGE W.....	—	U.S.	P.	*Old Creole Days.*
CÆDMON (kăd'mon).....	680	E.	C.	*Poems.*
CAHILL, REV. DR. D. W.	1864	I.	C.	*Letters and Lectures.*
CALHOUN, JOHN C.. ...	1850	U.S.	P.	*Speeches.*
CAMBRĔN'SIS,GIRĂL'DUS	1220	E.	C.	*Topographia Hibernicæ.*¶

* *The Religion of a Physician.* It is written in English. Besides giving Latin titles to his works, Dr. Browne went to an extreme length in loading his style with ponderous Latin words.
† An infidel work, written in brilliant English. The logic falls far short of the rhetoric. It is incomplete.
‡ Bunyan was a coarse, illiterate Puritan tinker, who finally became a Baptist minister. His *Pilgrim's Progress* is a much overpraised book. Fanatic that he was, Bunyan takes care to picture the Pope and the Catholic Church as two odious monsters. It has been asserted that the *Pilgrim's Progress* is, in the main, pilfered from a Catholic work of the fifteenth century.
§ The full title is, "Historical Memoirs of the English, Irish, and Scottish Catholics since the Reformation." It is in four volumes.
‖ A great thinker, but a very poor writer.
¶ *Description of Ireland.* It is written in Latin. Geraldus Cambrensis signifies Gerald of Wales, for he was a Welshman. His real name was *Gerald Barry.* He was a slanderer of Ireland and

NAME.	DATE OF DEATH.	COUNTRY.	RELIGION.	CHIEF WORK.
CAMDEN, WILLIAM	1623	E.	P.	*Britannia.*
CAMPBELL, GEORGE	1796	S.	P.	*Philosophy of Rhetoric.*
CAMPBELL, THOMAS	1844	S.	P.	*Poems.*
CAREY, HENRY C	—	U.S.	P.	*Principles of Political Economy.*
CAREY, MATTHEW	1839	I.	C.	*Ireland Vindicated.*
CARLETON, WILLIAM	1869	I.	C.	*The Poor Scholar.*[2]
CARLYLE, THOMAS	1881	S.	P.	*The French Revolution.*
CAXTON, WILLIAM	1491	E.	C.	*The History of Troy.*
CARY, ALICE	1871	U.S.	P.	*Poems.*
CHALLONER, BISHOP	1781	E.	C.	*Memoirs of Missionary Priests.*
CHALMERS, REV. DR. T.	1847	S.	P.	*Astronomical Discourses.*
CHAMBERS, ROBERT	1871	S.	P.	*Cyclopœdia of English Lit.*
CHAMBERS, WILLIAM	—	S.	P.	*Things as they are in America.*
CHAPMAN, GEORGE	1634	E.	P.	*Translation of Homer.**
CHATTERTON, THOMAS.†	1770	E.	P.	*Poems.*
CHAUCER, GEOFFREY	1400	E.	C.	*The Canterbury Tales.*[1]
CHURCHILL, C	1764	E.	P.	*Rosciad.*[1]
CLARE, SISTER M. F.	—	I.	C.	*History of the Irish People.*
CLARENDON, EARL OF	1674	E.	P.	*History of the Great Rebellion.*
CLARKE, RICHARD H	—	U.S.	C.	*Lives of the Deceased Catholic Bishops of the U. S.*
CLAY, HENRY	1852	U.S.	P.	*Speeches.*
CLEMENS, SAMUEL L.‡	—	U.S.	P.	*The Innocents Abroad.*[2]
COBBETT, WILLIAM	1835	E.	P.	*Hist. of the Reformation.*§
COLERIDGE, SAMUEL T.	1834	E.	P.	*Poems.*

the Irish people, and a very inaccurate writer. For instance, he informs his readers that Ireland's greatest river, the Shannon, discharges itself into the North Sea.

* This was the *first* English translation of Homer. "Chapman's *Homer* still survives," says Hart, "and is even now in good repute, and is preferred by many to that of Pope."

† Chatterton died in his eighteenth year. He is the *youngest* author holding a place in English letters; but he was an erratic and unfortunate genius.

‡ He is better known by the *nom de plume* of "Mark Twain." He was for some time a steamboat-pilot on the Mississippi; hence the name " Mark Twain," which means *two fathoms.*

§ The full title of the work is, *A History of the Reformation in England and Ireland, in a Series of Letters.* The letters, sixteen in number, were written in 1824, 1825, and 1826. The volume is one that will well repay a careful perusal. It is the best specimen of vigorous idiomatic English that has appeared during the present century.

BRITISH, IRISH, AND AMERICAN AUTHORS. 427

NAME.	DATE OF DEATH.	COUNTRY.	RELIGION.	CHIEF WORK.
CŎL'OAN, REV JOHN....	1658	I.	C.	Lives of the Irish Saints.
COLLINS, WILLIAM......	——	I.	C.	Poems and Songs.
COLLINS, WILLIAM. ...	1759	E.	P.	Poems.
COLUMBKILLE (kolum-kill'), SAINT	597	I.	C.	Poems.
CONYNGHAM, D. P......	1883	I.	C.	Lives of the Irish Saints.
COOKE, JOHN E	——	U.S.	P.	The Virginia Comedians.²
COOPER, JAMES F	1851	U.S.	P.	The Spy.²
COWLEY, ABRAHAM*...	1667	E.		Poems.
COWPER, WILLIAM.....	1800	E.	P.	Poems.
CRABBE, GEORGE.......	1832	E.	P.	Poems.
CRAIK, GEORGE L......	1866	S.	P.	Hist. of the English Literature and Language.†
CRAIK, MRS. D M......	——	E.	P.	John Halifax,Gentleman.²
CRASHAW, REV. R......	1650	E.	C.	Poems.
CREASY, E. S., SIR.....	1878	E.	P.	The Fifteen Decisive Battles of the World.
CROLY, REV. DR. GEO..	1860	I.	P.	Poems.
CUNNINGHAM, ALLAN...	1842	S.	P.	Poems.
CURRAN, JOHN P.......	1817	I.	P.	Speeches
CURTIS, GEORGE W....	——	U.S.	P.	The Potiphar Papers
CŪ'SACK, MISS..........		E.		(See "Clare, Sister M. F.")
DALGAIRNS, REV. B. J..	?	E.	C.	The Holy Communion—its Philosophy, Theology, and Practice.
DĀ'NA, RICHARD H.....	1882	U.S.	P.	Two Years Before the Mast.⁴
DANA, JAMES D........	——	U.S.	P.	Geological Story Briefly Told.
DARWIN, CHARLES R...	1882	E.	P.	Origin of Species.
DĀV'ENANT, SIR W. ...	1668	E.	C.	Gondibert.¹
DAVIDSON, J. W........	——	U.S.	P.	The Living Writers of the South.
DAVIS, THOMAS O..:....	1845	I.	P.	Poems and Essays.
DAVY, SIR HUMPHRY...	1829	E.	P.	Last Days of a Philosopher.
DE FOE, DANIEL........	1731	E.	P.	Robinson Crusoe.
DE QUINCEY, THOMAS .	1859	E.	P.	Confessions of an Opium-Eater.
DERBY, EARL OF	1869	E.	P.	Translation of Homer.
DESMĒT', REV. P. J.,S.J.	1872	Belg.	C.	Indian Letters and Sketches.
DEVAS. C F	——	E.	C	Groundwork of Economics.
DE VĒRE, AUBREY......	——	I.	C.	Poems and Dramas.

* "Abraham Cowley," says Hart, "was accounted in his day the greatest of English poets. This verdict has long since been reversed."

† This is one of the very best works on the subject. Craik was a sound, learned critic.

Name.	Date of Death.	Country.	Religion.	Chief Work.
De Vere, Sir A........	1846	I.	P.	Dramas.
De Vere, M. S.........	—	Swd.	P.	Studies in English.
Dickens, Charles.....	1870	E.	P.	David Copperfield.[2]
Digby, Kenelm H......	—	E.	C.	The Ages of Faith.
Dillon, W	1684	I.	P.	Poems.
Disraeli (diz·rā'el-ee), Benjamin*...........	1882	E.	P.	Endymion.[2]
Disraeli, Isaac........	1848	E.	Jew.	Curiosities of Literature.†
Dixon, Archbishop...	—	I.	C.	Introduction to the Sacred Scriptures.
Dodd, Rev. Charles...	1745	E.	C.	Church Hist. of England.‡
Donnelly, Miss E. C..	—	U.S.	C.	Poems.
Dorsey, Mrs. Anna H	—	U.S	C.	The Flemmings.[2]
Douglas, Bishop.....	1522	S.	C.	Translation of Virgil.
Doyle, Bishop James..	1834	I.	C.	Letters on the State of Ireland.
Drake, Joseph R.§....	1820	U.S	P.	The American Flag.[1]
Drayton, Michael....	1631	E.	P.	Polyolbion.‖
Dryden, John	1700	E.	C.	Poems.
Dufferin, Lord.......	—	I.	P.	Letters from High Latitudes.
Duffy, Sir Charles G.	—	I.	C.	Young Ireland.
Dunbar, William......	1530	S.	C.	Dance of the Seven Deadly Sins.[1]
Dunstan, Saint.......	988	E.	C.	Concord of Monastic Rules.
Duyckinck (dī'kink), E. A...	1878	U.S	P.	Cyclopædia of American Literature.

* Afterwards Lord Beaconsfield. A vein of scandal runs through nearly all his fictions.
† A *curious* work indeed, but in many respects a bad, bigoted production. The elder Disraeli had a hearty hatred of everything Catholic, as is proved by many of the lying " Curiosities" which he so carefully gathered together.
‡ A valuable work on which Father Dodd is said to have spent thirty years. It was written in reply to the Protestant historian Burnet.
§ On the death of Drake, Halleck wrote the beautiful poem beginning with the oft-quoted stanza:
" Green be the turf above thee,
Friend of my better days!
None knew thee but to love thee,
Nor named thee but to praise."
‖ The *Polyolbion* is a poetical ramble over all England, and fills thirty ponderous books.

BRITISH, IRISH, AND AMERICAN AUTHORS.

NAME.	DATE OF DEATH.	COUNTRY.	RELIGION.	CHIEF WORK.
EDGEWORTH, MARIA....	1849	E.	P.	Tales and Novels.
EDWARDS, JONATHAN *.	1758	U.S.	P.	On Freedom of the Will.
* EL'IOT. GEORGE "†....	1880	E.	—	The Mill on the Floss.[2]
EMERSON, RALPH W....	1882	U.S.	P.	Representative Men.
ENGLAND, BISHOP.. ...	1842	I.	C.	Essays and Discourses (in 5 vols.).
ERIGENA, JOHN S	875	I.	C.	On the Division of Nature.
EVERETT, EDWARD.....	1865	U.S.	P.	Orations and Speeches.
EXTER, JOSEPH OF....		E.	C.	The Trojan War.
FABER. REV. DR F. W.	1863	E.	C.	All for Jesus.
FALCONER, WILLIAM....	1769	S.	P	The Shipwreck.[1]
FARADAY, MICHAEL ...	1867	E.	P	Chemistry of a Candle.
FIELDING, HENRY....	1754	E.	P.	Tom Jones.[2]
FISHER, BISHOP.	1535	E.	C.	Sermons and Letters.
FITZPATRICK, W. J.....		I.	C.	Life and Times of Bishop Doyle.
FORD, MRS. A. ("Una")	1876	I.	C.	Poems.
FORSTER, JOHN..	1875	E.	P.	Life of Goldsmith.
FRANCIS, SIR PHILIP....	1818	I.	P.	Letters of Junius.
FRANKLIN, BENJAMIN..	1790	U.S.	P.	Autobiography.
FREDET, REV. DR.	1856	F.	C.	Ancient and Modern Hist.
FREEMAN, EDWARD A..	—	E.	P.	History of the Norman Conquest of England.
FRENEAU, PHILIP......	1832	U.S	P.	Poems.
FROUDE (frood), J. A.‡.	—	E.	P.	History of England.
FULLERTON, LADY G...	—	E.	C.	Too Strange not to be True.

* He was a learned Calvinistic minister.
† "George Eliot" is the *nom de plume* of the late Mrs. Cross. Her maiden name was Marian Evans. She was a woman of uncommon genius, and her works of fiction show great power, originality, mental grasp, and high artistic finish. Unhappily, however, she belonged to the rationalistic school of writers. Mrs. Cross was an admiring disciple of Herbert Spencer.
‡ Froude is a very unsafe authority. His style is elegant, but his statements are often so twisted and colored that they must be received with a wise caution.
"When Mr. Froude is most *inaccurate*," says the historian Freeman, "when he is most *thoroughly ignorant* of the subject on which he writes, he still writes with an air of quiet confidence which is likely to take in all whose own studies have not qualified them to answer him. It is because the air of confidence is so quiet that it is so dangerous. Never, surely, did a false prophet succeed so thoroughly in putting on the outward garb of the true."—*Contemporary Review*, 1878.
Froude's *History of England* is in twelve volumes, and extends from the fall of Wolsey to the death of Elizabeth.

NAME.	DATE OF DEATH.	COUNTRY.	RELIGION.	CHIEF WORK.
GALLĪT'ZIN, REV. D. A..	1840	Rus.	C.	Defence of Catholic Principles.
GAY, JOHN	1732	E.	P.	Poems and Dramas.
GEOFFREY OF MONMOUTH	1154	E.	C.	History of the Britons.
GIBBON, EDWARD	1794	E.	P.	Decline and Fall of the Roman Empire.
GIBBONS, ARCHBISHOP.	—	U.S.	C.	The Faith of our Fathers.
GIFFORD, WILLIAM	1826	E.	P.	The Baviad.[1]
GIL'DAS, SAINT	565	S.	C.	History of the Britons.
GILES, HENRY	1882	I.	P.	Lectures and Essays.
GLADSTONE, W. E.	—	E.	P.	Studies on Homer.
GOLDSMITH, OLIVER	1774	I.	P.	The Deserted Village.[1]
GRIFFIN, GERALD	1840	I.	C.	The Collegians.[2]
GOOD, JOHN MASON	1827	E.	P.	The Book of Nature.
GODWIN, PARKE	—	U.S.	P.	Life of W. C. Bryant.
GOTHER, REV. JOHN	1704	E.	C.	A Papist Misrepresented and Represented.
GOWER, JOHN	1408	E.	C.	The Confessio Amantis.
GRATTAN, HENRY	1820	I.	P.	Speeches.
GRAVES, ARTHUR P..	—	I.	P.	Irish Songs and Ballads.
GRAY, THOMAS	1771	E.	P.	Elegy Written in a Country Churchyard.
GREELEY, HORACE	1872	U.S.	P.	Recollections of a Busy Life.
GREEN, GEORGE W	1883	U.S.	P.	Historical View of the American Revolution.
GREEN, JOHN R	1883	E.	P.	Hist. of the English People*
GRISWOLD, RUFUS W...	1857	U.S.	P.	Prose Writers of America.
GROTE, GEORGE†	1871	E.	P.	The History of Greece.
HĂK'LUYT, RICHARD..	1616	E.	P.	Voyages.
HALL, MRS. S C	1881	I.	P.	Lights and Shadows of Irish Life.
HALLAM, HENRY	1859	E.	P.	Literature of Europe.
HALLECK, FITZ GREENE	1867	U.S.	P.	Poems.
HAMILTON, ALEXANDER	1804	W.I.	P.	The Federalist.
HAMILTON, SIR W.	1856	S.	P.	Lectures on Logic and Metaphysics.
HARPER, REV. THOMAS	—	E.	C.	Metaphysics of the School
HAR'E, BRET	—	U.S.	P.	Luck of Roaring Camp.[2]
HASSARD, JOHN R. G...	—	U.S.	C.	Life of Archb. Hughes.
HAVERTY, MARTIN	—	I.	C.	History of Ireland.

* It is a work of great merit.
† Grote was an English banker, but a marvel of Greek scholarship. His *History of Greece* is a work of great power and originality—the greatest work on the subject in our language.

Name.	Date of Death.	Country.	Religion.	Chief Work.
Hawthorne, N........	1864	U.S.	P.	House of the Seven Gables.[2]
Haz'litt, William....	1830	E.	P.	Lectures on the Eng. Poets.
Headley, J. T........	—	U.S.	P.	Washington and his Generals.
Hecker, Rev. Isaac T.	—	U.S.	C.	Questions of the Soul.
Hay, Bishop George..	1811	S.	C.	The Sincere Christian.*
Helps, Sir Arthur...	1875	E.	P.	Life of Hernando Cortés.
Hemans, Mrs. Felicia.	1835	E.	P.	Poems.
Herbert, Lady.......	—	E.	C.	Cradle Lands.
Herrick, Robert.....	1662	E.	P.	Lyrics.
Hewitt, Rev. A. F ...	—	U.S.	C.	Life of Father Baker.
Hildreth, Richard ..	1865	U.S.	P.	Hist. of the United States.
Hilliard, George S...	—	U.S.	P.	Six Months in Italy.
Hillhouse, James A ..	1841	U.S	P.	Hadad.[3]
Hoffman, Charles F..	1884	U.S.	P.	Knickerbocker Magazine.
Hoffman, Mary 1.....	—	U'S.	C.	The Two Orphans.[2]
Holinshed, Raphael.	1580	E.	P.	Chronicles of England, Scotland, and Ireland.
Holland, Sir Henry..	1873	E	P.	Recollections of Past Life.
Holmes, Oliver W....	—	U.S.	P.	Autocrat at the Breakfast-Table.[2]
Hood, Thomas.........	1845	E.	P.	The Bridge of Sighs.[1]
Hooker, Richard.....	1600	E.	P.	Ecclesiastical Polity.
Hopkinson, J..........	1842	U.S.	P.	Hail, Columbia.†
Howard, Henry.......	1547	E.	C.	Poems.
Howard, Timothy E...	—	U.S.	C.	Essays on Politeness and Education.
Howells, William D..	—	U.S.	P.	Suburban Sketches.[2]
Hughes, Archbishop..	1864	I.	C.	Letters and Discourses (in 2 vols.).
Hughes, Thomas.......	—	E.	P.	Tom Brown's School-Days.[2]
Hume, David..........	1776	S.	P.	History of England.
Hunt, Leigh..........	1859	E.	P.	Poems.
Huntington, J. V......	1869	U.S.	C.	Rosemary.[2]
Huntington, Henry of	—	E.	P.	History of England.
Huxley, Thomas H....	—	E.	P.	Lay Sermons.
Ingelow, Jean........	—	E.	P.	Poems.
Ingersoll, Charles J.	1862	U.S.	P.	Hist. of the War of 1812.
Irving, Washington..	1859	U.S.	P.	Life and Voyages of Columbus.
Ives, Dr. Levi S.......	1867	U.S.	C.	Trials of a Mind in its Progress to Catholicism.
James I. of Scotland.	1437	S.	C.	The King's Quire.[1]

* The full title is, *The Sincere Christian Instructed in the Faith of Christ, from the Written Word.* It is a work of great excellence.
† This patriotic song gives Hopkinson a place in literature.

432   A SHORT DICTIONARY OF

NAME.	DATE OF DEATH.	COUNTRY.	RELIGION.	CHIEF WORK.
JAMESON, MRS. ANNA..	1860	I.	P.	Sacred and Legendary Art.
JEFFERSON, THOMAS...	1826	U.S.	P.	The Declaration of Independence.
JEFFREY, LORD	1850	S.	P.	Essays in the Edinburgh Review.
JERROLD, DOUGLAS.....	1857	E.	P.	Caudle Curtain-Lectures.
JOHNSON, DR. SAMUEL..	1784	E.	P.	English Dictionary.
JONSON, BEN...........	1637	E.	P.	Every Man in his Humor.[3]
JOYCE, ROBERT D.....	1883	I	C.	Deirdre.[1]
KAMES, LORD..........	1782	S.	P.	Elements of Criticism.*
KANE, DR. E. K.......	1857	U.S.	P.	Accounts of his Arctic Expeditions.
KANE, SIR ROBERT.....	—	I.	P.	Resources of Ireland.
KAVANAGH, JULIA......	1878	I.	C.	Women of Christianity.
KEATING, REV. DR. G..	1644	I.	C.	History of Ireland.
KEATS, JOHN..........	1820	E.	P.	Poems.
KĒ'BLE, REV. JOHN....	1866	E.	P.	The Christian Year.†
KENNEDY, J. P........	1870	U.S	P.	Horse-Shoe Robinson.[2]
KENT, JAMES..........	1847	U.S	P.	Commentaries on American Law.
KENRICK, ABP. P. R...	—	I.	C.	The Holy House of Loretto.
KENRICK, ABP. P. F...	1864	I.	C.	Primacy of the Apostolic Sea.
KEY, FRANCIS S.......	1843	U.S.	P.	Star-Spangled Banner.[1]
KINGLAKE, A. W.......	1870	E.	P.	Invasion of the Crimea.
KIP, BISHOP..........	1872	U.S.	P.	Early Jesuit Missions in North America.
KNOWLES, JAMES S.....	1862	I.	P.	William Tell.[3]
LAMB, CHARLES........	1834	E.	P.	The Essays of Elia.
LAMBING, REV. A. A...	—	U.S.	C.	History of the Catholic Church in Pittsburg.
LANDOR, WALTER S....	1864	E.	P.	Imaginary Conversations.
LANGLAND, WILLIAM...	14th c.	E.	C.	The Vision of Piers Plowman.[1]
LANIGAN, REV. DR. J..	1828	I.	C.	Ecclesiastical History of Ireland.
LAYAMON	13th c.	E.	C.	The Brutus of England.[1]
LAYARD, AUSTIN H.....	—	E.	P.	Ninevah and its Remains.
LECKY, WILLIAM E. H.‡	—	I.	P.	History of England in the Eighteenth Century.
LESLIE, MISS ELIZA ...	1857	U.S.	P.	Mrs. Washington Potts.[2]

* It was the earliest work on the subject in our language.
† The full title is, The Christian Year; or, Thoughts in Verse for the Sundays and Holidays throughout the Year.
‡ An able writer of infidel tendencies. He is commonly bitter and offensive when speaking of the Catholic Church.

Name.	Date of Death	Country	Religion	Chief Work.
Le'ver, Charles J	1872	I.	P.	Charles O'Malley.[2]
Le Vert, Madame	—	U.S.	P.	Souvenirs of Travel.
Lin'gard, Rev. Dr. J..	1851	E.	C.	History of England.
Locke, John	1704	E.	P.	Essay on the Human Understanding.
Lockhart, John G....	1854	S.	P.	Memoirs of Sir Walter Scott.
Lodge, Henry Cabot ..	—	U.S.	P.	Short History of the English Colonies in America.
Lombard, Archbishop.	1632	I.	C.	Commentary on Irish Hist.
Longfellow, Henry W	1882	U.S.	P.	Evangeline.[1]
Lossing, Benson J	—	U.S.	P.	Field-Book of the Revolution.
Lover, Samuel	1868	I.	P.	Poems.
Lo'well, James R ...	—	U.S.	P.	Among my Books.
Lydgate, Father J ...	1430?	E.	C.	Poems.
Lyell, Sir Charles...	1878	E.	P.	Travels in N. America.*
Lynch, Bishop John.	17th c.	I.	C.	Cambrensis Eversus.†
Lytton, Bulwer.......	1873	E.	P.	Pelham.[2]
Macaulay, Lord	1859	E.	P.	Essays.
MacCarthy, Justin ..	—	I.		Hist. of Our Own Times.‡
MacCarthy, Denis F..	1882	I.	C.	Poems.
MacCabe, William B..	—	I.	C.	Catholic Hist. of England.
MacCullinan, Cormac.	903	I.	C.	Psalter of Cashel.
Macgeoghegan, Abbé.	1750	I.	P.	History of Ireland.
MacGee, Thomas D....	1867	I.	C.	History of Ireland.
MacGill, Bishop	1872	U.S.	C.	Our Faith the Victory.
MacHale, Archbishop	1881	I.	C.	Letters.
Mackenzie, Henry....	1831	S.	P.	The Man of Feeling.[2]
Mackenzie, Dr. R. S..	1882	I.	P.	Life of Charles Dickens.
Mackintosh, Sir J....	1832	S.	P.	Progress of Ethical Philosophy.
MacLeod, Rev. D. X...	1865	U.S.	C.	Devotion to the Blessed Virgin in N. America.
MacMaster, John B...	—	U.S.	P.	History of the People of the United States.
Macpherson, James...	1796	S.	P.	Poems of Ossian.
MacSherry, James ...	1869	U S.	C.	History of Maryland.
MacSherry, Richard	—	U.S.	C.	Essays and Lectures.
Madden, Richard R...	—	I.	C.	The United Irishmen.
Maginn, Dr. William.	1842	I.	P.	Miscellanies.
Maguire, John F.. ..	1872	I.	C.	The Irish in America.

* Lyell is the author of several learned works on *Geology*.
† *Cambrensis Overthrown.* It is a refutation of the errors and calumnies of Gerald Barry, or Giraldus Cambrensis.
‡ It covers from the beginning of the reign of Queen Victoria till 1880, and is an interesting and valuable work.

Name.	Date of Death.	Country.	Religion.	Chief Work.
Mahon, Lord............	——	E.	P.	*History of England.* *
Mahony, Rev. Francis	1866	I.	C.	*Reliques of Father Prout.*
Maine, Sir Henry S..	——	E.	P.	*Lectures on the Early History of Institutions.*
Mal′lory, Sir T.......	15th c.	E.	C.	*History of King Arthur.*
Malmesbury (mams′-ber-e), William of...	12th c	E.	C.	*Hist. of Kings of England.*
Mandeville, Sir J.....	1372	E.	C.	*Travels.*
Mangan, James C......	1849	I.	C.	*Poems.*
Manning, Cardinal...	——	E.	C.	*Four Great Evils of the Day.*
Marlow, Christopher	1593	E.	P.	*Edward II.*[3]
Marryat (măr′I-at), Captain†.........	1848	E.	P.	*Jacob Faithful.*[2]
Marsh, George P......	——	U. S.	P.	*Lectures on Eng. Language*
Marshall, T. W. M....	1878	E.	C.	*Christian Missions.*
Mas′singer, Philip....	1640	E.	C.‡	*New Way to pay Old Debts.*[3]
Masson, David.........	——	S.	P.	*Life and Times of Milton.*
Mather, Cotton.......	1728	U. S.	P.	*Magnalia Christi Americana.*§
Meagher (mäh′er), T. F	1867	I.	C.	*Speeches.*
Meehan, Rev. C. P....	——.	I.	C.	*O'Neill and O'Donnell.*
Mel′Ine, J. F...........	1873	U.S.	C.	*Mary, Queen of Scots.*
Merivale, Rev. C......	——	E	P.	*History of the Romans.*
Miles, George H......	1871	U.S.	C.	*Poems.*
Miller, Hugh.........	1856	S.	P.	*Testimony of the Rocks.*
Miller, Joaquin‖.....	——	U.S.	P.	*Poems.*
Milner, Bishop John..	1826	E.	C.	*The End of Controversy.*
Milton, John..........	1674	E.	P.	*Paradise Lost.*
Minot, Lawrence....	14th c.	E.	C.	*Poems.*
Mitchel, John........	1875	I.	P.	*History of Ireland.*
Mitchell, D. G¶..... .	——	U. S.	P.	*Dream-Life.*
Mitford, Miss M. R...	1855	E.	P.	*Belford Regis.*
Mi′vart, St. George**	——	E.	C.	*Lessons from Nature.*

* It covers from the Peace of Utrecht to the Peace of Versailles, 1717 to 1783.
† Marryat stands at the head of British sea-novelists as an easy, lively, and truly humorous story-teller.
‡ "A close and repeated perusal of Massinger's works has convinced me that he was a Catholic."—*Gifford.*
§ Great Works of Christ in America.
‖ His real name is *Cincinnatus Heine Miller;* but in 1870 he published a volume of poems, one of which bearing the name of "Joaquin," he has since that time assumed the name for himself.—*Hart.*
¶ He is better known by his *nom de plume* of "Ik Marvel."
** As a scientist, Prof. Mivart stands in the front rank. His *Genesis of Species* and *Lessons from Nature* are able offsets to the materialistic theories of Darwin, Huxley, etc.

BRITISH, IRISH, AND AMERICAN AUTHORS. 435

NAME.	DATE OF DEATH.	COUNTRY.	RELIGION.	CHIEF WORK.
MOIR, DAVID M.........	1870	S.	P.	Poems.
MOLLOY, REV. GERALD.	—	I.	C.	Geology and Revelation.
MOLYNEAUX, W.......	1698	I.	P.	Case of Ireland stated.
MONMOUTH, GEOFFREY OF..................	1154	E.	C.	History of the Britons.
MONTAGU, LADY MARY	1761	E.	P.	Letters.
MONTGOMERY, JAMES...	1854	S.	P.	Poems.
MOORE, THOMAS........	1852	I.	C.	The Irish Melodies.
MORAN, ARCHBISHOP...	—	I.	C.	History of the Catholic Archbishops of Dublin.
MORE, SIR THOMAS.....	1535	E.	C.	Utopia.²
MORE, HANNAH......	1833	E.	P.	The Religion of the Fashionable World
MŌRIĀR'TY, REV. P. E..	1875	I.	C.	Life of St. Augustine.
MORIARTY, REV. J. J...	—	I.	C.	Stumbling - Blocks made Stepping-Stones.
MORGAN, LADY.........	1859	I.	P.	O'Donnell.²
MORRIS, WILLIAM......	—	E.	P.	Poems.
MORRIS, GEORGE P.....	1864	U.S.	P.	Songs.
MORRIS, REV. J. S. J...	—	E.	P.	Troubles of our Catholic Forefathers.
MOTLEY, J. LOTHROP ..	1877	U.S.	P.	History of the United Netherlands.
MÜLLER (miller), MAX..	—	Ger.	P.	Chips from a German Workshop.
MULOCH, MISS D. M....	—	E.	P.	John Halifax, Gentleman.²
MURRAY, CHARLES A...	—	S.	P.	Travels in North America.
MURRAY, JAMES A. H..	—	E.	P.	Dictionary of the English Language.
MURRAY, LINDLEY......	1826	U.S.	P.	English Grammar.
MURRAY, ARCHBISHOP.	1852	I.	C.	Sermons.
MURRAY, REV. DR P...	1883	I.	C.	Poems.
MURRAY, PATRICK J....	—	I.	C.	Life of John Banim.
NAPIER, SIR W. F. P...	1866	I.	P.	History of the War in the Peninsula.
NEWMAN, CARDINAL....	—	E.	C.	Apologia pro Vita Sua.
NEWTON, SIR ISAAC....	1727	E.	P.	Principia.*
NORTON, MRS. C........	1878	I.	P.	Poems.
O'CALLAGHAN, DR. E. B.	1879	I.	C.	History of the New Netherlands.
O'CALLAGHAN, J. C.....	1882	I.	C.	History of the Irish Brigades.
O'CLERY, BROTHER M..	1643	I.	C.	Annals of the Four Masters.
O'CONNELL, DANIEL....	1847	I	C.	Speeches.

* This is Newton's great work. It is in Latin, the full title being, *Philosophiæ Naturalis Principia Mathematica*.

NAME.	DATE OF DEATH.	COUNTRY.	RELIGION.	CHIEF WORK.
O'CONOR, WILLIAM A..	—	I.	C.	History of the Irish People.
O'CURRY, EUGENE......	1862	I.	C.	Lectures on the Manuscript Materials of Ancient Irish History.
O'DONOVAN, EDMUND...	1884	I.	C.	Adventures in Merv.
O'DONOVAN, JOHN.....	1861	I.	C.	Grammar of the Irish Language.
O'FLAHERTY, R	1718	I.	C.	Ogygia.
O'HALLORAN, S...	1807	I.	C.	History of Ireland.
O'HANLON, REV. JOHN.	—	I.	C.	Lives of the Irish Saints.
OLIPHANT, MRS. M.....	—	S.	P.	The Days of my Life.*
O'MEARA, BARRY E....	1836	I.	C.	Napoleon in Exile.
O'MEARA, MISS K	—	I.	C.	Life of Ozanam.
O'REILLEY, REV. DR. B.	—	I.	C.	True Men as we Need Them.
O'REILLY, REV. DR. A. J	1878	I.	C.	Martyrs of the Coliseum.[2]
O'REILLY, J. BOYLE....	—	I.	C.	Ballads, Poems, and Songs.
OSGOOD, MRS. F. S.....	1850	U.S.	P.	Poems.
OSSIAN	3d c.	I.		Poems.
OTWAY, THOMAS........	1685	E.	P.	Dramas.
OSSOLI, MARGARET F.d'	1850	U.S.	P.	Critical Papers.
OTIS, JAMES..	1783	U.S.	P.	Vindication of the British Colonies.
PALEY, REV. DR. W....	1805	E.	P.	Natural Theology.
PAL'GRAVE, SIR F......	1861	E.	P.	Hist. of the Anglo-Saxons.
PARKMAN, FRANCIS.....	—	U.S.	P.	Jesuits in North America.
PARNELL, THOMAS......	1718	I.	P.	The Hermit.[1]
PARSONS, REV. R., S.J.	1610	E.	C.	A Christian Directory.
PARTON, JAMES........	—	E.	P.	Life of Horace Greeley.
PAULDING, JAMES K....	1860	U.S.	P.	John Bull and Brother Jonathan [2]
PAYNE, JOHN H........	1852	U.S.	P.	Home, Sweet Home.[1]
PERCIVAL, JAMES G....	1856	U.S.	P.	Poems.
PERCY, BISHOP........	1811	E.	P.	Reliques of Eng. Poetry.
PHILIPS, AMBROSE†....	1749	E.	P.	Poems.
PHILLIPS, CHARLES ...	1859	I.	P.	Life of J. P. Curran.
PHILLIPS, WENDELL....	1884	U.S.	P.	Orations.
PISE, REV. DR. C. C....	1866	U.S.	C.	St. Ignatius and his First Companions.
PIERPONT, JOHN........	1866	U.S.	P.	Poems.
PLEGMUND, ARCHB.....	9th c.	E.	C.	The Saxon Chronicle.

* An autobiography.
† Philips quarrelled with the poet Pope, but suffered for his temerity. Pope applied to him the novel epithet of "Namby Pamby," which has since been adopted into the language of vituperation.—Hart.

Name.	Date of Death.	Country.	Religion.	Chief Work.
Poe, Edgar A.	1849	U.S.	P.	The Raven.[1]
Pollard, E. Allan*	1872	U.S.	P.	The Lost Cause.
Pollok, Robert	1827	S.	P.	The Course of Time.[1]
Pope, Alexander	1744	E.	C.	Poems.
Porter, Jane	1850	E.	P.	The Scottish Chiefs.[2]
Prendergast, John P.	1881	I.	P.	The Cromwellian Settlement of Ireland.
Prescott, William H.	1859	U.S.	P.	History of the Conquest of Mexico.
Preston, Mrs. M. J.	—	U.S.	P.	Poems.
Preston, Mgr. T. S.	—	U.S.	C.	The Vicar of Christ.
Prior, Matthew	1721	E.	P.	Poems.
Procter, Miss A. A.	1864	E.	C.	Poems.
Procter, Bryan W.†	1877	E.	P.	Poems.
Quarles, Francis.	1644	E.	P.	Poems.
Quinn, Michael I.	1843	I.	C.	A Visit to Spain.
Radcliffe, Mrs. Ann.	1823	E.	P.	Mysteries of Udolpho.[2]
Raleigh (raw'lee), Sir Walter.	1618	E.	P.	History of the World.
Ramsay, Allan	1758	S.	P.	The Gentle Shepherd.[1]
Ramsay, David	1815	U.S	P.	Hist. of the United States.
Reade, Charles	1884	E.	P.	Peg Woffington.[2]
Read, Thomas B.	1872	U.S	P.	Poems.
Reed, Henry	1854	U.S.	P.	Lect. on Eng. Literature.
Reid, Mayne	1884	I.	P.	The Rifle-Rangers.[2]
Reid, Thomas	1796	S.	P.	Enquiry into the Human Mind.
Richardson, Samuel	1761	E.	P.	Pamela.[2]
Robert of Gloucester	13th c.	E.	C.	A Rhyming Chronicle.
Robertson, W.	1793	S.	P.	History of America.
Rogers, Samuel	1855	E.	P.	Poems.
Roscoe, W. T.	1832	E.	P.	Life of Leo X.
Roscommon, Earl of	1684	I.	P.	Poems.
Rowe, Nicholas.	1718	E.	P.	Dramas.
Rouquette, Rev. A.	—	U.S.	C.	Poems.
Rush, Benjamin‡	1813	U.S.	P.	Essays.
Rush, James§	1869	U.S.	P.	The Philosophy of the Human Voice.
Ruskin, John	—	E.	P.	The Stones of Venice.

* Pollard is the chief historian of the Southern Confederacy.
† Better known as "Barry Cornwall."
‡ Dr. Rush was the most famous American physician of the Revolutionary times. He was one of the signers of the Declaration of Independence.
§ He was the son of Dr. Benjamin Rush. The *Philosophy of the Human Voice* is a masterpiece; it exhausts the subject.

NAME.	DATE OF DEATH.	COUNTRY.	RELIGION.	CHIEF WORK.
RUSSELL, REV. MATT...	—	I.	C.	Poems.
RUSSELL, REV.DR.C.W.	1880	I.	C.	Life of Cardinal Mezzofanti.
RYAN, REV. ABRAM J..	—	U.S.	C.	Poems.
SABINE, LORENZO	—	U.S.	P.	The American Loyalists.
SACKVILLE, THOMAS	1608	E.	P.	Mirror for Magistrates.[1]
SANDERS, REV. DR. N..	1580	E.	C.	Rise and Growth of the Anglican Schism.*
SARGENT, EPES	1882	U.S.	P.	The Standard Speaker.
SAVAGE, JOHN	—	I.	C.	Poems.
SAXE, JOHN G.	—	U.S.	P.	Poems.
SCHOOLCRAFT, H. R.	1864	U.S.	P.	Historical Information concerning the Indians.
SCOTT, SIR WALTER	1832	S.	P.	The Waverley Novels.
SCOTUS, DUNS	1308	I.	C.	Commentary on Lombard's Book of Sentences (in Latin).†
SEDGEWICK, MISS C. M.	1867	U.S.	P.	Hope Leslie.[2]
SHAKSPEARE, WILLIAM	1616	E.	C.	Dramas.
SHEA, JOHN G.	—	U.S.	C.	History of the Catholic Missions.
SHEA, JOHN A.	1845	I.	C.	Poems.
SHEIL, RICHARD L	1851	I.	C.	Speeches.
SHENSTONE, WILLIAM	1763	E.	P.	The Schoolmistress.[1]
SHELLEY, PERCY B.	1822	E.	P.	Poems.
SHERIDAN, RICHARD B.	1816	I.	P.	The School for Scandal.[2]
SHERMAN, WILLIAM T.	—	U.S.	P.	Military Memoirs.
SHIRLEY, JAMES	1666	E.	C.	Dramas.
SIDNEY, SIR PHILIP	1586	E.	P.	Defence of Poesie.
SIGOURNEY, MRS. L. H.	1865	U.S.	P.	Poems.
SIMMS, WILLIAM G.	1870	U.S.	P.	History of South Carolina.
SMITH, ADAM	1790	S.	P.	The Wealth of Nations.
SMITH, SYDNEY	1845	E.	P.	Essays and Letters.
SMOLLETT, TOBIAS	1771	S.	P.	Humphry Clinker.[2]
SOMERVILLE, MRS. M.	1872	E.	P.	Connection of the Physical Sciences.
SOUTHEY, ROBERT	1843	E.	P.	Poems.
SOUTHWELL, REV. R. S.J	1595	E.	C.	Poems.
SPALDING (spawl'ding), ARCHBISHOP	1872	U.S.	C.	Hist. of the Reformation ‡
SPALDING, BISHOP	—	U.S.	C.	Life of Archb. Spalding.
SPARKS, JARED	1866	U.S.	P.	American Biography.

* It was written in Latin, but has recently been translated. Dr. Sanders was one of the theologians at the Council of Trent.
† Called *Opus Oxoniense.*
‡ The fullest and most exhaustive work on the subject in English.

A SHORT DICTIONARY OF

Name.	Date of Death.	Country.	Religion.	Chief Work.
Tighe, Mrs. Mary *....	1810	I.	P.	Poems.
Tinker, Miss M. A.....	— —	U.S.	C.	Grapes and Thorns.[2]
Trench, Richard C....	—	E.	P.	On the Study of Words.
Trevelyan, G. O......	—	E.	P.	Life and Letters of Lord Macaulay.
Trollope, Anthony...	1882	E.	P.	An Autobiography.
Tuckerman, Henry T..	1871	U.S.	P.	Essays.
Tyndall, John.......	—	I.	P.	On Sound.
Udall, Nicholas......	16th c.	E.	P.	Ralph Royster Doyster.[3]
Ussher, James........	1656	I.	P.	Antiquities of the British Churches.
Vaughan, Archbishop.	1884	E.	C.	Life of St. Thomas Aquinas.
Verplanck, G. C......	1870	U.S.	P.	Life of Shakspeare.†
Vet'romile, Rev. Dr. E.	1882	It.	C.	Travels.
Vitalis, Ordicus......	12th c	E.	C.	Ecclesiastical History.
Wace, Richard........	1184	F.	C.	Poems.
Wadding, Rev. Luke..	1657	I.	C.	Annals of the Friars Minor.
Walker, John........	1807	E.	C.	Pronouncing English Dictionary.
Waller, Edmund.....	1687	E.	P.	Poems.
Walpole, Charles W.	—	E.	P.	A Short Hist. of Ireland.
Walpole, Horace.....	1797	E.	P.	Letters.
Walsh, Robert........	1859	U.S.	C.	Essays.
Walton, Isaac.......	1683	E.	P.	The Complete Angler.
Walworth, Rev. C. A.	—	U.S.	C.	The Gentle Skeptic.
Ward, Rev. Hugh.....	1635	I.	C.	Irish Martyrology.
Ward, William G....	1882	E.	C.	Essays in the Dublin Review.
Ware, Sir James......	1666	I.	P.	Lives of the Irish Bishops.
Warton, Thomas......	1790	E.	P.	History of English Poetry.
Watts, Isaac.........	1748	E.	P.	Hymns.

* Her maiden name was Blackford. It was to the death of this lady that Moore refers in one of his Irish melodies, beginning:

"I saw thy form in youthful prime,
Nor thought that pale decay
Would steal before the steps of time
And waste its bloom away, Mary!
Yet still thy features wore that light
Which fleets not with the breath,
And life ne'er looked more truly bright
Than in thy smile of death, Mary!"

† Verplanck's "edition of Shakspeare's plays, with a life and critical notes, was an honor to American scholarship, and was the best American edition of Shakspeare prior to that of Richard Grant White." *Hart.*

Name.	Date of Death.	Country.	Religion.	Chief Work.
Spencer, Herbert....	——	E.	P.	Essays.*
Spenser, Edmund......	1599	E.	P.	The Fairy Queen.¹
Stedman, Edmund C...	——	U.S.	P.	Poems.
Steele, Sir Richard..	1729	I.	P.	Essays.
Stephens, Alex. H....	1883	U.S.	P.	History of the War between the States.
Sterne, Laurence	1768	I.	P.	Tristram Shandy.†
Stewart, Agnes.......	——	E.	C.	Life of Bishop Fisher.‡
Stewart, Dugald......	1828	S.	P.	Philosophy of the Human Mind.
Stoddard, Richard H.	——	U.S.	P.	Poems.
Stone, James Kent....	——	U.S.	C.	The Invitation Heeded.
Story, Joseph.........	1845	U.S.	P.	Constitution of the U. S.
Stowe, Mrs. H. B.....,	——	U.S.	P.	Uncle Tom's Cabin.²
Street, Alfred B. ...	——	U.S.	P.	Poems.
Strickland, Agnes....	——	E.	P.	The Queens of England.
Sullivan, A. M........	1884	I.	C.	New Ireland.
Swift, Dean..........	1745	I.	P.	Gulliver's Travels.²
Swin'burne, A. C......	——	E.	P.	Poems.
Swinton, William	——	E.	P.	The Twelve Decisive Battles of the War.
Taylor, Jeremy.......	1667	E.	P.	Holy Living and Holy Dying.
Taylor, Bayard.......	1879	U.S.	P.	Poems.
Temple. Sir William..	1699	E.	P.	Memoirs.
Tennyson, Alfred....	——	E.	P.	Poems.
Terhune, Mrs. M. V...	——	U.S.	P.	Alone.²
Thack'eray, W. M.....	1863	E.	P.	Arthur Pendennis.²
Thébaud (tay'bo), Rev. A. J., S.J	——	F.	C.	The Irish Race.
Thomson, James.	1748	E.	P	The Seasons.¹
Thoreau, Henry D....	1862	U.S.	P.	Walden; or, Life in the Woods.
Thorpe, Benjamin	1870	E.	P.	Old Eng. Translations. §
Tickell, Thomas......	1740	E.	P.	Poems.
Ticknor, George......	1871	U.S.	P.	History of Spanish Lit.
Tighernach (teer'nah).	1088	I.	C.	Annals of Tighernach.

* Spencer is a master of style, but he belongs to the infidel school of Darwin, Buckle, Huxley, etc.
† A famous but licentious novel full of wit and pathos.
‡ The full title is, *The Life of John Fisher, Cardinal-Bishop of Rochester; with an Appendix containing the Bishop's Funeral Sermons, Letters*, etc.
§ Thorpe was a most eminent Anglo-Saxon scholar. Among the many works of which he gave an English translation are Cædmon's *Poems, Beowulf*, and *The Saxon Chronicle*.

Name.	Date of Death.	Country.	Religion.	Chief Work.
Webster, Daniel	1852	U.S.	P.	Speeches.
Webster, Noah	1843	U.S.	P.	American Dictionary of the English Language.
Webster, John*	17th c.	E.	P.	Dramas.
Weninger, F. X., S.J.	—	A.	C.	Photographic Views.
Whewell (hū'el), W.	1866	E.	P.	History of the Inductive Sciences.
Whipple, Edwin P.	—	U.S.	P.	Literature of the Age of Elizabeth.
White, Richard G.	1885	U.S.	P.	Words and their Uses.
White, Henry Kirk	1806	E.	P.	Poems.
White, Rev. Dr. C. I.	1878	U.S.	C.	Life of Mother Seton.
Whitney, William D.	—	U.S.	P.	Language and the Study of Language.
Wickliff, John	1384	E.		Translation of the Bible.
Wilde, Lady	—	I.	P.	Poems.
Wilde, Richard H.	1847	I.	P.	Poems.
Willis, Nathaniel P.	1867	U.S.	P.	Poems.
William of Malmesbury	12th c.	E.	C.	History of the Kings of England.
Williams, Richard D.	1862	I.	C.	Poems.
Wilson, John	1854	S.	P.	Lights and Shadows of Scottish Life.
Wirt, William	1834	U.S.	P.	Life of Patrick Henry.
Wiseman, Cardinal	1865	I.	C.	The Connection between Science and Revealed Religion.
Wolfe, Rev. Charles	1827	I.	P.	Poems.
Worcester (woos'ter), Joseph E.	1865	U.S.	P.	Dictionary of the English Language.
Wordsworth, W.	1850	E.	P.	Poems.
Wyatt, Sir Thomas	1541	E.	C.	Poems.
Wyntoun (win'toṇ), A.	1430	S.	C.	The Chronicle of Scotland.
Young, Edward	1765	E.	P.	The Night Thoughts.

* "Of John Webster, the author of a famous tragedy called *The Duchess of Malfi*, not even so much as the year of his birth is known. The period of his greatest popularity and acceptance as a dramatist was about 1620."—*Thomas Arnold.*

www.ingramcontent.com/pod-product-compliance
Lightning Source LLC
Chambersburg PA
CBHW022137300426
44115CB00006B/234